Reclaiming Basq

THE BASQUE SERIES

Reclaiming Basque

LANGUAGE, NATION, AND CULTURAL ACTIVISM

Jacqueline Urla

UNIVERSITY OF NEVADA PRESS

RENO AND LAS VEGAS

THE BASQUE SERIES

University of Nevada Press, Reno, Nevada 89557 USA
Copyright © 2012 by University of Nevada Press
All rights reserved
Manufactured in the United States of America
Design by Kathleen Szawiola

Library of Congress Cataloging-in-Publication Data
Urla, Jacqueline.
Reclaiming Basque : language, nation, and cultural activism /
Jacqueline Urla. — 1st ed.
p. cm. — (The Basque series)
Includes bibliographical references and index.
ISBN 978-0-87417-875-3 (cloth : alk. paper) — ISBN 978-0-87417-880-7 (ebook)
1. Basques—Ethnic identity. 2. Basques—Politics and government.
3. Basques—Social life and customs. 4. Basque language. 5. País Vasco
(Spain)—Politics and government. 6. Pays Basque (France)—Politics
and government. I. Title.
GN549.B3U73 2012
305.89'992—dc23
2011040824

The paper used in this book meets the requirements of American National
Standard for Information Sciences—Permanence of Paper
for Printed Library Materials, ANSI/NISO Z39.48-1992 (R2002).
Binding materials were selected for strength and durability.

University of Nevada Press Paperback Edition, 2014
23   22   21   20   19   18   17   16   15
5   4   3   2   1
ISBN-13: 978-0-87417-965-1 (pbk. : alk. paper)

I write in a strange language. Its verbs,
the structure of its relative clauses,
the words it uses to designate ancient things
—rivers, plants, birds—
have no sisters anywhere on Earth.
. . .

Born, they say, in the megalithic age,
it survived, this stubborn language, by withdrawing,
by hiding away like a hedgehog . . .
. . . .

Its sleep was long, it bibliography brief
(but in the twentieth century the hedgehog awoke)

—"Prologue," Bernardo Atxaga, *Obabakoak* (1992).
Translated by Margaret Jull Costa

Contents

Illustrations

Figures

Maps

Table

Preface

In the corner of the western Pyrenees known as the Basque Country, people have disagreed about many things. They have disagreed about the kind of society they want to build, its proper name, its geographic boundaries, about whether it should be socialist or capitalist, whether they want to have independence and what that might mean. They have argued bitterly over the legitimacy of political violence and have also suffered deeply its consequences. But one issue about which there has been a remarkably strong degree of consensus over the years is that the Basque language, Euskara, is a valuable heritage that should be protected and reclaimed.

This book explores the pursuit of that conviction, examining some of the changing methods, modes of representation, and discourse of the Basque language revitalization movement as it was first expressed at the end of the nineteenth century and again when it reemerged as a social movement in the waning years of the Franco regime. Drawing on the analysis of historical documents, political treatises, and my own direct observations and interviews conducted through ethnographic fieldwork over the course of more than twenty years, I explore the reasons why people have thought it important to save Basque and how they have gone about it.

These efforts at language revival have been unfolding alongside and sometimes at the very center stage of the simultaneous Basque nationalist struggle for autonomy. For some language advocates, the two struggles are inseparable. For others, they are issues that should be kept clearly distinct. We will look at these and many other debates that language advocates have about what affects the social life of Basque and what it means to speak a modern language.

The principal protagonists behind these actions call themselves *euskaltzaleak*, Basque-language advocates. Though many are of Basque ethnic heritage, others are not. And while many language advocates speak Basque natively, some learned Basque as a second language, and yet others may not know Basque well at all. *Euskaltzaleak* are best thought of not as an ethnic group or a linguistic community in the usual sense of the term, but as a political-affinity group. Coming from various class and social locations, intellectuals, artists, musicians, linguists, educators, parents, and young people of varying walks of life, *euskalzaleak* make up a polymorphous social movement. Some of them have gone on to become part of official language-planning efforts working in town halls and provincial or regional governments, while others work in a wide array of civic organizations that are collectively referred to as *euskalgintza*. A compound work composed of the root *euskal* (Basque) and the suffix *gintza* (production, construction), the term *euskalgintza* conveys an understanding of language revival as an active and ongoing process of collective making and remaking Basque. *Euskalgintza* is the main focus of this book, and by all accounts, the results of this movement have been nothing short of impressive.

The ethnographer enters the lives of others and, if they are willing, stays for a long time to inhabit their world and experience it with them. The research on which this book draws comes from many such extended stays in the Basque Country, during which time I have received many kinds of support, advice, introductions, and extraordinary help, for which I am very grateful. I want to thank the dozens of people over the years at schools, radio stations, language-planning offices, town halls, research institutes, community associations, and newspapers in the Basque Country who allowed me to consult their archives, observe their events, and interview them. I learned much from these interviews and have tried as best I can to represent their viewpoints faithfully. To protect the anonymity of my interviewees, in most cases I do not give their real names. For most of my research, I have lived in the town of Usurbil (Gipuzkoa) and have benefited enormously from the help of its town hall and residents. There are more people who helped me there and elsewhere than I can list, but I would like to signal in particular the invaluable help and encouragement I have received from Olatz Altuna, Esther Barrutia, Olatz Osa, Lurdes Zubeldia, Jaime Otamendi, Alan King, Xabier Falcón, Arantxa Enetarriaga, Itziar Illaramendi, Joselu Aranburu, Feliz Aizpurua, Maialen Lujanbio, and Joxean Artze. I also want to thank the Patri Jatetxea and its extended family, the entire Zabalea household, Xabier Garagorri, Pedro SanCristobal, and students and colleagues in the anthropology department at the Basque University in Donostia who have hosted me and been encouraging of my work, in particular Jone Miren Hernández, Teresa del Valle, Txemi Apaolaza, and Aitzpea Leizaola.

The research on which this book is based first began with my doctoral research in 1982–83. I should like to recognize here the early and critical guidance I received from faculty in the anthropology department at the University of California, Berkeley. Paul Rabinow, John Gumperz, and Stanley Brandes in particular helped me in the early stages of my doctoral research. Also very influential on my intellectual formation was a cohort of graduate students at UC Berkeley that formed to study the work of Michel Foucault. My thanks to Arturo Escobar, David Horn,

Keith Gandal, Steve Kotkin, and Jonathan Simon. Our study-group meetings and work together with Paul Rabinow as editors of the newsletter *History of the Present* shaped many of the questions that run through this book.

Subsequent to finishing my doctorate, I joined the Department of Anthropology at the University of Massachusetts, Amherst, where I was able to continue and expand my research with further fieldwork until 2006. I have benefited from the advice and encouragement of colleagues and former students who have seen this project evolve over the years. I would like to thank in particular Reyes Lázaro, Oriol PiSunyer, and Susan DiGiaccomo for being wonderful interlocutors for my work. William Douglass, Joseba Zulaika, Begoña Echeverria, Sharryn Kasmir, and the late Begoña Aretxaga, all fellow scholars of Basque language and cultural politics, were terrific sources of advice and inspiration. Brenda Jo Bright and George Lipsitz helped to shape my approach to popular culture; Galician sociolinguist Celso Alvarez Cáccamo was helpful early on; Susan Gal and Kathyrn Woolard have been frequent readers of my work and mentors for the kind of politically informed linguistic anthropology I have wanted to carry out; Alan Swedlund, Lisa Henderson, Julia Urla, and my former students Mary Orgel and Susan Hyatt have offered great ideas, important conversations, and sustaining friendship.

I am very grateful for the financial support that has made the research on which this book is based possible. These include: the Social Science Research Foundation International Doctoral Dissertation Fellowship; the MacArthur Foundation Program in International Peace and Security; the Program for Cultural Cooperation Between the Ministry of Culture and the United States; the Basque Studies Program at the University of Nevada, Reno; the University of Massachusetts Amherst Faculty Research Grant; and the University of Massachusetts Amherst Department of Anthropology European Fieldstudies Program. Work on the writing of this book was also supported by a year-long fellowship at the School of Advanced Research funded by the National Endowment for the Humanities and by a postdoctoral fellowship at the Center for Historical Analysis, Rutgers University. I am very grateful for the opportunity these research institutes gave me to rethink my work and to all of my colleagues at SAR and CHA who provided me with insightful commentary on my work in progress.

Portions of various chapters have appeared in an earlier form in the journals *American Ethnologist* (Urla 1993b), *Pragmatics* (Urla 1995), *Critique of Anthropology* (Urla 1993a), and *Cultural Anthropology* (Urla 1988). My thanks to the editors and anonymous reviewers for those journals and to the reviewers at the University of Nevada Press for commentary that helped to shape my understanding of the materials. Thanks also to the wizardry of Michelle Turré for helping out with the maps.

I owe an inestimable debt of gratitude to my colleague Justin Crumbaugh, who enthusiastically read every chapter, often more than once, and who gave me the encouragement and stimulating questions that allowed me to bring this book to completion. On the serendipitous path of the book, one of my best pieces of good fortune was to have been befriended by Jone Izeta and Jakoba Errekondo. They made my work possible, and each in their own way taught me much of what I know about what Basque language, culture, and politics mean to its practitioners. They have been teachers, friends, and generous pillars of support. I dedicate this book to them and to the memory of my father, José Luis Urla, who died suddenly before this research began, and to Juanita Sagardia, a beloved mentor, who passed just as it was ending. *Mil esker denoi.*

Reclaiming Basque

Introduction

In 1963 a group of idealistic youth who had recently formed the revolutionary group ETA Basqueland and Freedom declared in their magazine *Zutik!* [Arise!]: "The day that Basque ceases to be a spoken language, the Basque nation will have died and, in a few years, the descendants of today's Basques will be simply Spanish or French" (Jáuregui 1981: 160). After the death of the dictator Francisco Franco almost twenty years later, Spain was reconfigured into a quasi-federal political system of autonomous communities. Soon after achieving its autonomy, the newly created regional Basque government, representing a much more moderate sector of the political spectrum than Basqueland and Freedom, nevertheless expressed a similar sense of compelling urgency about Basque-language revival in its first political program: "The Basque community has become aware in a gradually more intense and, given the circumstances, more desperate fashion, of the capital importance of Basque, understood simultaneously as a national language, as a fundamental sign of our community, and as a genuine instrument of thought and creativity.... Today we are completely convinced that Euzkadi will never be fully realized, in the full sense of the word, if the Basque language dies" (Eusko Jaurlaritza 1980: 72–73). Yet another twenty years later, on the cusp of the new millennium, this commitment was renewed once again as thousands of citizens in a coordinated simulcast event filled four soccer stadiums in capital cities across the Basque territory to mark the twentieth anniversary of the Basque language campaign *Bai Euskarari*! [Yes to the Basque Language!].

As a unique, non–Indo European language, Basque enjoys a kind of mysterious status in Europe. It is a language isolate with no known relation to any other existing language. It is spoken today by approximately 750,000 people, or about a third of the population who live in a geographic territory of the western Pyrenees spanning four provinces in northern Spain and three in France. The territory of Euskal Herria is larger than the three provinces that make up the contemporary Basque Autonomous Community of Spain—Araba, Gipuzkoa, and Bizkaia (see map 1). It is considered by many Basques to be a distinct nation and the homeland of the Basque language, Euskara, the traces of which can be found on archaeological

1

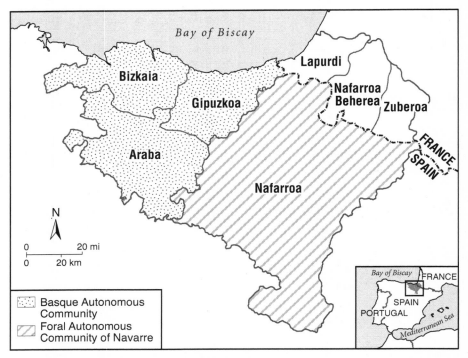

MAP 1. The seven provinces that make up the territory known as Euskal Herria. The three provinces of Araba, Gipuzkoa, and Bizkaia make up the contemporary Basque Autonomous Community, constituted in 1979.

remains dating back to the Neolithic (Trask 1997).[1] Contemporary Basque speakers are spread unevenly over this territory. In the province of Gipuzkoa, Basque speakers make up close to half the population. In the Gipuzkoan town where I lived during much of my research, the percentage of speakers is closer to 70 percent. In other areas like the province of Araba or the south of Nafarroa, Basque speakers can be few and far between.[2]

This complex and uneven linguistic landscape is due to a process of what scholars call language shift (Gal 1979; Fishman 1991) that had been going on for several centuries and became especially accelerated after the middle of the nineteenth century. By the twentieth century, language shift had led to a situation some sociolinguists call diglossia, in which the state languages—Castilian in the southern Spanish side, French in the northern territories—dominated as the taken-for-granted languages of education, commerce, and public life, while Basque survived largely as a home language. Language shift turned Basque for a long time into a language associated mainly with the countryside, spoken largely by farmers and fishing folk, few of whom knew how to read or write in it.

As we will see in more detail, socioeconomic changes, especially industrialization and urbanization, labor migration, as well as mandatory schooling worked together with deliberate state repression to accelerate Basque-language abandonment. In France formal state policies to eliminate Basque took shape at the time of the French Revolution. The ideologues of the French Republic viewed Basque, along with other regional languages, as obstacles to the spread of civic culture, liberty, and democracy itself. The French Republic, as Europe's first and most influential model of the democratic nation-state, set into place a strong association between minority languages and ideological backwardness, narrow-minded provincialism, and fanatical politics (de Certeau, Julia, and Revel 1975; Balibar and Laporte 1974; Higonnet 1980). The linkage it drew between monolingualism and democracy proved powerfully influential in Western political theory. To this day, the French state remains reluctant to officially recognize its ethnic and linguistic diversity and hesitant to fully endorse the European Charter for Regional or Minority Languages (Grin, Jensdóttir, O'Riagáin 2003; Safran 1999).

In Spain we encounter a very different scenario. Ironically perhaps, it is in Spain, where democracy has had a shorter political life, that Basque has faced both the most intense repression as well as the greatest support to date. In Spain as in France, elites widely regarded Basque as a backward language destined to disappear. But the Spanish state was historically weak (Linz 1973), allowing for the formation of powerful regional elites who began by the late nineteenth century to conceive of themselves as separate nations and take steps to preserve their languages. Their efforts were crushed under the Franco dictatorship (1939–75). The Franco regime promoted an aggressive Castilian-only language policy that created a climate of intimidation and repression for speakers of minority languages. My conversations and interviews with Basques about the Franco period were filled with stories of the many ways that Basque-speaking children were shamed by storekeepers or physically punished or humiliated by their teachers for speaking Basque. Under Franco, teaching or using Basque in anything other than a folkloric context was regarded as anti-Spanish. These hostile state policies toward Basque cultural expressions accelerated Basque-language loss and profoundly marked the generation that came of age under the dictator.

As leftist and progressive sectors began to organize more openly against the regime in the sixties, these language policies came increasingly under critique. Simultaneous with the reemergence of Basque-nationalist political groups, Basque-language revitalization efforts began to appear, led by university students, Jesuit priests, parents, and teachers. Without books or money, makeshift classrooms were created to teach children in Basque. Low-cost night schools emerged in many towns to teach Basque to adults, serving simultaneously as sites for consciousness-raising about linguistic inequality. The intense desire for social liberation that ran throughout Spanish society after the end of the dictatorship and the subsequent restructuring of the state into autonomous communities allowed these early grass-roots efforts at language revival to flourish and grow.

Basque-language revival is today one of the largest and most vital social movements of post-Franco Spain, involving people of many walks of life and a tremendous investment of human energy, time, and resources—much of it voluntary. Without this continued popular involvement and without the institutional support of the Basque Autonomous Community's regional government (established in 1979), it is entirely possible that the Basque language could have disappeared. But, as novelist Bernardo Atxaga says in the prologue to his novel *Obabakoak,* in the twentieth century Basque awoke, like a hedgehog, from its long sleep. Indeed it did. Basque language revival is today a social struggle spanning more than a century, made up of networks of intersecting activities and organizations. Over the years the struggle has become professionalized, and both its discourse and methods have changed in response to a changing political climate. The angry protests and street demonstrations of the sixties and seventies demanding Basque in the Basqueland, which successfully won the recognition of Basque as a co-official language in the Autonomous Community, have given way to less overtly nationalist and more systematic language planning. But the popular commitment to language revival has remained remarkably enduring, as evidenced by the thousands of citizens who participate in the many fund-raising events for Basque immersion schools, who continue to work for Basque-language media, music, and arts or have become dues-paying members of their local Basque-language association [*euskara elkartea*]. Basque-language revival continues to engage a wide array of people in varying degrees of commitment and very diverse activities.

This popular engagement makes the Basque-language movement stand out among Western Europe's many minority language–revival movements—Irish, Scottish Gaelic, Welsh, Catalan, Galician, or Breton. Language-revival efforts have been most vigorous and successful in the Basque Autonomous Community of Spain, where Basque promotion gained legal and institutional support in 1979. The Basque Autonomous Community created a Department of Language Policy to oversee and guide language revitalization, and public funding has helped to support these activities in the Autonomous Community and at times to assist parallel efforts in the larger Basque-speaking territories.[3]

But the movement is by no means a terrain exclusive to governmental planners or professional linguists. What makes the Basque case particularly exceptional is the high level of popular involvement and the numerous civic organizations working on behalf of language revitalization. In refusing to surrender language revival to official institutions, Basque-language advocates have held on to the view of language revival as a democratic project in social change rather than simply a policy regime.

Language Revival as a Social Movement

Language-revival efforts are on the rise around the globe. In the last decade of the twentieth century, public and scholarly recognition of language endangerment as well as new international nongovernmental organizations, Web sites, and publications addressing the decline of language diversity worldwide have grown dramatically. With over half the world's languages predicted to lose their last remaining speakers by 2100 (Nettle and Romaine 2000), the National Science Foundation and the National Endowment for the Humanities have made funding for endangered-language documentation a top priority. We have seen the concept of language rights become an increasingly salient issue in indigenous politics across the globe. Simultaneously, within Europe there has been a growing amount of public debate about the rights of linguistic minorities and the place of linguistic diversity in the deliberative bodies and policies of the expanded European Union (Wright 2004; Phillipson 2003). Policy frameworks like the 1996 Universal Declaration of Linguistic Human Rights, the 1992 European Charter for Minority or Regional Languages, and the 2003 UNESCO Convention for Intangible Heritage all signal to us a growing international recognition of the need for governments to value and protect human linguistic diversity.

The mobilizations we find today to protect language diversity and define language rights are exemplary of the trend in contemporary social movements to address themselves to forms of domination that are cultural in nature (Melucci 1980; Offe 1985; Taylor 1994; Crossley 2002; Hobson 2003). Nancy Fraser (1997) has described these as struggles for *recognition* rather than redistribution. That is, they are struggles that forefront forms of exclusion based on denigrating a group's social status, identity, or way of life. Such struggles and forms of inequality often have class dimensions, but as Fraser notes, they are not class conflicts as traditionally conceived. In the essay he authored that coined the phrase "the politics of recognition," philosopher Charles Taylor (1994) described recognition struggles as expanding our understandings of justice to include issues of inclusion, rights, and respect for group identities and differences. Taylor gave as one of his primary examples the struggle for the language rights of French speakers in Quebec, Canada. Curiously, however, despite this explicit reference to language in such a landmark text, and despite the growing salience of language endangerment and revitalization movements worldwide, the study of language revival remains a relatively marginal topic in discussions of multiculturalism, a specialty niche in sociolinguistics and folklore studies, and an extraprofessional activity for progressive linguists. This is not to say that language revitalization has gone unstudied. Sociologist Joshua Fishman has dedicated a lifetime to the study of language revitalization (1972, 1973, 1989, 1991, 1996, 2001), and many other linguists have joined him since (e.g., Hale et al. 1992; Reyhner 1997; Grenoble and Whaley 1998, 2006; Hinton and Hale 2001; Freeland and Patrick 2004; Nettle and Romaine 2000). Anthropologists have contributed a corpus of ethnographic studies of minority-language communities and movements that have generated many valuable insights into language struggles.[4] French sociologist Pierre Bourdieu (1991) had been writing on the political dynamics of language domination since the seventies, and in the fields of postcolonial and Latino studies the experiences of minority speakers have long been central objects of concern.

Curiously, then, mention of struggles to redress language domination has been strikingly absent from the lively discussions taking place today about the nature of social movements, power, cultural activism, neoliberalism, and structured forms of inequality. Neither a recent authoritative compendium on social-movement theory (Snow, Soule, and Kriesi 2004) nor a reader on the anthropology of social movements (Nash 2005) makes any reference to language revitalization. When they are not outright ignored, language-revival movements, particularly in Europe, suffer the condescension and stigma of association with backward-looking "regionalism" or, worse yet, divisive and potentially violent ethnic nationalism (Fishman 1991; May 2001). The result has been that language-revitalization struggles, the inequalities they address, and the particular kinds of discourses and strategies they deploy have yet to become fully appreciated or integrated into more general scholarly theorizing about multiculturalism, human rights, and strategies of collective protest.

Attention to language movements is long overdue, particularly given the heated public debates centering on language brought to the fore by debates over immigration and multiculturalism: "English Only" initiatives in the United States, the enactment of language requirements for immigrants in Europe, and the new initiatives by international nongovernmental organizations to make language a part of the discussion of universal human rights.[5] Political theorists in the last decade have begun to recognize that respect for language diversity must be a fundamental part of any program for a multicultural society and cultural democracy (Kymlicka and Patten 2003; May 2001; Freeland and Patrick 2004).

Revitalization, Resistance, and Modernity

The contemporary political climate would seem sufficient to justify more attention to language-oriented social movements, but their relevance is not only a question of timeliness. Such movements are worthy of analytical attention because they speak directly to contemporary theorizing about culture, identity, and power. In "Life After Primordialism," Arjun Appadurai writes: "It will no longer serve to look at ethnicity as just another principle of group identity, as just another cultural device for the pursuit of group interests, or as some dialectical combination of the two. We need an account of ethnicity that explores its modernity" (1996a: 139). The same holds true for language: we need an account of language that explores its modernity. This is precisely what this study of Basque-language activism seeks to offer. The study of language activism has a lot to teach us about modern ways that language and cultural identities are understood, documented, and managed in modern society. It has the potential to expand our understanding of mechanisms of exclusion that infuse everyday life and social institutions. Language struggles are not simply in the service of other ends; they illuminate the role of language as an axis of social stratification in its own right, while also deepening our appreciation of language as an instrument of resistance and creative cultural expression. Language revitalization and protection movements are also a fertile terrain for exploring the role that experts and expertise of various sorts—planning, demolinguistics, statistics, and management—have in activism, forming part of the field of discourses reshaping how the social life of language is imagined.

In analyzing how the Basque language was reclaimed and reconfigured in the latter half of the twentieth century, it is my goal not only to make some of the dynamics of this particular movement more well known, but also to take the study of language-revival activism out of its specialty niche and place it within wider conversations taking place about the nature of modern forms of power and resistance. As I hope to demonstrate, within the skirmishes over orthography and standardization, the development of language surveys, or the language play of pirate-radio broadcasters, we have fascinating windows into various ways of understanding and enacting what it means to be modern, to have a culture, to be a nation, and the challenges of trying to speak a "small language" in an increasingly transnational world. For this task I have assembled an eclectic analytical tool kit. Linguistic anthropology is one important source. In the last two decades, linguistic anthropologists have moved increasingly to bridge the gap between their more microanalyses of language use and macrotheories of ideology, culture, political economy, race, and ethnicity (Gal 1989; Hill 1985, 1993; Woolard 1985; Irvine 1989; Rampton 1995). Work by linguistic anthropologists on questions of language ideology has helped to denaturalize cultural evaluations made about languages and thereby show their historical development and political significance (Schieffelin, Woolard, and Kroskrity 1998; Kroskrity 1999; Woolard 1998a; Briggs and Bauman 2000; Gal 2006).

Colonial and postcolonial theorists provided me with an additional and crucial set of analytical inspirations for my work. The great Antillean anticolonial theorist Franz Fanon (1967) and African novelist Ngũgi wa' Thiong'o (1986) offer some of the earliest and most eloquent analyses we have of the place language has in the colonization of consciousness. Ongoing work by Latino artists, writers, and cultural critics has been especially instrumental in giving greater prominence to language in the analysis of the experience of cultural domination and the tactics of resistance (Anzaldúa 1987; Arteaga 1994; Flores, Attinasi, and Pedraza 1981; Flores and Yúdice 1990; Fusco 1995; Gómez Peña 1993). This divergent body of work, along with the analytics of power as developed principally by Michel Foucault, together inform my way of studying language-revival activism premises, tactics, and outcomes.

What is language revival, then, and what does it involve? As typically understood by sociolinguists, language revival, or "reversing language shift" (RLS) as it was called by Joshua Fishman (1991), refers to organized efforts to "increase the relative number of speakers of a language and extend the domains where it is employed" (Grenoble and Whaley 2006: 13). To achieve this goal, language-revival advocacy can involve a wide array of activities, chief among which tend to be teaching the language; seeking legal protections and/or official recognition; supporting the creation of literary works; and augmenting the visibility and use of the language via minority-language television, radio, and print media. In addition to education, law, and the media, a fourth arena of intervention by advocates is the language itself. Revival almost invariably involves some efforts to document and reform the language, as in the creation of a standard written variety. Goals are tempered by pragmatic conditions: resources, political backing, and social support. Language movements may aim for the modest goal of preserving a record of the language by creating a dictionary or the more ambitious goal of language maintenance—ensuring, in other words, the continuity of a community of speakers (Maffi 2000). At a minimum, language maintenance may simply aim to protect speakers' rights to use a language and incorporate a few hours of instruction into the schools. At a maximum, a language-revival movement may seek to expand the knowledge and use of the minority language in the general population such that it could become a frequent or possibly even the preferred language of use in a wide variety of domains.

In short, language revival can be played out in very different ways in different places. In some cases, it may be the action of a few intellectuals or a handful of teachers. In others, like the Basque, we find a broadly popular involvement. Even beneath a broad consensus supporting the revitalization of a language there may exist differing views and expectations about what revival entails for everyday language use (see Zalbide, Gardner, Erize, and Azurmendi 2006: 122). To use the term "revival" to describe what goes on in a language movement can be, in fact, somewhat misleading. For while language advocacy often frames itself as recovery of the past, the outcomes and objectives of the movement are as much about change and reinvention as they are about reproduction. Revival is fundamentally about creating a new linguistic future.

In attempts to reclaim Basque, the practices of language loyalism are simultaneously introducing distinctively modern ways of conceptualizing the Basque language, identity, and speaker. Much of this is quite deliberate. Social movements typically seek to change cultural attitudes, values, and meanings (Earl 2004). Minority-language advocates are keenly aware that some of the greatest obstacles to revitalization are the views they and others have internalized of their language as inferior, exclusionary, or impractical—something that they must inevitably give up to be sophisticated, good citizens or simply to be reasonable. In his important work on minority languages and political theory, Stephen May (2001) has brilliantly deconstructed these negative conceptualizations of minority languages and traced their origins to the philosophical matrix of the modern nation-state. Their association with obsolescence and the presumed inherent antagonism between minority languages and modernity, progress, and democratic values, he argues, has been one of the principal forms of symbolic violence through which minority languages have been marginalized to and contained in the private sphere or the museum. These sets of ideas continue to be one of the explicit targets of much of the discourse and strategies of language revival. Advocates of Basque preservation at the turn of the twentieth century, for example, spent a good deal of effort arguing that Basque was evidence of their distinct nationality, fully capable of functioning as a modern language. They sought to facilitate this by developing a set of standardized norms they thought would help adapt it to contemporary life. Minority-language advocates have drawn upon discourses of nationalism and the rationality of standards to promote and preserve their language, but they have done so with a strong degree of self-criticism—more so than we typically find, for example, in majority-language contexts. Within Basque activism we find trenchant critiques of bourgeois and primordialist notions of the nation. Contemporary Basque advocates have worked very self-consciously against nativism to develop a language movement that has been community based, participatory, and inclusive. Thus, as fraught as nationalism may be as a basis for staking claims to social justice, we should also recognize, as Sharryn Kasmir (2002) has argued, that not all nationalisms are alike. Even within the Basque country, there are clearly different ways of acting upon a sense of shared nationhood. Contestation and evolving critique are a part of the nature of Basque-language revival that we necessarily need to keep in view.

Examining the varied efforts of Basque-language advocates to challenge the marginalization of Basque and also improve its chances of survival provides us with a window into the evolving landscape of language ideology. I use the term language *ideology* to refer to commonly held conceptualizations about the social life of language that circulate in the discourses of experts, political organizations, and civil society at large. Within language ideology I include, for example, the ideas (shared or contested) that people have about what speaking a language (Basque, French, or Spanish or a specific variety of a language) implies about one's identity or political loyalties; beliefs about how a language should be spoken and with whom; comparisons people make about the value, beauty, or elegance of different languages or dialects; theories about what makes a language live or die, and so forth. In keeping with recent work on this topic (Schieffelin et al. 1998; Kroskrity 1999), I use the term ideology not in the sense of false ideas, nor in the functionalist sense of mystifications that are promulgated by a dominant class or state for the purpose of justifying historical inequalities. To be sure, ideas about language are interest laden. I follow Raymond Williams (1977) in seeing the critical task of analysts not to be that of debunking ideologies as false so much as understanding them as effective forces in society, constitutive of our worlds. Conceptions of language reflect the complex histories of social relations out of which they emerge and are themselves powerful forces in their own right, shaping social behavior and language use. As Kathryn Woolard has argued, ideologies have consequence (1998a: 10–11). They transform the social world they ostensibly just describe. The alternative perspectives and the shifts in language habits that revival movements seek to engender—the habit, for example, of assuming a stranger should be greeted in Spanish rather than Basque—can lead to meaningful material-semiotic changes in the world. Ben Rampton's fascinating study of young people's language use in Britain argues powerfully in this vein (1995). Language, he shows, is an axis of social stratification intersecting with other factors, like class, but not reducible to them and certainly not superficial. A lesson can be had, he argues, in the feminist movement's challenge to generic masculine pronouns. Feminist efforts were often derided by detractors as merely "symbolic" issues. But, as Deborah Cameron has argued, "a shift in linguistic practice is not just a reflection of some more fundamental social change: it is itself a social change. . . . Eliminating generic masculine pronouns precisely eliminates generic masculine pronouns. And in so doing it changes the repertoire of social meanings and choices available to social actors . . . [thereby] restructuring at least one aspect of how individuals interact with each other" (Cameron, in Rampton 1995: 12). Language, in short, is a powerful element that shapes how we are able to inhabit the world.

At a general level, then, I argue that language activism engages with culture and power not only when it achieves new state policies more accommodating to minority-language speakers—instituting language curriculum or funds for services in their language, for example—but also by illuminating how many everyday practices and beliefs relating to language operate as a form of power by naturalizing the dominance of one language over another. Activism reveals the terrain of language habits as thoroughly ideological.

Language revitalization both unsettles and reproduces dominant beliefs and habits of use to which speakers themselves may be very attached, while also seeking to introduce new understandings of linguistic practice. As others have shown, native speakers are not always happy about such changes, and resistance to language revitalization is consequently not uncommon (see Jaffe 1999). A useful way of thinking about the political-semiotic effects of language activism is provided in the analytical framework that anthropologists Jean and John Comaroff develop in their study of colonial missionaries in nineteenth-century South Africa (1991: 19–32). Despite their relative lack of political power, British evangelicals, they argue, set into motion cultural transformations that were of profound material, practical, and symbolic consequence to the evolution of colonial rule and to the form that subsequent resistance movements took. That scholars have failed to appreciate this comes from a poverty of thinking about the nature of cultural struggles and symbolic life more generally. Drawing on a rich ethnohistorical analysis, they show that the colonial encounter did not unfold as a whole-scale replacement of one set of beliefs by another, but as a clash of life worlds. Each side apprehended the other through the lens of their own taken-for-granted values, norms, and beliefs—what Bourdieu (1977) called "habitus," a set of dispositions and unspoken conventions about such things as time, space, or the self, embodied and enacted in everyday practices. These collided against one another, were adopted, or were at times wholly misunderstood.

In their view, the effects of Christian missionization over time are thus best understood as a series of disruptions in habitus such that beliefs once at the level of "common sense" became partially or fully recognized and articulated and, hence, explicitly defended or contested. One of the innovations of the Comaroffs' framework, as the above comment suggests, is to envision cultural struggles as setting the status of beliefs in motion. To capture this they find it useful to introduce a distinction between the terms *ideology* and *hegemony* in their analytical framework. They call beliefs and/or practices "hegemonic" when they are the most fully naturalized or taken for granted, reserving the category "ideological" for ideas or beliefs that are explicitly and verbally articulated. They draw a parallel between hegemonic ideas and what Bourdieu (1977) referred to in his work as *doxa*: "things that go without saying because, being axiomatic, they come with saying" (Comaroff and Comaroff 1991: 23). Beliefs or dispositions that are *doxa* are powerful, they argue, precisely because they are unstated, saturating everyday life, language, aesthetics, and the built environment, laying down the implicit grounding and limits of what counts as rational, credible, sayable, and thinkable. "They are internalized, in their negative guise, as constraints; in their neutral guise as conventions; and in their positive guise, as values. . . . the unspoken authority of habit, may be as effective as the most violent coercion in shaping, directing, even dominating social thought and action" (ibid.: 22).

Thus the Comaroffs characterize hegemony and ideology not as binary categories, but as *modalities,* end points along a continuum that ranges from the most taken for granted on the one hand to the most explicitly articulated on the other. This notion of a continuum provided them with a means of conveying the dynamic quality of the symbolic transformations that Christianization entailed. The colonization of consciousness (and resistance to it), they argue, is an untidy, drawnout struggle, entailing shifts in the modality of cultural beliefs as they become unmoored from the horizon of *doxa* and move into liminal territory, closer to the domain of the explicitly articulated and debated realm of values and beliefs (ibid.: 29). The cultural dynamics of domination and resistance are replete with ambiguity and best characterized not as a straightforward rejection or subjection, but as more akin to "a complex admixture of tacit (and even uncomprehending) accommodation to the European hegemonic order at one level and diverse expressions of symbolic and practical resistance at another" (ibid.: 26).

This analytical framework is a fertile one for conceptualizing some of the cultural dynamics of language activism as well. Like resistance to colonialism, minority-language advocacy is also a complex and untidy admixture of accommodation and resistance to dominant-language ideology that can give rise to a rupturing of an existing linguistic economy as well as to new framings for language. Much of the discourse and practices of language advocacy challenge explicit aspects of dominant ideology and tropes to which Basque speakers have been subjected: the idea, for example, that Basque is archaic, belongs to a fading rural life, is unsystematic or too difficult to learn. The advocates in minority-language movements question taken-for-granted ideas and in so doing make them objects of ideological debate. They also routinely challenge conventionally accepted ways of using language in everyday life. They do so in a variety of ways: sometimes explicitly via rationalized arguments and planning, via visual media and cues—a small sign in a store announcing, "we speak Basque"—or, more confrontationally, via spray painting Basque words onto Spanish road signs. Unsettling the habitus of language also occurs implicitly via new forms of expressive culture that use Basque in unexpected ways, offering up alternative images of what speaking Basque means. Drawing on the Comaroff model, we can understand language-revival activism as "pushing" the existing habitus of language use and attitudes out of the domain of the taken for granted and into the realm of the ideological. But the reverse takes place as well: language activism can play a role in naturalizing certain ways of understanding language, for example, as a measurable object of planning. New forms of self-awareness emerge about language, resulting in new moments of awkwardness among speakers as well as new senses of responsibility to the life of the language that are generated as individuals wrestle with the perceived consequences of what their language choices now seem to convey. Along with this, new forms of subjectivity take shape, deriving not only from the explicit challenges to prejudice and power, but from the very tools advocates use to preserve and understand Basque.

Language, Nationalism, and Governmentality

A second thread to which I have been indirectly alluding concerns the way the logics of nationalism and what Foucault called "governmentality" intersect in language activism. Movements to preserve or reclaim a language are almost always connected to cultural and political struggles for rights, empowerment, sovereignty, or land claims that shape them and need to be understood (Grenoble and Whaley 2006). In the Basque case, the language-revival movement in the twentieth century is powerfully influenced both by Basque and Spanish nationalist ideology and by the history of the Franco dictatorship. Basque-language treatises reproduce the idea firmly rooted in Western political theory of a fundamental equivalency between language preservation and the defense of a national cultural identity (Fishman 1972; Hobsbawm 1990). Basque nationalists have generally concurred in viewing Basque as evidence of the legitimacy to their claims to nationhood, even if they have disagreed about whether or how much they needed to actually speak Basque. We cannot forget, however, that Spanish-nationalist language ideology plays an equally central role in cementing the idea of one nation, one language. Expressed in its most virulent form under Franco and revitalized by the right-wing Partido Popular, Spanish nationalists continue to regard Castilian Spanish as the only legitimate language of Spain.

The nationalist imaginary—both Basque and Spanish—is omnipresent in language revival. Nationalism has clearly lent energy and support to the movement, but nationalist politics and tensions have presented revival with problems as well. Contrary to most of the existing political analyses of language movements, Basque included, I argue that the premises of nationalism do not fully explain to us the logics informing revival strategies. Nationalism does not explain a good deal of what language loyalists spend their time calling for, doing, and worrying about: how to manage and intervene in the social life of the language. My purpose is to revise the thesis that language revival is the outcome of nationalism and to show, rather, that revival strategies grow out of the conjuncture of nationalist imaginaries with the emergence of "the social" as a sphere of life demanding expert knowledge and intervention (Foucault 1991; Gordon 1991). As such, revitalization does more than confirm Basque as a symbol of the nation and Basque culture. Its methods also simultaneously draw upon and disseminate a view of language as an object to be governed and a social field of technical intervention.

My work joins that of many other scholars who are exploring how rationalities of governance shape the experiences of and struggles over cultural, class, and other forms of difference in diverse settings, contributing to an anthropology of modernity that aims to subject to ethnographic scrutiny modern forms of governmentality (Inda 2005). "Governmentality" is now a widely used term for a modality of power that Foucault began to address in his later work under the rubric of "biopower" (Foucault 1980a). Foucault conceived of biopower as a form of rule oriented toward the administration of life, at the level of either the individual body or the population. The aims and methods of biopower, he argued, differ from the way in which political theorists had usually defined power: that is, as something measured by and concerned with obedience to the sovereign and exercised through the imposition of law or force over a territory. Biopower is composed of strategies that aim at the correct and calculated management of the behavior of persons and populations. Governmentality or governance—terms I use interchangeably—is an expression of biopower and refers to "any rational effort to influence or guide the conduct of human beings through acting upon their hopes, desires, circumstances or environment" (Inda 2005: 1). Governmentality is, as Foucault said in shorthand, "the conduct of conduct" (1991). He saw governance as both a goal and a distinctive form of power exercised through wide-ranging modes of scientific knowledge or expertise, practical instruments and programs, and modes of subjectification, that is, ways of understanding one's relationship to oneself.[6] In contrast to social theories that defined power largely as the state's monopoly over force and law, governance is not the sole province of the state and its institutions. Rather, governmentalizing strategies are mobilized by multiple actors—authorities, planners, inspectors, and policy makers—that collectively, if not always coherently, seek to administer "the lives of others in the light of conceptions of what is good, healthy, normal, virtuous, efficient or profitable" (Rose and Miller 1992: 175). Foucault saw this political rationality to be at the heart of the modern welfare state and its ways of dealing with the factory worker, the urban dweller, and a host of social problems. As such, he wrote, "the problems of governmentality and the techniques of government have become the only political issues, the only real space for political struggle and contestation" (1991: 103). Since his original treatise on the subject, scholars have tracked shifts in governmentalizing tactics that have emerged with neoliberal conceptions of the state and the economy that abandon the notion of state welfare for concepts of empowerment, active citizenship, and entrepreneurialism (Rose 1999; Dean 1999). In contemporary modes of governmentality, the logics of the marketplace have become a pervasive framework for the management of social life and social problems.

Governmentality is thus best described as an evolving and pervasive political rationality that, as Wendy Brown puts it, "peregrinates between state, civil society and citizens" (2006: 79). It is pervasive in the frameworks and methods by which language advocates struggle to save Basque and build a new bilingual society. Their practices are clear indices of the way in which the tactics of governance—the creation of standards, norms, reliable indicators of progress, methods of planning—have become a part of the political struggles of social movements. As Colin Gordon explains, "As governmental practices have addressed themselves in an increasingly immediate way to 'life,' ... individuals have begun to formulate the needs and imperatives of that same life as the basis for political counter demands. ... the history of government, as the 'conduct of conduct' is interwoven with the history of dissenting 'counter-conducts'" (1991: 5). In seeking to reverse the effects of discrimination and to save their language, language-revival movements eagerly seek out, borrow from one another, and adapt from other fields of expertise methods such as surveys, standardization, strategic planning, and assessment routines that are deeply familiar, thoroughly modern, but which should not be taken for granted.

My approach follows Foucault's invitation to treat practices of resistance as *diagnostics* of power and modern ways of problematizing social life. As he explains:

> I would like to suggest another way to go further towards a new economy of power relations. ... It consists of taking the forms of resistance against different forms of power as a starting point. To use another metaphor, it consists of using this resistance as a chemical catalyst so as to bring to light power relations, locate their position, find out their point of application and the methods used. Rather than analyzing power from the point of view of its internal rationality, it consists of analyzing power relations through the antagonism of strategies. (1982: 211; see also Abu Lughod 1990)

Language-activist strategies can be seen as diagnostic of the ways in which the framework and assumptions of governmentality have in many ways set the terms of debate about language and shaped the way language practices and the speaking self are understood. At the same time, they are more than that. The emergence and naturalization of a particular governmental view of language and the speaking subject are also in part an outcome of the cultural struggle.

While language revival is a battle against prejudice, my main goal is to show that its cultural dynamics and effects go well beyond this. As a social movement, language revival contests negative views of minority speakers, opens up for explicit debate and critique conventional and often discriminatory ways of using or talking about language, and introduces new forms of subjectivity and imaginings of language, nation, and the self that can be experienced positively or negatively. At the same time, language-revitalization discourse and practices also reproduce dominant beliefs about the social life of language. This is often noted about counterhegemonic movements. Movements for racial, sexual, and gender equality, for example, are critiqued for reproducing essentialist notions of identity; ecology movements are revealed to uphold conservative notions of nature. This type of criticism has also been leveled at minority language movements: in working to assure greater respect and status for their language, activists' images, beliefs, and goals reproduce some of the dominant ways that nation-states conceptualize and treat languages: for example, the notion of languages as bounded, discrete objects; the belief in the necessity of internal uniformity; the erection of norms of good and bad use; and a presumed unambiguous link between nation and language.

Exploring these and other elements that minority activist discourse and practices share with dominant language ideology is necessary for understanding some of the tensions and ironies that are generated within minority language movements and the resistances to revival that often arise among native speakers.[7] This is important, but I am reluctant to leave the analysis there—the analysis of social movements requires more. We need to remember the unequal contexts of these struggles and to understand the larger frameworks in which they are constrained to work even as we scrutinize ironies and shortcomings. In her study of environmental activists, Anna Tsing (2005) reflects on precisely this issue. With public debate dominated by proclamations of the benefits of "universalism," it is tricky, she says, yet more important than ever, to make known the unequal and compromised terrain in which struggles for cultural differences are waged. My writing about Basque-language activism has been colored by a similar set of concerns and awareness of context. In the current moment, Basque cultural activism is being conflated with one violent strand of Basque nationalism. Accused of fundamentalism, ethnic cleansing, or fomenting terrorism, language activism as discussed in the popular press and scholarly writing is often disappointingly based on faulty or superficial knowledge. For this reason I have made an effort to discuss misconceptions that circulate about Basque-language advocacy and to convey a sense of *euskaltzaleak* as I have come to understand them to be: not exotic "others," but real people working very hard for something that is deeply meaningful to them— the Basque language and expressive culture. They are on the whole a highly creative, self-critical, and varied group of actors. Many embrace the idea of a common Basque nation, but the nation they imagine and enact looks nothing like the racialized nineteenth-century model that detractors continue to attribute to them. If this fact is not better known, it is because the voices and activities of language advocates, particularly those in local or nongovernmental groupings, are rarely heard beyond their own region, much less read in their own language. This awareness has led me to give priority to those perspectives and has pushed me to find other ways of approaching the politics and logics of language struggle.

My sense is that an anthropology of activism and social movements can more productively contribute to redressing inequalities when it is asking what the strategies of cultural activism, contradictory as they are, can reveal about experiences of domination, the mechanisms by which power is exercised through language, the sites of struggle, and the nature of contestation. Rather than stepping *backward* to assess in a kind of "bottom line" analysis whether minority-language advocacy is "truly" resistant, it strikes me as more interesting and valuable to step *forward* to get a closer look at the practices and discourses of activists and community-based movements as they engage with various modes of domination.[8] In so doing, we might be better able to appreciate the complexities of the social positions that minority-language speakers and activists inhabit and the insights that their location at the margins can often provide (Bhabha 1992; hooks 1990). For Foucault, "the task of the analyst is not to adjudicate between [solutions to social problems] but to 'rediscover at the root of these diverse solutions the general form of problematization that has made them possible'" (Rabinow and Rose 2003: xviii). I take this stance in my inquiry into the logics that inform the strategies of language revival. I do not ask whether nationalism is right or wrong, but rather how that imaginary has informed the discourse of revival. More importantly yet, I inquire into alternative formulations that envision language no longer as inherited patrimony, but as a performative practice. Similarly, I do not ask whether language revival, planning, or reform are the right things to do, but rather what makes standardizing, planning, or surveys seem to be so self-evidently useful courses of action for language preservation. What view of language and the speaking subject underlies these strategies? And what responses and unexpected effects do they engender?

I made a strategic decision to work across a number of sites, bringing into the same frame of analysis both "core" or dominant discourses of the revival movement—exemplified in the writings of academicians and intellectuals—as well as community-based language-revival groups and the marginal or "minor" tactics of the lowbrow language play of youth involved in the free-radio movement. This is only a selection of the range of activities one could study. The result might seem an eclectic assemblage with notable gaps; I do not examine the school movement, for example, in part because it has been widely studied. Rather than a comprehensive history, my aim with this strategy is to show that resistance to Spanish domination is an ongoing, multisited struggle. My intent is to convey a sense of the heterogeneity of ways that the cultural struggle around language unfolds. The meanings and status of Basque, like the methods of advocacy, are not fixed, but changing and disputed. Language revival is characterized by impulses to stabilize and manage the language as well as by spaces of creative ferment and new possibilities that emerge as the stability of the previous linguistic order is unsettled. This is my stance as I examine some of the rationalities and strategies at work in the reclaiming of Basque.

Locations

All views come from somewhere (Haraway 1991). Mine has been shaped by the analytical framework I discuss above, but also by the places where I lived in the Basque Country, the historical moment, and my own family history and political affinities. I entered the world of language activism as a graduate student of anthropology in the summer of 1979 when I went to the Basque Country to take my first Basque-language class. This was a momentous time in the history of Spain. The political climate was charged and exciting after Franco's death. Residents of the southern Basque territory were preparing to vote on a proposed Statute of Autonomy that would join three of the Spanish Basque provinces into the Basque Autonomous Community and make Euskara co-official with Spanish in that territory. Thousands of people at the time were taking Basque-language classes, while many other native speakers were enrolled in literacy classes in order to learn to read and write the newly created standard Basque. When I returned three years later in 1982 to begin ethnographic fieldwork on the evolving language politics, I took up residence in the small town of Usurbil (population 5000), just a few kilometers away from Donostia, the capital city of Gipuzkoa, near the French border.

Contacts and good luck led me to a family who ran a bar/restaurant in town. They had a couple of extra rooms they sometimes let out to truck drivers passing through and agreed to have me stay with them until I found something more permanent. An older cousin of mine drove me there, suitcases in tow. We were warmly received. María, the grandmother and matriarch of the family, had been the one to offer me this as a place to stay.[9] At the time she ran the kitchen of the restaurant I will call the Bar Martín, which served about one hundred modest but hearty midday meals to the workers of a nearby factory. María was an enormously vital, generous, and no-nonsense woman who had grown up in a local farmhouse. At the time I lived with them, all the members of the extended household had Basque as a first language but with different degrees of fluency, and none had formally studied it in school. While this family was generally supportive of Basque nationalism, its members had differing political opinions on the nationalist parties. María supported radical nationalism and did not hesitate to express her dislike for the Spanish police who used to come undercover to the bar fishing for information on ETA [Euskadi ta Askatasuna]. One of her sons shared her political views, while the other supported the more moderate nationalists. The division among nationalist sectors in society at large was extremely volatile at the time of my research; it often seemed more antagonistic than the one between Spanish and Basque political parties. Political violence was not a subject of our conversations. In general they, like most families I came to know, steered away from hot-button topics that could lead to arguments.

Language, on the other hand, was a topic about which it seemed almost everyone had an opinion and was willing to talk. Before arriving, as a dutiful new anthropologist, I had communicated to them that I wanted to live with a Basque-speaking family so I could learn the language well. I already knew Spanish with some fluency. And so, the night of my arrival and for many nights thereafter, we talked about where would be the best place for me to learn Basque. María's household, consisting of herself, her husband and his unmarried sister, María's eldest son and his wife and children, were all native speakers of Basque, but they often spoke in Spanish among themselves and with outsiders. The only exception was with the children. Adults in this family always addressed children in Basque. The linguistic environment was untidy to say the least. We got along well, but all of us wondered if, as a seminative speaker of Spanish, I would be able to learn Basque in this environment. Scouting about for other locations, a neighbor of theirs and well-known Basque-language advocate suggested a farmhouse family. They thought it was a marvelous idea. If I really wanted to learn Basque, they all thought that was the best place to go: a *baserri* [farmhouse].

The Zumarte farmhouse turned out to be that place. I did not move there permanently but spent many weekends with this other equally generous and welcoming family, living in what seemed an almost textbook example of the classic Basque farmhouse: three generations living under one roof, bedrooms located above the kitchen and cow stable below (Caro Baroja 1971). Like many farmers in this area, the husband of the family combined farmwork with his job as an unskilled laborer in one of the nearby factories. Several members of the family had spent time working in Argentina, while others had gone into service for the Catholic church as priests and nuns. These patterns were all very typical of rural Basque families. Basque was the language of everyday life at Zumarte; everybody spoke it with ease, and even the teenagers seemed more comfortable in Basque than Spanish. While they spoke Spanish when needed, they were consciously committed to Basque as the language of their home and willing to help me learn.

Though it seemed a distant world, the farmhouse was only a thirty-minute walk from the center of town, where María's bar was located. On my walk down the hill into town, I passed through another neighborhood known as "Santuenea," where workers from southern and western Spain had come to live in the sixties and seventies to take jobs in the nearby factories. They had become an important part of the contemporary makeup of Usurbil. I did a series of interviews with immigrant families in my early research, but I regrettably did not live with a family there.

These contrasts and processes of change were precisely what had drawn me to Usurbil as a place for fieldwork. I did not want to be isolated from change but to be right in the thick of it. Zumarte exemplified the rural farmhouse way of life that was iconic of "authentic" Basque language and culture in Basque nationalism. María's bar, on the other hand, located next to the main plaza, was a living display of language shift in the making. Meanwhile, from the streets of Santuenea, where barely a word of Basque was uttered, came some of the students, parents, and workers I would come to know in town and through my Basque-language classes.

For the better part of my first year of fieldwork, I was a traveler on this road, betwixt and between these very different experiences of Basque society, culture, and language. Usurbil and neighboring towns of Gipuzkoa have served as the primary location for most of the ethnographic observations I make about Basque language use and community-activist strategies. The boundaries of the language activism were of course not limited to this town. My research also took me to other locations—to attend language-loyalist conferences and events, lectures, and demonstrations as well as the well-known Basque Summer University in Iruña/Pamplona. I have learned about language revival by conducting formal and informal interviews with grassroots language loyalists throughout the southern Basque country, by spending many hours learning Basque alongside others in a variety of adult language classes, by reading local newspapers, and by spending unimaginable amounts of time socializing in local cafés—a defining feature of Basque social life. I also learned a great deal talking with the group of women who worked in the Martín kitchen about everyday life as it unfolded around us. I have been returning to this same area and the same kitchen for two decades. After my initial fieldwork in 1982–83, I carried out extended research stays in 1987, 1994, 1998, and 2003, and in these later trips I traveled significantly beyond Usurbil, exploring youth culture—music primarily—and Basque local media. Nevertheless, Gipuzkoa, and more specifically the Basque-speaking environs of Donostia, have been the vantage point from which I have experienced language activism. Of any of the Basque provinces, this one has some of the highest concentrations of Basque speakers, Basque-language schools, and grassroots language-activist organizations. Other locations like Navarra, where language revival is more contested, might have produced other perspectives, perhaps other emphases, particularly when it comes to my descriptions of the local dynamics of language use or local language associations. However, my overarching argument about governmentality and nationalism is, I believe, generalizable to the social movement as a whole.

My identity and my identifications with the Basque Country were not that of a complete outsider. I was born and raised in the United States to a Basque father and a Spanish mother who were refugees from Franco's Spain. My father's mother was born in the mountain town of Esparza. Basque was her first language. Whenever I was introduced as the visiting anthropologist, people would unfailingly mention my Basque heritage and knowing nods would follow. At the start of my research, this ethnic heritage supplied the most intelligible reason for why a young woman had come so far to learn about Basque. My family's political history added other kinds of connections. Both of my parents left Spain after Franco came to power, their families having suffered deaths, imprisonment, and economic hardship for their participation in anti-Franco resistance during and after the Spanish Civil War.

If heritage gave me a legible location and motivation in the eyes of people I worked with, what brought me inside the movement were my efforts to learn Basque. Bonds of solidarity rather than blood are what earned for me some modicum of access inside the world of *euskaltzaleak*. My effort to learn and use Basque were taken as evidence of the sincerity of my interests and were often necessary for me to be able to participate in and understand language-activist events. Trying to learn Basque alongside others also taught me a lot about the lived experience of the language and revival dynamics. This study would have been much thinner had I not had these many hours and firsthand experiences of studying and trying to speak Basque. The time I spent in and outside of classrooms put me in direct contact with other students of both Basque and Spanish origin, the efforts of consciousness-raising, and the discourse of the movement as it was popularly disseminated. It helped me to understand the practical difficulties of trying to translate that classroom learning into public spaces and the problems that differences between standard Basque and dialect presented, and it gave me insight into the social experiences of new Basque learners, called *euskaldun berriak*. Similarly, the hours I spent at the staff meetings of the local community magazine and free-radio station programmers, camping out at the gatherings of radical and alternative youth, listening in on the political discussions and workshops they organized on everything from the squatter movement to *bertsolaritza* [Basque oral poetry], and witnessing the concerts they held until the wee hours of the morning gave me a sense of other kinds of less regulated language dynamics and political strategies. The resulting analysis of the language movement's discourse and practices, while perhaps not an ethnography in the classic sense of the term, shares with ethnographies a reliance on personal learning, participation, and observation in particular places at particular historical moments. As fieldwork on an evolving and moving target, my work does not pretend to tell the definitive or whole story of the movement, but is an attempt to see why this long and vital struggle for linguistic equality merits a closer look.

Language Loyalism's Early Roots

Advocacy on behalf of the Basque language has a long history that begins well before the Franco era and even before the appearance of a Basque nationalist movement. Recovering that legacy of advocacy and disseminating a fuller understanding of Euskara's past has been an important part of the contemporary language struggle. Exposés on early *euskaltzaleak* [Basque language loyalists] were common in Basque cultural magazines of the seventies and eighties. These early scholars and writers served as a pantheon of ancestors whose work is seen as having paved the way for present-day revival efforts.

To convey some of this history of Basque language advocacy, I focus on three discursive moments widely considered to be pivotal in the history of language loyalism. The first of these is the publication of a dictionary and grammar in defense of Basque in the eighteenth century by the Jesuit scholar Manuel de Larramendi. The second is the florescence of the Euskal Pizkundea, a Basque literary and folkloric revival, and the emergence of the first Basque nationalist party in the late nineteenth century. Although there are many important figures in Basque revival from this era, I consider two principal political figures who were greatly concerned with the Basque language: the writer and lawyer Arturo Campión and Sabino Arana de Goiri, the founder of the Basque Nationalist Party. While they had many profound disagreements over politics, Campión and Arana are exemplary of the kind of nostalgic ruralist view of Basque language and culture that prevailed in this period. The third discursive moment takes place in the early twentieth century with the foundation of the Eusko Ikaskuntza [The Basque Studies Society] and Euskaltzaindia [The Basque Language Academy] in 1918. Though the latter two institutions are often portrayed as a part of the same generalized florescence of Basque nationalism and cultural revival of which Campión and Arana are a part, I think it wise to consider them separately. I argue that something quite distinct and important in the approach to language emerges with these latter institutions. The largely progressive reformers of The Basque Studies Society define and legitimate a decidedly modern sociological perspective on language that laid the foundations for the discourse of "language planning" that was to come. In juxtaposing these three discursive moments, my aim is to show that within the verifiable *longue durée* of language loyalism, there are notable shifts in the way that loyalists understood the relationship between language and something we might call national identity.

Basque has been admired, defended, as well as attacked for a very long time, but not always in the same way or for the same reasons. A comparison of these different moments in language loyalism shows us that what we have is not so much a linear progression, but a set of somewhat discrepant conceptualizations that in many ways continue to circulate and bear upon the language movement today. In examining the discourse about language, I try to avoid some of the problems that often plague histories of language revival. One of these problems is the tendency to view the past as a continuous expression of loyalty to language that endures unchanged over time. My own view is that there are important shifts in what Basque meant to language loyalists of the past and what it means in the present. Equally problematic are what I would call "superstructural" explanations of language revival. In the latter, language tends to be treated mainly as a political symbol in the struggle for some *other* form of power. In these kinds of approaches, language revival is not seen as a real issue, but rather as a guise for the pursuit of class or regional ethnic-elite interests or both. The issue is not whether language politics intersects with other axes of power and interests. Of course they do, and we should explore those intersections. But language advocacy is not necessarily reducible to those other struggles. In my own reading of these historical moments and treatises I take a third way that seeks to gain insight into the shifting nature of language ideology and to identify underlying assumptions, tensions, as well as rationalities that may be at work in contemporary language revival.

Larramendi and the Antiquity of Basque

The first written accounts discussing the origins and antiquity of Basque, as best we know, began appearing as early as the sixteenth century, proposing—via rather fantastical etymologies—Basque as the origin for Castilian and Latin words. But it is in the eighteenth century, when the Spanish crown was attempting to centralize the state, that the question of Basque origins really heats up. It is at this time that we encounter a flurry of writings describing the origins and grammar of Basque along with a defense of its status vis-à-vis Castilian. The historical record reveals an impassioned polemic over the political status of Spain's regions and claims to Christian purity of blood in which language was a key terrain of battle and the dictionary and grammar book held pride of place. As historian Pierre Bidart writes, the dictionary in eighteenth-century Europe was "a veritable instrument of political and historical debate," a means of "rendering of accounts, a manifesto, a counter-theory" (1986: 328).

In *Mitología e ideología sobre la lengua Vasca* (1980), linguist Antonio Tovar situates the rise of eighteenth-century *"apologias"* [language defenses] on behalf of Basque as a reaction to the creation of the Royal Spanish Language Academy. This academy's exhaustive six-volume *Diccionario de autoridades* (1726–39) as well as the writings of Spanish philologists of the time, argues Tovar, portrayed Castilian as intrinsically superior to the other languages of the peninsula. Euskara—typically referred to at the time as *vascuence* or *vizcaino*—was by contrast characterized as a crude vernacular, limited by a faulty grammar and a mongrel vocabulary borrowed from the many peoples who had passed through the region (Bidart 1986). Basque was considered a barbarism. These views about Basque, and minority languages in general, continue to surface even today, supported in part by a long and impressive list of scholars (May 2001: 20). As Stephen May notes, one of our most infamous examples comes from John Stuart Mill, the nineteenth-century theorist of liberal democracy in whose 1862 treatise, "Consideration of Representative Government," ethnic minorities are characterized as bearers of inferior cultures that stand in the way of a healthy nation-state. The following extract, which interestingly makes specific mention of Basques, is a particularly vivid example of how liberal political theory pits minority-language speakers in opposition to the democratic nation-state.

> Experience proves it is possible for one nationality to merge and be absorbed in another: and when it was originally an inferior and more backward portion of the human race the absorption is greatly to its advantage. Nobody can suppose that it is not beneficial to a Breton, or a Basque of French Navarre, to be brought into the current of the ideas and feelings of a highly civilized and cultivated people—to be a member of the French nationality, admitted on equal terms to all the privileges of French citizenship, sharing the advantages of French protection, and the dignity and *prestige* of French power, than to sulk on his own rocks, the half-savage relic of past times, revolving in his own mental orbit, without participation or interest in the general movement of the world. (Mill 1861: 293, emphasis in original)[1]

Among the most illustrious figures in the history of language loyalism is the eighteenth-century Jesuit priest Manuel de Larramendi, whose books challenged what he called the many "impertinences" and "calumnies" that were being perpetrated by Spanish philologists of the era (see Madariaga Orbea 2006). Larramendi offered his retort to their linguistic slandering with a cleverly entitled grammar, *El imposible vencido* [The Impossible Conquered] in 1729, followed by a trilingual dictionary (Spanish-Basque-Latin) in 1745. Both of these texts can be seen as early examples of an argument language loyalists would continue to make for another two centuries: namely that Basque was every bit as grammatically complex, complete, and logical as any other language of high civilization. But Larramendi went further than this. His other set of claims had to do with the ancient origins of Basque. Here we find his arguments to be notably different from that of later Basque advocates. In his very first treatise on the Basque language, *De la antiguedad y universalidad del bascuence en España* (1728) [On the antiquity and universality of Basque in Spain] he marshaled etymological and toponymic evidence to argue that Basque was much older than Castilian. Indeed, he argued that Euskara was the original language of Spain and had once been spoken throughout the peninsula. This antiquity led Larramendi to revive the thesis that had circulated since the sixteenth century that Basque was one of the ancient languages of Babel (Tovar 1980). The Babelian thesis held Euskara to be one of the original seventy-two languages created by Jehova at the Tower of Babel and brought to Iberia by Tubal, presumed in theological writings to be the grandson of Noah, founder and ancestral patriarch of the Iberian peoples. In short, "Spain"—that is, Christian Spain— argued Larramendi, had its origins in the Basque provinces, and the evidence for this was Euskara itself.

Why was Larramendi making such a claim, and what did it mean at this moment when the Spanish crown was attempting to rescind the political rights of the Basque provinces? To answer this it is necessary to understand that the origin of languages throughout Europe was a political terrain of battle precisely because, as Judith Irvine and Susan Gal (2000) observe, languages were regarded as the expression of natural collectivities. Histories of languages and their boundaries were read as the histories of nations and their rightful political relations. As Woolard has argued, in early modern Spain, philological debates were a means by which groups in a polyglot and polyethnic Spain jostled for status, defined alterity, and argued the terms of their coexistence and rightful rule (2004). The reconquest, the long battle against Muslim rule in the Iberian peninsula followed by the subsequent absorption of Muslim and Jewish converts, had given rise to a society hierarchically divided between "Old" and "New" Christians. People or groups who could convincingly lay claim to being descendants of "Old Christians," that is people presumed to have no Moorish or Jewish background, enjoyed superior status and access to prized positions in civil and ecclesiastical administration. The genealogy of a language was one of the more powerful ways that a collectivity could make or contest a claim to being Old or New Christians.

Mockery of a language, like praise, can be a potent weapon in larger battles for social status (Hill 1993). The attacks and defenses of Basque in this period are a case in point. The claims Larramendi made about the ancient biblical origins of Basque, just like the scorn and accusations of barbarism by Spanish philologists, have to be contextualized as part of the intensifying debate that was taking place in the eighteenth century over the relationship between the Basque provinces and the Spanish state. Historically, the Spanish Basque provinces had enjoyed special political rights, *fueros,* that gave them a substantial degree of self-governance. The kings of Spain came to the tree of Gernika to swear to uphold the *fueros* and in so doing sustain political and military alliances with the Basques. These rights were justified, however, not as an instrumental strategy of a weak state, but as an entitlement Basques had earned for their decisive role in numerous battles during the reconquest. The medieval *fueros* granted to the inhabitants the special status of "collective nobility" for supposedly never having fallen under Muslim rule. This status "gave Basques direct access to public offices in the Spanish administration and military" (Shafir 1995: 89) and may partly explain why we find the early growth of an urbanized Basque elite that was Spanish speaking and largely collaborative with the state. However, as the Spanish crown grew stronger and sought to centralize its power in the eighteenth century, the special rights of provinces began to be challenged (Elliot 1963). Catalonia lost its own special privileges early in the century, and it looked likely that Basques would be next. To reaffirm somewhat anachronistically, as Larramendi did, a Tubalian origin for Basque in this particular political moment was to affirm the special status of Basques as Old Christians and thus shore up the continuing legitimacy of their foral rights (Douglass 2002: 99–101).[2]

It bears underscoring that in Larramendi's eighteenth-century treatises, an argument claiming Basque difference or uniqueness was not conceived of as an entitlement to *separation* from Spain. Rather, claims of Basque antiquity and Tubalian origins were presented more as evidence of the Basque people's *belonging and centrality to the history of Spain*; it was a claim to having a respected, even privileged place in the social order, not a claim of alterity. As William Douglass (2002: 100–101) points out, this interpretation of Larramendi contradicts that of Davyyd Greenwood (1977), who, following Julio Caro Baroja (1971), presented Larramendi's work as the beginning of a mutually exclusive and conflicting conception of Spanish and Basque identities. Douglass coincides with Tovar (1980) and my own reading that "[Larramendi's] real targets are the frenchified Castilian toadies of the Bourbon rulers in Madrid who were undermining Basque privileges. And while he does launch a few pejorative statements against the Castilians in general, he is mainly on the defensive against the Castilian anti-Basque barbs of the day—notably that the language was sheer 'gibberish' and that the Basque claim to universal noble status was pretentious" (Douglass 2002: 100).

Larramendi argued that the existence of Euskara proved the Basque people were the "*legitimate pure Spaniards,* descendants of the ancient settlers of Spain" and thus entitled to their special rights (Tovar 1980: 70, emphasis added). These conceptualizations, however, shift. When the *fueros* were lost in 1876 and Basque nationalism as a political ideology subsequently began to take shape, we see that the symbolic significance of Basque does a complete reversal. Euskara no longer links Basques to Spain, nor gives them pride of place in it. Rather it is now presented as setting Basques apart as a separate nation. Once again, etymology and linguistic evidence figure prominently as proof.

The Basque Folkloric Revival and Early Nationalism: Spanish Cities, Rural Basques

This turnaround begins to take shape in the last third of the nineteenth century with the Euskal Pizkundea, a key moment in the historical evolution of language loyalism during which Basque cultural institutions and popular festivals portrayed Euskara as part of a romanticized rural life. This movement emerged at the same time that industrialization and urbanization were producing profound economic and demographic changes that accelerated the pace of Basque-language loss and accentuated class antagonism.

Politically, this era is often dated to 1876 when, at the end of the second Carlist war, the southern Basque provinces were administratively incorporated into the Spanish state. At this time economic and political power went from being in the hands of rural notables, known as *jauntxos,* to the cities.[3] Although the *fueros* were abolished, special economic privileges were retained through what were called *conciertos económicos,* economic pacts that granted protective tariffs, new export regulations, and decreased taxes for the Basque provinces. This situation, together with foreign capital investment that began pouring into the cities, enabled a tremendous spurt of economic growth in the iron and steel industries, as well as in mining, shipbuilding, and railroad construction (see Clark 1979: 35–37). In the last two decades of the nineteenth century, the industries of the capital cities of Gipuzkoa and Bizkaia began to attract laborers from southern and western Spain, as well as people from the surrounding Basque-speaking rural areas. Rapid immigration gave rise to congested working-class neighborhoods, especially near Bilbao, where Basque and Spanish laborers lived side by side and where the seeds of a powerful organized labor movement began to take root.[4] In most histories of the Basque language, the growth of cities tends to be thought of as the prime factor that intensifies contact of Basque and Spanish speakers and leads to Hispanicization and language replacement. Philologists of the time bemoaned an increase in language mixing in popular culture and point in particular to a preference for Spanish among young women who went to the city to work as nannies and maids (Zalbide 1988: 392–93; see also Zuberogoitia and Zuberogoitia 2008). It is during this period of social and cultural transformation, writes Mikel Zalbide, that Euskara took a dramatic downturn and a long-standing practice of more or less stable bilingualism turned into "a serious hemorrhage" (1988: 392).

Of course, *castellano,* the Castilian language, already had a long history in the southern Basque Country. There is evidence that it was spoken in the upper social strata from the thirteenth century onward, when the provinces of Gipuzkoa, Araba, and Bizkaia were incorporated into the Crown of Castile.[5] In his review of the evolution of Basque, Zalbide notes that bilingualism was commonplace in a broad range of people whose professions or trades placed them in ongoing relations with that elite or with other people who did not know Basque. As he puts it, there can be no doubt that well before industrialization: "even in the most Basque-speaking areas north of the watershed running into the bay of Biscay there were many [people] who used another language in addition to their native tongue, frequently more often than Basque itself: seamen and traders, clergy and authorities, teachers, doctors and lawyers" (1988: 391–92).

However, the two languages, Zalbide argues, appear to have existed in a delimited, patterned, and more or less stable diglossia; Basque and Castilian each had its distinct domains of use. With industrialization this pattern was destabilized as increasing numbers of native Basque speakers left the countryside to seek jobs in the cities and abandoned the Basque language, though not necessarily their attachment to being Basque.[6] This gave rise, particularly in Bizkaia, to the emergence of a significant group of lower- and middle-class urbanites who identified as Basque—*vascos*—but who were not *euskaldun,* Basque speaking. This linguistic divide has continued to be a crucial and ongoing source of tension and ambiguities within the Basque-identified community.

Several factors coincided to accelerate language shift at the end of the nineteenth century. In Bizkaia the rapid increase and large concentrations of Spanish-speaking labor migrants was certainly one and is probably the most frequently mentioned factor. Also relevant, however, was the growing importance of schooling and literacy in Spanish for the general population. Basque was not formally taught in schools, and as a result literacy in Basque was minimal in the general population. In 1857 the Ley Moyano establishing mandatory primary education turned the neglect of Basque in education to outright banishment by explicitly prohibiting Basque in public schools. Meanwhile, the hostility toward Basque in the more abundant and more prestigious schools run by religious orders was legendary (Tejerina 1992: 88–89; Michelena 1977). Basque effectively had no place in formal educational institutions.

Language shift, however, is rarely just a case of the actual numbers or proportions of speakers or even a result of institutional marginalization or prohibition. Linguistic anthropologists have amply shown that language choices and processes of shift are strongly influenced by how languages are symbolically linked to structures of power, such as class status, gender, or the way a language is identified with access to desired livelihoods or valued social networks (see Gal 1979, 1987; Woolard 1985; Kulick 1992). Immigration and the resulting demographic tilt that gave rise to concentrations of Spanish-speakers in the working-class neighborhoods of the expanding cities—particularly Bilbao—are undoubtedly factors responsible for the shift to Spanish. But it would be a mistake to attribute language shift solely to institutional prohibition or the large influx of Spanish speakers. As Zalbide (1988) is keen to point out, the linguistic profile of the upper classes in the new society is also relevant. The people of Basque descent who wielded economic and political power in the cities were no longer Basque speakers by the time industrialization took off, and this fact powerfully shaped the social status of Euskara. Language shift among Basque elites had been in the works for some time. As Benjamín Tejerina notes, already by the late eighteenth century, economic prosperity generated by commerce and the naval and iron industries had given rise to a class of merchants and industrialists in the coastal cities committed to modernization and identified with Castilian (1992: 84–85, 1996). In contrast to Catalonia, where for the most part the upper classes remained Catalan speaking, in the Basque provinces of Bizkaia and to a lesser extent Gipuzkoa, Castilian had come to be identified with upper-class status—the "jacket wearers" (urbanites)—well before the industrial boom of the late nineteenth century (Zalbide 1988). Thus, writes Zalbide, Basque speakers coming into the cities "would have seen clearly that to be a Basque of any standing one of the decisive new conditions was being not merely a stumbling speaker of the new language but a competent one" (ibid.: 392).

The overlapping class and rural/urban semiotics of language is attested to in popular literature through the well-developed tropes of the hispanicized urbanite, referred to in Basque as the *kaletarra,* and the Basque-speaking peasant, *baserritarra.*[7] Castilian was predominantly associated with class ascendancy, modernity, and urbanity on the one hand and Basque with a rural sector that was on a precipitous economic and political decline. The consolidation of this ideology is critical, argues Zalbide, to explaining why it is that newly arrived Spanish-speaking laborers would have experienced relatively little incentive to learn Basque and native Basque speakers looking for work in the cities would have been inclined to abandon Basque altogether (ibid.: 393).

The Euskal Pizkundea, or Basque cultural renaissance of the late nineteenth century, unfolds in this context. This movement was spearheaded by an amalgam of intellectuals, middle-class professionals, teachers, and townspeople, some progressive, others more traditionalist, who shared a disenchantment with the profound social and cultural changes taking place and the growing hegemony of the urban centers (ibid.: 394). Most historians see this as the moment when a Basque-identified protoelite began to coalesce into a political force that was able to tap into and give voice to the acute sense of dislocation experienced by people of the smaller towns and countryside after the loss of the Carlist wars. Euskara, on a steady decline, became a rallying point for articulating this discontent. The Asociación Euskara de Navarra was the first of a variety of Basque cultural associations that began to stimulate the study of and artistic production in Euskara. The association organized the highly popular celebrations known alternately as Juegos Florales or Fiestas Euskaras and cultivated a conception of authentic Basque language and rural life that would become iconic of "Basque culture" in the years ahead.[8] At the Juegos Florales one could attend performances of *bertsolaritza* [improvised oral poetry], competitive rural games of ox pulling, log chopping, and hay cutting, as well as dances, handball, and song and literary competitions. In their analysis of these events, Pauli Dávila and Ana Eizagirre argue that these gatherings did more than romanticize rural culture. Lasting in different forms until the Spanish Civil War, these festivals and popular literary competitions served as points of encounter for northern and southern Basques and laid the basis for the development of a common *euskaldun* reading and writing public—a Basque-speaking imagined community—that had not existed before (Dávila and Eizagirre 1995: 262–63).

The writings of Arturo Campión, one of the key figures of this movement, give us insight into the tropes with which Basque was associated during this period. A self-taught linguist and prolific writer, Campión played an instrumental role in founding the Asociación Euskara de Navarra [popularly known as "*los euskaros*"] in 1877 and its journal, *Revista Euskara* (1878–83) (see Elorza 1978; Jimeno 2000). Campión called his native province of Nafarroa "the land of ruins" [*el pueblo de las ruinas*], and none seemed to cause him more pain than Euskara itself (Iriarte 2000: 320). His writings and those of his fellow "*euskaros*" reveal anguish over the decline of Basque, which they saw as both a symptom and a cause of the erosion of a distinctive collective identity. Campión described the Basque language as the most profound aspect of the Basque personality or spirit, "the fundamental, unmistakable, and irreplaceable currency of the Basques" [*la divisa fundamental, inconfundible e insustituible de los Baskos*] (Iriarte 2000: 324). He also believed it to be on the verge of extinction and dedicated much of his writing both to identifying the causes and to proposing solutions to this decline. He considered many factors were to blame. The lack of a university as a site for higher learning in Basque as well as the absence of a common literary standard made the adaptation of Basque to modern society more difficult. Campión also heaped much criticism on primary-school teachers for propagating negative attitudes and shame about speaking Euskara. The expansion of public education had brought the mass arrival of teachers who did not know Basque and punished children for speaking it (see Dávila 1995: 27–28). But all the blame, he argued, could not be placed on institutions, outsiders, or the schools. Basques also had to look inward to face their own indifference to maintaining their ancestral language. Campión was especially critical of Basque elites, whose attitudes he regarded as having a powerful impact on language: "The day that the upper classes of our provinces cease to carry out the stigmatization and abandonment of the indigenous language, one of the most powerful causes of the gradual decline of the language will have been resolved" (Campión quoted in Elorza 1978: 47; see also Tejerina 1992: 98–101). In making these observations, we might say that Campión was developing one of the earliest sociolinguistic analyses of the intersection between class, language prestige, and language shift. The class character of language shift would continue to be an issue for language advocacy after the Spanish Civil War as well.

Sabino Arana de Goiri

There is a great deal of continuity between the discourse about language in the folkloric revival and early Basque nationalism. The folkloric revival created the social networks and symbolic repertoire from which Basque nationalists drew their image of Basque culture, harnessing these, however, to a distinct political ambition. Politically, Campión, like many other writers in the Euskal Pizkundea, favored the restoration of the provincial charter rights [*fueros*] that had been lost in 1876. He and other supporters of foralism, however, began to lose ground to a growing contingent of middle-class intellectuals, professionals, and business owners who were being won over to the idea of Basque nationalism. At the forefront of this project was the Basque Nationalist Party—Partido Nacionalista Vasco (PNV). Founded in 1895 by Sabino Arana de Goiri, the PNV, one of the earliest Christian Democratic parties of Europe, drew its first supporters from the urban middle class and petty bourgeoisie. Beginning with a small following in Bilbao, the PNV grew to become a significant political force that garnered the support of town and country folk, capturing, by 1933, 30 to 40 percent of the vote throughout the Basque provinces (Clark 1979: 40).

Basque nationalism made Euskara a symbol of Basque nationhood, thereby giving added significance to its preservation and impetus to its study and reform. The Basque Nationalist Party, which began to take part in elections in 1898, provided an institutional infrastructure that language-loyalist activity had not had before. Zalbide (1988, 405n3) points to a cascade of events in the 1890s that signal the beginnings of a self-consciously *national* language-loyalist movement. This is when the idea of a single Basque ethnocultural unity spanning all seven territories in Spain and France, conveyed by the concise slogan, Zazpiak Bat—meaning "the

Seven [provinces] Are One"—began to gain recognition. One also finds evidence, argues Zalbide, of more extensive networks of collaboration among language loyalists. Basque-language journalism takes off in the peninsula and Basque language schools and learning materials start to be produced.

Scholars have had varied opinions as to exactly how sincere nationalists were about the defense of the language or how essential language was to nationalist definitions of Basque identity. There is not a simple answer to this, in part because the political landscape was varied and there are differing voices within what can be called Basque nationalism. As the first and largest formal expression of Basque nationalism, the PNV has dominated nationalist politics to such a degree that over time it has become almost coterminous with "Basque nationalism" (see Elorza 1978 and Larronde 1977). However, there have been other voices in the spectrum since the early part of the century: the *aberrianos,* a collective of radical nationalists that formed around the publication *Aberri*; the Acción Nacionalista Vasco (ANV), a moderate leftist group that split off from the PNV in 1930; and the Jagi-Jagis, a more radical anticapitalist nationalist group.

If one examines only the writings of Sabino Arana (and most assessments usually do), we find that in his short life, Arana's views on language were passionate, changeable, and fraught with some contradiction. The complex process of language shift and the way this intersected with class dynamics played a role in producing this ambiguity, since many of Basque nationalism's early supporters came from sectors of society—the urban middle class in and around Bilbao—where fewer people spoke Euskara. This was certainly true for Arana. Born into a devoutly religious upper middle-class Carlist family, Arana, like Campión and other members of the professional and industrial classes, grew up speaking Castilian. Arana's family was bitter toward the Spanish state for having forced Sabino's politically active father into exile. Sabino Arana began to study Basque in his adolescence when, as a student at the University of Barcelona, he became quite influenced by Catalan nationalism and the decolonization movements in the Spanish Empire. Returning to Bilbao in 1888 at the age of twenty-three, Arana continued to study the language and the reasons for its decline, while at the same time he started formulating the basic principles of Basque nationalism in a series of articles published largely in the newspaper Bizkaitarra.

One of the most well known of his essays, "Qué Somos?" [What are we?], published in 1895, is often taken as the foundational nationalist definition of Basque identity. European scientists like Paul Broca had already established that Basques constituted a unique, possibly proto-European "race" (Douglass 2002: 102). In his famous treatise, Arana incorporates this idea as one of five fundamental elements he thought defined the Basque nation: Euskara; race; Basque traditional forms of democratic self governance—what Arana called *lege zaharrak* [traditions, literally, "old laws"]; character or customs, which included such things as nobility of character, intelligence, virility, cleanliness, industriousness, and religiosity; and a unique historical trajectory marked by uninterrupted resistance to domination from outsiders (Romans, Visigoths, Moors, and Spaniards) that demonstrated Basques to be a separate people endowed with a unique historical character.

As Douglass (2002) notes, Sabino Arana has been accused of the "sin of racism." Far too often, however, writes Douglass, this critique fails to place Arana's views in their historical context. Arana thought of himself as a part of the widespread anticolonial rebellion against Spanish rule. He saw the Basques to be like Cuba and the Philippines, a nation unjustly colonized by Spain. Claiming Basques to be a separate race was relatively unremarkable; this was how nineteenth-century Europeans thought about cultural diversity. Throughout Europe nations were frequently described as races and conceived of as the primordial or natural groupings of humankind analogous to lineages. "Languages" were considered to be the most salient markers of these natural boundaries between peoples (Irvine and Gal 2000; Kohn 1944). As Maryon McDonald (1986: 337) notes, "[i]t was more or less tacitly assumed throughout the 19th century that descent and differentiation of languages were congruent with, even consubstantial with, descent, and differentiation of people, race, culture, and polity." Arana's followed a similar logic arguing that Euskara was evidence that Basques were a separate people/race. It was regrettable, he thought, if many Basques had now lost the language. But whether spoken today or not, we find in all of Arana's political treatises a conviction that the Basque language constituted incontrovertible evidence that Basques were a separate nation possessed of a distinctive culture, customs, and character.

The young Arana's writings returned insistently to proving exactly what was probably not nearly so clear in urban Bilbao: the fundamental difference between Basques and all things Spanish. In his distinctively inflammatory rhetoric, Arana made use of the concept of race as an immutable criterion of difference on which to base the rights of Basques to nationhood and independence (Gurruchaga 1985: 111). Some of the most vehement critics of Basque nationalism point to this as a feature of the exceptionality of Basque nationalism. However, as Douglass rightly notes, Arana was hardly unique in his views. "In situating Arana within fin-de-siècle Europe the issue was not who was racist, the rarity was the non-racialist" (Douglass 2002: 96). If his ideas about race carry an idiosyncratic strain, it was perhaps in the way that he combined elements of the older religious discourse of purity of [Christian] blood with the ideas about racial stocks and their differences that were being developed at the time in France, Germany, and England (Elorza 1995: 143).

Arana shared with other European intellectuals of his age a view that humankind was divided into fundamentally different and unequal racial stocks: Caucasian, Mongoloid, and Negroid (Douglass ibid.). Racial vigor and character were commonly used to explain the political triumphs and fortunes of the ascendant powers of nineteenth-century western Europe. Arana marshaled these ideas in making his arguments for separation from a Spanish state that had proven itself to be politically and economically weak. He argued that Basques and Spaniards came from different racial stocks, and he used this to challenge the legitimacy of Spain's political control. His writings are filled with diatribes against the degeneracy of Spaniards and erroneous affirmations that Basques had never mixed with Jews or Moors. Inclined to quarrel and hyperbole, Arana, for example, would not hesitate to point to the Castilian ancestry of his political opponents as a means of disparaging their opinions. Woven into this racial discourse was an undisguised class antagonism both toward the Basque oligarchy and the Spanish working class. He vilified all Spaniards, but particularly the immigrant workers, whom he called *maketos* and described as "the immense wave of corruption, blasphemies, sectarian ideas and perverse customs which, like another Flood, surrounds and overwhelms us from all sides."[9] Arana's writings urged Basques not to mix with these "outsiders," claiming them to be fundamentally incompatible and contaminating to the Basque character.

What, then, did the decline of Euskara matter in this ideologue's framework? Arana valued Basque as a sign of difference, and he worked to cultivate his own knowledge of it. However, he did not advocate a policy of Basque/Spanish bilingualism for everyone. His conviction that Spaniards were a corrupting influence on Basques led him to propose in one of his essays that the Spanish labor migrants should not be allowed to learn Euskara for fear it would facilitate their assimilation. As he was to say: "Many who are Basques do not know Basque. This is not good. There are several *maketos* who know it. This is worse" (Arana 1995 [1897]: 258). But perhaps the most extreme and convoluted expression of Arana's fear of foreign "contamination" is revealed in his article "Errores Catalanes" [Catalan Errors], from which comes the following excerpt. His primary referent for Basque nationalism here is the province of Bizkaia.[10]

> The Catalans wanted that not only they, but also all the other Spaniards in the region should speak Catalan. For us it would be the end if the *maketos* residing in our territory spoke Basque. Why? Because the purity of the race is, like the language, one of the foundations of the Bizkaian motto and while the language can always be restored, even if no one speaks it, as long as there is a good grammar and a good dictionary, the race, on the other hand, cannot be revived once it is lost.

If given a choice between a Bizkaia inhabited by *maketos* that speak only Basque and a Bizkaia populated by Bizkaians who spoke only Castilian, we would choose without hesitation the latter because foreign irregularities can be eliminated from the Bizkaia substance [*sustancia bizkaina*] and substituted for natural elements. This is preferable to a foreign substance with Bizkaian properties which could never change it [i.e., make it Bizkaian].

. . . Bizkaians are as obliged to speak their national language as they are to refuse to teach it to the *maketos* or Spaniards. It is not the speaking of one or another language, but rather the differentiation of languages which is the critical means of preserving us from contamination by the Spaniards and avoiding the mixing of the two races. If our invaders were to learn Basque, we should have to abandon it, carefully filing away its grammar and dictionary, and take up speaking Russian, Norwegian, or some other language unknown to them for as long as we were subject to their domination. (1965: 404)

This part of "Errores Catalanes" is one of the more notorious of Arana's writings. It has given rise to claims that Basque nationalists are not interested in having immigrants learn Euskara and that speaking Basque was never in itself fundamentally important to nationalists. The former is true for some early Basque nationalists. Arana was not interested in winning immigrants over to Basque, and the early PNV restricted membership in the party to people who could prove Basque ancestry. Outside the PNV, however, I have not found evidence that differentiating between who should and should not be allowed to learn Basque was of any real concern to language advocates of this period. More importantly, quite the opposite is true today. In contrast to Arana, the grassroots language movement that took shape at the end of the Franco regime has consistently had as its goal affordable or free public education in Basque for everyone. Language revival today, as we will see, seeks very much to make Basque-language learning available to everyone and represents this as a way of becoming Basque. "Errores Catalanes," however, is worth analyzing for purposes other than illustrating Arana's already well-documented dislike of Spaniards. First, it makes clear the underlying premise of hegemonic language ideology of the time: namely the idea that languages are and should be clearly discernable, bounded, and mutually exclusive things. Language mixing and borrowing, like racial mixing, was seen as detrimental to the health of the language and best purged. Arana spent a good deal of his time doing just that: purifying Basque of Spanish loanwords.

Second, and more subtly, the logic that drives Arana to his bizarre suggestion that perhaps Basques might do well to learn Norwegian if Spaniards were to learn Basque points at a deeper level to a fundamental paradox in nationalist-language ideologies. European national ideologies treat languages as markers of natural boundaries, even though it is clearly known that languages can be acquired and that they are dynamic systems that change over time. Is, then, language a part of the natural order (what is given) or culture (what is acquired)? As feminists have shown for the equally troublesome concept of "woman" (Ortner 1996b), language is categorically slippery, sliding across the opposition drawn between nature and culture. The nature and history of language consequently undermines the essentialism of nationalist discourse at the same time that it is used to support it. Read against the grain, Arana's infamous racist text, "Errores Catalanes," actually points to Euskara's potential to be a point of encounter and mixture rather than a boundary of immutable difference.

In his various treatises, Arana appears to say quite clearly that knowledge of Basque was not indispensable to belonging in the Basque nation. Heiberg elaborates on this point, concluding that language was "more a symbol of the nationalist cause than a fundamental issue" (1982: 358).[11] Nationalism, she rightly notes, drew its initial main support from the urban middle classes—small business owners, artisans, civil servants, and professionals—who found themselves caught, as it were, between the financial and manufacturing oligarchy allied with the central government and an increasingly militant and largely Spanish-immigrant working class on the other. At the time of its creation, writes Heiberg, Basque nationalism was a political ideology created by urbanites to deal with urban problems. Her thesis is that neither Euskara nor any other aspect of Basque culture was considered to be in and of itself indispensable to Basque nationalists. She argues rather that the cultural features marking Basque identity were selected for instrumental reasons: ethnic symbols were mobilized by Bizkaian urbanites for the purpose of instantiating difference and legitimizing their struggle for economic and political power. They had little attachment, she says, to the language or culture itself. Following Barth's theory of ethnicity (1969), she argues that it was the boundary itself that mattered.

More importantly, Heiberg argues, although the boundary was articulated in national/racial/cultural terms, it was understood above all as a moral/ideological boundary between Basques and anti-Basques. It was a boundary that hinged, contrary to what some scholars have argued, not so much on race as on patriotism. Early Basque nationalism, she argues, turned Basqueness into a political identity: a true Basque was *abertzale*, a key term best translated as a "patriot." We can see the priority given to political sentiment over objective cultural markers in the scorn Arana expressed in some of his writings for his own compatriots who thought that by attending the Fiestas Euskaras, wearing berets, beating drums, or dancing an *aurresku* [Basque traditional dance], they could save their nation. In his exhaustive study of Arana's thought, Jean-Claude Larronde cites an 1897 essay by Arana,

"Euzkeltzale bateri" [To a language loyalist], which makes clear Arana's view that language revival had to be intimately linked to a nationalist awakening: "It means nothing to know Basque without being a patriot. Patriotism is everything, even when you do not know Basque. *Euskara* will not save our mother country; nationalism alone can do this. Ensure the spread of patriotism and the Basque language will also spread with it" (Larronde 1977: 134–35).[12]

Despite this, it would be wrong, I believe, to conclude, as some authors have (e.g., Conversi 1997: 261–65), that language revival was largely an incidental issue, window dressing, as it were, used for purposes of legitimating nationalist economic and political claims to power. Linguistic revival and interests are to be sure interwoven with other economic and political interests, but this does not by definition make language politics into a trivial matter. Approaching language loyalty largely as foil—that is, conceptualizing it *only* as a means to some other political end, such as statehood or class hegemony—works against a deeper inquiry into language revival as a field of power in and of itself, with its own particular assumptions and dynamics. It does not lead to questions about what nationalists were doing with and to language, nor to exploring beliefs they had about the social life of language and the factors they thought influenced that social life. What I am calling the superstructural framework short-circuits the exploration of how specific ideologies about language governed and promoted particular kinds of interventions. In short, it cannot take us very deep into language ideology or the governmentality of language politics.

The argument that the revival of Basque held only minor relevance for early nationalists may also be historically inaccurate. This is the opinion of Zalbide (1988), who argues that Basque-revival activities in the early twentieth century not only were not incidental, but actually were increasing and becoming a kind of common ground for Basque advocates with varying perspectives on independence (see also Tejerina 1992). Chief among these activities were the growing efforts to create Basque-language schools for children in which women, many belonging to the women's nationalist group Emakume Abertzale Batza, played a key role. The claim that language revival was a minor or unimportant activity to nationalists during this period is challenged if we recognize teachers, mostly women, as political actors and take seriously the large amount of volunteer labor they put into this Basque-language education (Fernandez 1995; del Valle 1994; Ugalde 1991).

If we go beyond the early ideological tracts of Sabino Arana and look more broadly at the social milieu of the early twentieth century, a different picture comes into view of Basque professionals and educators concerned with meeting the challenges of the industrial society that was taking shape and finding a place for Basque in it. This stance is expressed most explicitly in the Basque Studies

Society. Zalbide argues that by 1901–1902, Arana himself had begun to reformulate his priorities, focusing less on the necessity of acquiring political independence and expelling Spaniards and more on strengthening the Basque language and speech community and adapting it to modern life (Zalbide 1988; Tejerina 1992). In his later writings we find Arana quite dedicated to developing a writing system and a more modern vocabulary that reveal his changing views toward modernity and the city. In some of his last treatises (he died in 1903 at the age of thirty-eight), we find him encouraging nationalists not to refuse modernization, but rather to make their own industries, arts, trades and to incorporate Euskara into these new arenas. "Make *Euskara* necessary in its homeland and rest assured that no native son will forget it. Make it so that it is useful for educating oneself, for prospering, for living, for cultivating oneself, and then, he who possesses it will consider it reasonable to preserve it, and he who does not speak it, will be moved to learn it. Without this, the first will only find [Euskara] to be an obstacle and the second will find it to be a useless luxury" (Arana 1995 [1901]: 275). The assessment that Arana makes in this statement about what motivates language maintenance begins to sound less like either rabid or romantic nationalism and more like the rationality of contemporary language-planning discourse. This and other late writings of his point in the direction of an emergent conviction among language advocates that Basque could be something other than a victim of modernity. If Basque were to have any future at all, it had to become necessary for the modern society that was being created.

Eusko Ikaskuntza: Modernizing Language Reform

The formation of Eusko Ikaskuntza, the Basque Studies Society, and along with it Euskaltzaindia, the Basque Language Academy, in 1918 constitutes a third key chapter in the genealogy of contemporary Basque-language revival. Although overlapping chronologically with early nationalism, I treat these organizations separately because the latter offer a distinct and utterly crucial ingredient to modern language-revival discourse and practice. If Basque nationalist ideology's principal contribution was to make Euskara into a symbol of a unique nation and a marker of collective difference, it was in the hands of this subsector of modernizing reformers that it started to be explicitly constituted *as an object of planning.* Today, the idea that language is something that can be planned is completely taken for granted. But pausing for a moment to examine the perspectives and proposals of Eusko Ikaskuntza's founders helps bring into focus a time when the idea that language *could* be planned and *should* be planned was just beginning to take shape.[13]

The speakers at the first congress of the Basque Studies Society, held in 1918, come close to what Rabinow (1989: 13) has described as "middling modernists": a cadre of middle-ranking professionals and social reformers committed to progress and social engineering. These were the doctors, lawyers, teachers, writers, and engineers of the second generation of the Basque industrial boom (Clark 1979: 38). Many, though not all, supported some form of Basque nationalism or autonomy. As Heiberg notes, this generation of nationalists was on the whole a forward-looking group concerned with the problems unleashed by industrialization and "enthusiastic recipients of European intellectual and technological innovations" (1982: 358). What concerned them most was not separation from Spain, but dealing with the social and economic transformations taking place in their society (ibid.).

The detailed chronicles of the five congresses held by the society from 1918 to 1936 reveal an exuberant group of people who saw themselves at a vital crossroads in the history of their country. Industrialization and rapid urbanization had created a chaotic social order, and a host of social problems had emerged: pollution, congestion, disease, and insufficient housing plagued Bilbao, the heart of Basque industrial growth. The working class had become increasingly militant; socialist and anarchist labor movements had begun to gain force. Class differentiation was growing, and the social and economic divide between the cities and the countryside was sharp. These changes were interpreted as destabilizing the roots of Basque identity as it had been understood until then. The speeches and writings of scholars and scientists who came to the Basque Studies Congress described themselves as in a race against time both to find solutions to the new social problems and to document a fading culture (Elizalde 1918a: 429–30).

The organizers of the congresses of Eusko Ikaskuntza praised the efforts of folklorists, dialectologists, and archaeologists that had come before them, but they believed the time had come to bring more order and professionalism to the array of cultural and scholarly societies that had proliferated. The aim of the society was to promote a more rigorous scientific methodology and a pragmatic orientation in Basque studies and at the same time to develop the expertise to build a new and healthier society. The social and economic problems facing its industrializing cities—migration, labor militancy, housing, and health crises—were going unaddressed by the central government. Spain in the late nineteenth century had a stagnant economy and a weak state. It was losing its last colonies and lacked an industrial and commercial bourgeoisie (Heiberg 1982). These economic and political conditions made it such that in Spain, the cosmopolitan and modernizing impulses were developing more in the culturally distinctive and economically advanced Basque and Catalan "periphery" than in the "core" (see Hechter and Levi 1979). In the Basque Studies Society, the project of scientific social reform was wedded to the preservation of cultural particularity in the periphery. Indeed, they argued that it was necessary that cultural preservation and science be conjoined. Folklore, as it had been practiced, would not do: the treasures and traditions of Basque popular culture, they argued, needed to be collected and better documented. To that end, members attended international scientific congresses and established formal relations with major European and American libraries and academic institutions. Students were sent to France, Germany, England, Belgium, and Switzerland to bring back reports on the latest techniques in a variety of disciplines: pedagogy, archaeology, horticulture, fishing, cooperatives, and the rational organization of work. While the Basque Studies Society promoted the recuperation of Basque music, dance, and other cultural traditions, it understood itself less as an antiquarian society than as the forerunner to a future Basque university, committed to the resolution of the central social problems that were becoming manifest in their rapidly changing society,especially the growing urban centers.

The projects and areas of study spanned numerous fields, from social insurance and agriculture to urban planning and public health (Urla 1989; Estornes Zubizarreta 1983). The zeal for social engineering brought to these various projects of reform is exemplary of what Gilles Deleuze has called "the rise of the social" (Deleuze 1979). "The social," as used by Gilles Deleuze (1979), Jacques Donzelot (1988), and François Ewald (1986) among others, refers to the emergence of social life as a new kind of scientific object and a domain of technical intervention, the conceptual foundation on which governmentality is built. It emerges in conjunction with the development of the social sciences and the welfare state, becoming a pervasive notion among social reformers throughout Europe by the interwar years. "The new sciences of the social worked not only to reconstruct the problems of crime, work accidents, and low fertility but also to constitute the whole of society as an object of scientific knowledge and prophylactic technologies" (Horn 1994: 18).

In touch with these currents of thought in the rest of Europe, the members of the Basque Studies Society enthusiastically brought these same visions to bear on their own society, and in so doing marked a transformation from the more nostalgic discourse that had been defining of the Euskal Pizkundea. The revival of Basque becomes envisioned as a problem treatable through science and planning, like other problems of the city, health, education, or reproduction: that is, as social issues of government that required scientific management and expertise. In the view of this new generation of modernist Basque professionals, protecting the Basque language, culture, and identity required *intervention,* study, and management, not isolation from "contamination." Planning was the watchword of the new ethos. If Basques had survived into the modern age lacking an awareness of the need to take measures to cultivate their culture, it was, declared one congress member, "by pure miracle" (Eleizalde 1918b: 868).

This orientation was nowhere better revealed than in the creation of the Basque Language Academy. Euskaltzaindia, as the academy was named, was created in 1918 at the very first meeting of the Basque Studies Society. The problem for its founders was not whether language could or should be studied and regulated—that was seen as imperative—but how, according to what criteria, and by whom. Julio Urquijo was a major advocate of this rationalist orientation to language revival and a guiding force at both Eusko Ikaskuntza and the newly created scholarly journal, the *Revista Internacional de Estudios Vascos* (RIEV). He began his opening speech at the first congress with a strong reproach for what he saw as "the absolute lack of method" and "grotesque hypotheses" that had abounded until then in the study of Basque and an insistence that the project of study and reform be turned over to those with appropriate credentials (1918: 413). The patriotic love for Basque, Urquijo told his peers, while commendable, had to be reined in and subjected to the rigors of modern linguistic science. The institution to carry this out, they all agreed, would be Euskaltzaindia, a proper language academy comprised of experts, not simply enthusiasts.[14]

The Basque Studies Society, Eusko Ikaskuntza, ushered Basque-language studies and corpus reform into a new moment of modernity. Language was not only being nationalized, it was being governmentalized; that is, it was being conceptualized as an object of social—rather than simply philological—analysis and planning. The nature of these congresses makes this shift in perspective particularly apparent, because language had not yet been separated off as its own sphere of expertise. At the congresses all of Basque society was under the microscope. Speeches addressing the preservation of Basque sat alongside presentations on new methods of agriculture, forms of social insurance, and work accident prevention, thereby allowing us to see more clearly the similarities in the way language revival was approached and the way projects were conceived for the development of healthier urban developments or social insurance for the aged.

The governmentalizing of language—that is, its conceptualization as an object of social planning—and its conjoining with nationalism has its seeds here in the Basque Studies Society and continues to be elaborated in the course of the language-revival movement. It is a process that brings into being new relations of power and knowledge, distinctive ways of conceptualizing language, and new cadres of experts—for example, the academy and later language planners—entrusted and authorized to speak its truth and plan its future. Sociological data, in particular, become key resources and instruments for language reformers, with which they feel they can not only better understand the nature of language but also more convincingly ground the legitimacy of their revitalization effort. A telling sign of this conceptual shift is the increasing preference for language surveys over etymologies as ways of knowing Basque. As a first and necessary step in initiating projects of reform, for example, Urquijo urged the undertaking of a complete linguistic atlas of the Basque-speaking provinces comparable to that carried out by Bonaparte in the previous century. "It is necessary that each commune, on the one hand, each form, each word, on the other, have its monograph, purely descriptive, done first-hand, and traced with all the observational rigor demanded by the natural sciences" (Urquijo 1918: 425). Saving Basque required new forms of knowledge. Whereas the previous defenses and prescriptive grammars had tried to demonstrate the uniqueness and logic of Basque, the governmental or planning perspective taking shape now would bring into greater and more explicit focus the social life of the language, its demographic distribution, its absence from the domains of high culture, commerce, and urban life. Arguments based in a social analysis would be the grounds for proceeding in one of the academy's most urgent tasks: the creation of a standard.

At its foundation, the Basque Language Academy was given the task of "purifying and regulating" the language so as to achieve its perfection and continuity (Campión and Broussain 1922: 32). In a sense, their charge was not terribly different from the eighteenth-century motto of the Royal Academy of Spanish: to purify, standardize, and give splendor to the Castilian language [*limpiar, fijar y dar esplendor al Castellano*). But the Basque academy's challenge was envisioned also as decidedly restorative. As Estornes Zubizarreta has observed, for members of the society "It was not simply a question of dissecting and analyzing the language on the operating table, but also of returning it to health and life after being wounded by policies—local and/or national—of persecution or abandonment" (1983: 173).

The debates among language loyalists at this time focus heavily on whether and how Basque could be adapted to modern life. Could Euskara have a place in the new century? Miguel de Unamuno's essay "La cuestión del vascuence," published in 1902, declared this to be impossible: Basque, argued the philosopher, was permanently uncivilized. Like "one of those species of animals that die as soon as one attempts to domesticate them or take them out of their savage state," Euskara, said Unamuno, could not become civilized (Villasante 1979: 350; see also Ugalde 1979: 11).[15] Two programmatic pieces—Luis de Eleizalde's "Metodología para la Restauración del Euzkera," presented at the first congress of 1918, and Julio Urquijo's "International Language and National Languages," published the following year— disagreed vigorously with these assertions. They both argued that the problem confronting Basque had to do with its *social* characteristics, not the language itself.

Urquijo was emphatic on this point: "No! The difficulty does not properly lie with the nature or type of language, but rather with other circumstances, like the extraordinary dialectal fragmentation, the abandonment of Basque by the upper classes, and the reduced number of existing Basque speakers" (1919: 175).

Urquijo and his colleagues Arturo Campión, Luis de Eleizalde, and Resurrección María Azkue, president of the Basque Language Academy, all argued that Basque could indeed become, to use the terms of the day, a language of "civilization." But new instruments were needed. The folklore festivals, poetry competitions, and literary tributes celebrating the beauty of Basque and rural life would not suffice. If Basque was to survive in the modern world it had to be taught in the schools and gain entry into commerce, industry, and the institutional domains of power. For this to happen, these modernist reformers argued, Basque needed a standard. Campión, an advocate of standardization, had codified four literary dialects in the late nineteenth century.[16] Arana, for his part, had developed a standard orthography for Bizkaian Basque. But Arana did not support further standardization. In language as in politics, he saw Basques ideally conjoined in a regional confederacy in which each province preserved its distinctive identity with some degree of political and linguistic autonomy. Eleizalde, while a strong advocate of Arana's party, nevertheless disagreed. He presented the matter of standardization to the congresses as a matter of "common sense" and a necessity for the "common good" (1918a: 434).

That modern languages had to have authoritative and stable norms was already an established premise of European language ideology by the twentieth century (Gal 2006). The question is not why did Basque modernist reformers think they needed a standard, but why now? The lack of a standard seems to have become problematic when this growing sector of intellectuals began to think of Basque society as a modern industrializing society and potentially a nation-state. There are pragmatic as well as implicit ideological factors that make standardization appear necessary. As Irvine and Gal (2000) argue, debates Europeans have about standardization are often premised on a presumed correspondence between the features of a language and its speakers. They have called this the principle of "iconicity," whereby linguistic features are interpreted as depicting a social group's inherent nature, degree of civilization, morality, rationality, and solidarity (ibid.: 37). Just as standard weights and measures, policies, and laws were seen to be necessary to modern commerce, fixed norms in language were read as signs of the unity and rationality of a social grouping, both of which were features deemed necessary for a modern nation-state (see Scott 1998).

Leading figures of the Basque Studies Society were strong exponents of modernist reform, but as they encountered resistance from fellow nationalists unwilling to go against Arana's disapproval of a unified standard. Rather than convince their peers on political grounds, academicians and advocates of standardization pressed the issue on grounds of practicality and efficiency. As Eleizalde declared in his address to the inaugural congress, it was simply too difficult, expensive, and confusing to have multiple literary dialects given the exigencies of modern bureaucratic institutions, printing presses, and public schooling. The fixity, stability, and uniformity of linguistic forms were, in their view, as tied to modernity as the modern steam engine. Bourdieu's work has been especially important in helping us to see how this feature of language ideology is not simply a function of nationalist ideology, but also a function of the social, economic, and political shifts in modern capitalist society—the development of a national education system, the expansion of the state's administrative apparatus, and transformations of the labor market—which help lay the grounds for the "common sense" of a standard language and its ensuing hegemonic spread. The production, reproduction, and diffusion of standard languages, writes Bourdieu, are a "dimension of the unification of the market in symbolic goods which accompanies the unification of the economy and also of the cultural production and circulation" of the modern nation-state (1991: 50). The perceived necessity of a standard emerges concurrent with the demands of bureaucratic predictability and calculability, much as the new industrial workplace seemed to require a more interchangeable and standardized worker (ibid.: 48).

Thus the "taming of Basque," as it were, through standardization should not be seen as soley the outcome of the grammarian's zeal for prescriptivism or the nationalist's desire to confirm the unity and uniformity of the language. Its self-evident status is powerfully and simultaneously anchored by conceptualizations of modernity, the rationalization of capitalist production, bureaucratic efficiency, and a sense that this will benefit the social life of the language. As a process, standardization is at the nexus of the logics of governmentality, modernity, and a Herderian nationalist imaginary that links one language–one nation. These discourses worked in tandem to render life without Standard Basque unthinkable.

Nevertheless, corpus reform was not uncontested. Debate filled the pages of *La revista internacional de estudios vascos* and *Euskera,* the journal of the Basque Language Academy. One of the biggest fears had to do with artificiality. Linguists were concerned that the pursuit of grammatical logic and lexical purity might lead to a standard which would be so different from vernacular that native speakers would reject it. They also feared social divisiveness. Academicians were keenly aware that prestige accompanied the creation of a standard such that if the standard variety seemed too much like the dialect of a particular region, it could be seen as giving higher status to those speakers. The solutions proposed at the time fell into three types: choose one of the four existing literary dialects to be the common standard; create a new amalgamated standard enriched with elements from all the dialects; or do nothing and let the process of unification happen on its own.

This latter opinion was held by several important scholars, both Basque and non-Basque. Among the most well-known and respected scholars to argue for "non-intervention" was the Spanish linguist Ramón Menéndez Pidal. In his "Introducción al estudio de la linguística vasca" [Introduction to the Study of Basque Linguistics], written in 1921, Menéndez Pidal demonstrated interest in unraveling the mysterious origins of Basque, but unlike the Basque reformers, he had no stake in its preservation, much less adapting it to be a national language. Like many linguists of his day, he viewed the evolution of languages as fundamentally naturalistic. If one language or dialect prevailed over another, this was the result, he argued, of the superiority of the literature and "genius" of the authors in that language: "The dominant dialect will be that which, gaining the support of all by its own merit, saps the life of the other dialects without being the executioner which kills them. Let life and death be forged by Providence through the arcane working of nature" (Menéndez Pidal 1962: 56).

Urquijo and other Basque academicians disagreed. They shared Menéndez Pidal's respect for the complexities of language evolution and were enthusiastic to apply the rigorous methods of linguistic science to the study of Basque. But many did not share his detachment about its fate or his explanation for the rise and fall of languages. Urquijo and his colleagues did not believe that "nature" explained why some languages had gained prestige or official status while others had not. They rebutted Menendez Pidal's "survival of the fittest" argument with political-economic arguments that stressed the influence that class dynamics and the institutions of the state had in determining the dominance of some languages over others.

In their disagreement, some of the problems that the discourse of modern linguistics poses for linguistic minorities are revealed. As Deborah Cameron (1995: 5) writes, the idea that languages evolve naturally, that linguistic changes should be allowed to happen "spontaneously," has been a defining feature of modern linguistics. But the admonishment to linguists and advocates not to "interfere" and to "let nature take its course," she rightly notes, inevitably benefits dominant languages supported by states and ignores the ways in which language is always already being shaped by social and political factors. Urquijo and his fellow modernist Basque reformers were acutely aware of this fact, as are many minority-language advocates. The experience of marginalization led them to greater insights into the political economy of language and to viewing the project of tampering with "nature" (e.g., via standardization) as less sacrilegious, though not without social risks. In this respect, advocates of standardization agreed with their detractors. Whether it was regarded as the savior or the exterminator of Basque, all sides on the standardization issue seemed to attribute a great deal of social consequence— positive or negative—to corpus reform and other kinds of deliberate interventions into language. As Eleizalde warned his colleagues, "This is not a problem for fanciful linguistic experimentation. Rather, we are dealing with questions of the life and death of our country; questions in which all dilettantism is inappropriate" (1918a: 438).

To find a path through these weighty problems was the task of the Basque Language Academy scholars. They would proceed with caution, inviting commentary and proposals and calling for much more study and documentation of the language before engaging in corpus reform. Though some preliminary attempts were made, standardization was not achieved before the Spanish Civil War broke out. Their discussions were not, however, without consequence. The perspectives on language elaborated in this period mark the beginnings of a new rationality with regard to language loyalism that lays the foundation for language-revival strategies in the latter half of the twentieth century. In these arguments for scientific study and standardization, we can see clearly how Euskara was being wrenched, at least partially, out of the domain of "nature" (or the divine) where it had resided for so long and incorporated into the domain of "the social." Basque emerges out of these debates not only as a marker of identity or a kind of primordial nationhood, but as a governable *social* phenomenon to be regulated by experts and requiring new technologies of knowledge, measurement, and intervention. Language revival was being refashioned as a problem of "government," and good government begins with norms and regularized documentation. These conceptions, as much as patriotism—and sometimes despite patriotic sentiments—drive forward the common sense of standardization, and it is this common sense that is arguably the most consequential legacy of this period.

The term "language planning" was not yet used, but it was clearly in the making. Defenses of Basque have a long history to be sure, but a closer analysis reveals that they differ in conceptualization. As Einar Haugen, one of the first scholars to use the term, explains, language planning is not just another term for reform efforts that we can trace back to early prescriptive grammars. Language planning refers more specifically to that moment when "the whole enterprise of cultivation and reform of language [is brought] under the point of view of social planning . . . [understood as] the establishment of goals, policies, and procedures for a social or economic unit" (1972: 287). We see this perspective emergent in the growing belief among these intellectuals that in order to survive, Basque had to be modernized and properly managed according to a social-scientific understanding of language dynamics. There are elements of this perspective in the work of prior writers—Campión or even Arana—when they make reference, for example, to the class dynamics that underlie Basque language shift. Concerns with language purification and origins, even the nostalgic romanticism that surrounded Basque-language celebrations of this period, do not completely disappear. History does not show us an absolute abandonment of discourses of the past, but rather their coexistence and sometimes collision with new logics and sociological ways of envisioning language that become hegemonic in the years to come.

Euskara and Basque Nationhood

FROM HERITAGE TO PRACTICE

One winter afternoon in 1983, a few months into my first year of fieldwork in Usurbil, María, the grandmother of the family with whom I lived, knocked on the door to my room. The restaurant kitchen below had closed and it was quiet, as everyone was still resting after serving the midday meal. Maneuvering her way into my room cluttered with newspaper clippings and notebooks, "You are interested in Basque things," she said. "Here, you might want to see this." With a heavy thump, she set down a large book: *El libro de oro de la patria* [The Golden Book of the Nation]. It was a gorgeously illustrated and impressive leather-bound book published just before the Spanish Civil War, with chapters on Basque rural customs, history, folk traditions, and of course, Euskara. As I carefully turned the large pages, I could see it was something of an encyclopedia of Basque culture. Published in 1934 during the Spanish Republic, it exuded optimism about a new future for Basques and was inscribed with warm dedications expressing solidarity from fellow Irish and Catalan nationalists. María was proud of the book, and she proceeded to tell me how her family hid it in fear when the Spanish Civil War broke out. They kept it for years, she said, under the floor in the cow stalls of the farmhouse where she grew up. Later that evening, when I was having dinner with her son and daughter-in-law, I told them about it. Her son was surprised. Neither he nor his wife had heard of this book, much less that a copy had been in their house for so many years.

El libro de oro de la patria had been a dangerous book. Written mainly in Spanish, its description of Basques as a nation with a rich history and cultural heritage would have been read as treasonous in Franco's Spain. Years later, I curiously came across reference to the book again. This time reading the memoir of novelist, linguist engagé, and one-time founding member of ETA José Luis Álvarez Enparantza, better known by his pen name "Txillardegi" (1997: 10). Txillardegi recounts finding the very same book hidden in a drawer in his parents' house. For him, the discovery of this book was a kind of apocryphal moment in his own development, emblematic of the way in which he and a generation of Basques in the fifties would begin to question their identities as they uncovered the signs of

FIGURE 2.1. Painted in the 1990s, this mural in Usurbil was the joint effort of a local group protesting mandatory military service and the language-advocacy association, Euskal Herrian Euskaraz [Basque in the Basqueland]. The Basque speaker in the mural is shown being strangled by the Spanish and French flags and crushed by the army boot above his head. Political dissent often linked the Basque-language struggle with other forms of antistate resistance. Photograph by the author.

a Basque culture and language that had been forced, quite literally in some cases, underground.

To continue my exploration of the discourse of language loyalism, this chapter will examine the place that Basque-language revival had in this process of recovery and reawakening of a Basque nationalist movement toward the end of the Franco regime. As we have seen, the first wave of Basque nationalism took language to be evidence of the Basques' separate origin and their difference from Spain. Nationalist treatises tended to talk about language as a heritage that indexed the nation—or what at the time was often also called the Basque "race," but this was not the whole story. The impassioned rhetoric about language as symbol of the nation should not blind us to the way in which intellectuals were simultaneously constructing the language as a distinctly social object to be documented, regularized, and governed. A third element of early nationalist discourse that was especially relevant for language politics was the Basque Nationalist Party's conceptualization of the Basque nation, commonly referred to as Euskadi at that time, as a political or moral community. Early Basque nationalists celebrated Basque rural life—the farmhouse, oral traditions, sporting competitions—as well as Euskara as a shared heritage. But they also considered loyalty to the idea of Euskadi as a distinct territory and nationality to be an important aspect of Basque identity. Being *abertzale* [patriotic] would henceforth become interwoven with what it meant to be truly Basque.

Each of these three elements continued to exercise influence on the strategies and discourse of language advocacy at the end of the Franco regime. However, as a clandestine Basque nationalist movement began to surface again in the late fifties, the monopoly the PNV ideologues had in defining Basque nationalism was challenged by a new generation that was inspired by other sources: Marxist Leninism and third-world liberation movements. Taking the name ETA, Euskadi ta Askatasuna [Basqueland and Freedom], a new organization emerged that became the vanguard of this alternate nationalism. It played a key role in rejecting the older racial and religious groundings that the Christian Democratic PNV had given to Basque identity, seeking instead to promote a radical, that is, socialist nationalism that refigured itself in alliance with working-class concerns and made the end of class inequalities part of the project of a national liberation. The agglomeration of political groups that aligned themselves with this alternate nationalism became collectively known as the MLNV [Movimiento de Liberación Nacional Vasco, Basque Nationalist Liberation Movement]. This schism between Christian Democratic and MLNV nationalists has been a defining factor in all ensuing cultural politics.

While the landscape of Basque nationalism was being transformed at the close of the Franco regime, language revival gained a groundswell of popular support. The Basque Language Academy began to be active again and along with it a popular movement for Basque-language schools. The indexical property of Basque, in other words, its semiotic function as the principal marker of Basque culture, gained in force as nationalist discourse turned increasingly to define Basqueness in cultural and political rather than racial terms. In this later era, nationalists across the political spectrum were united in attributing value to the Basque language and expressed support for its revival. But they had intense internal disputes about how genuine nationalist commitments to language revival really were. A major goal of this chapter is to go beyond the surface of seeming agreement about the value of Basque in order to trace these arguments about the place of language in national liberation and in particular to examine the rising importance of language use to Basque identity and patriotism. A critical moment in this process came early in the formation of ETA, where we find an attempt by some members to develop a deeper analysis of how linguistic domination operates and its centrality to the politics of colonization, as well as a growing sense that nationalists should demonstrate their loyalty to Basque by actually speaking it. The idea that patriotism needed to be matched by linguistic practice, while not entirely new, was most explicitly elaborated and passionately defended in the writings of Txillardegi and has had long-lasting impact on the language-revival movement. It is worth exploring the logics and evidence he used to argue for the importance of speaking—not just preserving—Basque and of taking language domination more seriously.

A closer reading of nationalist discourse shows that behind the virtually universal support for Basque revival there were (and still are) differences in the way "language" and Basqueness are conceptualized that manifest in quite pitched battles over the importance of speaking Basque. For some, Euskara is a form of cultural patrimony, a heritage, a possession, something one has and possibly tries to recover and record for posterity. What I call the "heritage" view of language is not unique to Basques; it is the view of language that prevails in Western societies. But another view of language and its relationship to identity began to be articulated by Txillardegi and subsequently other, younger language loyalists in which learning and speaking Euskara was envisioned as a means of *being and becoming* Basque. For some Basques the language that they choose to speak has no bearing on their political identity. But for others, being Basque or Basque nationalist and not speaking Basque became increasingly to be seen as an unsettling contradiction. Why? The move away from notions of race and toward an ethnolinguistic understanding of Basque identity that scholars of Basque nationalism have often noted was certainly a critical factor in prompting a greater valorization of language use. But it is not the whole story. It is not just that Basqueness had become more centered on language and culture, but that the conception of language itself was being rethought among advocates from a heritage to a practice. A performative or pragmatic view of Basque identity and patriotism as something realized in and through everyday language use is a key innovation in the rhetorical strategies of the language movement in second-wave nationalism. It is especially salient in grassroots organizations that seek to incorporate the larger society into the project of Basque nation building. Grasping the difference between a heritage and a performative perspective on language is key to understanding the terrain of language politics in the late and post-Franco era. It gives rise to lingering tensions, interrogations, and discomforting silences that erupt at times into outright disagreement and questioning over the relationship between being Basque and speaking Basque.

Given the conflation nowadays between Basque cultural activism and ETA, and thereby terrorism, a clarification is in order for the English-language reader. Some of the most elaborated arguments in favor of Basque-language revival and language use are to be found in the writings of two individuals who were active in ETA in the sixties. Early on in its formation, ETA founders established language revival as one of the five "fronts" of the struggle for national liberation. The organization's deliberate use of Euskara helped to invest Basque with connotations of oppositionality and to establish the importance of language revival in the project of nation building among younger generations. As an organization, ETA took positions on specific language-revival issues, expressing support, for example, for language standardization and criticism of language purism. Language revitalization was a key part of the nation-building project that, at its origins, ETA understood to be a multifaceted one of economic, cultural, linguistic, and political decolonization. That key leaders of language revitalization had linkages to ETA is far from unusual, as ETA was in the vanguard of nationalist activism in the late Franco years. Many Basque intellectuals who are now ETA's greatest critics were once members. Txillardegi was among them. As one of the most vocal advocates of language revival within ETA, one of the reasons he subsequently left the organization was precisely because he felt it was not fully committed to the cause of a Basque-speaking revolution.

To explore the second wave of Basque-language revival, a brief review of the history of the Franco regime is in order. The dictatorship's policies had a crucial role to play in what speaking Basque would come to mean for the generation of language loyalists who came of age during this era. The regime's repressive stance toward minority languages and the Spanish national imaginary it articulated, as much as Basque nationalism, shaped the rhetorical strategies of social actors working in favor of Basque revival. Francoist repression also shaped the sympathetic stance that much of liberal Spain had toward Basques and the Basque language as the regime came to an end.

The Franco Years

Creemos en la suprema realidad de España: Fortalecerla, elevarla, y engrandecerla es la apremiante tarea colectiva de todos los Españoles. [We believe in the supreme reality of Spain. The urgent collective task of all Spaniards is to strengthen, elevate, and aggrandize her.] (Program of the Falange Española de las JONS, 1939, Gurruchaga 1985: 156)

The uprising in 1936 and ultimate triumph of Franco's forces in 1939 brought with it assassinations, mass imprisonment, labor camps, confiscation of property, and a state-authorized political and ideological repression that reached into virtually every corner of life. Social life after the war was deeply divided into victors and vanquished. Those who had fought against the uprising or continued after the war to resist the regime were declared anti-Spaniards and punished. Repression was particularly intense and violent in the Basque provinces of Bizkaia and Gipuzkoa and continued for at least another decade after the war ended (Barruso Barés 2005). As sociologist Alfonso Pérez-Agote (1984) has noted, in Franco's first decree after winning the battle for Bilbao in 1937, the dictator made an exceptional case out of the Basques; rather than targeting specific rebels, he declared the entire provinces of Bizkaia and Gipuzkoa traitorous. The projects for bilingual education were brought to an abrupt halt. The Statute of Autonomy that had been approved in 1936 was nullified. The Basque government went into exile. Hundreds of children were put on ships bound for England, escaping the destruction left behind.

Institutionally, the Basque Country no longer existed as its own administrative, juridical, or even religious entity (Gurruchaga 1985: 289). The rule of law was placed in the hands of the military, which proceeded to prosecute for many years citizens thought to be ideologically contrary to the regime. Under constant censorship and the threat of violence, the Basque provinces, like much of Spain, became what Pérez-Agote (1984: 111) describes as "a society of silence"—at least for the first decade.

Although the Franco regime is sometimes described as more authoritarian or autarchic than fascist, his regime shared in the rabid nationalism characteristic of fascism (cf. Payne 1973, 1980). The Spanish Republican government was accused of having betrayed the founding values and unity of traditional Spain by separating Church and State and by granting statutes of autonomy to Catalonia and Euskadi. Separatism was the ultimate enemy. In a now infamous speech delivered in Donostia–San Sebastián in 1936, the fascist leader Calvo Sotelo described the unity of Spain as sacred above all else. "Given the choice between a red [i.e., communist] Spain and a broken Spain, I prefer the first, which would only be a passing phase, whereas with the second option, Spain would remain broken forever" (Sotelo cited in Torrealdai 1982: 17). The image of Spain cultivated during the Franco years was that of a single race, with a single language, Castilian, and a single culture. The military uprising and defeat of the democratically elected liberal Republican government was presented as a war to restore Spain's integrity and traditional values. The fascists strategically evoked the mythos of the reconquest—the battle against the infidels and the Moors—as a way of framing Franco's military overthrow. The Spanish Civil War was characterized as a new reconquest, a second holy crusade for the glory of God and the glory of Spain, a necessary evil to defend Spain against the enemies of God: the atheistic Republicans, Basque nationalists, anarchists, Freemasons, and liberal Europeanizing intellectuals. The regime tolerated Spain's other nationalities only in the guise of quaint regional folklore. Castilians were cast as the founding "race" that created Catholic Spain, whose art and literature were treasures of Western civilization. Castilian, *castellano,* was commonly referred to as "the" Spanish language, *la lengua española,* always in the singular. It was also even more revealingly referred to as "the Christian language," *la lengua Cristiana,* or simply as *cristiano* [Christian].

The conditions of repression during the immediate postwar period were conveyed in a letter written in 1952 by the president of the exiled Basque government, José Antonio Aguirre, on the occasion of Spain's petition to enter UNESCO after years of banishment. Aguirre's letter requested that Spain's petition be denied on the grounds that the Basques were being subjected to "a systematic policy of cultural genocide, carried out at times brutally and other times with deception and hypocrisy" (Beltza 1977: 135). Included among the acts of cultural genocide cited by the letter were: censorship of all publications of a Basque nature; elimination of plans for a public Basque University granted by the 1936 Statute of Autonomy; prohibition of all cultural societies, including the Basque Studies Society; the closure and in some cases the burning of libraries and publishing houses containing Basque materials; and the prohibition of teaching Basque in the schools. The Basque Language Academy dispersed and several members went into exile (Alvarez Enparantza (1997).[1] "The prohibition of the use of the Basque language and culture," wrote Aguirre, "extends from the cradle to the grave" (reprinted in Beltza 1977: 135).

This choice of words was not arbitrary, for the attempted annihilation of all official traces of Basque literally extended from birth certificates to tombstones. An order issued in 1938 required the use of Castilian for personal names in the civil registry, in cemeteries, and in all public documents. An order of the Ministry of Justice on May 18, 1938, denounced the "morbid" habit of using non-Castilian names in the provinces where regionalist sentiment prevailed (Torrealdai 1998: 132–33). Prior police permission was required to publish in any language other than Spanish. A deluge of state propaganda in the Basque-speaking provinces reminded the citizenry to speak "in Christian." Posters proclaimed: "Spaniard: speak in the language of the empire" or "Spain, a Spanish speaking nation" (de Miguel 1976: 203; Torrealdai 1982: 60). Investigators have found records of people being fined for using Basque in public, including an order declaring it illegal to speak Basque at family reunions without prior police permission (DeCicco and Maring 1983: 42; Heiberg 1989: 90–92). A collection of documents, official orders, and newspaper articles published by Basque author Joan Mari Torrealdai under the title *El libro negro del Euskera* [The Black Book of Basque] (1988), conveys the climate of repression, suspicion, and ridicule of Basque and Basque speakers that profoundly shaped the meanings language would have for the generation that came of age during the Franco era.[2]

Francoist cultural and linguistic policies of prohibition and intimidation accelerated the abandonment of Basque and also contributed to making Basque a sign of resistance against fascism. Except in restricted spaces of friends and family, Spanish was the language required of public life. However, in their rich social histories of the Basque life in the Franco era, both Ander Gurruchaga (1985) and Alfonso Pérez-Agote (1984, 2006) have shown that the Basque language and a Basque-nationalist symbolic universe were sustained and reproduced in the private sphere of the family and close-knit *cuadrilla,* or friendship circles. Parish churches and seminaries were key refuges for the use and study of Basque. In small towns the local parish church, exempt from the kind of surveillance of secular organizations, could sometimes, if the priest was sympathetic, offer a haven for the expression of a distinctive Basque cultural identity in the form of cultural or artistic associations, choirs, dance groups, or mountaineering clubs. Brought together under these conditions of a traumatic repression, Euskara and Basque culture became yet more politicized and linked to a clandestine nationalist imaginary.

Thus we could say that the political effects of forty years of censorship did more than just "repress" the Basque language or Basque identity. Tejerina (1996: 225) argues that the intensity of political repression made Basques more acutely aware of the decline of their language, thereby prompting a stronger adherence to it as a badge of identity. I would argue even further that repression's semiotic consequences were to constitute Basque and Spanish identities and languages, ironically enough, exactly as Sabino Arana had vehemently claimed them to be: mutually exclusive. As a result of its stigmatization, being Basque and speaking Basque became signs of opposition to the regime, practices that, in the public sphere, could signal not only an alternative national identity, but also anti-Francoist sentiment more generally. By the end of the regime, the public use of Basque or support for its use was a way to demarcate oneself from the dictatorship and its cultural politics. In the sixties and seventies the Basque nationalist movement, the revival of Euskara, and even ETA enjoyed a great deal of support among democratic and leftist sectors throughout the Spanish state and were widely regarded as the vanguard of resistance to the dictatorship (Pérez-Agote 1984: 115–16).

Revolutionary Nationalism and the Language Question

In the fifties the political and ideological stranglehold of the regime began to crack as labor unions started to organize strikes in protest against repression and the lack of basic freedoms. In 1947 miners and metal workers of the northern industrial cities staged the earliest of a series of paralyzing general strikes that marked the first open challenge to Franco since the end of the Civil War (Beltza 1977). Students in the universities also began to organize their own strikes and walkouts in support of the workers and in protest of the rigid censorship that dominated intellectual life, culture, and the media. The police responded with violence, and the streets became frequent sites of open confrontation with the state.

The shift in political context prompted a reassessment of the strategies of resistance among Basque nationalists. After a decade of sustaining a government in exile and lobbying the United Nations for help in deposing Franco, Basque nationalists lost hope of receiving any assistance from the Western democracies that had previously fought fascism. The United States had refused to intervene in the Spanish Civil War but kept its distance from the regime. As the cold war progressed and the United States became interested in securing its military hold on the Mediterranean, Spain became viewed as a strategic ally in Western geopolitics (Payne 1975; Herr 1971). In 1947, when the Truman Doctrine declared communism to be the primary enemy of the free world, the realignment of world powers associated with the cold war spelled the definitive end to all such hopes for international help in ousting Franco. After World War II, the United States and other countries restored diplomatic ties with Spain, and in 1952, despite protests from the Basque president in exile, Spain was admitted into UNESCO and began to receive economic aid from the United States. One year later, Spain and the United States signed a bilateral agreement giving the United States rights to set up military bases on the peninsula. Spain's ministers would begin a process of refashioning the country's image into that of a modern society, a growing economy, and a tourist destination of sun and colorful traditions in which the unsavory history of the war and dictatorship were to be forgotten. The Basque nationalist leadership was formally expelled from the Spanish embassy in Paris, and the resistance effort in exile effectively came to an end.

The climate of growing social unrest and international abandonment brought about a shift in the leadership of the Basque nationalist community from the pre–Civil War leaders of the exiled PNV to a new generation forming within Spain under the dictatorship. In 1952 a small group of young men, several of them students at the University of Deusto in Bilbao, began to meet in secret to discuss the future of Basque resistance. They saw that the dictatorship was not going to be deposed by the Western democracies. Exasperated with the apparent state of paralysis among the exiled leaders, these youth took the Basque name EKIN (meaning "to do" or "to take action"). After a short-lived attempt to join forces with the PNV, EKIN split off, and in 1959 EKIN announced that it was taking on a new and separate identity as ETA.[3]

Meeting at first as a very small group, these young men set as their first task to educate themselves in matters of Basque history, language, and culture. One of the original members described these early years in the following way:

> The mood at the time was truly sad from the Basque point of view. People had lost hope. That which some had placed in the Americans and in the goal of restoring democracy dissolved in 1953. We then thought that we had to do something without relying on anyone else and so we began to work. . . . As our first task we proposed to educate ourselves. We realized that we were mere neophytes when it came to our own Basque education. (Hordago 1979, 1:9).

Members of the original ETA recount gathering and reading all of the classic nationalist works they could locate and then moving on to explore broader European intellectual movements, especially Marxism and existentialism. Smuggling across the border books on Sartre, Marxist sociology, the Algerian war, and other anticolonialist movements, they searched for tools with which to conceptualize their political and cultural history.

The ETA did not begin as the violent and highly militarized organization that it became later.[4] The ideology of its early members was shaped by a mixture of nationalism and socially progressive Catholic activism. Marxism was to come later, but in its origins, religion was a major influence. The lower clergy in Gipuzkoa and Bizkaia, many of whom came from rural Basque-speaking communities, had publicly denounced the prohibition of Basque as well as torture and repression both during and after the war. They provided contexts under the shelter of the Church for studying Basque and discussing Basque history, culture, and political repression. Many of the leading Basque writers, linguists, journalists, sociologists, and leaders of the cooperative movement either were priests or had studied at Catholic schools and seminaries (Pérez-Agote 1984: 98–105). While ETA would eventually adopt a secular leftist nationalism, Joseba Zulaika (1988) has shown that the imprint of Catholicism can be found in the early conceptualizations of political struggle and notions of martyrdom.[5]

Constituting at first no more than a loosely defined group, ETA founders began their battle by circulating clandestine Basque nationalist literature and filling the streets with anti-Franco political graffiti. By the mid-fifties, ETA was organizing lectures and *cursillos* [short courses] on Basque history, ethnography, language, and literature. The political reawakening of Basques necessitated, in their view, that people achieve an understanding of their Basque history and culture. The educational courses of ETA pointed to symbolic domination and language abandonment as one of the more sinister consequences of their political subjugation. They described their task as one of "national reconstruction," and to achieve this, they believed they needed more than a political party; they needed to "create new men, different, fully identified and integrated in the project of national reconstruction" (Jáuregui 1981: 92). Years of Francoist propaganda, they argued, had distorted if not completely erased a sense of Basque identity and history. As one militant explained, in order to "act like Basques," they had to first educate themselves as to what being Basque meant (Hordago 1979, 1:28).

Part of the organization's early years were devoted to analyzing and critiquing the exiled PNV's formulation of Basque nationalism (Jáuregui 1981). These youth criticized Sabino Arana's anti-immigrant chauvinism and rejected race as a criterion of belonging in the nation. Also in contrast to the PNV, they declared themselves secular, albeit not always convincingly, and committed to the joining of French and Spanish Basque territories into a single independent state. Members of ETA tended to give greater importance to making Basque the national language and gave Euskara a prominent place in their publications. European Marxism, the anticolonial movements in Algeria and elsewhere in the third world provided these Basque revolutionaries with a new framework for understanding their situation and articulating their demands that was quite different from the romantic *Volkgeist* of early Basque nationalism. In the course of the sixties, they became more directly concerned with conjoining the struggle for national liberation with that of class struggle, and in so doing developed a new nationalist project that envisioned a restructuring of the total socioeconomic order as part of a new independent Euskadi.[6]

This reconfigured leftist Basque nationalism is articulated in Federico Krutwig's book *La nueva Vasconia: Estudio dialéctico de una nacionalidad,* originally published in 1963 and widely regarded as a formative text in defining ETA's political ideology. A native of Bilbao of German descent, Krutwig, the pseudonym of Fernando Sarrailh de Ihartza, was an accomplished scholar of Basque linguistics and, in 1941, at only twenty-one years of age, he was one of the youngest people to be elected to the Basque Language Academy. Krutwig took the opportunity in his book to deliver a biting attack on the racial conception of Basque nationality, which he characterized as "an anti-scientific mistake from start to finish" (Krutwig 1979: 26). Basqueness, he argued, was a cultural, not a racial identity, acquired and expressed primarily through language.[7]

Krutwig allowed that one should perhaps forgive the early nationalist forefathers for failing to appreciate the place of language in the political struggle, but one should not tolerate this attitude, he argued, from contemporary nationalists who "should study and be on top of what modern science has taught us regarding the intrinsic value of language" (1979: 26). This reference to science as a legitimating and authoritative arbiter of the truth about language echoes back to the Basque

Studies Society and continues as a pervasive feature in debates surrounding the relation of language to Basque identity in the contemporary era.

Krutwig and his contemporaries mined Basque lexicon and grammar for clues about Basque history and identity and their relationship to the language. A prime example is the investigation into the etymology of the word *euskaldun*. Krutwig's book, for example, discussed at length the significance of the fact that in Basque, the word for a Basque person, *euskaldun,* is the same as the word for a Basque-speaking person. Derived from the word *euskara* and the suffix *dun* (the relative form of the verb *du* (to have), *euskaldun* literally means one who "has *Euskara.*" This, Krutwig argued, showed the centrality of language to Basque identity. In the Basque language, he pointed out, there is no term for a Basque person who does not speak the Basque language. Not mincing words, he called the word *euskotar,* a neologism invented by Sabino Arana to refer to a Basque person who did not know Euskara, to be "a nefarious aberration" (Krutwig 1979: 28). Creating such a word, he said, allowed nationalists to be complacent about the decline of Basque by suggesting that *language* was not an essential part of being Basque. For Krutwig, linguistics offered more than abstract knowledge; it was a means of penetrating the dominant ideology, a tool in the liberation of Basque consciousness.

In *Vasconia* Krutwig elaborated the ideological framework for a revolutionary Basque nationalism modeled on third-world anticolonialism that incorporated language domination into it. Just as Frantz Fanon, writing *Black Skin, White Masks* about the same time, criticized his fellow Antilleans for abandoning their native creole for French, Krutwig sought to convince his compatriots that the habit Basques had of accepting Spanish as the better language for formal speech and writing was a sign of the depths of their own colonization. Krutwig directed his harshest criticisms to the nationalist bourgeoisie, the PNV, whom he disparagingly referred to as *jelkides.* Derived from the initials JEL used for the motto of the PNV, *Jaungoikoa eta Lege Zarra* [God and Traditions], and the suffix *kide,* meaning "a member of," the term *jelkide* had become a moniker for members of the party earlier in the century. In Krutwig's vocabulary, *jelkides* were the equivalent of a colonial elite, whom he accused of cynically manipulating nationalist sentiment to advance their primary interests in strengthening Bizkaian capitalism; they were perpetrators of economic exploitation with no genuine interest in the Basque language and culture. The abandonment of the language was perhaps the elite's most intimate and damaging form of betrayal to the Basque nation. In terms reminiscent of Herder, Krutwig explains the significance of this kind of linguistic betrayal in the following way: "Language creates the soul of the individual and the soul of the nation. This is why it is so tremendous a crime against the mother country for parents not to teach their children the language. There are no words to categorize this crime if it is committed, in addition, by someone who calls himself a NATION-ALIST" (1979: 30, emphasis in original).

The capital importance Krutwig placed on language in the liberation struggle in this early formative text was carried forward by Txillardegi, who, in the subsequent thirty years, would become one of the most influential and tireless advocates in the MLNV for linguistic revitalization.[8] Recalling this early period of intellectual and political reformulation of the premises of Basque nationalism, Txillardegi wrote:

> ... we were young, we liked to read, and we felt the necessity to analyze the Basque problem; we rejected that excess of sentimentalism, of sentimental motivations and good will that we associated with "official" nationalism and that was manifest for us in the incomprehensible attitude of nationalists who decried the oppression of Basque but did absolutely nothing to learn it (cited in Gurruchaga 1985: 239).

Language was a particular point of dissatisfaction with the nationalists of the past. In his memoir, Txillardegi repeatedly describes the frustration he felt at the tendency of nationalists, including passionate advocates of language revival, to speak and write all their manifestos in Castilian:

> This was the most serious thing. Among those language loyalists who came before us, it seemed at least, that *Euskara* was outside, far away, in the stratosphere, we did not know where. But we, the young nationalists of the time, we wanted to see *Euskara* transformed into the language of our nation, the everyday people's form of expression. That was a point of rupture between the two generations of language loyalists. . . . that language loyalists spoke in Spanish seemed to us to be completely contradictory. This led us to an *euskaldun* praxis and, therefore, to a confrontation with many preceding language loyalists, to be honest, with the majority. . . . The rupture between real and symbolic life could not have been more noticeable. (Alvarez Enparantza 1997: 129–30)

The early educational and consciousness-raising materials of ETA followed the overall approach laid out in *Vasconia*, establishing the inter-relation between the political struggle and the recuperation of Euskara (Jáuregi 2000: 212). Txillardegi further called upon his fellow militants to enact the organization's commitment to the recovery of Basque in their own speech. It would be this generation's perceived duty to overcome the divorce between professed Basque-language loyalty and Spanish linguistic practice. For example, ETA's early handbook for militants had a section entitled "Personal Position regarding Basque," exhorting future militants of the national liberation movement to contribute to the recuperation of the language: "Every *euskaltzale* [language advocate] who does not contribute to solving the problem of *Euskara*, the national language of the Basques, should be considered anti-patriotic" (reprinted in Hordago 1979, 1:256). The ETA began demonstrating these commitments to language by issuing bilingual communiqués and devoting numerous pages in its magazine, *Zutik!* to analyzing the causes of language decline. Txillardegi was instrumental in persuading the organization to treat language revival as one of the fronts of the revolution and to publically take positions on specific issues in language revival.[9] In the pages of its magazine, the organization criticized linguistic purism and argued for standardization and the adaptation of Basque to a modern urban life as an element of nation building. While there were disagreements within ETA over Basque, vis-à-vis the public ETA has stayed largely consistent in its support for the language-revival movement.

The new generation of activists was a powerful force in consolidating an eth-nolinguistic definition of Basque nationality grounded in the idea of a common cultural heritage, history, and language. The idea that Basques may have unique genetic characteristics is now a subject of study for physical anthropologists rather than an argument today's nationalists invoke to legitimate their political program. The revitalization of Basque became for many people of this generation a funda-mental form of nation building in which ethnic and nonethnic Basques, native and non-native speakers, could participate. There remains even today, however, a great deal of ambiguity among nationalists about what this concretely means. How much knowledge of Basque is sufficient? Is it enough for Basque speakers to be able to use Basque in public, or should the whole of society learn Basque? What prior-ity should the effort to revitalize Basque have vis-à-vis other aspects of national liberation? Did nationalists have a moral responsibility to speak Basque? The answers were not clear either within ETA or in the larger nationalist community.

The debate over language became particularly acute in the sixties, as the orga-nization pursued with greater rigor the attempt to synthesize class struggle with national liberation and eventually articulate a "civic" rather than an ethnic defini-tion of Basque nationality. A starting point in this story is 1964, when ETA's Third Assembly published a document known as the "Open Letter to Basque Intellectu-als," announcing its dual commitment to national liberation and the overthrow of capitalism. This document signaled the organization's official turn to leftist nationalism. For several years subsequent to this, the pages of *Zutik!* were almost exclusively concerned with class dynamics and developing a historical-materialist critique of Basque history.

The turn to Marxism provided Basque revolutionaries with tools for making sense of the social and economic effects of industrialization taking place in this period. In 1959 the Franco regime, abandoning its previous stance of isolationism, brought in a new contingent of technocratic ministers who devised a "Stabilization Plan" aimed at modernizing the Spanish economy, miserably lagging behind the rest of Western Europe. A series of development plans issued from 1964 to 1975 provided tax relief, new tariff laws, and monetary and budgetary incentives, which triggered dramatic industrial growth and demographic shift as well as massive labor strikes and social tension. Spain in the 1960s became one of the fastest growing economies of Europe, and most of this growth was concentrated in Madrid, Catalonia, and the Basque provinces, where a manufacturing base was already in place (Heiberg 1989: 92). Basque industry—banking, oil refining, weapons manufacturing, shipping, and steel mills—centered largely in the provinces of Bizkaia (primarily greater Bilbao) and Gipuzkoa, was a centerpiece in the "Spanish economic miracle" of the 1960s. By 1969 the Basque provinces of Gipuzkoa, Bizkaia, and Araba ranked as the top three provinces in terms of per capita income in Spain. Such growth depended on large quantities of cheap labor. The local population was not sufficient, hence thousands of unskilled laborers hoping to escape the grinding poverty of their rural villages in Castile, Galicia, and southern and western Spain went to look for work in Madrid, the Basque provinces, and Catalonia. The scale of this wave of internal immigration was enormous. Between 1955 and 1975, Spain's population grew by 23 percent, while in the Basque country growth averaged 60 percent (Heiberg 1989: 94). Geographically, industrial growth was also more far-reaching than in any previous era. Industry and immigration booms affected not only the big cities, but also the smaller towns of Gipuzkoa and Bizkaia (Mondragón/Arrasate, Elgoibar, Lasarte-Oria, Elorrio) that were in the heart of the Basque-speaking areas (Heiberg 1989: 96).

While Franco's technocrats celebrated a new era of "development" and "planning," their plans did very little to anticipate or alleviate the negative social effects of growth. A regressive tax structure and the government's failure to invest in basic social infrastructure and services in the areas of growth left workers feeling the brunt of the economic miracle. As Robert Clark argues, housing, schools, hospitals, and many other basic social services were vastly inadequate to the burgeoning population, yet Basque provincial and municipal authorities "lacked the necessary power to tax and spend to remedy the dislocations caused by the industrialization process" (1979: 238).[10] Labor migrants entered Basque society at the lowest economic rung, taking up residence in the many poorly constructed apartment complexes that began to spring up in the industrializing river valleys and port cities.

The social impact of the industrial boom was tremendous. In many small towns residents saw their populations multiply by several hundred percent. The once majority Basque-speaking town of Ermua (Bizkaia) is a case in point, growing from 1,277 inhabitants to 14,563 in roughly twenty-five years.[11] In the many interviews I carried out in Usurbil with language loyalists, the story of immigration was the principal starting point for talking about language dynamics. Economic and urban growth throughout this region had been extremely chaotic and unregulated. Newly arrived laborers were ill prepared to understand the cultural and linguistic marginalization native Basque speakers suffered. Under Franco they had learned nothing about Basque culture or the marginalization it had endured. To the contrary, the media, the schools, the post office, the town hall, and all official domains of public life under the control of the Spanish state in the Basque region reproduced that marginalization. The official institutions of the state treated the language of the newcomers as more legitimate than the Basque spoken in the communities where they settled. Basque speakers as a group were not in positions of economic or political power and did not control the institutional mechanisms for reproducing or protecting their identity (Shafir 1995: 113).

In his analysis of immigration and Basque nationalist politics, Gershon Shafir argues that labor immigrants did not learn Basque because the existing socioeconomic and political structure gave them little incentive to do so. It was not an avenue for jobs or social mobility, nor did they need to know Basque, he says, to integrate culturally (1995: 119). My interviews with Spanish labor migrants in Usurbil about their migration experience partially confirmed this. They had no trouble getting factory jobs. But could labor migrants who went to live in the smaller towns like Usurbil, where Basque was the habitual language of everyday life, fully integrate into their social surroundings without learning Basque? Many of those I interviewed said they felt knowing Basque would help them to participate more fully in the life of their community, but the conditions for learning Basque were not very favorable. Castilian and Basque are quite different grammatically, so learning takes effort. But residential segregation was another equally important obstacle. In many towns, the spatial concentration of immigrant laborers in large, newly erected housing complexes led to Spanish-speaking islands within otherwise predominantly Basque-speaking communities. Officially prohibited from the public realm, Basque circulated in the everyday talk of intimate social networks of friends and family. In addition to these structural obstacles to Basque-language acquisition, one must add the long-established language habit of linguistic accommodation, common to many minority-language speakers, in which native Basque speakers typically switch to speaking Spanish when engaging with officials or outsiders. If there were any incentives to breech these barriers and learn Basque during this early period of labor migration, it seemed to come from a sense of political affinity with the Basque cause. Not obliged to learn Basque for economic survival nor offered any opportunity to do so in school, labor migrants had to learn what they could informally. The negative consequences of this state of affairs for social cohesion and language maintenance were precisely what gave rise to the grassroots language-education movement's focus on creating inexpensive night schools so that everyone from factory workers, retirees, and housewives to the unemployed would have an opportunity to learn Basque.

Historians and sociologists describe labor migration as leading to the emergence of two communities, one Spanish migrant, one Basque, whose relations were characterized by resentment, antagonism, and avoidance (see, for example, Heiberg 1989: 96–98).[12] This characterization, perhaps overly generalized, nevertheless captures the social crisis as the new generation of revolutionary nationalists understood it. As the 1964 "Letter to the Intellectuals" had announced, ETA was committed to a class analysis of Basque society and to creating alliances between nationalists and the combative labor movement that was simultaneously unfolding. Unfair labor conditions, wage freezes, and inflation were rampant, but antilabor legislation and the structure of state-run syndicates denied workers the right to independent trade unions or free collective bargaining, making it very difficult for workers to organize for real change. Workers resorted to mass work stoppages in Gipuzkoa, Bizkaia, and Asturias and were met with intense police reprisals. From 1956 to 1975, Franco declared eleven states of emergency, suspending all civil rights. Police were able to enter homes without authorization, freedom of association was prohibited, and thousands of people suspected of fomenting disobedience and unrest were arrested and tortured (Gurruchaga 1985: 292–309). This shared experience of state repression under martial law produced the grounds for solidarity among activists in the labor movement, many of whom were immigrant, and the Basque-nationalist struggle (see Jáuregi (1981: 283–84).

That same year ETA published yet another document defining itself as "a Basque socialist movement for national liberation." Internally, however, it went through intense debates over the competing priorities of Marxism and national liberation, with some factions eventually splitting off and abandoning the national cause altogether in order to join leftist movements. Those who stayed worked to reach out to the migrant working classes and create a single revolutionary struggle that integrated issues of economic justice, national sovereignty, and ethnolinguistic revival. By the mid-sixties, ETA's leftist turn was expressed in their use of slogans like "Gora Euskadi Sozialista" [Long Live Socialist Euskadi] and the use of the term *Pueblo Trabajador Vasco* [Basque Working People] to refer to the Basque nation. This nation was based on a common set of political values—nationalism, socialism, and democracy—not ethnicity. It was not Spaniards per se, but the capitalist Spanish state that they identified as the primary oppressor of the Basques.[13]

Kasmir (2002) provides compelling ethnographic evidence of the way in which radical Basque nationalism refigured the project of liberation in such a way as to open doors to incorporating the Spanish working classes as part of the Basque nation. She observes that scholars have not paid much attention to this kind of working-class identified nationalism. For the most part, conventional understandings of ethnic nationalist movements have tended to characterize these movements as ideologically uniform in nature, initiated by elites, antithetical to the interests of working classes, and indeed excluding working-class migrants. As Kasmir notes, Basque radical nationalism constitutes an exception. "By employing different criteria for enemy and ally, ETA embarked on a debate with the PNV over who was Basque. ETA's construction of workers, native or immigrant, who 'work for true democracy in our country' linked class and activism to produce a novel Basque figure: the patriotic immigrant worker" (2002: 48–49).

Radical Basque nationalism has had Spanish laborers among its leading figures. Kasmir points, for example, to the legendary ETA militant "Txiki" (Jon Paredes Manot), who was a working-class immigrant from Extremadura. Executed by the state in 1975, Txiki was ethnically Spanish, but in radical nationalist circles, writes Kasmir, he was considered undeniably Basque.[14] From her research in the late eighties and nineties in the working-class town of Mondragon/Arrasate, she provides other examples of Spanish labor migrants and their children whose participation in the social venues and activities of radical Basque nationalism gained them acceptance as members of the Basque nationalist community and through this, grounds on which to claim that were "more Basque" than some of their ethnically Basque neighbors.

But what of language? Were there varying political stances toward language within Basque nationalism similar to those we find in connection with class inequality? Where does language fit in the turn to what political scientists call a "civic" definition of nationalism? This was exactly the question asked by Txillardegi and other language advocates. Having been forced into exile in 1961, he began to write letters to the ETA political leadership and published a series of articles in the journal *Branka* expressing concern over what he saw as the diminishing priority the organization was giving to the linguistic battle.[15] He argued that the organization had surrendered itself to Marxist-Leninist ideology and that the critique of capitalism the organization was adopting was necessary and fundamental to the movement, but insufficient. The Basque Country, he argued, should not follow pre-established models of revolution. It needed to develop its own political strategy for dealing with the intersecting forms of oppression—cultural as well as class based—specific to its historical situation. Strongly influenced by Jean-Paul Sartre, Txillardegi was suspicious of orthodox Marxism if it was accepted uncritically. He was alarmed at the decreasing use of Basque in ETA's publications and the low number of ETA leaders who either knew or were learning Basque. His writings from this period warned his compatriots that the organization seemed to be forgetting the centrality of language to the politics of state repression. In his eyes, a socialist but Spanish-speaking Euskadi was ultimately a betrayal of the movement. Txillardegi argued that independence and class revolution could not guarantee language preservation and, indeed, were hollow without it. The motto that he and like-thinking dissidents in the organization adopted was "the only national revolution is a Basque-speaking one" (Unzueta 1980: 19). In April 1967, shortly after the end of ETA's historic Fifth Assembly, and in view of the fact that they could not persuade ETA to change its course, Txillardegi, José María Benito del Valle, and José Manuel Aguirre, key spokesmen for *Branka*, officially resigned from ETA.[16]

There were many in and outside the organization who regarded the attempt to make Basque the national language as utopian and extremist, given the large numbers of people who knew only Spanish, although what exactly makes language revival any more utopian than the overthrow of capitalism or obtaining an independent state is not exactly clear. Each of these goals involves profound social transformation. Is the goal of language revival extremist? Racist? Is it another example of Daniele Conversi's claim that since Arana, Basque politics has been exclusionary in nature (1997: 262)? Some scholars have thought so in part, I would argue, because they associate language revival with "ethnic" rather than "civic" definitions of nationhood. Sociologist Rogers Brubaker (2004), however, has helped us to see the vexed nature of this distinction and others like it (e.g., political versus cultural nationalism). The civic/ethnic opposition is used by scholars to differentiate between forms of nationality or citizenship that rely on ideological or chosen factors like political creed, versus those based on inherited factors like cultural background, ethnicity, or descent. Civic nationalism purportedly is more inclusive because it is based on shared common ideals and values, while ethnic nationalism draws the boundaries of its community based on a common heritage. While in the abstract the civic/ethnic distinction is seemingly clear cut, in reality, says Brubaker, the distinction breaks down. Civic-based nationalisms are always also imbued with cultural content. France is a good example. It is the archetypical representative of a civically defined nation based on principles of equality, liberty, and fraternity, yet the forms by which it expresses its nationality are clearly loaded with notions of a common "French" culture. One must, among other things, speak French to be French, and the state recognizes only one official language.

Language in particular is a conundrum for the ethnic/civic opposition. Where does it belong? Language is the medium through we are socialized and acquire culture. It is often described and experienced as something one is "born with," deeply embedded into the core of our identities, as suggested by the very term "mother tongue." But language can also be chosen; it can be learned. Language transgresses the opposition between nature and culture that is at the root of the civic/ethnic contrast: it is both.

The long tradition in European thought of treating languages as indices of peoples is reflected in the continued practice of scholars (and nationalists) of treating language as a primordial tie—something that we inherit, like our ethnicity, and that is immutable. But if we do treat it like ethnicity, we fail to understand the project of this generation of language loyalists. It would be misguided to read the intent of Txillardegi and other language advocates as a rejection of a civic Basque identity that was being elaborated at the time. Quite the contrary, language revival is conceptualized as a civic project of sociocultural transformation founded on political beliefs and values in which they sought to engage all of society. It is a form of activism simultaneously cultural and political. Language advocates brought to this struggle a keen awareness of the way that Basque language loss had been minimized or naturalized. They also understood that pronouncements of language loyalty alone would not change anything. For social patterns to change, they insisted to their fellow nationalists that Euskara could not just be a symbol of Basqueness— it must be a *practice*. Herein lies one of the most important discursive contributions that language-revival activism of this era makes to the definition of modern Basque identity.

Euskalgintza: The Politics of Practice

Txillardegi abandoned the hope of persuading ETA to take a leadership role in language revival and joined forces with a heterogeneous social movement of Basque literary, publishing, artistic, and educational groups working on behalf of what was called at the time *kulturgintza,* a term meaning basically [Basque] "culture making." Language loyalists now use the term *euskalgintza* to refer to the social movement on behalf of *euskaldun* language and cultural production. During its early years, this social movement incorporated an array of groups and activities that had emerged contemporaneous with the new wave of Basque nationalism. At the same time that EKIN had started to meet in the mid-fifties, the popular Basque-language cultural magazines *Anaitasuna* (1953) and *Zeruko Argia* (1954) emerged, followed by the academic publications *Egan, Jakin,* and *Euskera,* all of which began publishing in 1956. At their start, several of these publications were possible because they were affiliated with Catholic entities like the Franciscan monastery of Arantzazu. These Basque-language publications constituted an incipient Basque public sphere for dialogue about Basque culture and society that was able to slip by the strict censorship applied to secular materials written in Basque.

Influential on the language movement was an essay Txillardegi published in the first issue of *Branka* in 1966, just before his departure from ETA. Entitled "Hizkuntza eta Pensakera" [Language and Way of Thought] (Alvarez Enparantza 1966), it argued that language was central to cultural identity. Txillardegi drew upon an impressive array of works by structural linguists, psychologists, and anthropologists, including Ferdinand de Saussure, Edward Sapir and Benjamin Lee Whorf, André Martinet, Claude Levi-Strauss, and Jacques Lacan—theorists who stood outside the controversies of Basque nationalism. Reading these theorists, he argued that there existed solid evidence that language structured thought processes in a profound way. Echoing Krutwig, he argued that science showed language was an essential part of culture, and thus the loss of a language was never inconsequential. He was appalled by the passivity of linguists or philologists who were fearful or indifferent to ways in which they could help the revitalization of Euskara. For him, linguistics and science in general should be tools of social justice and critique, not ends in themselves.

The recourse to scientific theories and evidence speaks to the struggle for truth and authority in which activists were engaged. As Bourdieu noted many years ago, struggles over ethnic, regional, (and we may add linguistic) identity are: "a particular case of the different struggles over classifications, struggles over the monopoly of the power to make people see and believe, to get them to know and recognize, to impose the legitimate definition of the divisions of the social world and, thereby to *make and unmake groups*" (1991: 221, emphasis in original).

At stake in minority-language and cultural movements, wrote Bourdieu, are struggles over "cognition and recognition" (ibid.: 220). Reversing the trend of language shift required dislodging commonsensical ways of understanding language that underwrite and naturalize the abandonment of the minority language. Activists seek to literally *re*-cognize the relationship between power inequalities and the taken-for-granted order of linguistic life. It requires questioning and reframing the minority-language speaker's habitual deferral to majority-language speakers. In struggles over cognition, says Bourdieu, science is frequently a powerful weapon that not only serves to legitimate activists' claims, but also to help bring them into being. "Any position claiming 'objectivity' about the actual or potential, real or foreseeable existence, of a region, an ethnic group, or a social class . . . constitutes a certificate of *realism* or a verdict of utopianism which helps to determine the objective chances that this social entity has of coming into existence" (ibid.: 225).

Txillardegi mobilized science to challenge the subordination of language revival to class struggle. He drew from Lacan, De Saussure, and other theorists to contest what he saw as a reductionistic variant of Marxism among some of his contemporaries that relegated language issues to "mere superstructure" (quoted in Unzueta 1980: 16) rather than a real axis of power.

Language loyalists of this early period were profoundly influenced by the arguments in *Language and Way of Thought*. The idea that language was more than a historical patrimony—actually a critical element shaping their unconscious, cognitive structures and identity as Basques—was disseminated through many cultural magazines of the period such as *Zeruko Argia, Muga,* and *Punto y Hora de Euskal Herria* as well as through the network of community-based adult language and literacy classes. It also was conveyed in reading and discussion groups organized via chapters of the language-revival organization Euskal Herrian Euskaraz [Basque in the Basqueland] that emerged in 1979. If language was vital for shaping worldview and the psyche, then the language shift underway became a much more significant cultural transformation than previously thought and raised questions about identity that were difficult to answer.

An incident from my fieldwork in 1983 was a telling example. A newly formed branch of Euskal Herrian Euskaraz in Usurbil had decided to set up a study group on sociolinguistics so locals could better understand language dynamics. This was a common means by which consciousness-raising about language took place. Lecture series and study groups organized by local language-advocacy groups were vehicles through which laypeople encountered and discussed the perspectives on language that intellectuals in the movement were proposing. I attended these meetings with about half a dozen other people from the town. Our sessions were facilitated by a member of Euskalherrian Euskaraz who had just finished his university degree in Basque philology. We spent the first few meetings discussing the relationship between language, society, and worldview. As the facilitator, the young man walked us through the basic steps of Txillardegi's argument. We learned that language provides the basic elements for the expression of ideas; that ideas are the basis of thoughts; that thoughts are the fundamental elements of personality; that one's personality is fundamental to personhood; and finally, that people who share a common personality constitute the basis for collective identity.

I was struck at the time by the tidiness of this view of a world of neatly separated languages and identities, astounding for people who lived and breathed bilingualism as a part of their daily life. As a form of popular sociolinguistics, however, this and other lessons like it were not attempts at nuanced linguistics, but rather efforts on the part of advocates to contest years of dominant ideology under Franco that treated the loss of Basque as inconsequential when it did not outright applaud it. It also set the stage for participating in the language movement: language revival was important because language was a central part of Basque personhood and collective identity. At the end of our discussion, a middle-aged woman in the group confessed that though she often spoke in Basque, she felt sometimes that she was thinking in Castilian and translating into Basque. She asked in a perplexed tone, "I speak in Basque, but how do I know if I really think in it?" "Am I really *euskaldun*?" she wondered.

Richard Kearney (2004) has said that to be Irish is to always be asking what it means to be Irish. Irishness, he says, exists in the interrogative mode. Such is the existential condition of so many minority-language speakers. The questions the woman in my study group asked were just one example of the kind of introspection that minority-language revival elicits. It was an introspection echoed in many provocatively titled articles of the day such as: "Who Is a Basque?" "What Is Basque For?" "Why Speak Basque?"

Language revival is by its nature a process of calling into question the meaning of language for identity. It also calls into question the taken-for-granted habits of how language is used. In the study group, our discussions often began with questions: Why were product labels or train announcements only in Spanish? Why did Basque speakers switch to Spanish when they entered a store or spoke to the telephone operator? Slogans in the language movement called for changes in habits and assumptions that make up the linguistic environment. They called into question the assumptions about when and where it is appropriate to speak a language.

The most novel contribution language loyalists of the contemporary era made to the conceptualization of language and identity was, however, its emphasis on practice. As we have seen, the language practices of nationalists were placed under scrutiny and criticized by Txillardegi and, before him, Krutwig. Both argued that *speaking* Basque was how a nationalist demonstrated the authenticity of his or her loyalties. Continuing to speak Spanish, they argued, was a contradiction of patriotism. Using Bourdieu's terms, they were asking nationalists to "re-cognize" everyday language practices as a field of power. In short, they were asking nationalists to see that domination was exercised not only through legal repression, but also through the seemingly "practical" or "habitual" patterns of language use that kept Basque in the margins.

Language-revival activism at this time did more than treat language as a symbol of the nation; it politicized everyday language use and instantiated a pragmatic view of Basque identity in which being Basque—which for many people meant being Basque nationalist—implied speaking Basque. This is a fundamental message of the post-Franco language-revival movement and one that logically aligned with radical nationalism's way of understanding political struggle as a whole: that is, the idea that one's politics, loyalties, and commitments need to be enacted to be credible. Joseba Zulaika demonstrates this in his extraordinary analysis of cultural logics that inform radical nationalism. Three related concepts drawn from Basque rural culture, he argues, are key to the way these radicals conceptualized their political struggle: *ekintza* [action], *indarra* [strength] and *egitan* [truth, authenticity]. *Ekintza*, explains Zulaika, refers to a basic belief that "there is an abysmal gulf between speaking, promising, wishing, imagining, and the concrete deed" (1988: 165). Related to this is the Basque cultural notion of truth which holds that commitments, beliefs, values are only fully authentic and real [egitan] when they are demonstrated in actions. *Ekinzta*, he argues, was both the word ETA revolutionaries gave to their actions and an organizing metaphor for what it meant to "be" an *abertzale* [nationalist].

Anthropologist Teresa del Valle (1994) finds this logic at work in Korrika, one of the biggest events in the language loyalist calendar. Korrika is a massive two-week marathon or race organized by the adult language–education organization AEK (Alfabetatzen Euskaduntzen Koordinakundea) to raise funds for Basque schooling and awareness about language revival. The mass appeal and intelligibility of the Korrika marathon stems, she argues, from its resonance with deeper cultural values including that of *ekintza*. Running the Korrika is an arduous task, as the marathon goes on day and night without stop for several thousand kilometers throughout the Basque territory. Kilometer by kilometer, runners demonstrate the physical energy, *indarra,* that the whole society is dedicating to keep Basque alive. Building on Zulaika's earlier insights into the operation of these metaphors, del Valle argues that *indarra* is a central aspect of Basque political events because it is a basic feature of Basque cultural conceptions of selfhood. It is through work, understood as physical exertion, that one most authentically communicates and defines one's self (1994: 43).

Korrika, which began in 1980, is not the first manifestation of the cultural logic of *ekintza* in language revitalization. It permeates the writings of Txillardegi and Krutwig and the criticisms they leveled against Spanish-speaking Basque nationalists. This is perhaps not surprising, as the social fields of language activism and radical nationalism have a good deal of overlap in this period, both Txillardegi and Krutwig being former members of ETA. But the basic premise that beliefs should manifest in actions/work also has strong grounding, as Zulaika shows, in *euskaldun* culture. This lays the foundation for the emergence of a pragmatic or performative view of the relationship between Basque language and identity in which Basqueness and patriotism—habitually tied together—are thought to be most authentically demonstrated through action: by speaking—and, if need be, learning—Basque. It soon became the leitmotiv of language campaigns and consciousness-raising events of the popular *euskalgintza* movement.

This practice-based conceptualization of identity, quite different from the categorical view of identity as something one is or is not, has passed unremarked in most discussions of Basque nationalism and identity. Using the conventions of their discipline, historians and political scientists of Basque nationalism in the late Franco era typically describe only two contrasting ways of defining Basque national identity: an ethnic or ethnolinguistic definition adopted by mainstream nationalists, and the "civic" definition of leftist radical nationalism that includes all who live and work in Euskadi and uphold the right to self-determination, regardless of ethnicity. The former ethnolinguistic definition is frequently characterized as largely essentialist and exclusionary and the latter as more inclusionary, particularly to working-class people of Spanish or mixed ethnicity.

The assertions language loyalists make about the importance of language to Basque nationality and identity typically get treated rather unproblematically as an expression of the ethnic view of Basque identity. But such a classification does not hold up under closer scrutiny of language-loyalist discourse. The pragmatic stance on Basque identity, rooted in the logic of *ekintza,* is quite different from the understanding of language as heritage most often associated with ethnic nationalism. The two perspectives are frequently merged by language loyalists themselves, but the distinctiveness of the practice-based view of Basque identity should not be ignored. It introduces a fault line into what Paul Gilroy (1993) calls the discourse of "ethnic absolutism." Just as the socialist nationalists made it possible for the patriotic labor migrant to become Basque, so the pragmatic linguistic perspective of language loyalists opened up new avenues for inclusion into the nation and the nation-building project. The latter asserted the possibility of being and becoming Basque through language learning. The nonessentialist nature of this conception of identity cannot be captured by the ethnic/primordialist versus civic typology. The failure to perceive the nonessentialist qualities of this view of language may be due in part to the way scholars themselves understand language. In Western European thought, language tends to be viewed, along with blood and soil, as a primordial tie. We have a long tradition of this line of thinking that goes back at least to the German romantics. Language is routinely seen as a feature of identity one is "born with," rather than a practice through which identities are actively produced. This view of language continues to prevail in political analyses of Basque nationalism, producing significant blind spots with regard to the contributions and complexity of language-revival discourse.

The ethnic, civic, and pragmatic conceptualizations of Basque national identity exist in tension with one another and their disjunctures give rise to the dilemmas and lived contradictions that are the stuff of everyday life in this territory. An example can be had in the ethnographic account by Kasmir (2002) of political life in Mondragón/Arrasate, a town famous for its industrial cooperatives. Kasmir's ethnography describes the ways that the children of Spanish labor migrants "became Basque" through participating in the world of radical-nationalist youth culture: hanging out in particular bars, attending demonstrations, adopting Basque names, and taking on distinctive punk working-class styles of clothing and musical tastes. In the course of this study, Kasmir describes a moment in the municipal elections of 1991 in which the local radical nationalists of Herri Batasuna were in a tight electoral race with the Spanish socialist party (PSOE, Partido Socialista Obrero Español) for the mayorship of the town. In the fray of mutual name-calling that spilled out into the streets after the election, she recounts a shouting match that erupted between Txema, a son of labor migrants from Extremadura who supported Herri Batasuna, and a local PSOE council member of Basque heritage. She notes that at one point in the encounter, Txema yelled out to his adversary, "[I'm] more Basque than you!"

The verbal scuffle illuminates the way in which the rooting of Basqueness in (nationalist) political ideology competes with its ethnic definition. The Basque councilman's membership in the PSOE—a Spanish nationalist party—placed him in opposition to Basque nationalism. Txema's political loyalties to Basque nationalism outweighed language and ethnicity in legitimating his claim to Basqueness. But further on in her account, Kasmir tells another story paralleling many of my own fieldwork experiences that indexes the pragmatic understanding of Basque identity, pointing to the awkward moments and silences that can and often do occur among radical-nationalist youth who do not speak Basque. She describes a group of radical youth who are talking among themselves in Spanish. When the topic of conversation turned to language, they began to criticize themselves and other nationalists who "go around as very Basque, but don't even speak *Euskera*." The conversation continued in this vein, she recalls, until it finally came to an awkward halt when one of the youth exclaimed in exasperation, "what do I care if Euskadi is socialist, if no one speaks *Euskera*!" (2002: 57). Comments like these, by no means unique to Arrasate, echo almost verbatim the criticisms Txillardegi made of his fellow ETA militants some thirty years earlier.

As in most complex societies, there is not a single means by which Basque identity is gained, defined, or expressed. There are claims based on territory (I was born/live there), heritage, and ethnicity, as well as claims based on political sentiments. The pragmatic perspective on identity and the connection it makes between language use, Basqueness, and patriotism is such that one's linguistic choices are always potentially available for political readings. "Every identity," writes Stuart Hall, "has at its 'margin', an excess, something more. . . . The unity and internal homogeneity which the term identity treats as foundational is not a natural, but a constructed form of closure . . . and also an excess which destabilizes it" (1996a: 5). Within the contemporary Basque nationalist imaginary that gave greater prominence to the pragmatic view of language and identity, the Spanish-speaking *abertzale* (nationalist) was just such a potentially destabilizing force. Familiar and demographically common, to be sure, the nationalist who spoke only Spanish was conceptually problematic. To use Mary Douglas's phrase, she or he was always potentially "matter out of place" (1966).

There are many more people who support Basque nationalism and language revival than there are people who speak Basque, and thus, in the context of everyday life, people typically accommodate the disjuncture that can arise between linguistic ideology they may uphold favoring the use of Basque and the practice of speaking Spanish. They invoke other ties of solidarity such as being neighbors, coworkers, relatives, having common political beliefs, and so forth. One place, however, where that disjuncture is most acutely felt and the stakes around language choice seem highest is the public sphere of political performances. While all language is potentially available for "identity readings," on the public stage, where people claim to represent the nation, the presence or absence of Euskara will rarely pass without commentary, either in the form of critique, apology, or explanation. Such is the terrain of meanings that all speakers have to negotiate in their language choices. It is a terrain in which, as Kasmir's case makes apparent, pointing to the use of Castilian among a group of nationalists could sometimes stop a conversation dead in its tracks.

CHAPTER THREE

Making a Modern Language

Language teachers are the foot soldiers of a language-revival movement. At least this is how the teachers of the Basque-language classes I took in the early eighties saw themselves. At that time, teaching Basque was not just a job, as may be more the case today; it was a way of participating in the recovery of Basque culture. In language class we debated social issues, talked about why learning Basque was important, and often socialized together after class ended. It was common for teachers to organize extracurricular activities to get us to practice Basque out in the real world. But this was not always so easy. There was a big gap between the Basque we learned in class and what we heard native speakers say outside the classroom. When I haltingly spoke my new words and phrases with the native speakers in, for example, the kitchen of the Martín restaurant, more often than not they would look at me quizzically, smile, or become slightly uncomfortable. After a pause, someone might explain, "oh, yes, that's how you *should* say it," and a discussion of verb conjugations might unfold right then and there. Eager to learn how to communicate, I started to change the way I asked my questions in class. Instead of asking my teachers how something was said in Basque, I sometimes asked **kalean,** *nola esaten da?* [How is it said *in the street*?]. This second question was one that my teachers were not always comfortable answering.

One of the reasons this question was unsettling comes from the various agendas and responsibilities that language teaching often bears in contexts of revitalization. Basque teachers were not just trying to teach us Basque, they were also committed to what language revivalists call "bringing the language forward" (Hornberger and King 1996: 440). That is, they wanted to help in the process of making Basque into a modern "national" language suitable for new usages. Like many endangered or minority languages, Basque had survived mainly as a spoken language with strong dialectal variation. When the language-revival movement began to pick up again in the 1960s, the Basque Language Academy recommenced work on language standardization in the 1960s, and in 1978 they published the first guidelines for Euskara Batua [Unified Basque]. Basque-language classrooms—both the

Basque-medium primary schools, known as *ikastolak,* and the nongovernmental adult language and literacy–school network, AEK, took charge of disseminating this new standardized variety of Basque. Thus, for a good decade, an odd situation existed in Basque Country in which the Basque being taught in the classroom was not well known and was different from the local dialect that was spoken by native Basque speakers. The resulting disjuncture between classroom or, as we students called it, *euskaltegi* [school] Basque, and what was otherwise referred to as *herriko hizkera* [popular speech] was a frequent and sometimes heated topic of commentary as well as a cause of awkward interactions in daily life.

Today, much has changed. Unified Basque is no longer an oddity. Most young adults in the Basque Autonomous Community have received part or possibly even all of their primary-school instruction in this variety. It is used in official government business, in publishing, and in EITB, the publicly financed regional Basque Television and Radio network that began broadcasting in 1982. Batua is now a regular part of the linguistic landscape and, without a doubt, one of the most significant legacies of the contemporary language-revival movement. Here I examine the controversies that circulated among intellectuals at the time of its creation and how they manifested in the daily lives of the speakers with whom I lived. My analysis draws on the work of linguistic anthropologists who have helped us to see the complex ways that seemingly "technical" decisions about language norms are linked to relations of power and cultural frameworks of value (Schieffelin and Doucet 1992; Parakrama 1995; Silverstein 1996). While I describe some of the details of the corpus reforms that standardization brought about, my main concern has less to do with the linguistic aspects of standardization than with its ideological meanings and ironic effects.

The arguments made for standardization, the criteria used, and the reactions to those decisions offer us insights into some of the dilemmas that arise for minority-language advocates trying to make a place for their language in modern state structures and cultural institutions. Defining standards of usage is often one of the first steps in any language-planning effort (Haugen 1966b).[1] But exactly what is a "standard language"? The concept is actually murkier than it may first appear. It has been defined in various ways: as the language most widely understood, the language of prestige, or the official language (Joseph 1987). Michael Silverstein (1996), however, gives us a more provocative definition. Standard languages, he says, are not so much language varieties as they are ideological constructs—and quite powerful ones at that. The sense that people have of being a unified linguistic community, says Silverstein, is premised more on the belief that they share common norms than on how they actually speak. Standards are idealizations of language practice that mark people who have allegiance to them as members of a single community and also stratify them according to how they are perceived to deviate from the ideal. The necessity of having a standard is a cultural belief so ingrained in Western conceptions of language that it has been difficult, says Silverstein, for speakers of standardized languages to regard nonstandardized ones as "real" languages at all (1996: 286). Minority-language advocates are acutely aware of the connotations that derive from not having a standard, and this was part of what drove forward the creation of Batua. Their efforts are diagnostic of how taken-for-granted standardization is in assumptions about what makes one language better, more useful, more civilized, or more prestigious than another (Parakrama 1995).

This analysis of the debates about standardization continues my exploration of how the Basque language became a terrain through which the unity, governability, and modernity of a distinct Basque nation were constituted and represented back to the public. I am especially interested in how standardization functions as a means by which a national linguistic community is hailed into being. Because my periods of research in the Basque Country coincided with the phase when Batua was first being popularized, I was able to observe some of the awkward social effects the process engendered among native speakers and language advocates in Gipuzkoa, where I lived. I could also see that while standardization was desirable to many and seemed inevitable to most, it was not uncontested. A sustained debate accompanied standardization and continues to this day. Having examined the first efforts at standardization at the beginning of the twentieth century and what language advocates thought it had to offer for ensuring the future of Basque, here I focus more on the tensions that erupted in the post-Franco period and what these can tell us about the ways language reform collided with existing ways of experiencing Basqueness and the political divisions between conservative and radical nationalists. I am also concerned with why it is that many language loyalists and planners today are adamantly reclaiming vernacular Basque as necessary to their linguistic future.

Making Batua

Standardizing Basque is as much a story about the intentional imagining of a modern and translocal Basque linguistic identity as it is a linguistic process. Nevertheless, it is worth considering the variance that language advocates were facing. Basque has been described as having anywhere from six to nine dialects. The Bizkaian and Gipuzkoan dialects—which linguists now more commonly call Western and Central varieties, respectively—are spoken in the Basque Autonomous Com-

TABLE 3.1
Basque Dialects & Geographic Locations (after Zuazo 1988)

1. Western varieties (Bizkaia, Araba, and western Gipuzkoa)
2. Central varieties (Gipuzkoa and western Nafarroa)
3. Navarrese (communities and valleys of Nafarroa: Bortizierieta, Malereka, Baztan, Ultzama, and Aezkoa)
4. Eastern Navarrese (Erronkari, now lost; Zaraitzu, almost lost)
5. Zuberoan (also known as Souletin; northern Basque province of Zuberoa)
6. Lapudian and Low Navarrese (northern Basque provinces of Lapurdi and Nararroa Beherea)

munity and have the largest number of speakers, making up about two-thirds of the Basque-speaking population today (Zuazo 1988; Amorrortu 2000).[2] Opinions vary as to how mutually intelligible the dialects are to one another, but all scholars agree that the range of variation across the territory is significant. Table 3.1 lists the most commonly accepted dialectal categories.

As we have already seen, in the early twentieth century the modernist reformers of the Basque Studies Society found the lack of a single standardized way of writing Basque to be untenable for an industrializing society. In language as in other areas of social life, they saw it as both more practical and rational to have agreed-upon norms. The Basque Studies Society founded the Basque Language Academy in 1918 and charged it with the task of devising these norms as part of their overall mission to regulate and modernize the language. In 1934 Resurrección Azkue, at the time president of the academy, developed a unified literary variety he named Gipuzkera Osotua, based primarily on the Gipuzkoan dialect, but it was never officially adopted. The project to standardize Basque remained stalled until the 1960s, when a new generation of politicized writers, poets, and language advocates began to emphasize the need for norms.[3] The importance second-wave nationalists gave to language in defining Basque identity and the reemergence of the Basque-schooling movement placed pressure on the academy to resume work on standardization. Increasing literacy in Basque was considered of utmost importance to the future of the language. But what variety of Basque should be taught? In what dialect should textbooks be written? What was "good" Basque? And who should determine that?

The arguments advocates made in favor of standardization largely replicated those that were made before the Spanish Civil War. And once again, responses for and against were passionate. Some nationalists held firm to Arana's view that unified Basque, if needed, should be allowed to emerge naturally. But the new generation of radical nationalists thought otherwise. Krutwig and Txillardegi both saw standardization as an urgent necessity of the nation-building project and a requirement for introducing Basque into modern print culture. Uniform rules of grammar and orthography as well as an expanded vocabulary were seen as necessary tools for transforming Basque into a national language and also as tools for combating the often repeated claims that Basque was not suitable for serious intellectual pursuits.[4] This sentiment was advanced most emphatically by writers and advocates on the nationalist left, for whom standardization was also seen as a means of strengthening the unity of the various provinces. In their view, Batua was a mechanism for creating a truly national *euskaldun* public sphere.

As in the pre–Civil War period, members of the Basque Language Academy were concerned with establishing their expertise and their right to direct the process of standardization. On this point, Luis Villasante, former president of the academy, was unequivocal:

> In the long run, who does not see that the problem of unification is, above all, a technical problem and that it is the technicians (linguists and specialists of the language) who have to resolve it? It is true that for them to carry out their work it will be necessary that the whole community supports them, but the task of showing the way belongs to them. To believe that unification will happen by itself is like believing that a book will emerge by throwing type-set on the floor. (Villasante 1980: 98)

Villasante was clear: standardization properly belonged to the experts. He won that battle, and the academy's role as the ultimate authority on the language was recognized in the 1978 Statute of Autonomy (article 6.4).

Work toward standardization began with spelling and vocabulary. In 1964 a group of writers, including Txillardegi, met in the city of Baiona to discuss the need for a standardized orthography and modernization of vocabulary.[5] Later that year, the academy established guidelines for a standard orthography based on some of the proposals made at the Baiona meeting (Villasante 1980a: 62–63). Four years later, in 1968, on the occasion of its fiftieth anniversary, the academy voted to begin work on a plan for standardization.

The road map for the academy's work was developed largely by the respected linguist Luis Michelena (a.k.a. Koldo Mitxelena). Azkue's pre–Civil War proposal for Gipuzkera Osotua [Enhanced Gipuzkoan] and Krutwig's postwar proposal for Classic Labourdin literary variety were models on which they built (Zuazo 1998). The goal was to create a new amalgamated literary variety, integrating elements from the various dialects but based primarily on the geographically central dialects. According to Villasante (1980a) the academy's work was governed by an agreement to favor regularity of inflexional paradigms, the preservation of grammatical distinctions, antiquity, and maximum intelligibility. Purification often accompanies standardization efforts (Joseph 1987; Crowley 1989), and in the Basque case this was manifest in a concern with purging Spanish grammatical influences. However, the writings of the academicians, in particular those of Luis Villasante, the Basque Language Academy member charged with documenting the history of the process, show a strong inclination to pragmatism over purism and a concern with making the standard as easily comprehensible as possible. Among the reasons the academy gave for choosing the central dialects (i.e., largely Gipuzkoan) as the basis for Batua was their sense that Gipuzkoan forms would be intelligible to the greatest number of speakers. In creating Unified Basque, explained Villasante, the academy tended toward retaining linguistic forms once commonly found in all the dialects. However, he noted, unification should not become a search for the purest or most authentic Basque forms: "The unification movement should not give in to the temptation of archaeologism. It is not advisable to turn to older forms except in the case when these forms are still alive in at least an important part of the language. . . . We do not want an archaeology [*arqueologismo*] that threatens life; we want one that serves it" (1980a: 88).

The published record reveals experts trying to balance an array of sometimes competing values. They approached the task by setting up various committees that dedicated themselves to just one aspect of the language (e.g., verb morphology, syntax, phonology, lexicon). It took ten years of work (1968–78) before the academy published its first guidelines. Once it regularized the spelling of placenames and established a standard orthography, the academy took on grammatical features, beginning with the standardization of noun declensions. Declensions mark cases and perform many of the same functions as prepositions or articles in English. In Basque, these declensions take the form of suffixes added to nouns. So, for example, the noun *etxe* [house] may have the following declensions as suffixes: etxe*a* [the house], etxe*tik* [from the house], etxe*ko* [of the house], etxe*ra* [to the house], etxe*raino* [as far as the house], etxe*az* [about the house], and so forth.

Then came verbal morphology. Basque has a rich auxiliary verb system that marks person, number of objects in transitive verbs, and tense. Although the same information is encoded in the verbs of all the dialects, the morphemes vary. Below are three forms of the phrase "I gave them to you" with the meanings of each morpheme listed below. The phrase is composed of the main verb *eman* [to give] and an auxiliary verb that displays dialectal variation [*dizkizut; deutsudaz; derauzkit-zut*]. This example, taken from Estibaliz Amorrortu (2000: 43), illustrates some of the variation that dialects present in the auxiliary verb root and other morphemes:

(1) Batua and Gipuzkoan

Eman d-i-zki-zu-t: [I gave them to you]

D	Present tense
I	verb root "izan"
ZKI	plural object
ZU	you: dative
T	me: ergative

(2) Bizkaian:

Eman d-eu-tsu-da-z: [I gave them to you]

D	Present tense
EU	verb root "eutsi"
TSU	you: dative
DA	me: ergative
Z	plural object

(3) Navarrese:

Eman d-erau-zki-tzu-t: [I gave them to you]

D	Present tense
ERAU	verb root "eraun"
ZKI	object plural
TZU	you: dative
T	me: ergative

The academy's work on norms for pronunciation and syntax progressed more slowly. Until quite recently, the academicians preferred not to define norms for spoken Basque. They characterized Batua as a written code for use in education and official written documents. This was reflected in the academy's description of Batua as a "literary" or "cultivated" Basque, rather than "standard" Basque (Amorrortu 2000). But as Basque was introduced into television and radio, broadcasters began to request guidelines on pronunciation. The academy complied, in 1998 publishing norms for "Cultivated Pronunciation of Euskara Batua," which it offered as a guide for use in formal functions of the language (news broadcasting, public speeches or lectures, and school). Contrary to popular belief, lexicon was not a primary concern in the standardization project. The academy's stance has been to regard all lexical equivalents in the various dialects as appropriate for use in Unified Basque. Despite this fact, Amorrortu's research showed a strong association of Batua with Gipuzkoan among Basque speakers that is reflected in lexical choices: "As with other aspects of the language, Gipuzkoan lexicon is mostly used when using *Batua*, even by speakers of Bizkaian" (2000: 45).

Norms for Normalization

Batua had multiple connotations when it entered into the public realm: it was associated with modernity, legitimacy, rationality, national unity, and, in the eyes of some, radical nationalism. The establishment of standardized norms, proponents said, would help Basque achieve a "normalized" situation. Indeed, the two processes—normalization and standardization—were regularly conflated (Zalbide 1998). The term *normalization* was first used by Catalan sociolinguists to describe the goal of language revitalization as a whole, and it was soon was adopted by Basques as well in lieu of the pre–Civil War term *restoration*. Sociologist Rafael Ninyoles's 1972 definition stands as a generally accepted understanding of what this term meant for language loyalists at the time:

> On the one hand, to normalize means to dictate norms, reduce to a few rules, codify, and standardize a language on the basis of a supra-dialectal variety. The meaning is thus basically linguistic. On the other hand, when we speak of normalization we are suggesting that a culture be placed on or restored to a "normal" level. We imply a purpose, a goal which to a large extent, goes beyond the limits of linguistics, and with reference to which the linguist will be relegated to the role of a simple technician. "Normalizing" will be equivalent to placing a language on an equal footing with other languages (neither "above" nor "below"): on the same level. (1972:75)[6]

The use of the term *normalization* for language revival is unique to Spain's minority-language movements. It is a term dense with meaning in a country that was at the time seeking to abandon its image as a dictatorship and refashion itself as a modern European nation (Crumbaugh 2007b, 2009). One of the key ideologues in this process was Manuel Fraga, Minister of Information and Tourism from 1962 to 1969. He first introduced the term and concept of *normalization* into the official political discourse of the regime in the mid-sixties. Cultural critic Justin Crumbaugh (2009) describes normalization as a central element in Fraga's cultural policies. The phrase "*Hay que normalizar*" [we must normalize], Crumbaugh argues, was a veritable mantra of Spain's modernization efforts, applied to everything from the economy and diplomatic relations to culture and political life (ibid.: 6). Normalization promised an end to state repression and a new consumer society characterized by planning, progress, and economic development. Catalan- and Basque-language loyalists' use of the term *language normalization* intelligently tied their political struggle to reclaim Spain's minority languages to this broader state-authorized endeavor to become a "normal" (i.e., modern and democratic) society.

Normalization had the status of what anthropologists call a "key symbol" (Ortner 1973). Becoming normal was a powerful and agglutinating symbol, a social good with which seemingly everyone could agree. Like other key symbols, its concrete meaning remained productively ambiguous and flexibly open to interpretation, as some language planners would complain (e.g., Zalbide 1998: 365). As we see in Ninyole's definition, normalization seems to imply that deliberate reforms of the language are needed to increase the prestige and expand the social use of Basque. Under the rubric of normalization, Basque-language standardization acquires the status of a therapeutic intervention, a mechanism for returning the minority language to health by helping Basque become "normal." The definition of language normality—described as being "neither above nor below"—underscores that normalization is to be seen as a nonconfrontational discourse, aligning minority-language revival and its methods with values of fairness, equity, and democratic reform.

Under the rubric of normalization, standardization was presented as part of the process of social modernization and reparation of Basque. Nevertheless, Batua was the subject of intense controversy in its early years. The academy's proposed orthography and the decisions they made with regard to declensions and verbs were widely discussed in cultural magazines and regional dailies. The public debate on standardization was so intense that the academy published two short books in Spanish (Villasante 1980a, 1980b) intended to explain to a popular audience the process and rationale behind the creation of Batua. From the seventies on, there was an explosion of talk about the Basque language, from its grammatical peculiarities, historical origins, and political importance to the causes for its decline; its viability for philosophy, poetry, physics; as well as the proper methods for teaching it. Batua was a ubiquitous topic in this talk, eliciting both support, confusion, and fierce condemnations. In a 1983 Basque government–sponsored study, public debate about Basque was described as chaotic and semifanatical: "The controversy is aired in books, magazines, in newspapers, round-table panels, coffee houses, literary circles, in a round of drinks at a bar, and in the after dinner conversations among friends. Everyone defends his or her right to have an opinion, generalize, and to be dogmatic about any issue related to *Euskera*" (Eusko Jaurlaritza/Gobierno Vasco 1983: 149).

Opposition to the new Unified Basque was most vehemently expressed by a group of writers calling itself Kardaberaz, which advocated for the use of dialect or popular speech forms over Batua.[7] An explicitly anti-Batua perspective was also given voice in two books published not long after the 1978 guidelines. *Euskaltzaindia, el batua y la muerte del euskera* by Vicente Latiegui and Dionsio de Oñatibia (1983) and *El libro negro de euskara* by José Basterrechea (a.k.a. "Oskillaso") (1984). Both are vitriolic condemnations of Batua, which they described as a "monstrous" and "artificial" creation of ETA radicals—non-native speakers to boot—that violated the authentic nature of Euskara and would have long-term negative consequences on the language. One senses that Txillardegi and Krutwig, both strong advocates of Batua, second-language learners of Basque and, as we know, supporters of radical Basque nationalism, may have been the implied targets of these criticisms. The main problem with Batua, said Oskillaso, was that it is too different from spoken vernacular Basque and is highly Castilianized (Basterrechea [Oskillaso] 1984: 136–38). Batua, he said, was simply bad Basque and was a sign of the hegemony that non-native speakers had come to exercise over language reform. Latiegui and Oñatibia argued that the real intent behind the new standard was not to save the language, but to depose the orthography invented by Arana. In short, while detractors disliked Batua for sometimes different reasons, they seemed to coincide in arguing that the new standard was an attempt by the newer generation of leftist nationalists to establish control over the symbols of the nation. Batua's opponents argued that linguistic barbarisms were being committed simply to promote an "extremist" vision of Basque nationalism. Among the most pernicious manifestations of this "intransigence and fanaticism" in the view of opponents was the letter "H" (Basterrechea [Oskillaso] 1984: 136).

Orthographic Storms: The Ideology of Letters

In places where identity and nationhood are being negotiated and challenged, virtually every aspect of language has the potential to become a culturally and politically meaningful symbol (Woolard 1998a: 23). As Megan Thomas argues, "the work of orthographic distinction has often been particularly attractive to those who perceive themselves to be asserting self-sovereignty against foreign, colonial, or imperial domination" (2007: 956). As she shows in her study of late-nineteenth-century Filipino revolutionaries, particular ways of spelling operated as a means of "flagging" the nation and supporting their claims to sovereignty, as in: "we have *our own* language; we should have *our own* government" (ibid.: 955).[8] This view is echoed in the work of other scholars who show that orthography may index boundaries with outsiders, as well as competing "ways of imagining the past and the future of a community" (Schieffelin and Doucet 1992: 285). In the Basque case, we see both processes in the debates concerning how to render sound into writing. Two controversies in particular—over the letters "z" and "s" before the war and over the letter "h" in the contemporary period—illustrate the passionate political investments in spelling that erupted and *dis*rupted the work of the language reformers.

Orthography came to be an issue, as we might expect at the formation of the Basque nationalist movement in the late nineteenth century, and Sabino Arana was in the thick of it. An avid student of Basque, he published numerous treatises relating to the language as well as a grammar book and was a prolific creator of new words, some of which have become part of common usage today, notably Euzkadi [the Basque nation], *aberri* [fatherland], and *askatasuna* [freedom]. Among Arana's many legacies was a new orthography for the Bizkaian dialect, *Lecciones de ortografía del euskera bizkaino* [Orthographic Lessons of Bizkaian Basque] in 1896 [1965]. An abiding concern in all of his work was to purge the signs of Spanishness from the language. Writing in Basque was not terribly common at the time, and when authors did so, they used the roman alphabet and tended to rely heavily on the spelling conventions of French or Spanish. Northern Basque writers reflected the influence of French orthography in using "ç" for sounds that southern or Spanish Basque writers represented with either "z" or "s." Writers from the south, for their part, often used the Spanish orthographic practice of placing tildes [~] over palatized "n." On both sides of the frontier, writers followed the conventions of Romance orthography in representing Basque sounds, for example, in the syllables *que, qui,* and *gue.* These conventions gave rise to spellings like *guiçonac* for the modern *gizonak* [men] or phrases like *antçiñaco adisquide* [old friend] and *itz eguiteco* [to speak] for the modern *antzinako adiskide* and *hitz egiteko.*[9] Romance orthography could not deal well with Basque sibilants [written today as "s," "x," "z," "ts," "tx," "tz"], resulting in varying spellings for these sounds and a fair amount of confusing solutions (see Trask 1997: 75–79).

Arana's orthography introduced changes into these conventions that made Basque difference from Spanish and French more visually apparent. He eliminated the letter "h" that was used by some French Basque writers and extended the use of the tilde [~] over various palatized consonants in ways that were not consistent with the Spanish use of tildes. Arana replaced the letter "j" with "x" and, in contrast to Spanish, he introduced an accent mark over the letter "r" to mark the rolled sound written with "rr" in Spanish. One of the more notable departures of his orthography was to introduce the letter "k" where "c" or "qu" had previously been used. Absent from Romance languages, the letter "k" was also seized upon as a symbol of orthographic decolonization in the language reforms of anticolonial movements elsewhere in Spain's colonies. It is quite possible that in young Arana's sojourn in Barcelona, he had already encountered this use of "k" in the writings of the diasporic leaders of those movements who had gone into exile in that city.[10]

New spelling conventions served to mark difference from Spanish and French, but they also became a road map to the political divisions internal to Basque political life at the time. Partisans of the early-twentieth-century Basque nationalist movement embraced Arana's "new Basque," while writers of other political persuasions continued to use the conventions of the past. How a writer chose to spell a word reverberated with ideological meaning. Spelling was so politically loaded, writes historian José Javier Granja Pascual, that the use of certain letters in fact became a way of designating ideological factions among the pre–Civil War Basque intelligentsia: "those writers who wrote with 'x' instead of 'j,' and 'k' instead of 'c'" (1984: 155).

A particularly heated spelling debacle revolved around Arana's use of the letter "z" instead of "s" in the words *euzkera* [the Basque language, now spelled Euskara in standard Basque] and *euzkadi* [the Basque nation, now spelled Euskadi]. Arana based his spelling with a "z" on an etymological theory that the common root of these words was derived from the word "sun" [*eguzki*]. He, like many of his contemporaries, subscribed to the theory that Basques had once been sun worshippers. Archaeological evidence from burial sites, including the four-headed symbol *lauburu,* believed to be a sign of the sun, were in his view incontrovertible evidence of this. Using etymological analysis, he argued that *euzkera* meant "language of the *euzkos,*" that is, sun worshippers, and thus should be written with a "z." Arana's contemporary, Arturo Campión, rebutted this theory in the *Revista internacional de estudios vascos* in 1907. He marshaled evidence for a distinct and autonomous root, "*eusk*" [Basque]. *Euskera* more likely derived from *eusk,* he argued, and should be spelled with an "s." Campión further argued that it was not necessary to create a new term, Euzkadi, for the Basque Country, as a term already existed, Euskal Erria (spelled at that time without an "h") meaning "land of the Basque language" (1907a, 1907b). As Granja Pascual (1984) notes, Campión's linguistic evidence was dismissed by Arana and regarded as an attempt to undermine his nationalist project. Campión was politically aligned with foralists, who wanted to restore the special accords [*fueros*] the Basque provinces had before the second Carlist war. The divergent spelling proposals for these key words soon spiraled into emblems of nationalists on the one hand and foralists on the others. So strong was "the union that Arana's followers made between nationalism and the neologisms . . . that any person who refuted the etymologies and grammatical or linguistic concepts of Arana was automatically seen as anti-nationalist" (Granja Pascual 1984: 165). Arana's etymology was eventually overturned in favor of Campión's, but for many years, the term *zetakide* [Z-ists] became a moniker for those aligned with Aranista political ideology (ibid.: 166–67).[11]

In the contemporary era, the debate over "z" and "s" faded away and all eyes turned to the letter "h." The Basque Language Academy incorporated "h" into the standardized orthography of Batua. Of all the innovations that the academy proposed, this one was the most publicly criticized and debated. The letter "h" was, as the president of the academy at the time, Luis Villasante, put it, *la cuestión batallón* [the bone of contention] (1980b), illuminating again the power of orthographies to symbolically flag internal political divisions among Basques.

"H," both as a letter and as a sound, has been one of the marked distinctions between the writing and pronunciation of northern and southern Basques. Speakers of northern Basque dialects (Lapurdian, Low Navarrese, and Zuberoan) have an audible aspiration in certain words that southern-dialect speakers do not. Writers of northern literary varieties of Basque, as noted above, used the letter "h," but Spanish Basque writers did not, and Arana did not include the letter in the Bizkaian orthography that had become widely used by the PNV.

For Spanish Basques, "h" was consequently a marker of the northern territory commonly known as Iparralde, and it was precisely because of this that the academy's decision to include it became such a symbolically loaded issue. The place of French Basques in the Basque nationalist project—a movement clearly based in the south—was an ongoing and complicated issue for nationalism since its beginnings. No one disputed that the north was a part of the greater Basque cultural continuum and territory of Euskara; many of the earliest and most accomplished writers in Basque came from that region. There are clear and recognized linguistic continuities and a long history of mutual aid and traffic of goods and people across the Pyrenees that unite north and south. But there were also notable differences. The Basques of Iparralde have had different political and economic histories. Living in France, they also had crucially different wartime experiences that gave rise to their more distant and ambivalent relationship to Basque nationalism (Jacob 1994; Ott 2008).

The issue of the north had become an especially contentious one for nationalists at this particular moment in history, when Basques were debating different scenarios for their political future. While radical nationalists have insisted in their political rhetoric and symbolism on a political vision that included Iparralde, the PNV has generally been willing to compromise for a more reduced territorial scope. Consequently, when the academy decided to include "h" in the new orthographic norms, this was taken by critics of Batua as yet more conclusive evidence that radical nationalists were controlling the standardization process. The academy responded to these criticisms by publishing a short book entitled *La "H" en la ortografía vasca* (Villasante 1980b) to calm the outrage and explain, in as accessible a fashion as possible, the linguistic reasoning for its decision. Author Villasante explained that the inclusion of "h" in the new Basque orthography was a logical extension of two of the general principles that guided all their standardization efforts: to treat all the dialects as related variants of a common "language"; and to preserve as many of the meaningful grammatical distinctions as the dialects in their totality present, even if those distinctions were no longer in current usage. From their research, the linguists of the academy judged the aspirated "h" to be an archaic form with phonemic value that has been lost over time in the southern dialects. Villasante's explanation for the inclusion of "h" emphasized its antiquity: "h," the linguists argued, was part of a common linguistic heritage from which the various dialects derived. "H," they argued, was authentically "Basque," not simply "northern."

As Joshua Fishman (1973) has argued, the deliberate creation of a standard language involves a delicate process of balancing the "authentic" with the "modern," the "rational" with the "national." The preceding discussion exemplifies the complexity of this balancing act. The case of Basque standardization illustrates how the logics of linguistic rationalization aimed at making the grammar rules more regular or preserving phonemic markers at times collide with other kinds of symbolic investments in linguistic form. Academicians tried to show that their choices were based on neutral, rational reasoning, but in the early years they had a hard time keeping the meaning of "h" within a purely linguistic framework of value and separate from the tensions of nationalist politics. The resistance they faced speaks to the ways that letters can operate as condensed signs of differing political ideologies, imagined geographies, and even ways of paying homage to past ideologues like Arana. It also underscores how socially fragile the idea of a translocal "Basque" linguistic community still was at that time. The academic engineers of Basque modernity refer to a discoverable substrate of common language as an observable fact, but for many Basque speakers the concept of a greater Basque language was tenuous due partly to the absence of a strong literary tradition and partly to the way they "lived" Basque. Speakers could recognize similarities across dialects, of course, but few had ever formally studied the language. Basque was experienced and lived out as a local language, in which variances were not something to look beyond, but were valued and meaningful markers of place and identity. The belief in a common Basque on which standardization depends is something that experts, together with the social movement, bring into being, not simply discover.

CHAPTER FOUR

Batua and *Euskalki*

REFIGURING AND REAPPROPRIATING
THE VERNACULAR

Crafted in the ferment of anti-Franco resistance, endorsed by radical nationalist writers as well as erudite linguists like Mitxelena who bore impeccable scholarly credentials, Batua managed to emerge from the controversies that originally surrounded it and elude being pigeonholed as the emblem of any particular political camp. It was adopted by Basque language schools and enthusiastically promoted by the grassroots adult language–education movement and early cultural magazines. As Bourdieu tells us, the rise and spread of official languages are processes closely linked to the rise of mass education and the economic and institutional structures of modern nation-states (1982: 42). In the case of Unified Basque, the institutional structures and statelike powers that the Basque Autonomous Community acquired after 1979, together with the growth of Basque medium education and the blossoming of Basque-language media, undeniably helped the spread and normalization of Batua, shaping the connotations it would have for speakers. When, in 1982, the newly created Basque government passed the Basque Normalization Law, which called for introducing Basque into public administration, public schooling, and media, Batua became the de facto official variety of written and formal spoken Basque in all of these arenas. The media have been especially important in establishing Unified Basque as the language of an emergent public sphere. Its adoption as the code of choice by the governmental-funded television and radio network EITB (Euskal Irrati Telebista) and later on by the first independent all–Basque–language newspaper, *Euskaldunon Egunkaria*, founded in 1990, further contributed to the production of a Basque public that was coming to recognize itself in and through a translocal variety of Euskara. The expanding institutional usage of Unified Basque diffused earlier accusations of linkages to radicalism and solidified the identification of Batua as legitimated national standard in a way more convincing than any pronouncement or debate ever could.

As Batua was becoming a spoken as well as a written variety, its use provoked a range of reactions. I want to turn now from analyzing the public discourse among linguists and political activists about standardization to discuss some of the ways that the introduction of Batua affected the communicative economy of native

Basque speakers of Usurbil, where I lived and did ethnographic research. I saw a notable difference between the way residents and local language advocates talked about and made use of vernacular and standard Basque in the nineties and the way they had responded to it in the early eighties when I had done my first fieldwork. A few incidents from life in Usurbil help to illustrate the shifting language dynamics in action and the more recent turn among language advocates to revalorize and find a place for vernacular Basque in the project of language revitalization.

When I began research in 1982 and 1983, conversations about Batua were a part of everyday life in Usurbil. The first generations of children to attend Basque medium schools were getting all or part of their education in Batua. Hundreds of adults had some exposure to it from attending the low-cost Basque language and literacy classes offered in town. Youth looking for jobs in teaching or civil service were avidly studying Batua to obtain diplomas certifying their knowledge of Basque in the hopes of gaining an edge in a slim job market. Batua was on the new Basque television channel and in magazines and newspapers.[1] It circulated in the world of native Basque speakers in this town as an emblem of a resistance movement and as a slew of new words and unfamiliar spellings in the newspapers or in the hard-to-read letters children brought home from their teachers. It also entered into the lives of local residents through the halting speech of the visiting anthropologist. Sitting in the kitchen of the Martín restaurant helping and talking with the women while they prepared the meals, washed dishes, attended to children, and dealt with the many suppliers who came in and out, I would occasionally ask a question about something someone had just said, a phrase or word I did not understand. The differences between the language I was learning and what I was hearing often turned our discussions into questions about what was better or more correct, the new Basque or the local dialect—what residents called *herriko hizkuntza* [local language] or *gure hizkera* [our speech]?

Language revival can be tricky business, and the studies we have of such efforts warn time and again that native speakers of minority and indigenous languages can become quite alienated by standardization and other reforms taken to modernize and preserve their language. The reasons are multiple. Language advocates may be outsiders who are perceived to be criticizing and trying to rearrange meaningful ways of speaking. Measures taken to save the language can disrupt habitual ways of using the language at the microlevel of interpersonal discourse patterns and at the macrolevel of societal distribution (Hornberger and King 1996). For example, minority languages typically operate as in-group "languages of solidarity." They may be restricted in use to particular social circles, private or sometimes highly specific ritualized domains. Steps taken to teach the language, to put it into broader public circulation, or to encourage formal usages can undermine some of the traditional social functions and values as well as pleasures associated with the language when it operates as a restricted "insider" code. Purism can also have alienating consequences. Language advocates may reject some forms of language mixing and borrowing as signs of "contamination" and try to introduce reforms that return the language to what they consider to be a purer and more authentic state. If native speakers as a result come to perceive their way of speaking to be a source of low prestige compared to a more "correct" variety of the language, they may reject the language movement and abandon speaking the language altogether.[2] One of my first Basque teachers, Imanol, a young native speaker, warned us of this quite explicitly in one of the many discussions our class had about Basque-language dynamics. Raised in a fishing family in the old port of Donostia, Imanol grew up in an environment where Basque was the language of everyday life. His mastery of and appreciation for colloquial Basque set him apart from many of the other teachers I had. One day in class, Imanol was talking about the generational gap between older and younger speakers of Basque. He was criticizing his fellow Basque speakers who, upon taking literacy classes and learning Batua forms, then went home and corrected the colloquial forms of their parents or grandparents. In his own community, he said he could see that this was giving older speakers an inferiority complex about the way they spoke Basque. Our elders have been told their language is wrong, and as a result, he said, grandparents sometimes stop speaking Basque with the youth. Imanol urged us to regard native speakers as our teachers, rather than uneducated or illiterate speakers. New speakers [*berriak*], he said to us, must get close to native speakers [*zaharrak*] in order to learn how to speak.

Imanol taught Batua, but he did not regard it as superior to colloquial Basque. It was, however, notably different, and that difference often confounded the interactions between native and new learners. Nancy Dorian, one of the most astute observers of minority-language dynamics, points out that part of what accounts for the differences observed between the standardized varieties that minority-language advocates create and everyday vernacular has to do with the different kinds of things that language revivalists and lay speakers value about a language (1994). She gives an example of this from the standardization of Irish that has relevance for the Basque case. The speech of native Irish speakers, she says, had over time found it possible "to dispense with some of the more complex features of the traditional grammar, but in each locality they preserved the distinctive speech of their own region with its own forms, phraseology, and idioms" (ibid.: 485). However, these features, notes Dorian, were not the ones that concerned the Irish-language advocates. What language reformers cared about was preserving grammatical complexity and creating uniformity. Thus, in the effort to facilitate interregional communication, Irish standardization created uniformity at the cost of stripping the language of precisely those specific and variable markers that gave speakers a sense of intimacy with their language. As has been documented for a number of other cases, this is a danger for any standardization effort; it can trigger responses that can ironically lead speakers to oppose revitalization and, at worst, inhibit them from speaking their native language.[3]

What can we learn about these dynamics from the way Batua was received in Usurbil? In the part of Gipuzkoa where I did most of my research, Batua did initially generate some disruption of the local speech economies. But on the whole, in Gipuzkoa Batua was accepted more easily than in other parts of the Basque-speaking territory. This might be partly a result of the fact that the Gipuzkoan dialect spoken in Usurbil was fairly similar to Batua norms. But I believe that standardization was tolerated as well as it was for ideological as well as grammatical reasons. This was an area characterized by widespread popular support and involvement in the school movement and adult-literacy classes, both of which were important agents in in disseminating a sense that standardization was necessary. In the classes I attended, Batua was presented as a way of creating social cohesion among Basque speakers, making it possible for everyone to understand one another. The endorsement of standardization by the grassroots education movement and its linkage to progressive politics worked to make Batua seem less like an imposition and more like a tool of resistance, still wooden and "clunky," perhaps, but widely seen as socially necessary.

This did a lot to grease the wheels of acceptance. Yet even in Usurbil, where the political and linguistic conditions were all favorable for standardization, the unsettling effects of Batua on a shifting linguistic economy were palpable. Many native speakers said they simply did not understand it. *Ezin entenditu!* [Cannot understand!] María shrugged her shoulders and declared when she encountered an article in the newspaper written in Batua. There were certainly many words and spellings that she and other native speakers did not recognize. However, in contrast to the situation for speakers of Bizkaian Basque, the differences between her Gipuzkoan dialect and Batua were not great. Noun declensions and verbal morphology between the two are very close. While there were some pragmatically salient differences in how some verbs were conjugated (the auxiliary verb *ukan* [to have], was an often-noted example) in this area of the Basque Country, problems of intelligibility seemed to have less to do with deep grammatical differences than with lexicon, pronunciation, and discourse style. Speakers of standardized Basque did not generally display the vowel harmonies and contractions that were distinctive to vernacular speech styles.[4] As linguist Estibalitz Amorrortu (2000) has noted, written or spoken Batua tends to exhibit a more formal, bookish discourse style, in which every verb is conjugated, every syllable pronounced. Similar to the case of Irish described by Dorian, the speechways of native Basque speakers dispensed with the grammatical explicitness distinctive of Batua in favor of a more elliptical, synthetic, and performative discourse style. The differences between standard and colloquial Baque were also sometimes described to me as a question of intonation and accent, or what locals called *doinua* [melody]. When I asked directly about differences, it was more common, however, for people to point to lexicon and verb-conjugation rules as the main source of difference with Batua. In the first couple of decades of Basque-language standardization, a torrent of new coinages and vocabulary were being developed as Basque was introduced into new domains of use.[5] The often odd-sounding neologisms that were appearing almost daily were commonly associated with Batua, while Spanish loanwords like *telefonoa* [Sp. *teléfono,* telephone], *leetu* [Sp. *leer,* to read], *entenditu* [Sp. *entender,* to understand] became markers of the speech of native dialect speakers. In the popular talk about standardization, vocabulary often operated as concrete markers of the differences between new standard and local speech forms that were otherwise hard to name.

Linguists may view such language variation as benign, but in popular language ideology, variation is typically loaded with social meaning. A basic premise of the ideology of standard in which we are all socialized today is "the belief that, if there are two or more variants of a form, only one is 'correct'" (Hill 2008: 35). The pervasiveness of this belief presents a conundrum for minority-language revival. As Susan Gal observes, one of the ironies standardization poses for minority-language revival is that "every creation of a standard orientation also creates stigmatized forms . . . among the very speakers whose linguistic practices standardization was supposed to valorize. Contrary to the common sense view, standardization creates not uniformity, but more (and hierarchical) heterogeneity" (2006: 171). These diversifying and hierarchizing effects were both noted and contested among Basques. Despite grumblings about how dry, unintelligible or artificial Batua sounded, despite the declarations on the part of the academicians that Batua was never intended to replace vernacular, native speakers did often talk about it as more correct than their own speech. Older people, like María, seemed less prone to this kind of negative view of their own speech than somewhat younger Basques who had grown up under Franco and were more insecure about their language skills. When conversations arose as to how to say something in Basque, María's daughter-in-law, for example, was more inclined than María to describe the Batua form she had learned in her literacy class as the "correct" or proper form: *hola esan **behar** da,* [that is how we **should** say it]. The fact that these forms were formally taught at school, endorsed by the Basque Language Academy, and presented as good for the nation has everything to do with the authoritative status they acquired for so many. Teachers addressed criticisms of Batua saying that it was easier for non-natives to learn and socially advantageous because it could be used "anywhere" and with "anyone." Their confident assertion of the all-purpose utility of Batua was diagnostic of the degree to which standard languages are taken to be ways of facilitating communication and fostering social integration (Gumperz and Cook-Gumperz 2005: 271; Joseph 1987). If you are a speaker of a "well normed, wide currency" language, writes Dorian (1994), you encounter language norms at school and often discount them as old fashioned. But speakers of "smaller," recently normed languages, she says, are often less confidant, and for good reason. Such speakers have rarely studied their language and have typically seen it disparaged. This was precisely what my teacher Imanol was saying when he talked about the "inferiority complex" of older native-Basque speakers. The indexical ties of Batua both to education and to nation building loaded it with prestigious and political connotations that muted most challenges.

In the Bar Martín kitchen, the strains this produced for native-Basque speakers came up often in the question—do we speak correctly? If he was in the restaurant, María or her daughter-in-law would call upon the poet Joxean Artze, one of their favored clients and neighbors, to give his opinion on a language question that might arise. When he came into one of our kitchen debates, he would inevitably regale us with stories about how a local farmer used a word, the etymology of a forgotten place-name, the meanings of an expression, or the various ways that something could be said in Basque. Artze was an artist of language, not a grammarian. He would pause, and with his sonorous voice he would slowly and meticulously voice out syllables of words like they were his own poems, unpacking their contents and letting the sounds of them resonate. He did not offer lessons in grammar rules. Rather he almost always encouraged his neighbors to appreciate the *goxotasuna* [sweetness] of their vernacular. Though he never claimed Batua to be bad, as a poet he saw variable speech ways as richness, rather than problems that needed regimenting.

Countervailing voices like that of Artze or of my Basque teacher, Imanol, have always been a part of the discussion of Batua. If one was listening, one heard a certain amount of "back talking" to the hierarchizing effects of standardization and the primacy it gives to referential meaning and transparency over more poetic dimensions of language (see Samuels 2004). Popular ideology nevertheless powerfully links standards to authority, an authority sustained by educational systems, government bureaucracies, mass media, and other powerful social institutions that inculcate a respect for its forms and provide material reward for those who master the norm (Bourdieu 1991). For most Usurbil residents, Spanish had been the language of authority, power, and upward mobility. It was the language of Basque upper classes and urbanites. However, language planning and political autonomy were changing this. Knowledge of Spanish continued to be indispensable, but at the same time, the creation and adoption of Batua introduced a new resource in the communicative economy. The following conversation in 1983 with a group of young women from Usurbil was a telling example of the kind of new linguistic capital Batua was starting to represent, as well as an example of the resentment some native speakers felt about the implied demotion of their local ways of speaking Basque.

One afternoon, a group of young women in their twenties, all childhood friends of the same *cuadrilla* were gossiping about boys and relationships. Isabel, a native speaker of Basque who worked at the time in janitorial services, started to tell her friends that a mutual friend of theirs, Maite, might be romantically interested in a teacher at the local *ikastola*. Being slightly younger than the rest of the group, Maite was on the fringes of this friendship circle. She was from a more solidly middle-class family that was strongly language loyalist. Unlike Isabel and the rest of the group, Maite had attended a Basque medium school and was consequently fluent not only in local Basque, but also in Batua. She had also recently secured a coveted civil-service job in the provincial administration for which knowledge of Batua had been a plus. In speculating on Maite's love interest, Isabel described what she took to be the usual kinds of crushlike behaviors; she commented on how Maite looked at the teacher, made a point of going to the same places as he, but also on Maite's language use. I recorded the following description she gave of Maite in my notes: "The other day she [Maite] was talking to me, normal, you know, in Gipuzkoan, the way we usually talk. And then *he* came along and she suddenly started talking to him in Batua. Right in front of me! 'Look at her!' I said, 'talking like a *berria!*' [*euskaldun berria*, new Basque]."

Isabel's tone was disparaging and had all the markings of class resentment. Like many of the Basque children of her generation, Isabel had attended the local Catholic school for girls and received a basic high-school education entirely in Spanish. She had also enrolled in a Basque-literacy class at the local night school but did not master Batua with anything like the fluency Maite acquired at her school. I asked Isabel why she thought Maite had switched to Batua, and she replied, "Oh, to impress him; she wants to act superior, more sophisticated, and educated than the rest of us." Unstated but known to all the participants was that Maite's supposed love interest was an *ikastola* teacher who had learned Basque as a second language and was actively involved in the radical nationalist party, Herri Batasuna. His speech, while fluent, was recognizably Batua. Most people in town, out of habit or because they were unable to do otherwise, spoke to the teacher in the Gipuzkoan dialect. It was rare for native speakers to speak Batua with one another, especially in informal contexts. Maite's switch to Batua was consequently unusual, and her friend interpreted it as meaningful. I had often heard Usurbil residents claim that Basque women spoke Spanish in public to appear more sophisticated.[6] In this case, the use of Batua was being perceived in a similar way, that is, as a way of "putting on airs." The incident revealed that for native speakers, standard Basque was an unevenly distributed form of cultural capital and an emergent or potential mark of "distinction," convertible, as Bourdieu (1984) would say, into other forms of sexual, economic, or political capital.

Controversies erupted in town life over the proper place of Batua. Standardization was promoted particularly emphatically by the new generation of radicalized nationalists as a necessary vehicle for achieving the normalization of Basque and building a unified and modern nation. Using Batua in official public communications was regarded by younger and more radicalized generations as a social duty. This was illustrated in a language skirmish that took place in Usurbil around the same time as the gossip session described above. The principal players in this episode were, on the one hand, a recently formed youth group calling itself the Gazteen Asanblada [Youth Assembly] and, on the other, Usurbil's town council, controlled at the time by the PNV. Radicalized youth assemblies were appearing in many towns of Gipuzkoa in the eighties. Usurbil's Gazteen Asanblada was not a language-revival group—their concerns were more with organizing events for youth in town—but for them, like many groups in the world of alternative politics, support for Basque normalization was an integral part of their political identity as progressives and anti-establishment.

The provocation for the dispute was a series of public notices the town council had issued in the spring of 1983 after the town had suffered severe floods. The notices described, in Gipuzkoan dialect, the flood damage and actions they were taking. Gazteen Asanblada put up a poster in the plaza denouncing the notices. Their poster consisted of a copy of the council's original announcement with a comment written in Batua that I translate as: "How are those of us who are learning EUSKARA going to read this? In Usurbil, those who know Castilian have an easier time than those who are learning EUSKARA. Where is your *euskalzaletasuna* [Basque language loyalty]" (capitalization in original).

The spelling of the word "Euskara," following Batua orthography, made it clear that their criticism was about the failure of the council to use standard Basque. At a meeting at the town hall held shortly thereafter, it was proposed that the council adopt a policy of using Batua in all its official documents. A PNV member of the council replied in a bilingual announcement distributed and posted in the town:

History has shown that the unification of a language is not achieved by imposition or by decree, but by an evolution carried on over the centuries. Secondly, at least as far as we know, there are no stipulations that regulate or obligate any institution to use one form or another of EUSKERA. We believe, without taking an extreme opposing view that whoever writes the documents should be able to have complete freedom to write in BATUA or in LOCAL EUSKERA. We furthermore think that written documents are intended for the people to read and that if we want them to be read, they must be intelligible. It is public knowledge and commonly noted that BATUA is very artificial. For this reason, we do not accept this proposal and vote no. (capitalization in original)

The announcement included an additional interesting note of clarification: "The council members of the PNV also want it to be noted in the minutes that the reason for the deficiencies that may have existed in the recent translations regarding the floods were due to the fact that the translator was not available. Therefore the translations had to be done with the Basque that we knew."

This exchange between an oppositional youth group and PNV town-council members was an exceptional occasion for witnessing a public debate over the indexical codings that Batua and dialect had for local Basque speakers at this time. The youth chastised the older town-council members for using local dialect in official notices. Some of the youth were members of the language activist group, Euskalerrian Euskaraz [Basque in the Basqueland], which at the time strongly encouraged the use of Batua as a duty and sign of *euskalzaletasuna,* a word connoting both authentic language loyalism and patriotism. As the youth group's poster implies, they thought that Batua should be the variety used in public communications so as to help popularize it and assist in the project of linguistic/national unification.[7] Interesting and more ambivalent is the response of the adult PNV council members. They refused to accept the equation of language loyalism and patriotism with Batua. They apologized for the possible deficiencies in their Basque, publicly underscoring the sense of inadequacy that so many native speakers of Basque were feeling at this time about their language skills. At the same time, their response points not just to insecurity but also to the positive values associated with local speech: intelligibility and closeness to the people.

These and other incidents from everyday life in Usurbil in the early eighties—the kitchen discussions at the Martín restaurant, the youth group's challenge to the town hall's poster, and the young women's afternoon gossip—point to some of the connotations and dynamics Batua generated for these native Gipuzkoan speakers in the first decade of standardization. We see insecurity, but also expressions of value for local vernacular. Anthropologist Sharon Roseman documents similarly ambivalent feelings about vernacular in her study of language attitudes among rural Galician-speaking villagers. She found that vernacular Galician speakers, like many native Basque speakers, often described themselves as speaking poorly, calling their variety of Galician a corrupted *castrapo* (mixture) (1995: 14). However, she wisely cautions researchers against taking self-deprecating statements at face value. Longer-term fieldwork revealed to her that while dialect speakers would publicly "bow down" to the higher status of Castilian or even standard Galician, they also expressed strong loyalty and preference for their own speechways. Rather than an unambiguous sign of linguistic insecurity, she suggests that such devaluating statements about their language may be an example of the "quietly ironic" gestures of deference that peasants habitually would perform for outsiders.

Without downplaying the hierarchizing effects and dominance of standard-language ideology, we have reason to be cautious about assuming that vernacular is uniformly perceived as inferior. Linguistic anthropology based on more in-depth ethnographic observation shows language attitudes toward vernacular and standard can be multifaceted, dependant on the interactional context, and vary according to generation (see Strand, forthcoming). Attitudes are also dynamic. When I returned ten years later in the mid-nineties to do new research on local Basque media, I found an almost completely different scenario with respect to Batua. Knowledge and usage of Batua was greatly expanded. Identified with Basque schooling, mainstream media, and governmental institutions, standardization had ceased to be a point of contention between radical and conservative nationalists.

Normalizing Batua

The 1983 debacle in Usurbil over how the flood notices were written soon became a distant memory. The same year as the poster dispute, the local town council initiated a plan to increase the use of Basque in municipal government. The first step they took was to hire Arantxa, the translator that the council member referred to in the debate about the flood notices. A native of Usurbil, she was one of the very first of a new corps of civil-service *técnicos,* as they were called, municipal language professionals who began to be hired to design and carry out language normalization. If teachers were the foot soldiers of the first wave of language revival, *técnicos* like Arantxa were the professionals of the second wave. In an interview we had in 1994, Arantxa reflected on her first decade of work. When it all began, she explained, no one really knew what to do or what "bilingualism" meant in practice. In her first years on the job, bilingualism meant translating. Arantxa spent most of her day copying all official documents, minutes, and notices that had typically been in Spanish into Basque. She took it for granted that this should be done in Batua, as this was the literary standard approved by the Basque Language Academy (and the language in which she had taken her certification exams). As part of her job, she also offered simultaneous translation from Basque to Spanish at town-hall meetings for one or two elected council members who did not understand Basque. Her role, as she saw it, was to make it possible for Basque speakers to use their language in mixed settings like the town-hall meeting and to thus be relieved of what sociolinguists call the "accommodation norm" (Woolard 1989), according to which native-Basque speakers would switch to speak Spanish in the presence of nonspeakers. But even with translation, Arantxa pointed out that not all Basque speakers took advantage of the opportunity to speak in Basque publicly. Some, she said, were uncomfortable with the process of being translated in front of their peers and either translated themselves or spoke Spanish.

As the language technician, Arantxa experienced firsthand the artificiality and hierarchizing effects of standard Basque, and she confessed she thought much of her translating work was in vain. She explained, "To begin with, the [Castilian] language of official documents is already baroque. Translating this bureaucratic Spanish into Basque . . . it came out very artificial. No one could really make any sense out of it, even those of us who studied Basque." She was also very critical of the way that she, as translator, was the only person responsible and accountable for using Basque and knowing it well. "Everything was delegated to the translator and everyone else could continue to do as they please!"

Above her desk Arantxa had hung a sign with a phrase by Joxean Artze that had become popularized by the language movement. It read: "Basque is not lost because those who do not know it do not study it, but because those who know it, do not speak it." Arantxa referred to this statement often as a philosophy that guided her life. No nationalist revolutionary herself, she nevertheless embraced a pragmatic view of Basque identity as something expressed through language use. She was worried that standardization was making some native speakers anxious about speaking in Basque and, ironically enough, choosing to speak in Spanish with local officials like herself. The local farmer was embarrassed to speak to her in what she called their "home" Basque, "*beren etxeko hizkera.*" It was not uncommon, she told me, for a native *euskaldun* to come in with a notice they had received written in standard Basque and to ask her what it meant. For Arantxa, Batua and dialect [*euskalki*] should be seen as complementary. "It's good to use Batua for writing," she said. "But here in Usurbil, we should speak our own way, especially with one another . . . that is part of our identity . . . we should use and transmit that *goxotasuna* [sweetness] among neighbors."

These experiences led Usurbil and other town halls located in predominantly Basque-speaking areas to gradually abandon the obligatory translation of perfunctory bilingualism in favor of normalizing the use of Basque, translating into Spanish when needed or requested. In so doing, the municipal *técnicos* have led the way in developing a more accessible standard, because, as Arantxa put it, it was precisely there, at the municipal level, that the need for an accessible formal Basque was most acute. The UEMA [Udalerri Euskaldunen Mankomunitatea], an association of self-identified Basque-speaking town halls, formed to help out with this project. With help from UEMA, the town hall hired a local writer to develop a more user-friendly Basque.[8] In talking about this work, one municipal language planner in UEMA explained, "We had no choice." If town officials were going to really function in Basque, rather than just translate all the time, then they had to write in a way that everyday readers could understand. Otherwise the Basque would be purely symbolic and everyone would read the Spanish. "Today is the day," he said, "that we have forms in Basque that are better than those in Castilian. I don't say this out of arrogance, but because we have really taken a lot of care to develop a good, clean Basque [*euskara txukuna*]."

Arantxa was certain that these efforts had helped to improve attitudes towards Batua as a variety and standardization in general among the elected official and workers at the town hall. This was yet another demonstration of the benefits of popular involvement in language revitalization. If Basque standardization has proceeded as well as it has in Usurbil, this no doubt has something to do with the participation, advocacy, and ingenuity of local actors—elected council members, the mayor, and staff—who, in their determination to make Basque an everyday language of their workplace, have creatively intervened to find solutions to the dilemmas of revitalization. In short, local actors can play a critical role in mediating the hierarchizing effects of standardization. In normalizing Basque usage in new domains, they have also proven to be leaders in initiatives to make a more accessible Batua. If Batua norms once came from above, what the nineties showed is that Batua would continue to be retooled from below.

Returning to Usurbil again in 1998 provided me with other signs that practices and attitudes toward the use of Batua and vernacular Basque in were shifting in the world of language advocacy. A language-awareness campaign carried out that year and the formation of a new community magazine were an especially telling contrast with the debate over the flood notices of 1983.

Eztu Prezioyik! [It's Priceless!]

Language-awareness campaigns were a routine part of cultural life in this part of the Basque Country. Carried out by various entities, from nongovernmental language advocacy groups, to the regional government, and town halls in the form of posters, buttons, and signage of all kinds, these campaigns called attention to language ideology and challenged the habitual practice of reserving Basque for private use. In contrast to the nationalist revolutionary slogan, "Basque in the

Basqueland," language campaigns most often took the form of simple reminders—for example, to speak Basque, to answer the telephone in Basque, or, as one sign in a restaurant in Donostia's tourist zone put it, "we speak Basque, of course."

Usurbil's town hall repeatedly designed language campaigns of various types to encourage residents to speak in Basque. In 1998 the town was designing a new campaign to encourage local shops and businesses to use Basque in their internal paperwork and in their dealings with the public. To develop the campaign, the town hall hired a twenty-six-year-old university student, Olatz, a resident of Usurbil who had some experience in sociolinguistics. Olatz had no trouble developing a plan of implementation and steps by which store owners could make a gradual transition to Basque. But I knew from our frequent talk about the project that she was having a hard time deciding how to carry out the publicity part of the campaign, that is, how to advertise it to residents.

She wanted to have a slogan that would really grab people's attention. After fifteen years of language-normalization campaigns, she said, people had become jaded. The streets were plastered with posters, signs, and stickers urging them to speak Basque; "they've heard it a million times," she said. Olatz was not an advertising professional, but she sensed that she needed to be clever in order to stand out among the glut of graffiti and billboards. She needed a publicity campaign that made residents feel they were being personally addressed. Only then did she think she would stand a chance of getting residents to be identified and involved in the language-normalization campaign.

Olatz's solution was to use vernacular Basque in the local advertising campaign. She chose for the slogan, "It's Priceless," and intentionally spelled it as it sounded in local vernacular, "*Eztu Prezioyik!*" rather than its Batua spelling, *ez du preziorik*. For the campaign poster, she chose a photograph of a recognizably central street in town, and she designed a sequential series of posters that each started with the question, "How much is it?" *Zenbat da?* Over the course of a few weeks, the campaign released one poster a week, each with the same photograph but with different responses, first one hundred pesetas, then one thousand, then one million. Finally, in the last poster closing the campaign, the slogan appeared with the answer: *Zenbat da? Eztu prezioyik!* [How much is it? Priceless!].

> *Zenbat da, 100 pta?* [How much [is it], 100 pesetas?]
> *Zenbat da, 1000 pta?* [How much, 1000 pesetas?]
> *Zenbat da, milloi bat?* [How much, a million?]
> *Zenbat da? Eztu preziyoik!* [How much is it? It's priceless!]

Olatz liked the playful and surprise ending. Since this was a campaign directed to local residents, business owners, and shopkeepers, the theme, *zenbat da?* [how much?], was intended to evoke the language of commerce. I was struck by the similarity between the rhetorical structure of this "It's priceless" campaign she designed and U.S. television ads for American Express credit cards. When I asked if the U.S. ads had served as a model, Olatz said she was unaware of the campaign, nor did she feel they were actually very similar. As important as the referential message was the linguistic form. This, to her, made her campaign quite different from the American Express ad. *Eztu prezioyik,* the campaign's final message, was not just saying that Euskara was priceless—it did so, as she said, "exactly how we would say it here, in Usurbil."

But this was exactly what initially made the town council and sociolinguist to whom she presented the campaign skeptical. It was customary to conduct all public campaigns in Batua. Olatz had to persuade them that the vernacular form was crucial. Precisely because it was highly unusual to see dialect in billboards, the posters for the campaign would be eye grabbing, she told them. She also argued that residents needed to see this campaign as their own, not something coming from elsewhere—for example, a government office. To achieve this, she argued, the campaign slogan needed to be simple and something with which residents could identify. The language had to be what she described as "closer" [*gertuago*] than Batua. *Herriko hizkera,* local speech, elicited a different kind of affective relationship to Basque that she felt could penetrate the numbing effect of two decades of political campaigns.

In contrast to other arguments in favor of dialect, Olatz's proposal to use vernacular in the public sphere was not coming from a position of linguistic conservatism or antistandardization. Olatz was fluent in Batua, a strong supporter of language revival and leftist nationalism. Yet her strategy of advocacy was virtually the opposite of what her peers in the Youth Assembly had done fifteen years earlier: designing a public language campaign in vernacular. "*Eztu Prezioyik!*" was a sign of a new political moment and a set of shifting attitudes toward vernacular Basque among language loyalists. To people of her generation it was not as urgent and necessary to flag the nation, as it were, in every public use of Basque through Batua. She took Batua and Basque nationality for granted and wanted to do more with language. For this campaign, she approached her work more like an advertiser seeking to carve out a particular market niche by mobilizing the indexical qualities of dialect as a marker of local identity. In contrast to earlier language advocates, she felt able to shed the pedagogical burden that had been placed on them, to set aside the never-ending burden to model standard spelling and standard conjugations. For people of her generation, vernacular Basque was no longer a source of insecurity, but rather a communicative resource they would increasingly refashion for use in a variety of new contexts.

Noaua!

Usurbil's brand-new community magazine, *Noaua!* illustrates in spades this emergent new attitude toward vernacular. The magazine was created in 1997 by a group of residents concerned with promoting Basque-language use in their community. Local language-revival groups like this were springing up throughout Gipuzkoa and Bizkaia in the nineties, and one of their main activities involved local media in Basque. The goal was to promote literacy skills and community identity in Basque. Advocates of this and other magazines believed that people were more likely to want to read and write in Basque if the subjects were short and about local life— sports, people, and any number of other bits of news that touched them directly. In these local *euskaldun* media, one found a new space for imaginative uses of vernacular and informal registers of Basque. In the case of Usurbil's magazine, the use of vernacular began with the title: *Noaua!* The word is a very informal colloquial greeting that peers call out to one another on the street, meaning literally, "where are you going?" The spelling of the word indicates that this greeting is in an informal register, *hitanoa,* typically only mastered by native speakers in this region of Basque Country.[9] Written in nonstandard Basque in a register not used in mainstream media, *Noaua!* indexed a decidedly local rather than a national *euskaldun* public sphere.

The first issue of the magazine included three popular "legends" about the origins of the term *noaua* as a greeting. These stories give us insight into some of the pragmatic value of the term and thus what it connoted as a title for the magazine. According to the first origin story, a man, Ramon Urkiak, nicknamed "Ezkerra," was sitting on a particular bench in the neighborhood of Zubieta when he called out "*Noaua!*" to the priest, Don Francisco, who was passing by. Nonplussed, the priest told him never to address him that way again. Ever since that day, so the legend goes, Ezkerra and anyone else who has sat on that bench greet passersby with *noaua!* The second story tells of Marquis Perriko, a native of Usurbil and friend of the Spanish King Juan Carlos, at the time prince of Spain. It is said that when Perriko was attending the prince's wedding in Greece, he called out "*Noaua!*" as a procession of soldiers walked by. Upon hearing the phrase, one of the soldiers recognized it as from his town. He shouted back, and the two were able to find each other in the huge crowd and had a long talk. The third legend is the story of a man named Julian Borda and his friends, who frequently sat on a bench next to the main church of Usurbil. While there, they would often greet the *guardia civil,* the Spanish rural police, as they walked by calling out "*Noaua!*" After hearing this many times, one of them stopped, walked up to them, and said: "*No os quiero oír más decir 'no agua'!*" [I don't want to hear you say "no water" anymore!]. The joke comes from the Spanish policeman's confusing the similar sounding Basque word "*noaua*" with the Spanish phrase "*no agua*" [no water].

We cannot know, of course if any of these stories are true. They are meant to be entertaining. Submitted by residents, each one sheds some light on the pragmatic value of this word and, by extension, vernacular Basque. The first story establishes *noaua* as a sign of common or indecorous language. It is not the language with which one addresses someone of high social standing, as revealed by the irritation of the priest when he is greeted this way. The priests in Usurbil and throughout most of this strongly Catholic Basque region would normally be addressed with respect if not reverence. The second origin story underscores the vernacular's connotations of social solidarity and shared hometown identity. Called out into the crowd, the greeting *noaua!* operates as a badge of common identity and a vehicle for social connection. The third story adds another interesting layer of meaning. It functions as an inside joke, in which townspeople, normally fearful of the *guardia civil,* are able to enjoy a moment of mockery at the guard's expense. The scene is a comic reversal of the long-standing stereotypical representation of the rural Basque as uncultured country bumpkin who speaks Spanish poorly. In this inversion, mastery of the vernacular provides a source of pleasure and power that at least momentarily contradicts dominant ideology.

These stories signal the variety of connotations that vernacular Basque could have for speakers at this particular historical moment: solidarity, intimacy, the antihierarchical, the populist. Some ten years after the flood notices, we see residents of Usurbil working on behalf of Basque-language revival were now strategically deploying vernacular with the aim of giving their magazine a local appeal and identity. They do not reject Batua—in fact, most articles in the local magazine are written using its norms. But dialectal forms and colloquial phrases are playfully and creatively used in subtitles for various sections of the magazine. This was very deliberate. At meetings I attended, I observed one of the board members, a language activist who had actually been part of the original Gazteen Asamblada protests a decade earlier, urge his peers to develop a more vernacular style that drew on popular culture and the historical knowledge that older residents had about community life. If they wanted the magazine to be read by residents, he said, they needed to make it appealing and to distinguish themselves as something other than the town-hall bulletin. He saw vernacular as a way to do this. He helped suggest some of the titles for various sections. For example, the section for short announcements is titled *Gazi-gozo-geza* [salty, sweet, bland], an expression meaning "a little bit of everything." Another colloquial phrase, *ika-mika,* meaning "controversy," is the title of the op-ed section, where a member of the community expresses his or her opinion on a debate. Informal colloquial phrases were chosen over more standard news categories. *Berriketan* [chatting] rather than the more formal *elkarrizketa* [interview] is used as the title for a section that interviews a member of the community. Similarly, while Basque-language news media invariably use the word *kirolak,* sports, for the sports section, *Noaua!* uses *izerdi patsetan,* a phrase meaning "soaked in sweat." Other creative uses of colloquialisms are: *porrusalda* ["leek soup," signifying mishmash or jumble] for an ad hoc collection of short news items, or *pil pilean* [simmering] for late-breaking news. The refunctionalizing of bits of vernacular links the magazine—a new medium for many Basque speakers—to the world of popular speech forms. To understand some of these expressions requires knowledge of Usurbil's landscape and routines of social life. *Marquesaren petriletik* [from the bench of the Marquesa's [house], for example, refers to a spot on the main street of town where older men and young people sometimes sit to watch people go by. It has been appropriated as the title for a section commenting on town happenings.

Eztu Prezioyik and *Noaua!* are in many ways products of the accomplishments of the language movement as well as some of new terrains that have opened up for Basque usage. Among language advocates, the political discussions no longer concern whether to have a standard or not. The question is no longer "Batua, yes or no?" as the magazines of the seventies asked. Nor is it "Batua or dialect?" Rather, it is now a question of deciding the best ways to make use of the varieties of Basque and what spaces they should occupy.[10] In a study of language attitudes among university students from the late 1990, linguist Estibaliz Amorrortu found that dialect loyalty remains high, particularly in Bizkaia, where the vernacular is more distant from standard Basque (2000).[11] Her study showed that Batua was respected by Bizkaian speakers, but it was not trumping vernacular in terms of prestige, and it took second place to vernacular when it came to social attractiveness. Amorrortu's empirical tests, my own observations, and those of Begoña Echeverria (2000) from similar time periods all show young people describing vernacular as the most authentic or true Basque: *jatorra* [authentic], *petoa* [genuine], *benetako euskara* [true Basque]. The specific meanings that using vernacular has will vary and depend on the interactional context of its use. So while it is difficult to generalize, we can see from this research that vernacular was acquiring new meanings and performing new kinds of communicative functions as a result of the emergence of a new standard. Speakers may have experienced their speech as stigmatized in relation to the new "power code," but this stigmatization itself became protested, appropriated, and transformed. As Dell Hymes once famously noted, language is a symbolic resource people use "in the continuing project of the reconstruction of the social order" (Hymes 1974 in Hill and Coombs 1982: 232). As the Basque linguistic and social order was being reconstructed by revitalization and political autonomy, usages of vernacular show us that a new communicative economy was emerging. For new generations of Basque youth, vernacular became a way for them to signal a kind of identification with "realness," authenticity, and populism in relation to a progressively institutionalized Basque political culture.

With the debate over whether to standardize settled, we see new usages and a new set of discussions about vernacular and standardization among language advocates. By the second half of the nineties, a move to reclaim vernacular as legitimate Basque and to promote its oral and written use was manifest among language loyalists, particularly in Bizkaia. There, as in Usurbil, one finds a greater incorporation of Bizkaian dialectal features into public media.[12] Popular culture, local media, and comedies are the most notable arenas in which vernacular is making its comeback. Basque television, once Batua's exclusive domain, has introduced much more vernacular into shows, especially humorous ones. One of the earliest indications was a game show, *Balinda,* that aired in the nineties in which contestants competed to correctly guess the location of a person based on his or her speech. Basque dialectal diversity was celebrated in the show, and knowledge about it was rewarded. The nineties also saw the creation of the smash-hit soap opera *Goen Kale,* in which actors occasionally used vernacular and informal registers, followed by the equally popular comedy show *Wazemank.* The latter show, organized as a series of sketches parodying well-worn icons of Basque cultural life, included in its repertoire a hilarious recurring spoof of a Basque language academician, dressed in priestly cassocks, who miraculously turns up on his motor scooter, dictionary in hand, to enforce Batua when the characters in a scene have committed a language blunder.

The ability to make fun of themselves and the excesses of language regulation, correctness, and norms that characterized the early part of the language-revival movement is a sign, to be sure, of change. There is less anxiety about continually proving that Basque is valuable and fully modern. However, if the necessity of Batua was at some level seen as incontrovertible, this analysis has shown that the process of standardization has been characterized by dissent, caution, and critique from the start. Basque writer Koldo Zuazo's book *Euskararen sendabelarrak* [Basque's Healing Herbs] provides, for example, one of the most trenchant critiques of the prescriptivism that attended standardization. Unlike past critics who attacked the political pedigree of the creators of Batua, Zuazo's criticism focuses on the social stratification and insecurity that standardization generates and which led, he argues, to such strange situations as parents believing that they had nothing to teach their Batua-proficient children about Basque, because they saw their own ways of speaking to be inferior. Zuazo chastises himself and fellow language advocates for having become so dependent on the rulings of the Basque Language Academy, waiting with baited breath, as it were, for the latest norms to tell them what was right and wrong. The average Basque speaker, says Zuazo, had ceased to trust his or her own judgment about language. The result has been impoverishment of the linguistic repertoire. "The creative capacity of the Basque speaker, the capacity to play with and enjoy the language, is being lost. And when that is lost, the language itself is on the way to being lost" (2000: 132).[13]

Zuazo's work is exemplary of the continuing effort of language scholars and activists to revise and rethink their priorities and strategies. The push for standardization was a reflection of the priority given to possessing a uniform print culture and making Basque suitable for use in high-prestige domains of social life. This was a legitimate purpose, writes Zuazo, but the language movement went astray when people misconstrued dialect, as most people do, to be incorrect or inferior to the standard. This is hardly a problem unique to the Basques (see Gal 2006; Sliverstein 1996). But Zuazo goes further, saying it was equally wrong to regard standard Basque as the absence of dialect and to position Batua and dialect as "formal" and "informal" registers. Vernacular is better understood, he argues, as a local variety, not a register, and in that sense appropriate to any context or activity where speakers share this code. Therefore, he reasons, standard Basque should be refigured as a variety for translocal communication that should flexibly incorporate dialectal forms into public ways of using Basque.

This ongoing reconceptualization of the dialect/standard relationship in the Basque movement has interesting parallels with conversations taking place among postcolonial writers who wrestle with the consequences of speaking nonstandard varieties of European languages. Sri Lankan activist author Arjuna Parakrama (1995) offers, for example, a penetrating exposé of what Silverstein called the "aggressively hegemonic" nature of standards to become measures of all other speechways (1996: 286). Standard-language ideology, Parakrama argues, is a mechanism of colonial and postcolonial domination that requires constant vigilance. Criticism, he says, is not enough; the way forward is to work on reshaping normative standards of English to include elements of nonstandard varieties. Taking the case of standard English, he writes, "This standard needs to be broadened, continually revised and even then, it is not to be trusted" (1995: 16). Parakrama demonstrates this in his own writing by deploying Sri Lankan forms of English and calls upon others to do the same.

The message we may take away from this is that a closer look at the discussions and cultural productions of Basque, and no doubt other language advocates, shows us a more complex set of positions, greater degree of play with standardization, and awareness of ironies than we might otherwise assume. Located on the periphery of dominant European languages, writers, artists, and even the *técnicos* of language normalization reproduce standard-language ideology at the same time that they offer up perceptive critiques and creative alternatives to standardization as it is dominantly practiced.

CHAPTER FIVE

The Will to Count

MAPPING AND MEASURING BASQUE

I did not go to the Basque Country thinking my questions about the cultural politics of language would lead me to statistics, but they did—and right away. Newly arrived to Usurbil and not knowing exactly where to begin, I went to the town hall to introduce myself. I got no further than the administrative secretary, who listened to my explanation of my project, then paused and told me she had something for me. She disappeared and returned with a three-volume sociological study of the town commissioned in the late sixties. The study, carried out in preparation for a new Municipal Urban Plan, was packed with tables and charts that quantified everything about the town: land use, numbers of telephones, educational profiles, rates of immigration, unemployment, births, and yes, language. "Everything you'll want to know is there," she said as she unloaded them into my arms. "Read it." And I did.

We learn as anthropologists that the art of ethnography relies on never taking for granted that which our subjects find utterly obvious (Rosaldo 1989). This is not always easy to do with something that the anthropologist herself also finds unremarkably familiar, which was the case with the report I was handed. I knew the report would be useful, of course, but ultimately I saw survey data as "background" to the cultural debates and dynamics I had come to study. Months would pass before I began to take notice of statistics as a very central part of the discursive practices of language revival, a mode of representing social life, and an increasingly important way the language movement had of talking about the health and future of Euskara. Numbers, I came to discover, were not outside the realm of symbolic struggle and debates that interested me; they were and still continue to be a key part of it.

Quantification, like standardization, has been perceived as an indispensable tool for saving the Basque language, and an enormous amount of energy and resources have been devoted to this enterprise. The normalization efforts of the last quarter century have produced, to borrow philosopher Ian Hacking's phrase (1982), an "avalanche of numbers." From the census and surveys of the early eighties to ever more rigorous quantifications of the "linguistic landscape" have come pages and pages of statistical surveys, pie charts, bar graphs, and percentages, telling us among other things who reads Basque, who can write it, who learned it at school, who learned it at home, how much it is spoken, and their demographic characteristics.

The logic, programs, and imaginary of contemporary Basque-language revival have become deeply intertwined with statistical thinking and practices. I would like to look at the arguments made *for* language statistics and also *with* them. Examples from my observations of language activism in Usurbil figure occasionally to provide some concrete examples of these discourses in action. My ethnography also revealed some notable differences between statistical and "folk" or popular ways of talking about language. My larger questions are: Why has measurement been considered so vital? What did advocates think quantification had to offer the project of language revival? And how has the practice of counting changed over the last twenty-five years? My aim is not to comment on the accuracy of language statistics, but on their truth effects. It is to explore numbers as a form of rhetoric—arguments intended to persuade—and also as a political technology of "government"—an instrument by which language is made into an object of planning and expert knowledge. In this analysis I hope to continue the exploration of how it is that the technologies of knowledge through which the struggle against language inequalities is carried out do not just resist domination but, more importantly, actually transform how language and the language speaker are understood. Before delving into the specifics of Basque-language maps and graphs, I will first lay out a framework for conceptualizing the power that numbers can have in language-resistance efforts.

Language, Power, and the Statistical Imagination

We live in an "age of statistics." That is to say, today we do not just count things. Statistics and their kin—averages and probabilities—permeate our ways of talking about ourselves in the modern world. They are a privileged way of knowing and representing the social body, diagnosing its ills, and managing its welfare. Theorizing the stakes that statistical practices have for language struggles, or any social movement for that matter, requires us to recognize the multiple functions that numbers can have. Official statistics and census counts have concrete material consequence in contemporary democracies, determining political representation, entitlement to funding, education, and the provision of numerous and vital social resources (Kertzer and Arel 2002; Alonso and Starr 1987). In various parts of the Basque Country, for example, assessments of percentages of speakers are used to allocate bilingual services; numbers can determine whether you are likely to be able to speak in Basque with your town-hall clerk or to have a Basque-speaking nurse at the municipal health clinic. In that sense, what gets counted, and how, are questions of direct consequence for the experience of everyday life. Numbers, as Nikolas Rose (1999) has argued, lend a sense of rationality to these allocations that meshes well with democratic political values. The idea that numbers are impartial makes the distribution of services seem to be less arbitrary, more legitimate, fair, and democratic (Rose 1999: 208). The politics of numbers and the controversies that surround them, however, go beyond issues of equity and apportionment. Statistics are also technologies for producing truths about the social world. And not just any truth, but truths typically accorded authoritative, scientific validity. Consequently, at stake in minority concerns with statistics are not only competing claims to resources, but also competing claims to truth.

Foucault's analytics of modern forms of power/knowledge are useful for further unpacking and reframing the politics of statistical truth production. At a very basic level, his analytics start with a rejection of what we might call statistical realism—the idea that the object of enumeration exists independent of its measurement—in favor of a social constructionist approach. However, his argument goes beyond a simple kind of social constructionism; it goes beyond arguing that discourse shapes reality rather than just reflecting it.[1] For Foucault, statistical sciences have a very specific role in the configuration of the form of power that he called governmentality. Governance, wrote Foucault, is effected through a "whole complex of *savoirs*," modes of documentation and registration that turn social phenomena into objects of knowledge and administration (1991: 102–103). As Nikolas Rose and Peter Miller explain, "Governing a sphere requires that it can be represented, depicted in such a way which both grasps its truth and re-presents it in a form in which it can enter the sphere of conscious political calculation" (Rose and Miller 1992: 182).[2] Statistics constitute what Rose and Miller call a technology of governance. As they argue, governmentality may be analyzed in terms of political rationalities, that is the discursive fields within which the exercise of power is conceptualized, its objects defined, and moral justifications for governing made. But it must also be analyzed in terms of what they call "governmental technologies, the complex of mundane programs, calculations, techniques, apparatuses, documents, and procedures through which authorities seek to embody and give effect to governmental ambitions" (ibid.: 175).

Historically, the push for an ever more detailed numerical inventory of the population in the course of the nineteenth century was linked to ambitions of social reform and social hygiene, to the development of policies to improve sanitation, detect criminals, curtail vice, prevent accidents, and, in general, produce a more harmonious society (Hacking 1981, 1982; see also Linke 1990; Horn 1994). Statistics, from a Foucauldian perspective, are not just modes of legitimating the aim of government; they are a means through which governmentality works by bringing into being domains of social life—"the economy," "crime," "language," "health"—as objects or problems "subject to determinant rules, norms and processes that can be acted upon and improved by authorities" (Rose and Miller 1992: 183). They are emblematic of the Enlightenment project's axiomatic faith that the world could be "controlled and rationally ordered if we could only picture and represent it rightly" (Harvey in Rose 1999: 221).

As several authors have noted, statistics are a mechanism in the technocratization of social conflicts—that is, they are an instrument in the trend toward handing decision-making power over to expert analysts and policy makers, whose formulas and procedures are trusted to better understand and resolve our problems than legislation (Dreyfus and Rabinow 1982: 196; Shore and Wright 1997; Rose 1999). This aspect of governance bears close resemblance, of course, to Max Weber's well-known analysis of the effects of bureaucratization and rationalization (Gerth and Mills 1958). Weber decried rationalization and all that it entails as leading to the disenchantment of the life worlds. For Foucault, however, there is more than disenchantment at stake in these processes. Foucault asks us to go further and to explore what he calls the "regime of truth" that is set into place when an issue is transformed from a "political" to a "technical" problem (1980b).

Before considering these issues for Basque language statistics, it may be useful to identify at a general level some distinctive features of statistical discourse. In my view, three basic semiotic processes—holism, classification, and normalization—are key to this discourse. The first among these is what Robert Thornton (1988) has called the rhetoric of holism. Counting, listing, and other quantitative measures inherently conjure up a larger collectivity. Percentages are clear examples of this. Every percentage, of necessity, evokes a whole of which it is a part: a nation, an ethnic group, a language, or a risk group. The census is a prime example of how counting evokes the imagined community we call the nation (Anderson 1991). More specifically, however, in the statistical imagination, the imagined whole is understood as a *population*: a bounded and quantifiable entity capable of and demanding measurement. Populations, as Barbara Duden notes, are distinctly modern conceptions, artifacts of demographic science that have quickly become self-evident entities that "grow, consume, pollute, demand, are acted upon, developed, and controlled" (1992: 146). Populations are by definition objects of calculus, presumed to have knowable rates, generalizable laws, and predictable aggregate patterns.

The second semiotic process associated with quantification is classification. Statistical knowledge classifies; it carves up the population in a myriad of ways, sorting and dividing people, things, or behaviors into groups: the bilingual speaker, the native speaker, the Hispanic, the immigrant. It is in the sorting and dividing of the social world that statistical practices may have their most profound ideological effect on the social construction of reality (Hacking 1982, 1986; Kertzer and Arel 2002; Kitsuse and Cicourel 1963). Incorporated into institutional practices and discourses, the categories of counting can come to be seen as self-evident units of social life, lasting well beyond the specific statistical counts themselves.

Counting implies the divisibility of populations into discrete categories and creates the sense of equivalency of entities within a category. In this fashion, statistical classifications rationalize sociolinguistic reality by reducing that complexity into separate and therefore countable units. This is one of the reasons why quantification is appealing; it helps us to map a messy reality. However, it can also elide things we know to be true. For example, dividing up the world into countable languages makes it seem as if our social reality is made up of distinct and bounded languages with internally homogenous groups of speakers (Hill 2002). The fluidity of boundaries, mixtures of languages, and multilingualism of speakers is ungraspable in numerical counts of "native speakers" of language X or Y. Language boundaries are easily taken to be facts of nature, rather than historically produced artifacts, entangled with social interests and disputes that often go beyond language itself (Arel 2002; Gal and Irvine 1995; Harries 1988; Khubchandani 1983; Lieberson 1981).

The third semiotic process and powerful effect of statistical knowledge is normalization. Hervé le Bras (1986: 325) called statistical science a "machine for exploring society," but it is always also a machine for the creation of norms. Statistical studies are often aimed at revealing what is average or frequent in a population, notions that slide easily from descriptive norms to prescriptive standards. This is encoded in the semantic ambiguity of the term "normal" itself, meaning both "average" in a quantitative sense and "healthy." Part of what it means to be modern today is to experience statistical averages and rates for such things as height, weight, intelligence, and accidents, as standards against which we measure ourselves or are measured by others as normal, abnormal, healthy, diseased, risky, or safe. In the Basque case, we see that metaphors of social health and pathology have been a frequent companion to the discourse of statistics. In early uses of statistics by Basque-language loyalists, it was common for data on the linguistic population to be presented as necessary for "diagnosing" and "curing" the ill health of Basque and restoring it to normalcy. The use of these terms is a clue to the historically close relationship that has existed between statistical analysis and social reform. One of my aims, then, is to try to deduce implicit ideas about what is "normal" or "healthy" for Basque from the talk about and with statistics.

Finally, statistical categories operate as ways of describing who we are (or are not) and to that extent may be factors in the formation of collective identities of all kinds. In theorizing how statistical categories shape identity claims and politics, it is useful to remember that statistical discourse is not simply representational—it is material and practical. Statistical categories and norms gain force in our lives as they become embedded in institutional practices, policies, and public discourse. The power of quantification to shape the ways we have of understanding ourselves would seem to hinge on the extent to which their institutionalization has material consequence for our lives, dictating, for example, the ways in which political claims can be articulated and the categories that are available for entering into public debate as a subject (Scott 1998: 87–88). While census categories do not magically supplant other ways of understanding social reality, they can be influential in shaping how social experience and inequalities get publicly framed in ways that can have consequences for potential political alliances and mobilization (Abramson 2002). In the United States the categorizations of official statistics about language, for example, exert ideological effect when they routinely present minorities as people lacking English rather than as people fluent in languages other than English. In this and many other ways, official statistics powerfully *shape,* rather than just reflect, how we understand the world of language.

Philosophers of science believe that statistical thinking has revolutionized how we understand ourselves as kinds of social beings.[3] To the extent that statistical practices offer up ways of thinking and talking about ourselves as part of particular collectivities and aggregate social trends, to the extent that they shape the way we categorize the world and interpret behavior as normal or pathological, as incurring certain risks, statistics operate as more than administrative techniques for the extraction and distribution of resources. They contribute to the crafting of modern subjectivity or sense of the self, shaping how we relate to ourselves and to our behavior. Statistical discourse produces what Foucault has called "subject effects" (1982) with material, semiotic, and practical consequences that need to be investigated.[4]

Much of what has been written about the politics of statistics has concerned their use by the state, colonial administrators, and other powerful institutions and authorities (see Appadurai 1996b; Carter 1997; Cohn 1987; Cohn and Dirks 1988; Kula 1986; Scott 1988). Looking at how statistics are deployed in the context of minority-language resistance to state power and discrimination allows us to see the strategic reversibility or tactical polyvalence that Foucault saw as inherent to governmental technologies (Gordon 1991: 5; Foucault 1991). As has been noted, numbers have become iconic of science and objectivity (Gould 1981; Porter 1995). Frequently compared to mechanical recordings, photographs, and X-rays, they claim the status of pure description, or what Bourdieu called "a science without a scientist" (Bourdieu 1990: 169; see also de Certeau 1986). As Jonathan Tagg has argued for the documentary photograph (1988: 172–73), we want to bear in mind that statistics' binding relationship to "the real" is not a result of their intrinsic nature, but is something which has been produced and reproduced by the social sciences and a variety of governmental and legal practices. This authoritative status, not always uncontested, of course, renders statistics a potent political tool in the arts of persuasion for both dominant and subaltern groups. This dynamic plays out as Basque citizens wanting to save their language turn to surveys and demolinguistics as tools of knowledge and resistance.

The Will to Count in Euskadi

In the heady years after the Statute of Autonomy was passed and official language planning became a possibility, language loyalists who joined in the newly created Department of Language Policy, as well as those who remained working outside it, were keen on acquiring systematic and reliable quantitative information on the linguistic population. Until then, figures on speakers had to be cobbled together via sample survey, disparate records, or estimates produced by individual researchers. This changed in 1981, when the census began collecting data on Basque- and Spanish-language skills in the Basque Autonomous Community. The Foral Community of Nafarroa began to collect similar data after 1986.[5]

If the introduction of the census marked the first stage of statistical assessment of language, a second major turning point in language statistics came about in the 1990s, when partnerships among Basque-language organizations in the Autonomous Community, France, and Nafarroa made it possible to develop a reliable statistical portrait of all seven provinces of Euskal Herria. Two major surveys assumed the role of taking the pulse of the language in this decade. The first of these was begun in 1989 by EKB [Euskal Kulturaren Batzarrea], an independent Basque sociolinguistic association. The EKB survey, called the Kale Neurketa [Street Survey], used sampling techniques to assess the amount of spoken Basque-language use throughout the seven provinces. It was followed in 1991 by the Basque Autonomous Government's Department of Language Policy survey, known as The Continuity of Basque. Carried out every five years, this survey was created to supplement the government census data with more detailed periodic measurements of the linguistic population's demographics, reported language use, and attitudes. To these massive surveys must be added the hundreds of smaller scale surveys that are commissioned by local entities, municipalities, businesses, and community-based associations in conjunction with language-revival campaigns and planning efforts of all kinds.

Today, the language survey is a quotidian technology in the normalization of

Basque. In some ways we can see this as the realization of an aspiration that began much earlier with Eusko Ikaskuntza, the Basque Studies Society. Entire sections of their congresses were dedicated to the importance of reliable statistics for effective social policy. As one of the opening speakers to the 1920 congress declared to his colleagues: "It is impossible to conceive of any collective policy, whether social or economic, that is not based on statistics" (Olarriaga 1920: 234). Statistics, said another, might not govern the world, but they instruct us as to how the world should be governed (Gortari 1920: 235). The business leaders, intellectuals, and middle-class professionals who were the early architects of the Basque Studies Society bemoaned the poor state of official statistics. Comparing the statistician to the medical examiner, José Orueta, an industrialist and one of the authors of the first Basque Statute of Autonomy, argued that it was only through numbers that true knowledge and the health of Basque society could be obtained: "just as for one's health one must weigh oneself, take one's pulse and temperature, know the amount of one's nutritional intake and analyze one's blood and its components—in sum, know oneself through numbers—the same has to necessarily apply to the health of the collectivity, and with even greater reason, since *it is only numbers that can represent and measure the actual vitality of a people*" (1920: 276, emphasis added). Orueta's words would be echoed many times in the discourse of language advocates to come.

These aspirations would not be realized until after Franco's death. As soon as the 1979 Statute of Autonomy was passed, the regional government in the Basque Autonomous Community established its own statistical service, EUSTAT. Shortly thereafter, in 1981, language questions were incorporated into the census, and in 1982, the Law of Basque Language Normalization, disposition No. 2, mandated the creation of a sociolinguistic map for language-planning purposes. Autonomy gave Basque-language advocates the opportunity and resources to know Basque in new ways. Language had become more central to the definition of Basque nationality, and this fact, together with the new possibilities for developing language policy, invested language data with great interest and value.

On the threshold of a newly gained but limited autonomy, two reports appeared in which statistics were mobilized to take stock of the past, present, and future of the Basque language. The first, *Conflicto lingüístico en Euskadi/Hizkuntz borroka Euskal Herrian* [Language Conflict in Euskadi], published by the Basque Language Academy in 1979, used sample survey data (SIADECO 1979). The second, *La lucha del Euskara/Euskararen borroka* [The Battle of Basque], published by the Basque government a few years later, utilized the newly available census data as well as additional survey data on language attitudes (Eusko Jaurlaritza 1983). Both reports were issued in a Spanish- and a Basque-language version.

I would like to look closely at these two texts as a way of understanding how language advocates in and outside the government talked about the possibilities that statistics offered. How did language advocates represent the status of Basque to themselves and the general public at this critical moment in their political history?

The first text, *Language Conflict in Euskadi,* henceforth *Language Conflict,* sported on its cover a dramatic image of a horse's head that recalled Picasso's famous painting of the bombing of the Basque city of Gernika during the Spanish Civil War (see figure below). As the site of the oak tree where Spanish kings had historically come to swear allegiance to Basque foral laws, the city of Gernika has special significance in the Basque Country. Its bombing was emblematic for many Basques of their repression under the Franco regime, and images of Picasso's painting circulated a great deal in the iconography of Basque resistance after the transition. The research for *Language Conflict* was carried out by SIADECO, the Sociedad de Investigación Aplicada del Desarollo Comunitario [Society for the Applied Study of Community Development], a progressive Basque research organization that had been conducting studies of the impact of labor migrations and industrial growth on Basque communities. This book's self-professed aim was to use the methods and concepts of sociolinguistics, a field largely unknown at that time in the Basque Country, to bear on the process of language shift. *The Battle of Basque,* on the other hand, published in 1983, was a study carried out by the Autonomous Government's Office of Sociological Survey Research, headed by José Ruiz Olabuenaga. Both publications were written for a lay audience and available in local bookstores. One year later, the Basque government published the *Atlas Lingüístico Vasco* [Basque Linguistic Atlas] (Olabuenaga 1984), containing colored maps and graphic summaries of *The Battle of Basque's* data for popular usage.

The titles of both studies, *Language Conflict* and *The Battle of Basque,* underscore language advocates' attempt to provide a political understanding of the history of Basque regression. Both texts also convey excitement about the prospect of bringing statistical tools to the description of Euskara. Like their turn-of-the-century predecessors, they each suggest that political passions had made it difficult to gain an accurate assessment of the language. *Language Conflict* is introduced by SIADECO, saying: "This volume . . . is the product of a team of specialists [working] in accordance with scientific methods. It was necessary to leave behind approximations and subjectivism, those of the adversary as well as our own" (1979: 13). We see in both an eagerness to deploy this expertise to create a neutral space of observation and to transform language revival into a more evidence-based and rationalized process. These books show us that for these language advocates, rendering language revival a field of technical expertise was positively seen as a tool

FIGURE 5.1. This image, reminiscent of Pablo Picasso's famous painting *Guernica,* served as the cover art for the 1979 book *Conflicto lingüístico en Euskadi* [Language Conflict in Euskadi] by SIADECO. Metaphors of battle were frequent in language-revival discourse immediately after the transition. Courtesy of Euskaltzaindia.

for enabling planning. It is helpful to take a closer look, then, at how these two reports deployed statistical representations in this key moment of political transformation in which Basque language policy was just beginning to be designed. How were citizens counted and what conventions of visual representation were used?

Mapping the Language/Mapping the Nation

Deeply embedded in Western language ideologies is the idea that languages belong to particular places. We territorialize language, and those territories are often thought of as bounded national spaces, or homelands. This linkage between language, territory, and nation or culture was foundational to the thought of the German Romantics, and most especially Herder, and is conveyed in most European nationalist and language-revival movements. But it is also a taken-for-granted premise in the social sciences (Wolf 1982) and the visual rhetoric of the world atlas (see Segal 1988: 301–303; Anderson 1991; Kostelnick 2004).

The territoriality of Euskara was instantiated in the ways both these books visually presented data on the Basque language. Both *Language Conflict* and *The Battle of Basque* simultaneously quantified and territorialized Basque through the recurrent use of maps as backdrops for displaying numbers of speakers. However, with the formation of the Basque Autonomous Community, we find some flux among language advocates in their units of measure.

Language Conflict, produced by nongovernmental advocates, has maps, tables, and charts that use all seven of the Basque provinces as their unit of analysis. Basque-place names are given, and the Spanish and French territories are referred to as "the South" [Hegoalde] and "the North" [Iparralde] Basque Country respectively. Implicit in the mapping is that this territory is a single whole, Euskal Herria, rather than "regions" of Spain or France. In using this territorial unit, *Language Conflict* was following in the tradition of mapping Euskara that had been in use since Louis Lucien Bonaparte's first dialectological map of Basque was published in 1863. The Statute of Autonomy, however, put a new unit of measurement into circulation: the Basque Autonomous Community (BAC). The BAC, as we know, incorporated only three of the historic Basque Provinces—Gipuzkoa, Araba, and Bizkaia—leaving out Nafarroa, which became its own autonomous region, and the northern territory in France. In marked contrast to *Language Conflict,* the Basque government's publication and the subsequent popularized linguistic atlases of 1984 and 1989 used the BAC as its map.

In the highly charged political climate of the southern Basque Country, differences in terminology and ways of representing the Basque country resonated with political meanings. Whether an author used Euskadi, Euskal Herria, or the now-outdated term Las Vascongadas, for example, said something about his or her political leanings when it came to Basque nationalism. Language loyalists as well as activists and scholars in the broader nationalist movement had some concern that along with autonomy might come a gradual acceptance of the Autonomous Community as the natural context for discussions of Basque cultural or political issues. Would the BAC statistics and map—the outline of which coincidentally resembles the overall shape of Euskal Herria—come to stand in for the Basque homeland?

As Michael Billig (1995) writes, these are not trivial concerns. It is precisely in these seemingly ordinary ways that a sense of nationhood is conjured. Nationalism, he says, is not something remote in contemporary life; it is not "confined to the florid language of blood-myths. Banal nationalism operates with the pro-saic, routine words which take nations for granted and which in so doing, inhabit them" (1995: 93). Billig points to sporting events and chants, the weather map, and modes of address used by newspapers and opinion polls as collectively operating as the "deixis of the homeland" (ibid.: 106), reproducing a sense of a collective "we" and a common "here" (see also Anderson 1991). Deixis, he says, normally works "unobtrusively" (ibid.: 107), but in this precise moment of the emergence of the BAC, Basque nationalists and language advocates were made acutely aware of it. The boundaries as well as the categories used in newspapers, maps, and yearbooks were loaded with significance. Advocates of the broader vision of a Basque home-land have continued to keep the vision of a greater Euskal Herria visually present in maps, but also through such things as popular *urtekariak,* a type of "year in review" book distributed to subscribers of the cultural magazine *ARGIA*. These and other kinds of statistical compendiums (e.g., Aztiker 2002) instantiated what we might call a counterdeixis by providing news highlights, summaries of remarkable events, and directories of cultural organizations for all seven provinces. During its operation from 1990 to 2003, the Basque-language newspaper *Egunkaria* similarly included weather and news about Iparralde, the French Basque territories, as a normal part of its "national" news.

While theses books show that the units of measurement were in flux, they also show that both governmental and nongovernmental advocates shared a vision of Basque as a language in geographic peril. The maps from this period create a visual narrative of the spatial retrenchment of Basque. The maps below show us various ways in which this retrenchment has been represented. *Language Conflict* depicts a Basque-speaking territory that is gradually shrinking over the centuries, reced-ing in the face of Spanish and French linguistic domination. An image from this book, entitled "The Primitive Territories of Euskara" (see map 2), shows that the Basque language at one time in the past extended well beyond the seven-province boundaries of Euskal Herria.

Another image from this same book, entitled "Linguistic Areas" (see map 3), gives us an image of the Basque-speaking territories in the twentieth century. Here we see another way that language shift is territorialized. The Basque-speaking community in this image is represented as a small but solid core, surrounded at its outer limits by a shaded area called a "contact zone," a frontier, as it were, between peoples and languages.

The collection of census data after 1981 in the Basque Autonomous Community allowed for an increasingly more detailed picture of this retrenchment, showing the percentages of Basque speakers municipality by municipality. The next image (see map 4) is a sociolinguistic map of the Basque Autonomous Community pro-

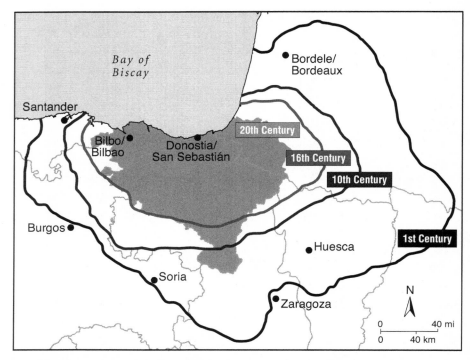

MAP 2. This map, entitled "The Primitive Territories of Euskara," is adapted from the book *Conflicto lingüístico* (SIADECO 1979). It shows how language shift was visually conceptualized as a shrinking territory. Here as elsewhere in that book, Euskal Herria is presented as a unified territory. Courtesy of Euskaltzaindia.

duced with census data from the late eighties (Eusko Jaurlaritza 1989). By showing percentages of speakers according to municipality, the Basque-speaking community in this image has gone from a solid but shrinking core to what one analyst called a linguistic "archipelago" (Olabuenaga 1984: 12). The landscape of Basque is revealed as fragmented and highly uneven.

Published as they were not long after the end of the Franco regime, both texts, not surprisingly, present a portrait of a language, and by extension a national and cultural identity, besieged. In both reports the encounter of the state language and Basque is framed as a battle. The rhetoric and imagery of endangerment is pervasive, particularly in *Language Conflict* published in the flush of liberation after the Franco regime. This is evident in the following extract: "Declining moment by moment, they are rendering us empty. The weapons that can be used against Basque are infinite; they have been used and will continue to be used—all of them.

They are the result of a long state of siege and aggressions. We, Basque speakers, are now reduced to the status of the American Indians on the reservations. Because that is what we are, the Indians of Europe; let us set aside euphemisms" (SIADECO 1979: 17). This book wanted to show readers that the marginalization of Basque in the present came from the history of Basques as an internal colony, not as a result of the poverty of the language, as some philogists had argued. Given this history, say the authors of *Language Conflict,* it is miraculous that Basque had survived at all. Attached to this sociopolitical reading of language contact is also a political imaginary. The images of retrenchment and the embattled narrative of struggle suggest the existence of a once linguistically whole nation: a time when all or almost all the population knew Basque. This is both the way the remote past is imagined and also a seeming aspiration for the future: what once was and what can be again.

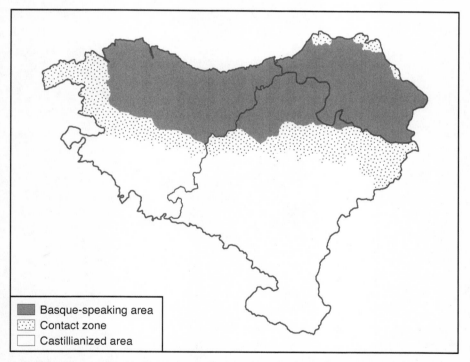

Basque-speaking area
Contact zone
Castillianized area

MAP 3. This map, entitled "Linguistic Areas," is adapted from the book *Conflicto lingüístico* (SIADECO 1979). It depicts the territory of Euskal Herria unconnected to its surrounding states, showing the Basque-speaking community as a shrinking core surrounded by a bilingual "contact" zone. Courtesy of Euskaltzaindia.

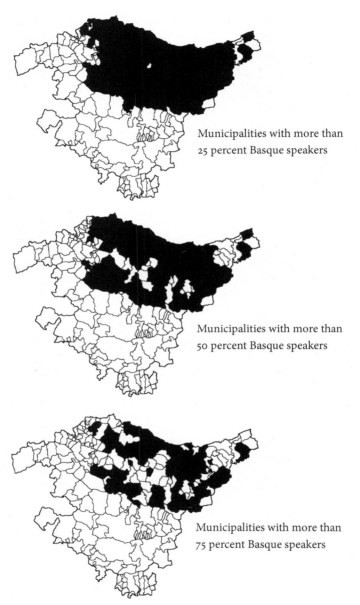

Municipalities with more than
25 percent Basque speakers

Municipalities with more than
50 percent Basque speakers

Municipalities with more than
75 percent Basque speakers

MAP 4. These images from the *Basque Linguistic Atlas* use census data to map the percentages of Basque speakers in the Basque Autonomous Community. Census data allowed for more detailed mapping according to municipality and a shift from an image of the Basque-speaking territory as a shrinking core to one of a linguistic archipelago (Eusko Jaurlartiza 1989: 71). Courtesy of Eusko Jaurlaritza, Servicio Central de Publicaciones.

In addition to references to battlegrounds, reservations, and fragmented home-lands, we also find metaphors of health and disease in describing the status of Basque. The decline in speakers and the linguistic fragmentation of the territory revealed in maps and figures are on more than one occasion equated with degeneracy and the "amputation" of Euskal Herria (SIADECO 1979: 24, see also 19, 202). Contrary to what most Basques would have learned in school, in this book language shift is not presented as an inevitable outcome of modernization, but as a product of colonization, a social pathology for which language planning was a cure. Statistics serve as instruments for diagnosing the ills of Basque and language revival—tellingly called "normalization"—is described as a way of giving to Basque what presumably all languages should enjoy: health, longevity, vitality.

In both of these texts, the depictions of a nation struggling to recapture its linguistic and territorial integrity are interestingly paired with calls for scientific and rational planning. In both texts we hear the rhetorics of national liberation alongside the voice of the more dispassionate technician, intent on identifying rates and norms. Quantification is doing double duty. On the one hand, it is providing the incontrovertible evidence of the legacy of repression in the present. The "hard facts" of declining numbers make visible, quantifiable, and therefore *real* the persistence of Spanish-language hegemony despite the new freedoms for Basque nationalism in the political arena. On the other hand, statistics are bringing into being the linguistic community as a population that is knowable, trackable, and in desperate need of the kind of planning that, they point out, is virtually commonsensical for other spheres of social life.

Language Conflict and *The Battle of Basque* provide insight into the use of statistics in language-revival discourse shortly after Franco. A decade later, in the presentation of the first results of a new and comprehensive language survey by the Basque government, the planning voice or perspective gains primacy over the narrative of the besieged nation. The preface to the first edition of *The Continuity of Basque,* written by Mari Karmen Garmendia Lasa, who headed the Department of Language Policy throughout the formative 1980s, appears to be almost lifted from the pages of Orueta's 1920 speech to the Basque Studies Society. She writes:

> Just as in the field of medicine, the cure of an illness requires an accurate diagnosis, so in social questions it is not possible to find rational solutions without having first done a good analysis of the problems and factors at work. Until today, the agents of linguistic planning in *Euskal Herria* have had to rely in general on their own experience, intuition and incomplete knowledge of the sociolinguistic situation, both in terms of its geography and the globality of the object of study. . . . Nevertheless, as the resources dedicated to language planning have increased, the need for a global vision and complete X-ray

of the situation of our language has become increasingly evident. As a response to this need we have carried out the investigation you have before you in this book (Aizpurua 1995: 11).

In this first edition of the survey, entitled *The Continuity of Basque*, as well as in later reports, statistics become increasingly presented as a form of impartial diagnosis and visualization. There is a decided move away from metaphors of battle. As the very title—the *continuity* of Basque—indicates, references to conflict and confrontation have been supplanted by a more neutral language and a focus on Basque survival rather than its disappearance. We see an evolution away from talking about Basque and Spanish as languages in competition for the same social and geographic space to a focus on tracking what the authors call the demographic evolution of the linguistic population. By the nineties, a new field of expertise, demolinguistics, had become a familiar part of the way talk about language was undertaken and an indispensable instrument in the implementation of language-normalization policies (i.e., according to percentages of speakers in a given area). Within a relatively short span of time, the linguistic population had become a routinely referenced part of the social imaginary. Investigators would henceforth seek to know in ever-greater detail how the Basque-speaking population was changing in terms of any number of variables: age, residence, education, gender, and political ideology.

By the nineties we also see that the use of all seven provinces for presenting data on the status of Basque has become much more normalized. After much work and lobbying, the territorial rubrics for language statistics have ceased to become a source of tension between government and nongovernmental sectors, as partnerships established in 1990 among the Autonomous Community's Department of Language Policy, the Autonomous Community of Nafarroa, and the French Basque Cultural Institute now facilitate sharing of data. When it comes to language, the Basque government is just as likely as nongovernmental groups to use the seven provinces of Euskal Herria as a unit for their statistical reports. Hence we find a reference in the preface to the government's report, *The Continuity of Basque,* to this study's providing data covering the "full geography" of the language. In addition, we see Basque increasingly described and figured as a language of Europe—a reflection, no doubt, of the growth of the European Union as a referent for minority-language activism and rights in the nineties and the creation of the European Charter for Regional or Minority Languages in 1992.

The image of a shrinking territory of speakers, so distinctive of the seventies and early eighties, seems to be largely retired from the visual culture of language revival. In today's posters and pamphlets, pie charts and bar graphs dominate. This kind of graphic display is prized in technical and professional media for its ability to "impress at a glance" (Kostelnick 2004). Of course the pie chart still evokes a singular whole, and in that sense, the rhetoric of holism continues. But it does so in a much more abstract way than did the map of Euskal Herria. This is just one of the ways in which we see Basque-language revivalist discourse shifting its priority to the production of comparable and standardized measures over flagging the nation.

From *Euskaldun* vs. *Erdaldun* to Bilingual vs. Monolingual

As the linguistic population's features are increasingly quantified and percentages are tabulated, what features of speakers started to be counted and how? How did the classifications of the first statistical studies configure the makeup of the linguistic community, and how do they do it now?

Statistical tabulations of experts enter a world that is already rich with cultural categories. To help us defamiliarize the self-evident way that language statistics divide up the world, it is helpful to look at some of the popular or everyday ways of sorting speakers that I found Basque speakers of Gipuzkoa using when statistics first began to be gathered. From my fieldwork in Usurbil in the eighties, I found that Basque speakers divided the linguistic universe into two main categories: *euskaldunak* (Basque speakers) and *erdaldunak* (non-Basque speakers). More specifically, they tended to reserve the term *erdaldun* for monolingual speakers of the majority language—Spanish in this case. Speakers of foreign languages, by contrast, tended to be identified by their nationality. This was more or less the extent of explicitly language-based categories. Living in Usurbil, however, helped me to see that linguistic classification was conveyed indirectly in other popular forms of identifying and categorizing people. For example, in everyday talk a person's hometown or place of birth was probably the most common way of identifying someone. Hometown is an identity that sticks for life, and it was used as an identifier far more often than a person's surname. Hometowns carried certain kinds of linguistic information. Basque speakers generally understood the way that language mapped onto geography. Consequently, to know that a person was from the town of Azpeitia or Tudela or from a particular neighborhood would generate expectations about whether that person was likely to know Basque, and if so, whether they would understand that person's variety of Basque or not. Geographical markers were signposts in the uneven linguistic landscape that native speakers could read with varying degrees of sophistication. This also worked in reverse. If geography was a way of signaling language, language was a way of placing people in a geography. For native speakers, Basque speech forms, nuances in pronunciation, and word choices were legible markers that identified them as from a particular region or town. The categories through which speakers understood the linguistic universe were consequently more complex and nuanced than the binary terms *euskaldunak* and *erdaldunak* suggest.

Language loss or shift can produce classification problems. In the Basque context, the non-*euskaldun* Basque is a good example. This is someone whose heritage is recognizable as Basque, usually through a distinctive Basque surname—Echeverria, Aranburu, Mendizabal-but who does not know the Basque language. This phenomenon was a source of intense discussion for radical nationalists like Krutwig. Arana had developed a word for this category of person: *euskotar,* but this neologism never really took root. The category presented a bit of a conundrum, since the word in Basque for a Basque person, *euskaldun,* means Basque speaker. Basque-language advocates made reference to this fact continually. Tellingly, however, this was not a problem in Spanish, as such people would be called *vascos,* the Spanish word for Basques, regardless of whether a person knew Basque or not. Wondering how Basque speakers dealt with this, I asked native speakers of Usurbil about labels for and attitudes toward this kind of person—the non Basque-speaking Basque. I had to describe what I meant, as it was not something one could say efficiently in Basque. My question was usually met with some consternation. I heard the pejorative *belarrimotz* [short-eared], which people sometimes used to chastise Basque children who spoke Spanish. This tells us something about the value native speakers in this community placed on knowing Basque, but it did not seem to be a commonly used label for a Basque who did not know Euskara. In Usurbil, where most ethnic Basques did speak Euskara, residents did not comfortably categorize such people as either *erdaldun* or *euskaldun.* In contrast, they were usually comfortable calling someone *euskaldun* if that person knew Euskara, whether or not they were ethnically Basque.

If language loss generated classificatory lacunae in local language ideology, language revival was giving rise to new category labels to describe a shifting universe. Thousands of people were now learning Basque as a second language, and with this, a new set of terms had emerged onto the landscape. People contrasted *euskaldun zaharra* [literally "an old Basque"] to refer to people who had learned Basque as their first language at home and *euskaldun berria* [literally "a new Basque"] for those who learned it as a second language. While referencing native versus nonnative status, part of what made the difference between these groups so salient, particularly in the early years of the movement, was not just the predictable differences in competency between natives and learners, but also the different variety of Basque they spoke. The "new Basque" was typically a speaker of standard Basque while the native or "old Basque" speakers most often spoke in dialect. This contrast, quite salient in the eighties, has since ceased to be so marked as most native speakers also know standard Basque.

In the statistical surveys, the categories sort the linguistic world in somewhat different, somewhat overlapping ways from the popular practices. Most notable is the fact that dialect variations, meaningful markers of local or hometown identity, were not an object of measurement in most of the language-planning surveys. Dialect studies, of course, exist, but the census and most language surveys measure Euskara as a single category. In this way, quantification, like standardization, powerfully reproduces the idea of Basque as a linguistic unity. What counts in the census, or what the census counts, are not dialects, but numbers of speakers and types and degrees of linguistic competency. The census and most of the surveys break down language knowledge into four skills: speaking, reading, writing, and comprehension, then asking respondents to characterize their level in each skill as something they do "well," "with difficulty," or "not at all." It is useful to look at the focus given to measuring these particular skills as an indication of the centrality of literacy to contemporary conceptions of citizenship, as well as the practical importance of measuring literacy skills in a society seeking to build a bilingual administrative apparatus, schooling system, and media. These data, for example, were used for gauging the potential market for Basque-language news and television.

While the unity of Basque as a language was routinely instantiated by these ways of measuring, other kinds of divisions and complexity came to the foreground. The sorting of speakers into degrees of competency brought into focus a middle ground of speakers between *euskaldun* and *erdaldun* who had varying masteries of Basque. Statistician-planners began to develop new terminology to talk about this middle ground and the features of in-between types of speakers. Reports in the eighties start to use the term "quasi-*euskaldun*" to designate people who reported speaking Basque "with difficulty," followed later by the term "active new Basque" to refer to second-language learners who report being able to read and write in Basque well (see Eusko Jaurlaritza 1989). While the public discourse about language continued to use the binary categories of speakers and nonspeakers of Basque—for example, *euskaldunak* and *erdaldunak*—the statistical studies reveal the planners' interests in the spaces and movement in between.

In the nineties, something remarkable happened. *The Continuity of Basque* surveys dropped the categories of *euskaldun* and *erdaldun* and started to categorize speakers as bilinguals or monolinguals.[6] It happened quietly without fanfare or a press release. But its significance indexes a decisive exit out of the hegemonic worldview of majority-language discourse that conceptualized a social world made up of two mutually exclusive linguistic communities. The binary division of the population into Basque and non-Basque speakers conveyed an image that was at odds with a more complex reality of people with varying degrees of knowledge. But perhaps even more significantly, such a categorization continually elided the reality that almost all *Basque speakers are also speakers of the state language.* The unequal political histories of Basque and Spanish are such that Basque speakers, like most linguistic minorities, learn the majority language. Aside for the very young, few monolingual Basque speakers remain. Basque bilingualism (and often multilingualism) was invisible in the previous schema of counting. It was invisible precisely because of the design of early Basque surveys, which, like most language surveys (see Singh 1998), was premised on an implicitly monolingual view of the world (one language per person).

The decision to start counting in terms of bilinguals and monolinguals, instead of Basque and non-Basque speakers, offered a more faithful representation of Basque speakers' ability to function in both languages. In so doing, it made the biases of dominant-language ideology available for discussion. One wonders why it took so long to talk about Basque speakers as bilinguals. According to May (2003), the habitual tendency to "forget" the minority-language speaker's multilingualism is symptomatic of the widespread association of minority-language speakers with linguistic deficit and a view of their attachments to their language as provincial, isolationist, or uneducated. These kinds of accusations were in fact gaining ground in Spain precisely when the shift in counting categories occurred. Critics of minority-language normalization in Spain had begun to accuse language loyalists of wanting to impose Basque monolingualism and to eliminate Spanish. *The Continuity of Basque* is an indirect retort to this accusation. Backed by the legitimacy of international experts who served as advisors, *The Continuity of Basque* has shown with each new edition that Spanish monolingualism is far and away more common than Basque.[7] In sorting the population into bilinguals and monolinguals (see figure below), these new studies provide a quantified representation that challenges the idea of the Basque linguistic community and the Spanish-speaking one as mutually exclusive. It presents language revival as a process of *expanding* citizens' linguistic resources rather than contracting them (imposing monolingualism), as detractors decried.

As statistical inquiry progresses in the Basque Country, we find an evolution from a rather straightforward counting of speakers and their abilities to developing *typologies* of speakers. There is, for example, an increasing sophistication in cross-tabulating information on linguistic behavior, competency, and attitudes with demographic information on the respondents—their age, gender, employment, level of education, place of residence, political ideology, and self-described identity (Basque, Spanish, Both Basque and Spanish). The development of typolo-

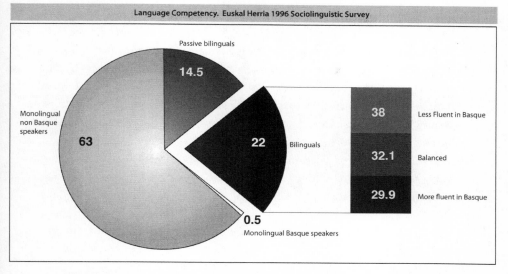

Language Competency. Euskal Herria 1996 Sociolinguistic Survey

Passive bilinguals

14.5

Monolingual non Basque speakers

63

22   Bilinguals

38   Less Fluent in Basque

32.1   Balanced

29.9   More fluent in Basque

0.5

Monolingual Basque speakers

FIGURE 5.2. This image summarizing the results of the 1996 language survey *The Continuity of Basque II* shows the turn toward more abstract and standardized graphemes such as pie charts and bar graphs for representing the linguistic population. Here we also see the shift in counting practices toward measuring different types of bilingualism rather than counting Basque versus Spanish speakers (Eusko Jaurlaritza 1996: 19, translated by author). Courtesy of Eusko Jaurlaritza, Servicio Central de Publicaciones.

gies is a key instrument of governmentality that grows out of statistics (see Sekula 1986). In the Basque case, language planners use this data to generalize about the characteristics of different kinds of speakers and show important shifts taking place in the demographic profile of Basque speakers.

Typological analysis by Miren Mateo and Xabier Aizpurua (2003) reveals, for example, that Basque speakers, especially those under twenty-five, are very different in their linguistic habits and backgrounds from those just one generation ago. Many more have learned Basque from a very young age as a second language at school, rather than as a language of their home. These young people are able to read and write in standard Basque but often do not master informal registers and are not likely to speak it with their close friends. This is a dramatic turn-around from earlier generations, who tended to speak Basque at home or with close friends and use Spanish in public or on formal occasions. Those patterns that defined Basque language use in the past have little bearing on the language patterns of many young people today. From a statistical point of view, the profile of the "typical" Basque—that is, bilingual—speaker is changing. Consistent with this, the visual representation of Basque tends now to be more focused on charting these kinds of generational typologies, usually through bar graphs and histograms, rather than mapping the physical territory of Basque as was common in the past.

A decade after the Law of Normalization mandated the introduction of Basque into education, media, and public administration, language loyalists were becoming increasingly concerned with usage. Were the successes at gaining institutional support resulting in more everyday usage? What about intergenerational transmission? Planners were keen to know who was most likely to speak Basque as their home language and pass it on to their children? What activities, relationships, or spaces seemed to be associated with greatest use of Basque? As a new generation of young people schooled at least partly in Basque began to emerge, the test would now be whether they actually speak it, and if so, when and with whom? (see Martínez de Luna 2002).

The original initiative to measure the everyday use of Basque came from nongovernmental sectors of the language movement. Until then, most data on the usage of Basque came from the estimates speakers reported to surveyors of how often they spoke Basque. By the early eighties, the sociolinguistic institute SIADECO had begun experimenting with what they hoped would be more objective methods for measuring the amount of Basque spoken in public. Usurbil was one of the first sites where the new survey method was tested. In contrast to self-reporting, the idea of this survey was to actually document usage from direct observation. Surveyors were recruited from among the schoolteachers and university students to walk a specified route along the streets and through a variety of public spaces in the various neighborhoods of Usurbil—the plaza, open-air market, handball court, and playground. The goal, as a member of SIADECO, described it, was to get beyond subjective impressions and "take a snapshot" of the presence of spoken Basque in public life.[8]

The "street measure" of language use subsequently went on to become a periodic nation-wide survey, called the Kale Neurketa. The nongovernmental language-advocacy group EKB carried out the first nation-wide survey in 1989, and the survey has continued to be carried out every four years since that time.[9] Conducted simultaneously in towns throughout the seven provinces of Euskal Herria, the survey is a major organizational feat involving the training of hundreds of recruits who, on the same days at the same hour, all walk down the primary streets of their towns recording the language(s) they hear being spoken. With surveys now spanning more than twenty years and more surveys on the way, Basque sociolinguists hope they will be able to measure changes in the amount of public Basque usage over time.

Numbers from the various surveys have become the tools with which language advocates assess and dispute among themselves and in the media the relative success of language-revival efforts. There is no question that survey results also operate as a kind of "report card" on the language-revival policies of the governing political party. For example, at a training seminar I attended in the spring of 2003 for language technicians, a high-ranking member of the Department of Language Policy was presenting the results of the 2001 *Continuity of Basque* survey. The data showed in no uncertain terms, he said, that where supportive language policies exist, language shift has been arrested. Government surveys in the Basque Autonomous Community showed very clearly that that intergenerational transmission seemed to be secure and that there was even modest gain in speakers. Where protective language policies are weaker, as in Nafarroa, or virtually nonexistent, as in the northern territories in France, we were shown that Basque speakers are declining rapidly. One of the participants at the seminar, however, raised his hand to remind everyone about Street Survey data on usage. The young man agreed that the overall results of language planning looked good and were cause for celebration, but that usage was not keeping up with the increase in knowledge. The 2001 Street Survey showed that while knowledge of Basque had increased to 25 percent of the total population as a whole, public use of Basque averaged only 14 percent, up slightly from 11 percent in 1989 (see Altuna et al. 2002). Even the government data showed that the number of youth (born after 1977) who report speaking Basque habitually is only half of those who say they know how to speak it correctly. These and other discussions of language advocates reveal the anxieties and high-stake questions that are brought to bear on the volumes of language data that are now produced. In the changing demographics of Basque speakers, what should be the priorities of planning? Is Euskara now safe? Or will it always be at risk?

Perpetual Calculation

Orueta's twentieth-century dream to measure Basque in the language of science, to diagnose it in the rational light of numbers, is now a reality. The social life of Basque is, if nothing else, monitored, counted, and tabulated. Planners listen to the heartbeat of Basque in the language of percentages. In the twenty-first century, the auditing of the language and language revival has, however, changed some of its methods. The Basque government has finally realized its long-desired goal of creating a fully digitized sociolinguistic data bank. Known as the EAS, Euskararen Adierazleak Sistema [System of Basque Language Indicators], it consolidates the information of the latest government surveys into a searchable data bank. Language technicians who need, for example, the latest percentages of bilinguals in their community can have these instantaneously. The intention behind the data bank is to permit continual statistical evaluation and to provide systematic, reli-

able, and, very importantly, *standardized* measures that are compatible, and therefore comparable, with those used internationally (Aizpurua and Mateo 2003). As
Theodore Porter (1986) notes, standardization standardizes by pursuing uniformity in its measures and its measurers. Thus, we find that yet more of the unique
or idiosyncratic ways Basque advocates developed to talk about the world of
speakers are replaced by new terms that harmonize with the terminology used
by international scholars: the category *euskaldun berri* [new Basque] is replaced
in the databank by "L2" speaker; the category of a "quasi-*euskaldun*" is replaced
by "passive bilingual." As Basque enters the realm of calculus, standardization in
categories of counting transforms the discourse of language revitalization itself.

New ways of quantifying language also continued to emerge. In a 2003 visit to
Usurbil, I learned that a new sociolinguistic survey commissioned by the town
hall had just been completed. This time, it was given to me as a zip file. Unlike the
three-volume study I was given on my first trip to Usurbil, this one was written
entirely in Basque. The sophistication and detail achieved in language surveys is
impressive. A topographic map of the town is overlain with statistics on population, knowledge and use of Basque by neighborhood, even by street. A tremendous
amount of data is offered on the linguistic competency, rates of language transmission, reported usage, attitudes, and the consumption of Basque-language media
and cultural products. New in this report was an effort to quantify the "linguistic landscape," a concept I had not seen in earlier reports. As used by the French
Canadian researchers R. Landry and R. Y. Bourhis (1997), the linguistic landscape
refers to the way in which a language is visually present in the public space of a
given territory via advertising, billboards, the signage of commercial and public
buildings, street names, official notices, posters, and so forth. The linguistic landscape, argue these authors, is a part of the broader symbolic universe we inhabit;
as such, the visibility and place that a language has can tell us something about
the social status of its speakers. The youth who angrily painted the Basque name
Donostia over the Spanish name *San Sebastián* or *kalea* over the Spanish word
calle in the seventies understood this symbolic struggle over cultural space. Today,
studies conducted within the framework of linguistic landscape (e.g., Cenoz and
Gorter 2006) analyze public language with a technical terminology, making it into
a quantifiable phenomenon to be measured and monitored by experts with standardized and reliable indicators. This research on linguistic landscape has grown
along with the growth of language planning. Catalan researchers have led the way,
in 1999 developing OFERCAT, a method for taking a picture of what they call the
public "supply" of a language. Basque-language advocates followed suit, collabo-
rating with Catalans to develop Euskaini, a tool through which town halls and

organizations of all kinds could systematically measure and track the presence of Basque in the linguistic landscape.

Usurbil's 2003 language survey exemplifies the ubiquitous use of surveys as a way of measuring all aspects of language, from competency to speech to visual and material culture. In evaluating the social, cultural, and political consequences of the turn to quantification, I have wanted to point out effects at multiple levels. Among these are effects of legitimation that come from the association of statistics with empirical fact. Measurement rendered verifiable the marginalization of Basque, thereby legitimating protective policies and justifying the need for language planning. At the same time, quantification has facilitated a certain degree of depoliticization of language-loyalist discourse. Language normalization has become a more rationalized field of technical expertise, carried out by a new cadre of trained individuals and institutions/organizations that produce and interpret this information. The surveyor today stands alongside the grammarian as a voice of authority charged with telling the truth and assessing the health of Basque.

Language demographics can have material consequence in shaping the kinds of normalization plans that are designed and the chances citizens have to be able to use their language in public institutions.[10] The formation of UEMA, the Association of Euskaldun Municipalities, is a good example. In the early 1990s, predominantly Basque-speaking municipalities formed this association to help one another begin to normalize Basque as the habitual language of public administration and circumvent the time-consuming obligation of continual translation that normalization policy seemed to mandate. The legal possibility to do this was written into the Law of Normalization of 1982, which allowed local public administrations to operate entirely in Basque "when the sociolinguistic situation of the municipality indicates that this will not prejudice the rights of citizens" (Article 8.3). The UEMA seized upon survey data and argued for conducting local administration in Basque, translating only as requested, in those municipalities that had 80 percent Basque speakers. More recently, this was revised to allow communities that had 70 percent Basque speakers participate. However, in all cases, UEMA required that there be unanimous support for this among the entire town council. In short, the numbers had to be there, but also the will.

Demolinguistics can have important consequence for the provision of services when language policies conceive of services in the minority language not as an absolute right of the individual, but as a privilege that is contingent upon the relative proportion of one's linguistic group in the unit of measurement.[11] This is the case for the Basque Autonomous Community, and it is also consistent with the policy recommendations of the European Charter for Regional and Minority

Languages. Like the BAC, the European Charter urges member states to undertake protective measures for linguistic minorities "where numbers warrant" (Grin 2003a, 2003b).

In addition to legitimating and material effects, we have seen that routines of counting and units of measure carve up the population and create certain ways of understanding it, particular ways of categorizing speakers giving salience to some kinds of differences (competency) over others (dialect). Looking at counting practices over time, we see an ideologically profound shift away from a framework of mutually exclusive language groups—*euskaldunak* and *erdaldunak*—in favor of "bilinguals" and "monolinguals." Accompanying the changes in the statistical imagination of language, we are beginning to see the emergence, at least in the parlance of the experts, of a new species—the *normal* or *typical* Basque speaker—whose socioeconomic status, average age, residence, and education can be specified and on the basis of which policies are made.

The discursive effects of statistical discourse, like biopolitical discourses more generally, are both totalizing and individualizing (Foucault 1978). That is, they shape conceptions of both the collectivity and the self. The routine collection and public display of language statistics give rise, on the one hand, to the idea that Basques are a linguistic *population*, a boundable entity with rates of growth and attrition and patterns of behavior. At the same time, a new form of linguistic subjectivity is produced. Being an *euskaldun* today is no longer predominantly defined by some hard-to-pin-down set of expressive sensibilities, as the nineteenth-century folklorists thought, but by a set of common behaviors or skills that can be measured and understood quantitatively. Language-awareness campaigns, popular books, and the media ask individuals to think of themselves and their behavior as part of these larger social patterns. The invocation to speak Basque, set against the backdrop of statistics, tells the individual that his or her language choices in the home or in the street have a direct impact on the social life of the language and therefore on the language's historical fate. Pervasive in public culture, statistical representations encourage a sociological self-consciousness and a monitoring of one's linguistic habits. Revitalization strategies can be said to cultivate a notion of linguistic citizenship, in which speakers are asked to assume responsibility for behavior, to judge and to think ahead about the impact of seemingly quotidian and personal practices of everyday life.

While it is fair to say that the statistical view is hegemonic in language-revival discourse, other projects and ways of knowing Basque do exist within language-loyalist circles. At the turn of the twentieth century, language advocates celebrated Basque in poetry and song competitions. The vitality of the language was seen to be rooted in its expressive culture, in its poetics and artistry. This way of celebrating and perceiving the value of Basque continues to exist, for example, in the still very active participation of youth in the Basque improvised art of oral poetry, *bertsolaritza*. Alongside efforts to quantify the linguistic landscape, we find projects in language preservation that conceptualize the relation of language to space differently. Usurbil's toponymic project is one worth noting. This project in recovering local place-names was commissioned in 1988, just as new zoning and development projects were in the works. Members of the town council had seen how earlier development schemes introduced standardized nomenclature that rode roughshod over the cultural as well as physical landscape; they wanted to do things differently this time. Recognizing that the fields, abandoned houses, and "barren" land scheduled for development were already meaning-filled and richly storied places, they commissioned two young philology students, Mari Karmen Etxabe and J. J. Furundarena, to go out, notebooks and tape recorders in hand, to explore in archives and talk directly to farmers and elderly people in order to elicit and record the local lore on place-names. After a year and a half of research, they produced an eighteen-volume compendium of the almost two thousand names of streams, hills, fields, houses, and paths that they had collected. They organized community lectures and created a local public exhibition where they put these on display through pictures of the places and maps. This was a project in the recovery of what Allan Pred (1990) has called, "lost words, lost worlds." It was a means of recovering memory and traces of history as much as linguistic tokens. This local project, repeated by other towns in the area, linked language to place in a very different way than linguistic landscape measures. As one of the young investigators said at the public presentation of the project, "the words are treasures that link today's world with that of our elders." The place-name project sustains an understanding of words not as "things" to be counted, but as stories to be listened to, memory traces, and bearers of practical knowledge, cultural norms, and values (Basso 1996). This, too, is a form of language revival by other means unfolding in the interstices of normalization and quantification.

Language revival may speak overwhelmingly in the language of numbers, but this method does not go uncontested. I close with a description of a lecture by the novelist, language advocate, and schoolteacher Anjel Lertxundi that he delivered in 1999 to the municipal Basque language association of Tolosa. Titled "The Measure of Who We Are," Lertxundi began by stating that the language-revival movement was at a unique historical crossroads. The last year of the century is an auspicious moment for Basque, said Lertxundi. Twenty-five years after the death of Franco, the Basque-language movement finds itself on the threshold of a new millennium, wanting to close the door on a dark past and begin a new, more hopeful future. Basque advocates, he said, need, however, to break the silence and talk about where they have failed. Statistics tell us there are more Basque speakers but not as much use of Basque as was hoped. As an experienced teacher, Lertxundi said he was keenly aware that many of today's youth were seriously lacking in expressive resources. We, *euskaltzaleak,* language loyalists, he suggested, were partly to blame. The methods of revitalization we have been using were too heavily modeled on the premises of dominant languages. We measured who we were in terms of numbers, and we taught our language using the same kind of pedagogy and exercises we use for majority languages. These have failed us. Lertxundi's lecture called for a more radical approach in the new millennium. He called upon advocates to stop trying to make theirs into a dominant language. Let us embrace (rather than try to correct) the condition of being a "small language" and create strategies that fit the particularities that pertain to this unique situation. We live and work with cultural models of language and of resistance, premised on Castilian. Mimetic desire, he said, pervades our strategies.

It would be a mistake, I think, to see Lertxundi's lecture as a condemnation of numbers. He was not so much rejecting enumeration as questioning the blind spots of the taken-for-granted and routine ways that language loyalists had been approaching Basque revival. He suggests that in the desire to become equal to Spanish, language-revival strategies have ignored what makes Basque unique. It is precisely the incommensurate qualities of the language, its particularities, the nuances and multiplicity of its registers and dialects that constitute [play]grounds of creativity and sources of vitality. Taking the pulse of a language, Lertxundi says in his 1999 lecture, is not a simple or self-evident task. He makes allusion to ideologues and "language police" who tend to make a barricade out of language, drape a flag around it, or convert it into a sacred temple. He cautions against giving primacy to quantity over quality, uniformity over plurality. And he reminds his audience of language loyalists that many aspects of language—its symbolic richness, aesthetic and affective qualities—escape the grasp of language planners and technicians. Our movement, he says, calls for constant self-critique.

CHAPTER SIX

Beyond the Classroom

NEW TACTICS FOR NEW TIMES

Language revitalization is, and really has to be, a dynamic and evolving process. In the sixties, the priorities of advocates were to secure official status for Basque, to standardize it for written use, and to spread the teaching of it to the general population. But by the late eighties and nineties, a new set of concerns and priorities was emerging for Basque-language loyalists. Chief among these was to move beyond increasing language competency to encouraging language use. How could advocates motivate people who had learned Basque to use it beyond the home, beyond the pamphlet, and beyond the classroom? Along with this greater focus on language use came a perceived sense of urgency, especially acute among nongovernmental activists, to disentangle language revival from the nationalist problematic and, indeed, to sever any connection to "politics" at all. These two concerns—with increasing usage and decreasing politicization—inform the new directions in language activism that were taken at this time. Without abandoning the aspiration of a national-language movement, new strategies and organizations emerged in civil society that were oriented toward a less explicitly political and more community-based activism, intent on normalizing the use of Basque in the everyday life of their own communities.

Tracking these developments shifted the spatial practices of my fieldwork from the kind of in-depth dwelling in a single place for which ethnography is known to tracing the broader network of groups in this new wave of community activism. Returning to the Basque Country for several periods of fieldwork in the 1990s, I continued to live in Usurbil but found myself spending more of my time in a car traveling the highways as well as smaller windy roads of Euskal Herria, on the trail of the boom in local cultural associations and media projects around the southern Basque Country. Interviews and workshops took me from the small, predominantly Basque-speaking towns of Arretxabaleta and Aulesti to the diverse, industrial urban centers of Lasarte-Oria, Renteria/Orerreta, and Arrasate/Mondragón and to the capital cities of Gasteiz, Donostia, Bilbo, and Iruñea. I negotiated my way down congested city streets and cobblestone lanes, sat—sometimes in cafés or busy modern offices, other times in damp, uncomfortable basement rooms—

talking, tape-recording, and taking notes with volunteers in community language-advocacy groups, leaders in grassroots language organizations, people in Basque publishing, and an emerging corps of municipal language professionals dedicated to taking language revitalization beyond the classroom.[1] While the developments I describe go well beyond the town of Usurbil, living there offered me a context in which to observe the formation and workings of the kind of local-community language activism that I was hearing about in my interviews.

This research—carried out largely in 1998—is the basis for the story I want to tell about the shifting strategies and discourses of the grassroots language movement. Drawing from a dozen formal interviews, many informal conversations, documents, and observations, I reconstruct the frustrations that nongovernmental language advocates in the 1990s were experiencing and the new organizations and strategies they created to meet the challenges they were encountering. Fruit of their reflections in the late eighties was the proliferation of *euskara elkarteak*, community-based Basque cultural associations that, among other things, sought to promote language normalization through local television and magazines.

In the vision nongovernmental language loyalists had of the political context in which they were embedded, as well as the repertoire of practices and representations that they turned to for reorienting their activities, one can see the important role that theories of language scholars and other expert discourses play in the field of language activism. These theories provide models of language and conceptual tools that language loyalists use both to understand the social life of language and to strategize about how best to advance the process of language normalization.[2] Grassroots language activism in the nineties changed significantly as theorists and strategies of the past receded and new ones took their place. Txepetx succeeded Txillardegi as the theorist who ignited the imagination of activists. His work provided them with a theory of language revitalization framed in terms of ecology and multiculturalism, in contrast to the frameworks of third-world liberation or internal colonialism that had influenced earlier generations. At the same time, advocates looked to forms of expertise in the fields of marketing, entrepreneurialism, and quality management as a way of becoming more efficient and effective in their efforts. The nongovernmental language movement entered a decidedly new phase of professionalized language planning that carried with it significant shifts in the ways language revival as a practice was envisioned.

The Politics of Frustration

The boom of *euskara elkarteak* happened in the 1990s, but some of my interviewees traced its roots to a decade earlier. As early as 1983, they said, it was becoming clear to activists that the language-revival movement was entering a new era.

Under Franco, they explained, the movement had been united under a common enemy. Basque revival had taken shape as a heterogeneous conglomeration of groups and activities that drew its leadership and volunteer labor from a diverse group of people: university students, teachers, scholarly clerics, writers, and parents. Although it had many and diverse groups, its core organizations were the Basque schools, *ikastolak,* for children; the adult language and literacy organization AEK; the Basque Language Academy; and small publishing houses. Emblematic of the struggle for democratic freedoms throughout Spain, Basque revival enjoyed strong popular support. But by the early eighties, the involvement of ordinary citizens waned somewhat, as the newly created regional governments of the Basque Autonomous Community and to a lesser extent Nafarroa began to take on responsibilities for promoting language normalization.

The dynamism for language revival would henceforth be centered mainly in the Basque Autonomous Community, where a variety of governmental entities were created to develop language policy. Key among these was what was then called the Secretariat of Language Policy [Hizkuntz Politikarako Idazkaritza Nagusia, or HPIN] and is now renamed the Deputy Ministry of Language Policy [Hizkuntz Politikarako Sailburuordetza]. This entity was charged with putting into practice the mandate of the Language Normalization Law of 1982. As laid out in that law, governmental language policy was to be focused on three main arenas: education, public administration, and media. Various departments within the Basque government were created to begin the work of implementing the law by defining linguistic requirements for civil-service jobs, providing mechanisms for teaching Basque to public employees who did not know it, developing the curriculum for public schooling, developing different models for bilingual education, and creating the new, government-funded Basque-language television and radio network, EITB. Basque-language revival no longer belonged exclusively to civil society—it was now a government activity as well.[3]

What did this mean for the language-movement organizations already in place? It meant new economic resources: subsidies, largely from the Ministry of Culture. But with subsidies came new regulatory controls and clashes of power and ideology. Governmental policy makers and programs came into increasing conflict with the grassroots language organizations that operated outside its control. Tensions were most acute between the government and AEK, the adult language and literacy organization that had been the vanguard of the movement, and Euskal Herrian Euskaraz [Basque in the Basqueland], the Basque-advocacy organization notorious for the spray painting of Spanish traffic signs, billboards, and other tactics of linguistic guerilla warfare. The political appointees of government language-planning departments were controlled largely by the Basque Nationalist

Party, while the leadership of these nongovernmental groups included many more people sympathetic to the leftist wing of Basque nationalism.

The confrontation between popular language-revival organizations and the regional government was pervasive in Basque-nationalist political culture and had its roots in the split between moderate and radical nationalists at the time of ETA's formation. This ideological split became yet more solidified at the time of the formulation of the Statute of Autonomy. In 1979 many supporters of Basque nationalism had abstained from voting for the statute in protest against the limited form of political and territorial sovereignty it offered. Basque nationalism divided into two main camps: a majority that accepted the statute's limited level of autonomy and a minority, albeit a significant one, that wanted to work for the self-determination of the greater Euskal Herria. They rejected the statute and called for a new referendum. These differing stances are politically identified either with the center-right Christian Democratic Basque Nationalist Party (PNV), which held the presidency of the government of the Basque Autonomous Community from its inception until 2009; or with the *izquierda abertzale,* also sometimes referred to as the MLNV and identified with the political coalition party Herri Batasuna, created in 1979 and now, after several reincarnations, generally known as Batasuna.

In addition to their disagreements over the Statute of Autonomy, a second major point of contention between these two nationalist camps has been the public stance each takes on the issue of political violence. With the transition to a more democratic political system, the majority of Basque nationalists argued that armed struggle was no longer necessary. The PNV wing of Basque nationalism, as well as the more recent nationalist party Aralar, condemn the use of violence and have been emphatic in calling for an end to ETA. While Herri Batasuna and its successor parties on the nationalist left do not advocate violence, their stance toward it has been more complicated. They have argued that state police repression has continued in the Basque Country and that a true democratic transition has not yet happened. The stance of most official leadership in the *izquierda abertzale* has been that any condemnation of violence must also include public condemnation of the state's practice of torture or other forms of violence toward Basque political prisoners. Anything short of this, they say, is an unfair and one-sided condemnation of political violence. Thus, whenever anyone was killed by ETA, leaders in the MLNV would publicly say they lamented the deaths but would lay the blame for continuing violence at the feet of the existing political system that refused, in their view, to genuinely work for a peaceful solution. A shift in the stance of the radicals was announced in 2011, with the creation of a new political party called Sortu, which is the first self-identified party on the radical nationalist left to explicitly condemn all forms of violence, including ETA. For most of the last thirty years, however, this was a major bone of contention. Critics called the radicals' refusal to condemn ETA violence to be evidence of the group's links to the organization, and indeed, this argument led to the banning of Herri Batasuna in 2003. Their stance on political violence was held up as evidence that they, and all other sympathizers with the radical left, were in fact under the political control of ETA. A vicious cycle continues unabated on the question of public words and political violence. While there are other issues, such as class and economic ones, that distinguish the nationalist camps, their differing stances toward political violence came to overshadow virtually all other issues.

Throughout the eighties and nineties, the polarization between leftist or radical nationalists and center-right nationalists reverberated in the language movement at all levels, both regional and municipal, as it did in the rest of political culture and society as a whole (Abad et al. 1999). Language-revival groups or events were seen through the lens of this opposition and identified with either the PNV—that is, the regional government—or the radicals. During my fieldwork in the eighties, it was common to hear members of the radical left and nongovernmental language groups question the authenticity of the regional government's commitment to language revival. Grassroots language organizations, conversely, were accused of being controlled by the political forces of the *izquierda abertzale*. These mutual suspicions made it difficult for the two camps to work together on language-revival projects. The end result was that in the first two decades of autonomy, the language movement experienced a large growth in economic resources and institutional support, but it was also tensely divided into two camps that often criticized, mistrusted, and duplicated each others' efforts (see Mendiguren and Iñigo 2006).

Frustrated on many grounds, language advocates felt that a time for reassessment was at hand. In 1983 at a sociolinguistic conference in Bergara and at the annual Basque Summer University [Udal Euskal Unibersitatea, UEU]—a gathering place for language loyalists from all over the Basque Country—members of the grassroots organizations were assessing the goals of the language movement, their place in it, and new directions for their work in this new political context.[4] They were convinced that for language normalization to be successful, it needed to sustain a broad-based social movement; it needed both to continue popular involvement in language revival and to better coordinate the efforts of the various organizations working for it. Two nongovernmental organizations emerged that year with the goal of creating a new dynamic, albeit in very different ways: The Confederation of Basque Culture (EKB) and Arrasate Euskaldun Dezagun [Arrasate (We) Can be Euskaldun] (AED).

The purpose of EKB was to facilitate the sharing of information and technical skills among the many autonomous organizations throughout the seven provinces (i.e., in both France and Spain) working on behalf of Basque normalization. Among its member organizations were: the language-teaching organization AEK; Euskal Herrian Euskaraz; a number of the largest Basque-language publications, *Jakin* and *ARGIA* and later *Egunkaria*; the Basque Summer University; and a number of other smaller organizations. The EKB worked in favor of language normalization and occasionally waged highly visible media campaigns to encourage, for example, parents to enroll their children in Basque-immersion classes. In contrast to the more conventional protest tactics of street demonstrations and consciousness-raising used by Euskal Herrian Euskaraz, EKB focused more on applied research, lobbying, and consultancy in language planning. It served as a clearinghouse of information on the language movement, had an extensive archive of documents on Basque-language politics, and created BAT, which has become the main journal for sociolinguistic research in and on Basque.

The AED saw itself as a very different kind of organization than EKB. Its scope was decidedly local—to foster Basque language normalization in its own municipality. The town of Arrasate/Mondragon was exemplary of the way industrialization and labor migration had impacted formerly Basque-speaking towns of the interior. It had experienced a large and rapid influx of labor migrants from Spain and had become a town known for its working-class politics. But at the same time, this once predominantly Basque-speaking town saw the percentage of Basque speakers decline to less than half the population. These circumstances had prompted the formation of AED in 1983. By the time I was doing my interviews in the nineties, AED had become legendary in the grassroots movement for its unique and successful method of community-based language activism, pioneering in the production of local Basque media as well as Basque after-school programs of various kinds. I visited the town in 1993 and again in 1994 mainly to get to know its magazine—*Arrasate Press.* In an extended visit in the spring of 1994, I spoke to two of its key figures: a young woman who was the director of the magazine, and a young man I will call Joxean, who had been a member of AED since its foundation and was now managing the group's Basque after-school program. Competent and professional without being a technocrat, Joxean listed the statistics on declining numbers of speakers and then described to me the group's origins in ways that helped explain the ideological and practical reassessment that was taking place in the nongovernmental movement:

> We felt the situation was desperate and decided something had to be done. But at that time, eleven years ago [1983], language had become very politicized. We had to find a way to rise above our differences—politics, ideology, personality, above differences in sex, age, social class. Basque speakers needed to organize in order to expand [the use] of

Basque in Arrasate. AED was created with this integrationist stance. This is very important to underscore. Everyone should be able to fit under the common goal of language
revival. That is our only goal; we never give any kind of [political] opinions or ideological perspectives about anything that isn't related directly to Basque language recuperation or Basque culture. And this is very important—people come together around
language itself. Everybody was talking about language revival, but society was functioning in Castilian. We saw that there was a need for a new practice.

Joxean's comments point to his and other activists' sense of urgency about finding more effective strategies for promoting Basque-language use and dealing with
the problem of "politics" affecting language revival. In virtually every interview I
conducted, advocates described the social movement as having become paralyzed
by the climate of conflict and polarization in Basque nationalist politics. Sociologist Tejerina found this to be a common perception among Basque-language professionals he interviewed in the early nineties as well. As one of his interviewees
put it: "I think that for *Euskara* to be the language of *Euskal Herria,* it should be
totally separate from politics. It seems to me each party makes use of *Euskara*
in its own fashion, to attract people--that is what it's all about. So, I think that it
[politics] should be completely separate from *Euskara*; given the situation today, it
should be a separate issue, and have nothing to do with that" (1992: 253).

The situation Basque-language advocates were describing bears a resemblance
to that which Camille O'Reilly (1999) encountered in her study of Irish-language
revival in Northern Ireland during this same time period. She found that the climate of intense political polarization and the specter of political violence led many
pro-Irish language organizations to eschew any relationship to political parties,
"the troubles," or Sinn Fein. She traces how appeals using the images and rhetoric
of internal colonialism, once favored by language advocates of the sixties, were
increasingly abandoned in favor of a tamer advocacy discourse framed in terms of
"heritage" preservation.

O'Reilly suggests that political violence and economic interests motivated this
shift in the case of Northern Ireland. Most language-revival entities depend on
government subsidies that require groups to frame their aims in less contestatory
or political terms (O'Reilly 1999; see also McEwan-Fujita 2005). And while the
need to secure subsidies cannot be disregarded in the Basque situation, my interviews suggest that more than economic calculus was behind the shift in strategy.
Nongovernmental advocates were confronting inertia and looking for ways to
generate a participatory citizenry. By the early 1990s it was clear that EKB was
not going to be able to mobilize the broad-based movement it had envisioned. It
carried out important research and technical consultation on language normal-

ization, developing a diploma in language planning and in-service training for teachers, among other initiatives, but its original hope to inject a new dynamism in the popular movement by creating local EKB chapters had failed. Despite its valuable and broad ranging work, EKB had become too closely identified with the radical left and could not bring people together across political lines. It had not been able, for example, to get the Federation of Ikastolas—a major player of the language movement—to join EKB, a fact that EKB insiders attributed specifically to their perceived association with the *izquierda abertzale.* The time had come for new strategies, and AED was the model to which increasing numbers of activists would turn.

A Future for Our Past

May 1994: I was videotaping an interview with a sociolinguist working at the time at the sociological research institute SIADECO. I will call him Koldo. Koldo was comfortable in front of the camera, having had experience working in Basque-language television as a humorist and game-show host. I had gone to speak with him, however, not to talk about television, but about his opinion as a sociolinguist on the emergence of community-based language groups. He had recently written a report on the topic, and I wanted to follow up. "Two factors," Koldo explained, "helped to initiate the movement: AED and"—he held up a large five-hundred-page tome so I could get an image of it on my camera—"this book." The book he held up was *Un futuro para nuestro pasado* [A Future for Our Past] (1987), by José María Sánchez Carrión. For many language activists, Sánchez Carrión, who has come to be affectionately known by the nickname "Txepetx," was responsible for a turning point in their way of thinking about strategies of minority-language revival. *A Future for Our Past* was credited by many of my interviewees with providing an entirely new grounding for language activism and the theoretical underpinning to the strategy of community language groups.[5]

Written as his doctoral thesis, *A Future for Our Past* is a huge and eclectic tome about the nature of language and identity and language acquisition, as well as a blueprint for reversing Basque-language shift. It is also a call for researchers to use their work to better understand and help communities reverse language domination. Sánchez Carrión explains that he published the book because "I had the absolute conviction that a new discourse was needed to avoid the final collapse of such a valuable language as *Euskara.* The need for a new dynamic, a new approach that would, via the theory of linguistic spaces, permit escape from the monster of impotence, desperation, and annihilation that those in power and their intellectual agents proclaimed as inevitable for the great majority of our linguistic communities" (1987: 16).

At the heart of this text is the premise that language revitalization needs to be guided by a theory of how language acquisition happens. In his view, all language acquisition—first or second—depends on a combination of psychological/emotional, cognitive, and behavioral elements that fall into three main categories: motivation, knowledge, and use. In order to effectively reverse language shift, language advocates, he argues, must understand the role that each of these factors plays in language maintenance and how they have been affected by the history of language domination. A good part of the book is dedicated to explaining the ways in which motivation, usage/speech, and varying elements of linguistic competency (e.g., oral competency and literacy) interact. The message for language-revival advocates was that any strategy they develop must work on all three fronts if they wish to be successful.

A Future for Our Past provided them with a theory about the social life of language that challenged how language activists had been conceptualizing and approaching language revitalization. Language advocacy, closely tied to nationalism, had focused on explaining and contesting the marginalization of Basque in public life. The priorities and styles of language militancy of the past—demands for legal rights, modernization, schooling, institutional legitimation—were not negated by Txepetx; they just were not enough. Advocacy had to give priority not so much to making Basque into a national language, but to ensuring it was a *biziaren hizkuntza,* meaning literally "a language of life," a language for living. What sustains a language, he argued, was the use of that language in everyday life. Txepetx provided advocates with a theory that explained to them why that was so. His text did not tell advocates to forget about political rights, autonomy, or even the struggle for national independence, but it did not lead with those issues. Instead, it made a forceful case that to save the language, advocacy needed to attend to the creation and maintenance of a variety of spaces or domains of Basque-language use.

Txepetx argued that spaces where language is used in an unrestricted and natural way operate like magnets, drawing people to the language, or more precisely drawing people to the activities and the relationships forged in these spaces and in this language. His theory explicitly recognized the affective dimension of language learning and use where previous theories focused on the political dimension. The desire to participate in relationships generated in these spaces, he argued, are what give less-able speakers the motivation to learn more. Regular usage also helps to sustain the identification with the language among those who already know how to speak it. The classroom might be a necessary *starting* point for language acquisition, but an emotional attachment to the language and motivation for use comes about, he argued, when language learning takes place in the context of social activities or what he called "the grammar of a culture," not just the classroom. The vitality of Basque, he argued, depends on its having a diverse and sustainable range of natural "habitats."

Many language advocates I spoke with described the excitement Txepetx's theories elicited in the world of *euskalgintza,* the grassroots language-revival movement. Most had entered into language promotion out of a desire for social justice, and very few had any formal studies of sociolinguistics. Koldo explained it thus: "Here in *Euskal Herria,* we have a lot of people working hard on language revival . . . but we write very little. We do not have many theorists." Txepetx's book approached language in a completely different way than that of either philology or linguistics, which were the main ways of studying language in the Basque Country at the time. It drew on sociolinguistics, educational psychology, and the sociology of language to provide both a sociopolitical analysis of language dynamics and a theory about what drove language use and acquisition. At the same time, his text discussed language in ways that were undoubtedly familiar and meaningful to activists. In *A Future for Our Past,* languages are discussed as if they have a life of their own, living, dying, and competing for space. This way of thinking about language as discrete, bounded organisms, along with his negative view of language mixing as a sign of degradation, common to most Europeans, meshed well with the prevailing conceptions of language that Basque advocates already had.[6]

Part of what made this text resonate with language advocates was, then, the fact that it entered into an already prepared ideological field. Where the text seemed to break new ground was in suggesting new terrains of action and a new ethos for language revival. *A Future for Our Past* grounded language normalization in the values of ecological diversity and, overall, more positive, integrative, and life-affirming values that transcended confrontational nationalist politics. One language advocate, for example, told me that discussions of Txepetx's work seemed to allow greater room to talk introspectively about personal sentiments and experiences with language learning, in contrast to the focus on the political battle [*borroka*], that had dominated language advocacy.[7] Txepetx drew upon concepts from Native American spirituality, for example, to call for a more respectful attitude to language diversity as a valuable part of nature. As one leading figure in the language movement put it, Txepetx's text offered Basques "a framework that is valid for human language—for *all* languages and it also provides for us the ethical principles for relations between nations and languages of the world . . . based on equality, mutual respect, and a recognition of our common humanity, not uniformity."

In grounding minority-language revival in these kinds of values, we can see Txepetx's text as an early example of the now growing trend we find among international language-advocacy groups to link linguistic with biological diversity. The image of nature that it mobilized—discrete language communities inhabiting discrete habitats—resonates comfortably with commonsense ways of linking languages and territories. So while some of its framework was familiar, it nevertheless launched activists into new tactics of organizing. For language revival to succeed, Txepetx argued, it required unity among all its advocates as well as a strong sense of individual responsibility. Particularly novel was the idea that the agent of linguistic revival was not to be figured as a nationalist political party or as the *abertzale,* the Basque patriot, as it had been in Txillardegi's texts. Rather, the agent had to be what Txepetx called "the linguistic community" in all its political and ideological diversity. As one devotee of Txepetx's work explained, the message of his text was that Basque citizens had to learn how to work across their ideological differences. They had to transform their political culture. Language revival had to be a society-wide endeavor. It could not be delegated to institutions, experts, or the next generation. Nor could it be postponed until after independence. Txepetx's followers adopted the idea that the *euskaldun* community was best thought of not as a future utopia, but as something always in the making. This urgency was condensed in the slogan *orain eta hemen* [here and now] adopted by one of the largest of the Basque community language groups (Abad et al. 1999).

Txepetx's ideas were taken as a guide for the popular movement and disseminated through the members of a study group, Adorez eta Atseginez, based near Arrasate. Numerous workshops there and elsewhere were arranged to discuss his ideas and teach them to others. In particular, advocates looked for ways they might answer Txepetx's call for creating pluralistic spaces of Basque-language use that would draw together and motivate people to want to speak and learn from one another. The momentum generated around these ideas culminated in a conference, "The Universe of Basque" [Euskararen Unibersoa], held in March of 1997 and attended by four hundred people representing forty-nine different nongovernmental language-advocacy groups. It was an attempt to respond to Txepetx's call to consolidate the Basque-language community. Out of this moment of solidarity in popular language advocacy came two very concrete results: the dissolution of EKB and the formation of a new organization known as Kontseilua [The Council of Basque Social Organizations]. Another outcome was a refocusing of language advocacy at the local level.

Euskara Elkarteak, the Community Language Group

Sitting with me in 1998 in the town hall of Eibar, where he worked, was Fernando, the graying director of Topagunea, the association of Basque Community Language Groups formed in 1996. Like many language advocates of his generation, he had been exposed to leftist ideas in France, where he had studied and lived with other expatriate Basques for a part of his youth. Now, back in his home-town, in addition to leading Topaguneak, he also worked as a language planner in the Basque Service Department of Eibar's town hall. Like Koldo, Fernando saw *A Future for Our Past* as a key influence on the formation of community-based language groups. A turning point, he said, was a series of seminars on sociolinguistics held in Bergara with Txepetx.

> About eighty people attended these Saturday seminars, and from that point the theme of localism began to acquire greater importance. Until then all the movements in favor of Euskara were movements that had a national focus. The EKB is a good example. They would come from Donostia, the capital city of Gipuzkoa, with their plans, their reports and ideas, with the goal of having local groups adopt these. Our method is the opposite. We come from below so that with time we can build a national movement. The dynamic is exactly the inverse.

With AED as an example, community language associations began to appear in various localities, at first in Gipuzkoa and then spreading to Bizkaia, with fewer numbers in the rest of the Autonomous Community (Amonarriz and Arruti 1993). By 1993 there were over ten thousand dues-paying members in local language associations, one of the main activities of which was to enlist residents in producing local magazines in Basque.

"We are not alternative. We are not oppositional media," explained Malen, the energetic twenty-six-year-old woman who was director of *Arrasate Press,* one of the first of the local magazine projects to be created. A journalist and *bertsolari* [improvisational poet] in her spare time, Malen exuded enthusiasm for her work. I went to Arrasate to interview her in 1993 and again in 1994, trying to understand the explosion of what I called at the time "alternative media." But she was careful right away to distinguish AED's media project from the dissident free radios we will look at in the next chapter. *Arrasate Press,* she said, "wanted to be for the whole community. We do not want to be marginal; we want to be for everybody." *Arrasate Press* emerged out of AED and shared its commitment to ideological neutrality. As she toured me around to see their offices and the television station they had created, she spoke about their goals with the ease of someone used to doing many interviews. She was eager to explain how they were working to attract readers for the magazine. "Many *euskaldunak* find it difficult to read in Basque if they didn't go to an *ikastola.* They aren't used to it. . . . Until we opened last year, all the information people could read about their town was in Castilian. . . . The census showed us that approximately twelve thousand people in Arrasate were literate in Basque. We saw the possibility of providing better, more interesting local news for that group of readers. And we saw this as a very interesting way of promoting

Euskara. We didn't want to make a magazine *about* Basque, but a local magazine *in* Basque."

The philosophy and organizational structure created by *Arrasate Press* was a model for Usurbil and most of the thirty or so other community magazines that had emerged by the end of the decade. Chief among the strategies of the community language groups was to appeal to distinctly local audiences. Language advocates understood that the strength of local identity and solidarity of neighbors had been an important element in the success of the *ikastola* movement, and they sought to replicate this. A former participant in the Txepetx seminars described to me the shift in strategies that took place in his home town of Lasarte-Oria and how it led to the creation of a new group, Ttakun, along the lines of AED's model.

> We realized after having been working on this for eight or ten years that we needed to form a group that involved people of all ideological tendencies who had a concern or affinity with Basque; who felt that Basque must be recuperated now and by us. We had to work very consciously to create a center in Lasarte, what Txepetx calls in this theoretical language a symbolic space [for Basque]. And we realized that, given our history [with political conflict] this would not happen just automatically. We had to work very hard to create this ourselves.

He went on to describe the group's very self-conscious effort to assemble a diverse list of fifteen or twenty people "of different ages, different political loyalties, and in different professions . . . not just teachers," who had taken an interest in language revival in the past. He described how they began contacting individuals to talk about the possibility of forming a language group. The *ikastola* movement, he said, had been a model for them: "You couldn't start explaining the sociolinguistic theories of Txepetx, so we had to find something more accessible and familiar. The clearest reference was the *ikastola* movement; they had gained credibility in the community and an identity as locally run and politically neutral. This was the kind of movement we were trying to build, except that our domain of action was not education but other social spaces of language use."

Critical to their success, said this young activist, was their emphasis on personal contact. "We contacted people directly; one of us would sit down and talk with the person individually, explaining our goals and that we thought their participation was important." He stressed for me just how different this approach was. "In the sociopolitical context that we live in, this is not normally done. People stick to their own groups. We don't interact across them." It is easier, he said, to integrate people of different sensibilities at the local level precisely because you come to them as the grandson of their neighbor, the friend of their cousin, a parent whose kids are in the same soccer club.

Careful thought was given to such features as the name of the group, the potential connotations that the locations of meetings might have, as well as other spatial and visual signifiers of their identity. One of the founders of the Lasarte group explained that they chose the name Ttakun because it is the word they use to describe the sound of the *txalaparta,* a traditional wooden percussive instrument used to call people to the cider houses when the cider is ready. "This fit," he told me, "with the way we wanted people to think of the group: as a place for bringing people together." In a similar vein, Fernando recounted that the community group of Ermua chose to have its first meeting in the town square: "We met in the town square, not in the periphery, but in the center. It is important to occupy the center because until now most groups working on Basque normalization were situated in the margins of society. . . . We took a photograph of the group in front of the town hall . . . there were business people, priests, technicians, politicians, youth, rockers. . . . People came away with the impression that this was something else; it had a different dynamic. This had a big impact."

Representational strategies now, as in the past, have been an integral part of language advocacy in their endeavors to reframe how they and the general public conceptualized Basque and the movement to recover it. Advocates stopped describing language revival as a radical or oppositional movement and developed a semiotics that conjured images of plurality and communal effort. In this endeavor, they turned away from the language of confrontation, *borroka,* to creatively appropriate elements of Basque culture that evoked traditional models of communal work and solidarity.

Rather than present themselves in the familiar rhetorical strategies of nationalism, community language groups conceptually aligned themselves with the popular (*herrikoia*) traditions like *auzolan* [neighborhood work] and associational culture—gastronomic societies, mountaineering clubs, cooperatives—familiar and distinctive institutions of Basque social and political life (Pérez-Agote 1984).[8] The activities of community language groups were no longer primarily the consciousness-raising discussion groups of the past. They were focused on fostering socializing and community building. Their activities ranged from excursions for youth, after-school programs, and cooking classes to producing a weekly magazine, achieved through residents' dedicating countless hours of unpaid time. Interesting were the ways groups sought to engage their neighbors in this kind of cultural activism. Groups appealed not so much to a sense of nationhood or patriotic duty as to communal traditions rooted in Basque rural culture. In the posters that the group of Lasarte-Oria, Ttakun, put up to call for help in renovating a building for Basque cultural activities, we find residents enjoined to participate in *auzolan,* a practice of mutual aid by which neighboring farmsteads worked together to repair roads or harvest hayfields.

The *hitzarmenak* [*ak,* plural] is another interesting example of how language-advocacy groups repurposed cultural elements linked to Basque rural life. The term is one that historically referred to the verbal or written agreements among neighboring farmers on such things as where a boundary lay or how a piece of land would be used. Advocates working in and around AED that were studying Txepetx's work came up with the idea of putting this concept to work for language revival. As they understood Txepetx's message, the goal of a community language group was to integrate residents in the process of normalization. They saw the *hitzarmen* [pledge; *hitzarmenak* (pl) pledges] as a way to do this. Community language groups enrolled local groups, businesses, and individuals into language revival by asking them to sign a pledge, a *hitzarmen,* to become a dues-paying member of the *euskara elkartea.* Where possible, the community group also sought to obtain pledges from groups and businesses to take concrete steps to increase the usage of Basque in ways that made sense for their organization. This could be anything from pledging to put up signs in Basque or translate a menu to promising to carry out correspondence with local groups in Basque.

At a conference sponsored by AED discussing the new strategies of the Basque Community Language Groups, Juan Arexola-Leiba explained the logic behind the pledging strategy. The *hitzarmen,* he states, operates on very different premises from those of typical top-down language planning. A pledge is not imposed from above, he explains. Well before a pledge is ever declared, a great deal of preparatory work is done talking with associations, assessing their language abilities, and getting people within the association to become more self-conscious about their language habits. Furthermore, a pledge should not be seen as an isolated act; to be effective, these accords must be part of a broader social dynamic actively pursuing Basque normalization in the community. "The pledge is not the objective in and of itself—it is an instrument. Knowing how hard it is to change the practices, habits, inertia, of individuals and organizations, this is a means of slowly but surely trying to take steps toward changing that reality. . . . A pledge is and must be a living thing and the various organizations themselves must play the leadership role in fulfilling it" (1993: 46).

This bottom-up participatory method operationalizes an important principle in Txepetx's theory of language revitalization, namely that being successful requires a community-wide participation and sense of responsibility. It is interesting to consider this particular term, *hitzarmen,* in light of some of the premises of Basque-language ideology regarding notions of truth, personhood, and practice [*ekintza*]. We saw that Txillardegi's arguments for patriots to speak Basque drew moral force from the powerful cultural linkage between acts and words. The *hitzarmen* is another instance of the rhetorics and practice of language revival drawing on the language ideology of *euskaldun* expressive culture. The semantics of the concept of *hitza* [speech], writes Zulaika, link a person's utterances directly to his or her personal integrity (1988: 228–30). Parsimony is highly valued and words are not to be spoken lightly. One's words ideally should be few and should convey only what a speaker knows to be true through direct witnessing or personal experience. The same values are present in *bertsolaritza,* a traditional form of improvised oral poetry (ibid). These aesthetic and moral values invest the practice of verbal agreements with intensified moral force and make the *hitzarmen* an interesting and seemingly not arbitrary choice for framing commitments to language revival.

As with *auzolan,* the *hitzarmen* exemplifies the creative refunctionalization of elements of Basque-language ideology and culture. As a method, they serve to engage members of the community in the practice of language normalization, an important aim of the grassroots movement. But I want to suggest that they also recast language-revival activities as means of participating in *euskaldun* cultural values and ethics. These kinds of framings dissociate the communal work of language normalization—which must be a collective endeavor if it is to be successful—from the realm of party politics and conceptually link it to practices that are seen as distinctively and authentically [*jatorra*] *euskaldun* forms of sociality and culture (e.g., gastronomic clubs, *auzolan, hitzarmenak,* and *bertzolaritza*). These serve as what Clifford Geertz (1973) would call both "models of" and "models for" the practice of language normalization. In short, in this new moment of language advocacy, we find Basque cultural practices being creatively mined as templates for the practice of language revival, "indigenizing" it, anchoring it in Basque cultural values, so that working to save Basque is in a sense a way of being Basque. For ethnic and nonethnic Basques, participation in language-revival activities becomes a means for learning about and participating in Basque cultural practices and values.

A Future for Our Past was an inspiration for much of the nongovernmental language advocates of the southern Basque provinces in the 1990s, introducing a new orientation and terminology and inspiring a focus on community-based work. At the same time, however, other forms of expertise—strategic planning and total quality management—borrowed from the corporate world were making their way into language-revival discourse. Other interviews and observations illustrate what it was that made these management techniques appealing at this particular historical moment. If the goals of depoliticization and community engagement led some advocates to link language revival with traditional cultural practices, other efforts were creatively appropriating the language and logics of the marketplace and entrepreneurialism. The concept of the pledge, or *hitzarmen,* interestingly operates as a kind of semiotic bridge between these two approaches; an understanding emerges of language revival as a means of being both authentically Basque and innovative.

Total Quality Language Revival

A series of workshops I attended in 1998 provided me with the first signs of the coming together of entrepreneurialist methods and language revival. Funded by a grant from the provincial government, the workshops were organized by *Topagunea* for teaching marketing strategy to the many community language groups that were publishing local magazines. For three weekends I traveled to Eibar with the young woman serving as director of Usurbil's community magazine, *Noaua!* to listen to an experienced business consultant teach methods of competitive-strength assessment [SWOT analysis] to a room full of volunteer language advocates. The instructor talked to us about the importance of setting target objectives. If you want to have a long-lasting magazine, he said, think of your readers not as your political allies or even as fellow Basques, but as customers. Identify your market, he said, and try to provide those customers with a unique product. He walked us through the steps of SWOT analysis, identifying organizational strengths, weaknesses, opportunities, and threats.[9] Make an annual strategic plan, he advised. Concretize your goals and identify the factors that directly determine your ability to meet them.

As we stood in a bar having a coffee during one of the workshop breaks, my companion and I talked about the training. "Our forms are changing," she commented wryly. The workshops were aimed at helping volunteers be more effective producers of local media and agents of language normalization by teaching them the methods of quality management, self-assessment, and strategic planning. They were quite deliberate, and they had received a grant from the provincial government to do this, arguing that this would allow them to produce a higher quality product.[10] I was more than a little surprised at the linking up of what struck me on the surface as antithetical worlds: corporate management and minority-language promotion. Basque revival had for so long been ideologically tied to oppositional and decidedly nonprofit-oriented values. So when I had the opportunity to interview Fernando, Topagunea's director, I asked him how it was that capitalist business-management strategies fit into the populist project of Basque-language community media. For him the explanation was simple: securing economic indpendence.

If we hope to become self-financing, our only, or almost only, avenue is going to have to be advertising.[11] When you begin a magazine there is a sentimental factor. That factor plays a role when you go to a store and they say, sure, we will put an ad in the magazine. But after about eight months or so, that sentimental factor diminishes and you now have to be more professional; you have to enter the parameters of the market. You have to change your discourse. You have to have quality; you have to show you can sell, that you are useful. Because the market only understands profit and money. So the sentimental factor always exists, but the role it plays declines . . . you have to specialize. . . . that's where the workshops on marketing, internet, graphic design and layout . . . and so on. . . . What we have seen very clearly is that you cannot survive only on militancy and determination. This requires professionalism and constant dedication.

The perceived need for professionalism and less "politics" that Fernando described was manifest in the changing aesthetics and modes of language advocacy. Groups were making less use of street demonstrations, graffiti, stickers, and boycotts as ways of demanding Basque-language rights. Disappearing too were the unstructured participatory styles of meetings that had been a distinguishing feature of so many oppositional grassroots organizations of Basque civil society. In their place, leaders of language advocacy were displaying a greater penchant for mission statements, annual reports, organizational charts, and reliable measures of progress. We see from his statement that Fernando was not rejecting Basque nationalism nor abandoning a political perspective on language politics. What he was saying was that nationalist arguments were not going to be enough to gain and keep Basque magazines readers or advertisers. He presented a pragmatic argument that sees the logics of the marketplace as the inexorable context in which the preservation of language, identity, and heritage must operate. Like the early-twentieth-century intellectuals of Eusko Ikaskuntza, Fernando thought that patriotism was not enough to preserve Basque.

In the Basque Autonomous Community the emergence, or we might say more accurately, the *strategic appropriation* of the distinctive concepts and methods of entrepreneurialism by nongovernmental language advocates was manifest in multiple places and initiatives. The marketing workshops I attended were one sign of this at the level of community language groups. Another was the formation in 1997 of the new nongovernmental organization Kontseilua.

Emerging out of the excitement surrounding Txepetx's work and the perceived collapse of previous strategies, Konsteilua signaled a new moment in which the premises for language revival contained in *A Future for Our Past* were combined with a zeal for professionalism and efficacy that was receptive to the ethos of total quality management. The organization's stated aim was to act as a lobbying force for a more extensive and holistic language-planning effort that could take revival past the limited realms of the 1982 Law of Normalization. Like the community language groups, Kontseilua's founders thought carefully about their media image, selecting a leadership that would be recognized as politically neutral. Willing to collaborate with the Basque government on projects, they were nevertheless committed to sustaining broader civic participation in language revival. Autonomous nongovernmental organizations were seen as vital sources of critique and innovation with regard to language normalization. Kontseilua's first initiative was the "Bai Euskarari!" ["Yes to Basque!"] campaign. "Yes to Basque!" was the name of the Basque Language Academy's first historic language-revival campaign of 1979, created in the early moments of democratization, and Kontseilua saw the twentieth anniversary as a good moment to renew the enthusiasm that Basque revival had enjoyed during the transition. Kontseilua's founders planned to do this by getting a wide array of civic groups and private businesses to make pledges to take part in the project of language normalization. But they did not stop there. In keeping with the penchant of new management methods to bestow diplomas and certificates, Kontseilua created the Bai Euskarai Ziurtegiria, a certificate that organizations earned for various levels of accomplishment in advancing Basque-language normalization.

Konsteilua made techniques of strategic planning a part of its own internal operations and encouraged its member organizations to follow suit. Konsteilua's founders were interested in what they could borrow from the latest management methods to increase the success of language-normalization efforts and to increase the efficacy of their own workings as a coordinating and lobbying organization. This new generation of language advocates believe in showing that language-revival projects are serious, expertise-based efforts, reliant on well-conceived plans, and able to deliver results. It was from within the ranks of one of the member organizations, the sociolinguistic research group Soziolinguistika Klusterra, that the early experiments with using specifically TQM (Total Quality Management) in the design of language-normalization plans emerged.

Several years after the marketing workshops I attended in Eibar, I was able to meet and talk with Inazio (Iñaki) Marko, the person who had pioneered the incorporation of TQM methods into language planning. He had been the director of EKB for eight years and was now teaching at the university and a member of the Basque sociolinguistic research institute, Soziolinguistika Klusterra. Like most Basque advocates, he had a busy agenda balancing full-time teaching, research, and advocacy work. I met him at the university; he grabbed a couple of folders, cleared his running shoes off the passenger seat of his Renault van, and we drove off to have lunch and talk about what had led him to TQM.

He began by stressing to me the importance of sustaining a popular social movement if language revival was to be truly successful. Government cannot do it all, he said, nor can it reach all arenas of social life. Hence the social movement was vital. But, he said, the language movement currently had several weaknesses. Similar to Koldo, Marko explained that Basque citizens had demonstrated an incredible willingness to work on behalf of language revival and to *do* things, but their projects lacked a clear strategy and were unsystematic. As he put it, "we are strong on desire, but poor on techniques." The most serious deficiency they faced, he said, was the lack of any valid method for documenting and evaluating the efficacy of language-promotion projects.

Searching for solutions, Marko came upon the idea to look into TQM when he was working on a language-planning job in 1999. The Basque nationalist labor union, LAB, had signed a *hitzarmen* in the Bai Euskarari! campaign and wanted him to design a plan for implementing their commitment to use more Basque in their operations. Over the course of the 1990s, designing Basque-language plans for the workplace had become an important activity. Basque had been gaining a notable public presence in schooling and public administration and in Basque public radio and television. But outside those venues, Spanish continued to be overwhelmingly the language of work. Language advocates in and outside the government had started to publish position papers identifying the workplace as an emerging and urgent priority. In 1999 the Basque government came out with a new "General Plan for the Promotion of the Use of Basque," which specifically identified language policy for private enterprise as a priority. Private consultancies—EMUN, ELHUYAR, and ARTEZ—emerged to offer their services for designing language plans, and various pilot projects were launched in companies wanting to engage in language normalization.[12]

Meanwhile the Basque economy and world of business was also dramatically changing. Economic restructuring of the historically important shipping and ironworks sectors had led to massive job loss and economic stagnation in the seventies and eighties. Unemployment reached record high levels in the mid-eighties. Through reducing labor costs, increasing productivity, and technological modernization, Basque economic indicators started to show improvement, and Basque products began to compete well in the rest of Europe. Also notable was the growth of the service sector—banking, insurance, tourism, and advanced services to businesses. By the mid-1990s, the Basque economy once again began to outperform the rest of Spain, such that by 1998, its economic growth exceeded that of Spain by 3.8 percent and Europe by 2.8 percent (see Uranga 2003: 211).

Basque private industry, its world-famous industrial cooperatives, as well as its government shared a common interest in improving productivity and gaining ground within an international marketplace. They showed themselves to be very receptive to the innovations in management taking place in Europe, the United States, and Japan. After the formation of the European Foundation for Quality Management (EFQM) in 1988, Basque industries, for example, soon began winning the most prizes in Spain for excellence in the practical application of "Quality Methods." In 1992 the Basque Autonomous Government created its own equivalent organization, Euskalit, the Basque Foundation for the Advancement of Quality, to further consolidate, as its Web page (www.euskalit.com) announced, the reputation of the Basque Autonomous Community as a leader in "excellent and globally-minded" enterprises.

At the time Marko began to work on language planning for the labor union, interest in entrepreneurial and managerial innovation was at its peak. His genius was to link the two, bringing language planning to the workplace with the highly prized and well-regarded methods of quality management.[13] In the latter, he recognized tools that could help them go well beyond previous efforts, which had focused on providing translation and offering free classes to workers. Here were new means to bring Basque revival into the world of work and to bring the world of work into Basque revival. He was ahead of the curve, but soon other language advocates would join with him in arguing that the same kind of commitment to "research, development, and renovation" seen in the world of business should be applied to language normalization (see *ARGIA*, February 25, 2007, pp. 52–53). In our interview, Marko identified several factors that made TQM, in particular, attractive. First was the legitimacy it enjoyed in the private and public sectors. The TQM concepts of teamwork and leadership and its mechanisms of assessment and continuous improvement were, he said, already familiar and associated with "excellence" in the progressive globally competitive workplace. If the process of language normalization could be organized in a way that was consistent with already existing ways of working that made sense, appeared rational, and were technically sound, so much the better.

But TQM was not simply a means of garnering acceptance for language revival. Its principles of organizing work, in his view, could help resolve some of the perennial problems that plagued Basque-language normalization projects. In our conversation he stressed two problems: passivity when it came to changing language habits and an inability to measure substantive progress. Basque-language preservation has widespread popular support, he explained. No one is against Basque revival, at least not overtly. But in practice, it is tough to bring about, even when people ideologically support it. Resistances arise. We have learned, he said, that changing the entrenched habits of language use in an organization—the taken-for-granted patterns of interacting, verbal and written repertoires, documents, forms—requires a collective and self-conscious effort. Language shift is not something that can be delegated to a single person, a language "officer," or even a committee. In line with Txepetx's theories, Marko argued that normalization could not be successful if imposed from above. Everyone must be personally implicated in achieving the goals; everyone must be a stakeholder in a language-normalization process for it to work. Many language advocates I spoke with concurred with him on the danger of "delegating" language revival to a single office. They also complained about what they saw as tokenistic use of Basque, masquerading as real language normalization. We need methods, Marko insisted, that can help us to get better results. In his estimation, TQM offered solutions to some of these problems.

Emerging in the eighties as a managerial philosophy that sought to increase an organization's competitiveness, TQM is based on the premise that laborers produce more and better quality when they are "empowered" to take responsibility for the quality of their work, their productivity, and even their career trajectory (Inoue n.d.). Workers are assisted in this by a trademark system of competitive goal setting, teamwork, awards, and an elaborated program of periodic assessment. A a prime example of what theorists call neoliberal or "advanced liberal" styles of governance, TQM, as a method, mobilizes both technologies of *agency* oriented to enhancing worker participation and sense of responsibility in meeting performance goals and technologies of *performance* that aim at making results visible and measurable via standardized quantitative indicators (Dean 1999: 164–71). Distinctive of TQM is the way it blurs the hierarchical division between managers and workers. In TQM standards for performance are not to be externally imposed by bosses. Rather, in a TQM workplace, workers are participants in goal setting and self-evaluation so that, the reasoning goes, they come to have an investment in the outcome of their productivity. In TQM the worker is not described as a separate class to be disciplined, but rather hailed as a responsible, self-monitoring team player whose interests are fused with those of management and whose sense of satisfaction comes from a job well done. A second important premise of TQM is the commitment to continuous improvement. Toward this end, TQM develops highly elaborated and systematic mechanisms of feedback and assessment with which to measure the degree to which target goals are being met (Swift, Ross, and Omachonu 1998).

Leaning over the table where we were talking, Iñaki described in the following way the evolution of his thinking. What if we could persuade companies to approach language normalization in their workplace with the same methods of structured planning and assessment they use in other areas of their operations? What if they could come to see language as one of the many elements that make up the work-flow process subject to monitoring and continuous improvement?

We could then treat the project of deliberate language shift from Spanish to Basque not as a form of politics, but *as a labor process,* that is, as a form of productivity like any other, that could be managed via the same kind of principles of teamwork, leadership circles, and assessment regimes now being used for the production of widgets or customer service. And what if we also applied these same methods to ourselves as advocates of language revival, treating the work of language-advocacy organizations as *labor* to be systematically measured and continuously improved? I listened and was intrigued at the reconceptualization of language revival as work. Later, in his office, he showed me some of the organizational flow charts and calendars of assessment he had developed for the implementation of these ideas. Here were techniques that he believed could bring seriousness and systematicity to language revival and help to overcome the frustrating gap between widespread professed support for Basque revival and a reality of habitual and hegemonic Spanish-language use.

Since my conversation with Marko in 2006, Total Quality language planning has gone well beyond the hypothetical and experimental phase to become a powerfully new discourse in both governmental and nongovernmental language-normalization efforts. The terminology and managerial methods of TQM in language planning received official sanction with the launch later that same year of LanHitz, a governmental program to promote language normalization in the private sector. This was followed in 2007 by the signing of a new partnership between the Basque Autonomous Government's Deputy Ministry of Language Policy and Euskalit, the Basque foundation to promote Total Quality practices. Mirroring in many respects Kontseilua's Bai Euskarari campaign, the LanHitz project also drew upon pledges and certificates of achievement in their project. LanHitz created its own Certificate of Quality in Language Management, called Bikain, to be awarded to organizations for their achievements in language planning. And while LanHitz did not use the term *hitzarmen,* it also used the method of pledging. In both the governmental and nongovernmental projects, the strategy is not to impose language plans, but to have groups or businesses take on the management of their language practices with the assistance of consultants and, in the case of LanHitz, with subsidies as well. In asking companies to make a commitment to language normalization, the method of pledges does double duty. It fits well with the importance placed on giving one's word in Basque-language ideology, and it is consistent with neoliberal management strategies that seek to engage workers in their own management.

At the December 2007 press conference announcing the creation of the Bikain certificate, the Basque Minister of Culture at the time, Miren Azkarate, presented the certificate as an example of the refashioning of language revival that was underway. The following excerpt from her statement is interesting in the way it focuses not only on the public image of Basque, as we might expect, but also on language planning. It reveals a conviction that language revival can and should be invested with the normalcy, seriousness, and unquestioned desirability of wealth production in a progressive, future-oriented society.

> . . . within fifteen years the majority of the children who will be leading our society and our businesses will be bilingual. We have to show these young people, these future adults, that Basque is a useful language for all spheres of life. And not only on the basis of rights, identity or sentiments, but also on the basis of productivity and competitiveness. Basque, Spanish, bilingualism and multilingualism, in addition to being instruments for social cohesion, are also intimately linked to the creation of wealth and added value for money. Language management is increasingly a strategic element of management for businesses of the 21st century.[14]

Consequently, she goes on to say, the measuring and monitoring of language in the workplace should be seen to be as normal and legitimate as the monitoring of "any other economic activity." The Basque Nationalist Party, which had appointed Azkarate, has historically had close relations with the Basque business elite. It was successful in gaining endorsements for LanHitz from some of the most powerful sectors of private industry, including CONFEBASK, the Confederation of Basque Businesses; the Association of Entrepreneurs of both Gipuzkoa and Bizkaia; as well as the Confederation of Cooperatives of Euskadi. Through the rhetorical framework of this project, Basque language, culture, and identity were joined together with values of the contemporary marketplace: competitiveness, innovation, branding. The presentation of the LanHitz project to the public explained what companies had to gain through their participation. Businesses that incorporate Basque into their practice are promised various kinds of rewards; they are told that their actions will demonstrate their capacity for innovation and their commitment to progressive entrepreneurialism and will help them to be more integrated into Basque society. The incorporation of Basque is said to have the potential to bring greater "value added" to a company, serving its needs for "branding" and helping to project a more socially conscious and unique identity in the marketplace.[15]

The emergence of what I am calling as a short-hand "Total Quality" language planning in both independent and governmental sectors of the Basque Autonomous Community can be seen to exemplify the spread of the practices, norms, and values of the marketplace—such as responsibility, initiative, competitiveness, awards—to an ever-wider array of social spheres. Scholars have noted this as one of the distinctive features of neoliberal or advanced liberal forms of governance (Rose 1999). This reconfiguration of language normalization from an issue of social justice to one of "value added" bears a strong resemblance to the commodi-fication of ethnicity in the burgeoning heritage industry and can be seen as part of the widespread and profound metamorphosis taking place today in the way culture is conceptualized under neoliberalism (see Comaroff and Comaroff 2009). Alternately characterized as the spread of "enterprise culture" or the "new manage-rialism," this process has been received with mixed results to say the least. Marko was aware of this. TQM has received high praise as the most important innova-tion for improving productivity since the invention of scientific management by Fredrick Taylor. At the same time, its neo-Taylorian practices have been heavily criticized as an invidious form of worker exploitation, initiating speedup, eroding trust and collegiality, and masking inequalities within the language of "empower-ment" (Shore and Wright 2000; Inoue n.d.). What does looking at TQM from the perspective of this movement for linguistic equality have to add to this debate? And conversely, what are the implications of TQM for how language revival and language itself are conceptualized?

As with statistics, the appropriation of TQM exemplifies what Foucault called the tactical polyvalence of discourses (1980a: 100–102). Case studies like this help us to see differences in the ways that governmentality and managerialism unfold in various contexts. The Basque case is a lesson to us about the importance of investigating the circumstances that give rise to these practices as well as the var-ied motivations, and even meanings, that managerial methods can have for actors. Studies of governmentality, as it plays out in particular places, have not given us a very actor-centered view of this process. We have seen, for example, that non-governmental language advocates gave these practices their own "symbolic spin," aligning teamwork, for example, with *euskaldun* traditions of social solidarity and mutual aid. We also see that the emergence of Total Quality language planning is not best described as either the imposition or simply a "migration" of an expertise from one arena to another in either a passive or a conspiratorial sense. In con-trast to the forced imposition of neoliberal forms of governmentality over the poor (Maskovsky 2001), these shifts to managerial methods originated among nongov-ernmental advocates aligned with progressive, quasi-leftist sectors that were pow-erfully shaped, to be sure, by specific historical circumstances they did not entirely control. As we have seen, the contingent alliance of neoliberal modes of manage-ment with Basque-language revival occured out of a conviction that the world of entrepreneurial management had very specific tools of teamwork, standardized measurement, and legitimacy that could serve the project of minority-language revival caught in a certain degree of paralysis about how to move forward. This is something we should not discount, given the growing criticism of language nor-malization that was being voiced at the time by conservative Spanish intellectuals who were continually associating normalization with nationalist extremism (Neff van Aerstaeler 2006). Rather than a co-optation of activists unwittingly falling into the grip of neoliberal ideologies, the move toward Total Quality language revival is a deliberate appropriation of a set of highly valued techniques in response to specific practical and political exigencies. Neither exploitative nor progressive in any simple or straightforward way, it is better thought of as a creative—though not uncomplicated—response to particular challenges minority-language revival was facing at the time in Spain.

Might these methods, with their emphasis on continuous improvement and continuous monitoring, create an increased sense of pressure on workers to be accountable for how they speak as well as how they work? No doubt they could. But the studies published so far do not point in this direction, probably because language plans in the Basque Country have come about voluntarily in predominantly Basque-speaking zones at the initiative of workers who want to participate in language revival (Consejo Asesor 2005). It is also possible that their efficacy and seriousness could bring a sense of accomplishment and satisfaction to people who have wanted to be able to use Basque at work and yet seen declaration after declaration of support for Basque flounder and evaporate in practice. As Cris Shore and Susan Wright have argued with respect to audit technologies, "although their name and form seem to be everywhere the same, each time these technologies enter a new context, their impact varies, often in unpredictable ways" (2000: 58). The expansion of managerialism, like neoliberalism more broadly, is an uneven process that is not always experienced or practiced in identical ways.[16]

While I am suggesting that managerial techniques in language planning are neither inherently beneficial nor repressive, they are not neutral or without consequence. The Basque case shows us that they engender effects at multiple levels, bringing into being new practices, modes of expertise, priorities, and modes of subjectification. New institutions like Euskalit, new subsidies, resources, and rewards like Certificates of Quality, now inhabit the social field along with new planning consultancies. Shore and Wright have argued that managerialism contributes to the creation of new kinds of subjectivity (ibid.: 57). Engagement with the practices and discourse of TQM deliberately introduces shifts in subjectivity both for speakers in general and for language-revival advocates. The targets of language plans, for example, are encouraged to be self-aware and self-managing about their language use. At the same time, as we saw in the seminars in SWOT analysis, volunteers in community magazines were being coached to think of the Basque reading public they were trying to create not only or primarily as a nation, but as a market, a set of consumers. Advocates were implicitly asked to think of themselves as entrepreneurs and the community language group as a quasi enterprise. The struggle for social change and justice blends into the competitive struggle for a market share.

Approaches to language normalization like TQM, I am suggesting, shift the way speakers are asked to think about their language habits, what language is, or what the movement for revival is about. What, in the long run, might this mean for how struggles around minority languages are conceptualized and resolved, not just in the Basque case, but in other minority-language movements where managerial discourses are on the rise? Here we find no consensus but some cause for concern and greater analytical attention. G. Williams and D. Morris (2000) express some concern. Their close study of The Welsh Language Board describes an increasingly neoliberal approach to language planning, in which the objectives of strategic planning, strength and weakness analysis, and measurement seem to effectively sideline the general framework of democracy and rights within which the state had until then conceptualized protection for minority-language speakers. "In common with other forms of planning it is far more likely to be seen in terms of the strategic planning of the business enterprise, with a focus upon forward planning, prioritizing, evaluating strengths, weaknesses, opportunities and threats. It will involve seeking to replicate in other locations the success obtained in one location" (ibid.: 180). In her study of Scottish Gaelic language policies, Emily McEwan Fujita (2005) adds that the maze of record keeping and formulas for remits instituted by neoliberal-policy approaches present obstacles, not avenues, that ironically work against the use of Gaelic for speakers unaccustomed to such bureaucratic language. Nevertheless, other scholars are more optimistic. In his assessment of the European Charter for Minority or Regional Languages, longtime policy consultant François Grin (2003; Grin, Jensdóttir, and Riagáin 2003) praises the charter precisely because it does not argue for language promotion in terms of "rights" but rather opts for a "diversity management" approach. A less conflictual scenario is created, he argues, when language diversity, like health care or immigration, is approached as a field to be managed. Grin sees this as a positive step for minority-language preservation, and his perspective appears to be the dominant one for language planning in the European Union today.

The Management of Language

A more technical managerial discourse appealed to constituencies eager to depoliticize language revival and to "normalize" not just the use of Basque, but also language preservation and planning as a legitimate and valuable activity. The alignment of Basque revival with the discursive logics of wealth production and efficient and competitive management is a powerful, some might say ingenious, retort for a language movement that, while making great strides, has nevertheless been beset by recurring accusations of being impractical, too costly, and motivated by political radicalism.[17]

Two remaining questions are particularly relevant for the political future of language advocacy. How is the struggle for language rights reconfigured in this new framework? And what happens to language? Scholars have noted that governmentalizing discourses depoliticize social problems by turning them into problems of technical management. In the Basque and other cases, advocates thought this could help resolve some immediate problems, given the tense political climate. These methods can also potentially make language planning more accountable and possibly more effective. But what possible dangers does this approach entail? Political theorist Wendy Brown's analysis of discourses of cultural "tolerance" is a good starting point, as it raises some issues that are pertinent to the appropriation of TQM discourse. In *Regulating Aversion* (2006), she exposes the ways in which state policies advocating tolerance for cultural diversity work via a process of depoliticization. In other words, the conflicts, inequalities, and marginalization that arise around cultural difference are treated as problems arising fundamentally from individual or group prejudice. Differences, she says, whether they be ethnic, religious, sexual (we might add linguistic), are seen as natural sites of conflict that can only be attenuated by the practice of tolerance (ibid.: 15). Such a framework, argues Brown, makes conflict around cultural differences appear inevitable. In so doing, it effectively retreats from the kind of substantive political analysis we need to do of the histories of structural power inequalities that underlie these differences. It is but a short step to go from the idea that differences must be tolerated to the idea that differences must be managed. The predilection for managerial "solutions" is indicative, argues Brown, of a worrisome trend toward rejecting politics as a domain where conflict can be productively addressed and where citizens can be transformed by their participation. Extrapolating from her argument, we can say that Brown's retort to the praise Grin gives to management approaches to linguistic diversity would be to warn us of the dangers that come with sidestepping conflict. Managers' concerns with defining best practices and standardized performance indicators must not be allowed to bury the thorny but urgent discussion that democracies must have about linguistic diversity and citizenship.

In raising this issue, my intent is not to argue against the use of any of these strategies in the Basque-language movement. They emerged out of some very well-founded anxieties and political pressures. At the same time, Brown's argument suggests that innovation in the methods and marketing of language normalization is insufficient. To move forward, there must be continue to be a robust public debate about inequality and the values on which citizens want to construct their linguistic future. It is my sense that almost all the language advocates I interviewed would heartily agree.

In addition to depoliticization, it also seems valuable to consider the epistemological effects of the shift in discursive tactics of the language movement. What kind of understanding of language comes with the managerial methods? We have seen that TQM-inspired language planning continues the process of bringing language practices into an ever more precise and standardized grid of visibility and regime of calculus initiated by statistics. Language tends increasingly to be thingified on grids of assessment that work on the basis of countable units. But what falls off the radar of quantifying techniques? What difficult-to-quantify ways of using Basque become undervalued or dismissed entirely? There seems to be an inexorable tendency in language-planning schemas to reduce linguistic practice to language choice—"Basque," "Spanish," "English," "French"—and to quantify those choices with a resulting highly impoverished understanding of syncretic or translanguage phenomena. There is little room or seeming utility in this environment for researchers to study the nuanced and complex nature of linguistic interaction or linguistic registers, and indeed, this kind of scholarship is dwarfed by statistical measures of the linguistic landscape and demographic counts. Shore and Wright have argued convincingly that audit is surreptitiously coercive, easily becoming an end in itself. It is incredibly difficult to curb or say no to auditing practices (and the competitive ethos that accompanies them), because they "present themselves as rational, objective and neutral, based on sound principles of efficient management—as 'unopposable as virtue itself'" (Pollitt 1993: 49 quoted in Shore and Wright 2000: 61). How are the priorities of language research narrowed and harnessed to the development of standardized measures of language choice? From what source will the incentives emerge to study the nuanced symbolic meanings of linguistic interactions that can help us to understand when and why a person will speak one language or another?

In closing, we have seen that the late nineties and early twenty-first century gave rise to important shifts in the discourses and strategies of language activism and new fashionings of Basque and of Basque revival, some of which evoke traditional Basque culture, while others appropriate methods from the world of business, and yet others seamlessly bring tradition and entrepreneurialism together. It would be wrong to see language advocates and planners as external to the effects of these developments. In implementing new tactics, they were themselves caught up in them, placing not just language, but their own activities in the flowchart of managerial calculus. They were themselves becoming self-monitoring workers, aiming for continuous improvement. It was not without a sense of irony that one of my language-advocate friends gestured to the book on her nightstand that she and her fellow scholar/activist colleagues had decided to read: it was not Fanon; it was not Fishman. It was a translation of management guru Steven Covey's *Seven Habits of Highly Effective People.*

CHAPTER SEVEN

The Voice of the Street

BASQUE IN THE FREE-RADIO SOUNDSCAPE

Revolution announced itself everywhere when I made my first visit to Molotoff Irratia, the free-radio station of Hernani, an industrial town not far from Usurbil. It was 1994. The very name of the station—after the Molotov cocktail—conjured up images of barricades and urban guerilla warfare. The door was never locked. I pushed it open and made my way up the dank stairwell. Posters and graffiti punctuated the walls with slogans calling for "freedom of expression" and "Basque in the Basqueland," interspersed with anarchist and antimilitarist symbols. The spray paint and grungy feel announced my entry into the world of radical youth culture. Arriving at the top floor, I came into a bright, colorful space: young people were sitting hunched over papers at a table, writing stories for the nine o'clock news program, while others drifted in and out, picking up mail and sorting through CDs and old audio cassettes.

I had come that evening in February to ask Molotoff's steering committee for permission to observe the station and talk to programmers. Numerous small and quasi-illegal radio stations had emerged in the eighties, shortly after the transition to democracy, and I was curious to understand their relationship, if any, to the Basque language–revival movement.

Media making is an important concern and activity in many language-revival movements. Advocates of lesser-used languages understandably worry that mass media in the dominant language will drown out their language and draw their children away from its use and from their own cultural values. But if electronic and print media are often seen as threats to small languages, they have also been seized upon as weapons of resistance and survival. When broadcasting satellites were launched in the seventies, indigenous communities in remote areas of the Arctic and Australia suddenly found themselves flooded with commercial media in the majority language. Some responded at first by trying to block the satellite signal (Ginsburg 1991). But for European minoritized language groups like the *euskaldunak,* blocking out mass media was not an option; instead they set their sights on getting their own piece of real estate on the airwaves and fiber-optic networks. Producing minority-language media—from lowbrow to highbrow, newspapers,

television, and soap operas to Internet blogs—opens up new creative opportunities, social tensions, and challenges as the language is adapted to new modes of
circulation and broadcasting genres. Media are seen by minority-language policy
makers as playing several vital functions: giving speakers opportunities to hear
and use their language; enhancing the social status of the language in the eyes of
its speakers, helping them to see it as a part of the contemporary world rather than
of a dying past; helping to cultivate a sense of community or common belonging;
and contributing to the unification of the language.

In the Spanish Basque Country, Basque-language media making has been
seized upon for all of these functions. Gaining a media presence was perceived as
part and parcel of the transition to democracy and the achievement of some measure of political and cultural sovereignty after the death of Franco. Shortly after
the Statute of Autonomy was passed, one of the first measures the Basque regional
government took was to create the Basque Radio and Television Network (EITB).
There are presently four television channels, one emitting entirely in Basque, and
five radio channels that transmit in both Basque and Spanish (Díaz Noci 1998).
And this now pales in comparison with the growing amount of media distributed on the Web. Batua, Unifed Basque, was the defacto variety chosen by most
Basque-language media producers who emerged in this new era, coming out of
the strong sense among most language activists that Batua, as a standardized amalgam of different dialects, was the most suitable for translocal communication and
nation building. In recent years, attitudes about the necessity of spreading knowledge of Batua have relaxed considerably. Today we find much more use of dialectal forms of Basque, particularly in local media.[1] Language advocacy has secured
a notable presence for Basque in public media of the Autonomous Community,
although it still remains much smaller than that of Spanish. Basque, along with
Spain's other minority languages, has acquired new forms of circulation and visibility, but these are found almost exclusively within the territories of their respec-
tive autonomous communities. Until the advent of the Internet, Galician, Basque,
and Catalan media were not readily accessible outside these areas, contributing to
an understanding of them as regional languages rather than languages belonging
to the wider citizenry of Spain.

As Patrick Eisenlohr (2004) notes, one of the reasons electronic and digital
media are enthusiastically adopted in language-revitalization movements is the
strong association of these forms of media with modernity. Incorporation of the
minority language into a medium iconic of technological innovation disrupts
understandings of minority languages as obsolete, occupying "spatially and tem-
porally dislocated and distant positions, away from geographical centers and the
temporal present" (2004: 32; see also Cotter 2001). In this way, minority-language

electronic media, like other forms of media, permit what Eisenlohr calls a "rein-dexing" of the temporal and spatial qualities of marginality and limited value typi-cally projected onto minority languages by dominant ideology. Free radios, how-ever, have some unique qualities in this regard. Their distinctive political identities, broadcast goals, and methods differentiate them from mainstream media. Free radios are intentionally low wattage, usually broadcasting only within the limits of a town, with the intent of engaging a local community, town, or neighborhood as both audience and producers of their own media. They emphasize local rather than national identity; free radios present themselves as the radio of particular places: Hernani, Usurbil, Gasteiz, or Orereta. They invite members of the com-munity to participate by broadcasting call-ins and by inviting local residents to create their own shows. If mainstream media seek to disseminate information, to literally "broadcast" and spread information, free radio seeks to exercise a centrip-etal effect: to draw community members together in and through the making of local media. In this respect, free radio understands itself as a strategy of grassroots community building.

Free radios are also decidedly oppositional, having emerged in the eighties as a response of radicalized youth to their social and political disenfranchisement. Economic restructuring had brought unemployment among youth to an all-time high in the eighties. In addition, this period saw the Spanish state, in collabora-tion with the regional Basque police force, intensify its surveillance and harass-ment of radical youth activities as part of its campaign to eliminate the alleged "breeding grounds" of future "terrorists." Free radios were part of a broader set of efforts by radicalized youth to create autonomous spaces of cultural life and political expression, sympathetic to the leftist Basque-liberation movement but outside of political parties.[2] These media outlets were particularly closely linked to the *gaztetxe* [youth house] movement of the eighties, in which young people took over abandoned buildings to have concerts, organized workshops on everything from sexuality to natural foods, and in general created opportunities for social-izing outside of commercial establishments. They reported on arrests and harass-ments of young people, but they were by no means narrowly focused on the "Basque conflict." Free radios did live broadcasts at demonstrations and concerts. They had shows on a wide range of topics from global warming and antiracist organizing to discrimination against immigrants, Muslims, and gypsies. Station programming reflected eclectic mixtures of material and music from reggae, ska, hip-hop, jazz, heavy metal, and Basque improvised oral poetry. Their movement, like their own sense of Basque identity, was premised on exchange and solidarity with other dissident groups. In this sense, free radios were sites for the production of a kind of cultural politics and ethnicity akin to what Rampton (1995), following Hall (1996b), called "new ethnicities" of the periphery, organized not around exclusionary and essentialist notions of race and nation, but rather around common experiences of marginalization (Rampton 1995: 297).

The somewhat disapproving voices of some of my friends and collaborators in former research projects came back to me many times as I visited Molotoff and other radio stations in the mid-nineties. They did not understand my interest. Why was I spending time on them, they asked? These are the antics of a few radicals and pranksters; free radio, some seemed to imply, was not serious politics or language revival. I felt I had gone astray in their eyes as I descended from the more respectable study of language reclamation and congresses on language standardization and planning to the rather ignoble world of free radio. And in some ways, they were right. None of the free-radio programmers I came to know would say that Basque revival was their primary goal. They were neither trying to teach Basque nor to be models of exemplary or normative use. Rather, they most often described their goal to be that of countering the disinformation of mass media. Media distortion, censorship, and police harassment were the salient concerns of radicalized youth at this time. Their aim, they said, was to be the "voice of the street." Yet I knew that many free radios did use Basque in their programming. I wanted to explore that usage. I was intrigued to know whether the context of oppositional fringe media characterized by localism, a commitment to radical democracy, and a good deal of low-brow humor might allow for more playful and less normative uses of Basque. What, in short, did the "voice of the street" sound like in Basque?

In exploring the politics and poetics of language in two radio stations that formed part of the Basque free-radio media movement, I examine how this media movement, identified with irreverence and plain talk, intersected with the sociopolitical struggle and effects of language revitalization. Most of the ethnographic research on which my analysis is based comes from work I did in the mid-nineties. I begin with a controversy that started off my 1994 fieldwork at Molotoff as a way of illuminating the different language ideologies that operate in free radio versus language revitalization, differences that aligned them in some ways, but put them at odds in others. From there I turn to some of the distinctive stylings of programming at Paotxa, the free-radio station of Usurbil, as well as Molotoff, focusing on prerecorded radio introductions as performances of what I call "staged informality." I am interested in looking closely at how programmers—some native Basque speakers and some not—used particular features of vernacular to craft a deliberately unpolished, irreverent, and "in your face" broadcasting voice in Basque.

How people use language is always in some way commenting upon, reflecting, and constructing the political relations speakers inhabit (Gal 1989). This was especially true for the kinds of performances I examine here. As Richard Bauman and Charles Briggs (1990) have argued, performances are not simply artful uses of language separate from day-to-day life. Rather the form and meaning of any single performance, they say, is inextricable from other speech events it indexes and the broader sociocultural context in which it is produced (1990: 60–61). This premise guides the analysis that follows. The period of my observations was a time of real hardship for Basque youth. Economic recession in the early nineties brought unemployment in the Automomous Community to a record high of 25 percent in 1994 and 1995 and much higher, of course, for youth (Gatti et al. 2005: 43). Young people identified with alternative and oppositional politics had no prospects for jobs, were harassed by police, and felt shut out of a heavily policed public sphere, both Spanish and Basque. At the same time, the character of the language movement itself was changing and becoming increasingly institutionalized as Basque, or more specifically standardized Basque, was incorporated into the schools and regional governmental bureaucracy. These historically specific conditions as well as the genre of free radio itself shaped the verbal performances of radio programmers, inclining them to the use of vernacular forms of Basque as a means of locating themselves markedly "in the street"—a term resonant with populist political protest. Programmers resisted disciplined language, recycled and remixed elements of "authentic" Basque language in particularly gender-marked ways. The "voice of the street" is not just "out there" to be aired; it is fashioned through a creative reassemblage of resources that I want to examine here.

Free radio may not be a part of the language-revival movement, but its poetics are intimately linked to it. As we have seen, much of the language-revival movement had been focused on counteracting the marginalization of Basque by attempting to introduce it into prestigious and powerful domains of social life: education, government, and mainstream media. These efforts manifest a recurring concern with producing correct, standard, exemplary Basque in the public sphere. Free radio is a space of resistance that takes shape in the interstices of the discourse of language planning and revitalization. Its aesthetics have to be understood in relation to practices of governmentality that characterize the dominant strategies of resistance. Michel de Certeau's concept of "tactics" from his 1984 work on everyday forms of resistance may be helpful here. Tactics are contrasted with "strategies" as forms of resistance that are unsystematic, indirect, and follow an "errant" logic. They work by "bricolage," an assemblage that is improvised, inventive, and difficult to predict. "A tactic insinuates itself into the other's place, fragmentarily, without taking it over in its entirety, without being able to keep it at a distance. It has at its disposal no base where it can capitalize on its advantages, prepare its expansions, and secure independence with respect to circumstances" (ibid.: xix).

Tactics, says Certeau, are the archetypical methods of the housewife, the pedestrian on a crowded street, the vernacular speaker, those who maneuver to seize opportunities as they arise. This concept of tactics seems an especially appropriate way of envisioning the politics and poetics of a practice like free radio that poaches the airwaves, disrupts, but does not cohere into a formalized oppositional politics.

Free radio has now largely faded from the radicalized Basque youth-culture scene, but the linguistic performances enabled in these spaces merit attention on several grounds. They point to a reindexing and revalorization of vernacular that has continued to unfold in Basque cultural life. They also point to the complexity of the field of language revitalization. Strategies for challenging linguistic domination engender their own resistances. Reclaiming Basque from its abandonment and marginalization has led to an emphasis on its regulation, normalization (in all senses of the word), transparent standardized meanings, clearly demarcated codes, and quantitative measures that have gained prominence over other ways of experiencing and knowing language: dimensions of sensuality, musicality and sound play, open ended ambiguity and bivalency. The importance of this ephemeral form of media may be precisely that it points us to the realm of popular culture as one of possibly many sites where subjugated experiences and values find expression in parody, puns, and play (Samuels 2004). The seminal work of Mikhail Bakhtin on the dialogical nature of language, "double voicing," and carnivalesque aesthetics as modes of resistance are especially helpful analytical tools. I draw on them for unpacking the ways in which the playful performances of Basque free-radio programmers express tensions generated within the language movement and at the same time contribute to the ongoing process of creating new ways of being *euskaldun*.

Ideological Crossroads: Free-Radio Activism and Language Revival

Little did I know that my first visit to Molotoff would provide me with my first and somewhat dramatic lesson on free-radio language ideology. The members of the steering committee had begun to drift in and take their seats at a table in the center of the room. Maider was a twenty-six-year-old unemployed English teacher who worked on the news program. Fernando, the son of working-class immigrants from Cáceres, was a veteran of the station from its earliest days in the mid-eighties. He understood but did not speak Basque much. There were also Pello, a gay college graduate, currently unemployed, and Miren, a member of the militant language-activist organization Euskalherrian Euskaraz, who worked on a weekly program called *Erderaz eta Kitto?* [Is Spanish Enough?].[3] More committee members came in. Among them was Jone, who produced a women's program on

Sunday mornings. She was the youngest of the group and an activist in the squatter and feminist movement since high school. With striking jet-black dreads tied up with a black and white Palestinian scarf, a nose ring, spandex miniskirt, tights, and Doc Martin combat boots, she looked every bit the radical urban teenager. I found out later that Jone had grown up in a farmhouse and was a native speaker of Basque.

Announcements were made, reminders of upcoming events reiterated. Everyone spoke in Basque or tried as best they could to do so. I introduced myself and explained my interest in being at the station. They approved without much commentary. This evening there were clearly other, more pressing issues. Tension was thick in the air. They were there to plan a general assembly meeting of the entire radio collective to deal with a letter the steering committee had received. It was from the station's Basque-language committee, known as the *euskara batzordea*, formed years ago with the purpose of promoting Basque-language use at the station. Language committees were fairly common within the nongovernmental or grassroots activist world and reflected the way that language revival was seen as an integral part of being politically progressive. In the letter, the Basque-language committee accused the radio station, and the steering committee in particular, of failing to live up to the professed commitment to language revival. The committee's letter called upon the radio to pass a resolution that would require all new programs to be in Basque. After the letter was read, people started talking. Some of the members became outraged, while others seemed cynical. Before I knew it, talk escalated into shouts, accusations, and even tears. Molotoff was in crisis, and language was at the heart of it.

I was confused to say the least. Why was this proposal so contentious? From talking and observing programmers, from just looking at the graffiti and posters in the station, it was clear to me that there was awareness of the marginalization of Basque. It seemed that station members generally supported Basque revival as a cause and tried to speak in Basque if they could. This affinity between progressive politics and the Basque-language cause was widely shared in leftist and grassroots social movements throughout the southern Basque Country. Forty years of repression under the Franco regime had made the Basque language into a public sign of antistate, antiauthoritarian politics. The legacy was visible at Molotoff and other free radio stations I visited. It was not, in other words, accidental that almost all free radios had given themselves identifiably Basque names or used the Basque word for radio, *irratia,* in their title. Station identifications played at Molotoff— "you are listening to the voice of Molotoff Irratia"—were routinely said in Basque even though they had programs in both Basque and Spanish.

Why, then, the outcry against the proposal to institute a Basque requirement for new programs? Like most political conflicts, the reasons were overdetermined. Long-brewing interpersonal antipathies specific to this station played some role, I was told. But the argument that erupted in front of me also pointed to a fundamental difference between the means by which free-radio activism and the language-revival movement contested language domination.

The language movement was pushing to "normalize" or make habitual the use of Basque in all spheres of life. It had placed priority on gaining legal recognition, teaching, and taking measures to enable Basque usage in public and high-prestige spheres. Policies, planning, and standardization were the watchwords and tools for combating Spanish-language hegemony in the early years. In public, there was a strong inclination toward the production of "correct" Basque. Vernacular practices of code switching and borrowing from Spanish, common in everyday talk, were regarded as legacies of political and cultural domination of Basques. Language-revival discourse called upon speakers not to speak the way they had always spoken, but to speak in new ways, in new contexts, and with an awareness of their actions as impacting their own identities and the social life of the language.

Similar to language advocates, free-radio activists also regard speech as a form of political praxis. Speech is part of how free-radio activism contests power. But free-radio ideology clashed with language revivalists when it came to standardization and language norms. Language advocates saw norms as a tool for saving Basque. This was not easily reconciled with free-radio practice, which embraces an antinormative, antihierarchical approach to language. The earliest free radios in Europe came out of the autonomous/anarchist left in Italy and imagined themselves as "liberated zones" where the ordinary worker/citizen and the disenfranchised could speak for themselves in whatever form they chose—vernacular, regional dialect, stumbling, or non-normative talk (Guattari 1981). At the first broadcast of Radio Alice, the most infamous of Italian free radios, the station announced to its listeners its agenda: "Radio Alice transmits: music, news, gardens in bloom, conversations that have no purpose, inventions, discoveries, recipes, horoscopes, magical formulas, love, war reports, photographs, messages, massages, and lies" (Eco 1981: 223). These radios rejected what they saw to be the rigidities of leftist political discourse; they refused to uphold a consistent "party line" or correct ideology. They also rejected the notion of authorized spokespersons—people who speak for others—the party delegate, the journalist, the interpreter, the deputy. They saw these conventionalized forms of political talk as leading inexorably to a homogenization and reduction of voices and perspectives. Free radios wanted to open up the public sphere; they encouraged listeners to call in to give their account of events in their own words, as they saw it, or to send in their own tapes for broadcast. They were the antithesis of what feminist audio artist Frances Dyson (1994) describes as the dominant "Radio Voice": polished, authoritative, and singular.

> Generally, the dominant radio voice talks—its speech is clear, articulate, sometimes eloquent. Most of what it says is perceived by the listener as factual and informative, newsworthy. . . . It does not mumble or stutter, it pronounces full and meaningful sentences, it says something. As a voice, it is traditionally male, having a certain timbre and intonation that suggests a belief in what it is saying and a degree of authority in saying it. Critics of the dominant radio voice have dubbed it "the voice of authority." (167)

At free radio, wrote one its greatest enthusiasts, Felix Guattari, one encountered "the direct word, the live word, at one and the same time self confident and indecisive, contradictory, that is nonsensical, [and] charged with considerable desire" (1981: 234). Its unique form of politics is strongly linked to its unruly and humorous language. Though the Basque radio broadcasters I came to know in 1994 and 1998 had never read Guattari or heard about the legendary Radio Alice of Bologna, they shared with the Italians a preference for the unauthorized and unregulated voice. It did not seem to be an explicit policy for these Basque programmers, as much as an aesthetic that they shared and modeled for each other via the exchange of programs and at gatherings that free-radio activists held in various cities across Europe. The tactics of electronic disturbance were appealing to them and fit well with the punk-inspired oppositional aesthetics of Basque radical youth culture of the time (see Kasmir 1999). But while their oppositional politics incorporated affinity for the cause of language revival, the ethical commitment free-radio activists had to being the "uncensored voice of the street" made them averse to any form of regulating language. Policies proposed to require Basque-language use or prohibit sexist language were contentious at Molotoff. Herein lay the grounds for the emotional face-off over the proposal to implement a language policy that I witnessed on my first visit.

The tension between language-revival strategies and free-radio praxis was augmented, no doubt, by the changing nature of the language movement in the nineties. Language revival was receiving increasing institutional support. For young people coming of age after autonomy and the 1982 Law of Normalization, the Basque language, and more specifically Standard Basque, acquired associations it had not had for their parents. This generation encountered Standard Basque in institutions of authority, spoken by teachers, civil servants, and the regional government's media. The linguistic choices of oppositional youth culture are indicators of the shifts taking place in the ideological connotations of Basque. Their cultural productions show us that "Basque" in this unqualified sense was no longer an unequivocal sign of radicalism as it had been one generation earlier. The distinctive kind of "street Basque" I look at below is a means by which free-radio youth recycled and refashioned vernacular Basque to signal their antiauthoritarian and populist identity in an era when Basque was becoming more institutionalized.

With these basic parameters of free-radio ideology and the specific political and historical moment in mind, I turn now to a more detailed look at how programmers made use of Basque vernacular to craft their own voice and style. What resources did they use in fashioning what they called the "voice of the street"? Examples of Basque language use come from two different stations where I got to know current or former broadcasters well, watched them work or listened to tape recordings of their programs with them. The focus is on the linguistic forms used in program introductions rather than on the content or style of the programs themselves. As Debra Spitulnik (1993) has argued, linguistic form plays an essential role in how media generate meaning by both presupposing and constructing sender-receiver relations and evaluative frameworks for reception. A fixture of each program, the prerecorded introductions function as framing devices, highly marked and self-consciously produced verbal performances through which programmers establish their identity, define the kind of audience they imagine, and signal the kind of relationship they want to have with them.

These verbal performances are an especially interesting window into the heteroglossia of Basque political and popular culture. Colloquial registers and forms of speech on the airwaves of free radio indexed ideological perspectives, personas, or stances that were absent or deliberately marginalized in Basque and Spanish mainstream media. On free radio young feminists, unorthodox anarchists, hard rockers, and everyday residents haltingly, sometimes earnestly and many times hilariously, created programs that gave expression to their concerns, musical tastes, and identities. I look at just some of the ways they fashioned their voices in and through their forms of speech.

Several key premises from the Marxist philosophy of language articulated in the work of Bakhtin (1981; 1984a; 1984b) and Valentin Voloshinov (1986) are useful in analyzing this material. First is the premise that linguistic form is implicated in the expression of consciousness. Bakhtin and Voloshinov's sociopolitical approach to the study of language focused on identifying the way linguistic form communicated the ideological or evaluative stances of a speaker. Through choice of words, intonation, prosody, code switching, and other narrative devices such as reported speech, a speaker is said to animate a voice or set of voices that comment on the social world. As Jane Hill (1995) explains, "the voice system" of a text can be extraordinarily complex, requiring a keen understanding of linguistic forms, the social history of their usage, and the particularities of the social context of their utterance. A second related premise of this approach is the recognition of the intertextual or dialogical nature of language. Our words, wrote Bakhtin, are always shot through with the voices of others (1981: 293, 1986: 91). Word choice, turns of phrase, and intonation respond and bear witness to the ideologies, histories, class positions, and values associated with their previous uses. For this reason the Bakhtinian view of language is described as fundamentally dialogical, in the sense that the meaning of an utterance arises out of both the specific social context in which it is produced and the intertextual references it elicits.

The methods of Bakhtinian translinguistics, as it is sometimes called (Hill 1986), which approach language as an intertextual and dynamic system of voices, are more useful here than the analytics of governmentality I have been using so far. These methods are an aid to understanding the ideological messages in radio performers' linguistic stylings. They help one to see how their appropriation of vernacular Basque was a means of distancing themselves from conventional morality and state institutions and how, in the context of free radio, young people were carving out a voice for themselves in the shifting political and linguistic landscape that was taking shape after Basque autonomy.

Free-radio performances constitute creative linguistic play on the outside, but certainly in dialogue with governmentality and nationalist logics. The efforts to teach, normalize, and uplift the social status of Basque gave primacy to a standardized, uniform, and geographically nonspecific Basque, squeezing out other voices, other social locations, subjectivities, and meanings. It is tempting to fall back on a simple model of repression to account for these usages. But I would suggest viewing the street-Basque voice crafted in free radio not as voice *repressed* by mainstream nationalism, but rather as forms of language use and perspectives that evolve out of this new political context. If one considers language inherently to be, as Voloshinov states, a site of ideological struggle among voices (1986: 23), then the struggle that is being expressed in the free-radio segments below is not the more familiar struggle of Basque against Spanish, but rather a struggle from within to imagine a plurality of ways of being *euskaldun*.

Staging Street Basque

Usurbil's free radio was much smaller than that of Molotoff. It had about twenty active members (though many more occasional participants) during its five years of broadcast between 1987 and 1993. Unlike Molotoff, when Paotxa was created, the membership had voted, after much heated debate, to operate exclusively in Basque; thus most, but not all, of the people who took part in it had Basque as their first language and spoke it fairly fluently. In listening to tapes Paotxa programmers had kept of their programs, I was struck by the playful language, colloquialisms, vernacular, and conversational speech style in these radio broadcasts.

This was especially marked in the introductions that programmers made to their shows. Introductions typically consisted of prerecorded segments lasting a minute or two that were played at the start and closing each time a show was aired. These segments generally consisted of music and a stretch of talk that announced the name of the show and set the mood or tone for the program to follow. In the examples that follow, one can see how programmers drew upon particular linguistic forms—pronouns, vernacular pronunciation—and colloquialisms to evoke the informal and "direct" relationship with their audience that was distinctive of the free-radio broadcast style.

At Paotxa, one of the primary means of performatively evoking informality was through pronouns. Many of the program introductions made liberal use of a markedly informal mode of address, referred to as *hika* or *hitanoa,* named after the pronoun *hi* [you]. When people use these forms they are colloquially said to be speaking in *hika* (e.g., *hikaz ari da,* "they are [speaking] in *hika*"). To understand what it might mean to use this mode of address in radio introductions, some background is helpful.

Basque has two second-person singular pronouns, *zu* and *hi,* roughly equivalent to the English "you" and the now archaic "thou," or "*usted*" and "*tu*" in Spanish. *Hi* conveys intimacy and familiarity, and *zu* is generally considered to mark respect.[4] In addition to the pronoun itself, in certain instances the use of the informal *hi* mode of address can require markers on the accompanying inflected verb forms that indicate the gender of the person being addressed (-n for females and –k for males) even when that addressee is not a part of the argument of the utterance. To take a very simple example of the gender marking, the phrase "this is Paotxa [radio]" could be rendered in hika as either *hau duk Paotxa* when addressing a male or *hau dun Paotxa* when addressing a female. *Zu* verb forms, in contrast, do not mark gender, and indeed, nowhere else in Basque is gender grammatically marked. The difficulty of mastering these gender markings is legendary; as one observer writes, these forms are almost impossible for anyone who has not "heard it from the cradle" (Alberdi quoted in Echeverria 2003: 398). Nor was it easy to learn the forms, as the register had fallen out of use in many areas, and it was not generally a part of Basque-language instruction.

The contrast *hi/zu* is sometimes described as the Basque equivalent of the *Tu/ Vous* forms of Romance languages analyzed in Roger Brown and A. Gilman's classic work on the pronouns of power and solidarity (1960). But as more recent research has argued, the comparison is not exactly correct, since *hika* usage is significantly more restricted than is the case with most "T" forms (Rijk 1991; Alberdi 1993, 1995). Until the nineties, it is fair to say that the use of *hi* was largely limited to interaction in two of the most intimate and enduring social units of an individual's life: the family and one's immediate friendship circle. Within the family, *zu* and *hi* usage is asymmetrical. That is, siblings might use *hi* among themselves and parents might address their children in it, particularly as they get older (*zu* being preferred when they are infants). But children rarely or never use it with their parents or adult relatives. Within the family, the asymmetrical use of *zu* encodes authority and power. Outside the family, *hi* has tended to be used almost always reciprocally among close, same-sex peers.[5] *Zu* is generally used for most other social interactions.

Based on these patterns of use, linguist Rudolf de Rijk has suggested that we should not equate Basque *hika* with Tu/Vous. While it has some features of the general pattern of T/V pronouns, he suggests we "view *zu* as the normal, pragmatically unmarked form of address, and *hi* as a marked substitute encoding the feature 'solidarity' as defined by the social realities of local Basque culture" (1991: 377–78). As Rijk's comment indicates, appropriate usage of this register is locally defined and consequently highly variable. In one village it might be customary, for example, for a brother to address his sister as *hi*, whereas in another it might be seen as rude or offensive.

Knowledge of *hi* forms seems to have been much more widespread in the past. In the eighties and nineties, the forms were better known and more widely used in rural areas. At that time, knowledge and the ability to use *hika* forms was much less frequent among urban youth and virtually nonexistent among second-language Basque learners. People who had grown up on or in the orbit of farms seemed to know it best. In Usurbil, for example, *hika* was much more widely known than it was in Hernani or other nearby industrialized towns, and this was noticeable at the radio station; most of the programmers I interviewed in Usurbil seemed to have at least partial knowledge of *hika* verb morphology, and most could understand and recognize the forms even if they could not produce them fluently.

In general, knowledge of *hika* among native-Basque speakers was stratified by age, social location, and also gender. Older men and women tended to know it better than younger people. And young men seemed to be more comfortable and frequent users of this mode of address than young women. My Basque-speaking interlocutors in their twenties and thirties pointed to cross-gender talk as an arena where *hika* use was sometimes difficult. For example, in talking with me about her use of *hika* on the air, one of Paotxa's female broadcasters said: "At first I was very nervous. . . . I understand it, but I don't use *hika* that much. . . . It doesn't come out as easily for me as it does for him" (referring to her male partner in the broadcast). Other young women I knew in Usurbil expressed similar discomfort with *hika*. Similar findings have been reported by Echeverria, who gives us one of the most nuanced and careful descriptions we have to date of the multivalent and gendered connotations of this mode of address (2000, 2003). In her study of Basque-speaking high-school students in this area, Echeverria found boys using this register much more than girls, and mostly with other boys. From her interviews and observations, she concludes that "[t]here is a sense in which *hika* is associated with boisterous behavior in which boys are more likely to participate" (2000: 229). Drawing on Elinor Ochs's seminal work on the indexing of gender (1992), Echeverria argues that the gendered coding of *hika* is accomplished indirectly. In other words, "*hi* indexes certain social meanings (spontaneity, directness, naturalness, anger, fun, and being a *baserritarra* [farmer]), which in turn index masculinity" (2003: 404). While it seems it once was more generally used by both sexes, in the contemporary moment, Echeverria argues, *hi* has become an iconic marker of masculinity and male-like behavior (ibid: 407). These associated meanings of masculinity and roughness, I would add, also made *hika* a useful linguistic resource for youth involved in oppositional politics, given the strong coding of political battle with masculinity (see Zulaika 1988).

In addition to solidarity and gender codings, an additional indexical property of *hika* comes from its association with the vernacular Basque of native speakers, particularly those from farms or small villages. Since at least the nineteenth century, the rural farmhouse has been regarded as the prime locus of vernacular Basque, "unpolished" but authentic and rich in colloquial expression. Basque literature and early Basque-nationalist ideology reinforced these associations between Basque authenticity and rural life. Echeverria writes that her Basque-speaking interviewees described *baserritarrak* as people who are "really, really Basque" (2003: 404). I found the same to be true in Usurbil. It was with farm people, I was told, that I would be able to learn good, authentic Euskara.

Language standardization and the strategies of language teaching in the revival movement indirectly heightened this association between the vernacular of native speakers and *hika* forms. Basque-language instruction is carried out in Unified Basque, and typically only the *zuka* mode of address is used. The dialectal varieties of Basque spoken by native speakers, as well as *hika* forms, were not formally taught except in the most advanced levels of Basque-language courses. Although this is changing, at the time, unless one was studying for an advanced degree in Basque, *hika* forms had to be learned outside of class. There was one young man in Usurbil, for example, who was constantly pointed out to me as an unusual case, because he came from a Spanish-speaking home of migrant laborers and yet he had learned *hika*. Locals drew my attention to him and considered his use of *hika* a sign of this young man's exceptional degree of integration into the *euskaldun* community. He himself described not just learning Basque, but learning, as he put it, to speak like the local Basques, as something that had made him feel a part of the town. Once again, it can be seen how the language movement does not simply revive a language, but is itself a catalyst in changing the meanings of varieties of language use, in this case making the mastery of vernacular speech forms, dialect, colloquial pronunciations and *hika* into interchangeable indices of native-speaker status and Basque authenticity.

The *zuka* mode of address is undoubtedly the most commonly used by all Basque speakers, native and non-native. Interestingly, however, for young Basque speakers in this part of Gipuzkoa who have been educated after standardization, the *hika* and *zuka* modes of address have become the pragmatically salient markers of vernacular and standard Basque respectively. Youth at Usurbil's radio, like the high-school students Echeverria studied, described the contrast between *hika* and *zuka* using the very same terms that they used to contrast vernacular and Batua. Irvine and Gal call this kind of semiotic transposition "fractal recursivity" (2000: 38). In other words, youth described both *hika* and vernacular as being popular [*herrikoia*] and authentic [*jatorra*]. *Zuka,* on the other hand, seemed now to be functioning as a marker of Batua and was regarded as more formal and respectful, appropriate for use with strangers, authority figures, or second-language learners (Echeverria 2000: 222–43, 2003). Thus, at the same time that language planning and activism had succeeded in introducing Unified Basque into official and public institutions, vernacular Basque, with *hika* as its metonymic marker, appeared to be taking on new meanings to express a variety of new ends, including populism, authenticity, and disaffection from institutional norms and mainstream values.[6]

Keeping all this in mind—the layered indexical connotations *hika* has of solidarity, informality, directness, authenticity, and masculinity—as well as the broader political moment in which the Basque language was becoming more institutionalized and less identified with radicalism, puts one in a better position to look at some examples of how *hika* and other linguistic features emblematic of vernacular were used in free-radio program openers. It also helps us to appreciate the symbolic work that these performances accomplished, articulating critical stances vis-à-vis Basque cultural conservatism, instantiating new kinds of Basque voices, and reconciling cultural oppositions that have often made Basque seem out of place in the world of youth culture, radical or mainstream.

The first example comes from the opening to Paotxa's community news program, *Usurbil Hawaii da* [Usurbil is Hawaii]. The segment takes the form of two speakers, a young man and woman, who greet each other and have a brief chat. As the conversational format of this introducing segment and the pragmatically salient use of *hi* pronouns were features repeated in several other program introductions, it is useful to consider how these features served to frame the identity of the radio.

EXAMPLE 1

Usurbil Hawaii da!

> **Bold** indicates an *hika* form.
>
> Musical collage: begins with heavy-metal rock music, shifts to classical music, violins, then waltz, music fades down, announcers fade up:

(1) Female: ***Aizak, hi!***
               Hey, you!

(2) Male: ***Aizan, hi!***
               Hey, you!

> Basque folk music fades up for a few seconds, then down again.

(3) Female: *Gezurra badirudi, baina astean behin, ordu betez, Pacifikokoa baina ezagunagoa dugun, inpernatuko beroraren laguntzaz*
               It may seem hard to believe, but once a week, for a full hour accompanied by a heat from Hell more familiar to us than that of the Pacific [Ocean]

(4) Together: *Usurbil Hawaii da!*
               Usurbil is Hawaii!

(5) Male: *Ostegunero, zortzitan, erretirako angelusaren ondoen, Paotxa Irratia galantaren eskeintza berezia, bihotz bihoztarrez*
               Every Thursday at eight o'clock, when it comes time to retire for the evening angelus [prayers], Paotxa Radio makes this elegant and special offering from the bottom of our heartburn

(6) Together: *Usurbil Hawaii da!*
               Usurbil is Hawaii!

> Basque folk music comes up.

The opening musical collage and title for the news program, "Usurbil is Hawaii!" sets a playful, sarcastic, and nonsensical tone. It gains added hilarity when we know that the youth had set up their station in the basement of the now abandoned apartment building without a permit. They had built their makeshift studio themselves, and it was, indeed, hot and cramped when they first started broadcasting in July at the time of the annual fiestas. Soundproofing was nonexistent, and they could, in fact, actually hear the church bells ringing at eight o'clock when they came on the air to deliver their program. They make fun of their situation and adopt an irreverent, fallen-from-grace identity. This and other prerecorded introductions at Paotxa deploy what cultural critics Ella Shohat and Robert Stam (1994), drawing on the work of Bakhtin, have identified as the carnivalesque aesthetic. As theorized by Bakhtin (1984b), popular culture of the working classes and marginalized often expresses itself in this aesthetic. It is characterized by inversions of dominant cultural norms and abundant use of the oxymoronic, the asymmetrical, and the miscegenated. In place of propriety and correctness, we find a celebration of mistakes, puns, and the rebellious beauty of the vulgar. "In the carnival aesthetic, everything is pregnant with its opposite, within an alternative logic of permanent contradiction and nonexclusive opposites that transgresses the monologic true-or-false thinking typical of a certain kind of positivist rationalism" (Shohat and Stam 1994: 302). In these moments language becomes liberated from norms of decorum and vernacular prevails over standard.

Art critic Lucy Lippard (1990) identifies this aesthetic of comic reversal or "turning around on purpose," to be a prevalent one in the productions of many contemporary Native American and other minority artists. Paotxa programs use it quite a bit. The introduction to "Usurbil is Hawaii" seems an especially noteworthy instance of it, since, as the weekly community-news show, one could argue that this, of all programs, operated as the voice of the station as a whole. The opening is replete with metaphorical and musical juxtapositions: hell and heaven; heavy metal, classical, and Basque folk music. It marvelously brings into the same frame the realm of disaffected urbanized youth and the "traditional" Catholic moral universe of their parents' generation. Juxtaposing the solemnity of the evening prayers with reference to the tropics, and the allusions this carries of sexual license and exoticism, allows these lapsed Catholic youth a moment of hilarity as they indirectly poke fun at the religious traditions of the not-so-distant past. The humorous opening sequence of "Usurbil is Hawaii" establishes for itself an irreverent stance, poking fun at Basque tradition and propriety. Yet in carrying this out in unmistakably vernacular Basque, they animate a voice that is not commonly encountered in the public sphere: that is, the voice of *euskaldunak* (not just Basques, but Basque speakers) making fun of other *euskaldunak*. We need to pause to reflect on the significance of this. Part of what it means to be a minority is to always be on the defensive, to be trapped in the role of either victim or virtuous resister. The public performance of insider joking and mockery of one's own community is uncommon and felt to be risky. In the irreverent sphere of free radio, we encounter something that Basques rarely felt at liberty to display: a parodic voice from within the *euskaldun* universe.

The flyers announcing the radio's debut show Paotxa emerging into the public sphere. Likewise, the news show presents itself metaphorically erupting into the airwaves and customary life of Usurbil in the way that Bakhtin saw the subversive voice of popular culture erupting into the mannered voice of official or formal discourse. After the initial greeting to each other in lines 1 and 2, the announcers shift to a more formal voice, signaled in part through word choice and enunciation. The statements in lines 3 and 5 are elaborated and syntactically complex. The delivery is measured and exaggeratedly careful. They pronounce every syllable. This sense of a highly stylized formality is accentuated by the hyper-refined terminology the male speaker uses in line 5 to describe the show—a "special elegant offering" [*galantaren eskeintza berezia*]. The expression *bihotz bihoztarrez* is a comical wordplay on the polite and quasi-literary farewell expression *bihotz bihotzez*, meaning "with all [our] heart." The programmers have replaced *bihotzez* with the similar sounding *bihoztarrez* [heartburn]. Here we have a fairly typical example of the lowbrow humor that free-radio broadcasters liked to use, in this case based on sound play. In their mocking intonation, hyper-elegant phrasing, and deliberate final word gaffe, we have an example of what Bakhtin (1984a) called "double voicing," the copresence of two differently oriented social stances inhabiting the same words. The introducers speak in the tones of the imagined churchgoers, while winking their irreverence toward them.

A contrast between these two voices, one being the seemingly frank and genuine voice of the speakers—the persona in which they greeted one another—and the other being the rigid and hyperformal voice, is underscored as well by a switch from an *hika* to *zuka* register. The introduction (lines 1–2) has the speakers greeting each other in *hika*: "*aizak, hi*" and "*aizan, hi*" ["hey you"]. *Hika* is signaled by the verb morphology: the final –k of "*aizak*" ["hey," 2nd person singular "hi"] marks the male addressee, while the final –n of "*aizan*" indicates the female being addressed.[7] It is also underscored by each speaker's redundant use of the pronoun "*hi*" [you]. These initial greetings evoke a conversational format associated with friends from the same *cuadrilla*, or lifelong friendship circle. The indexical properties of *hika* establish the voice of the radio as genuinely *herrikoia* [popular] and anything but the formal and polite language of mainstream broadcast media.

In the exaggeratedly refined phrasing and vocabulary of lines 3, 4, and 5, the speakers adopt the *zuka* mode of address. As Hill has noted with regard to "mock Spanish," exaggeration or hyperpronunciations allow speakers to distance themselves from the words, register, or source language they are using, thereby establishing it as "other" (1993: 147, 167). Distancing seems to also be at work in these lines. After the informal greetings, the *zuka* voice comes off as inauthentic. Because verb forms in *zuka* lose their gender markings, these lines also lose the specificity of address. The register shift adds to the sense that in lines 3, 4, and 5, the speakers are no longer friends talking to one another, but are now "performing" a voice that is other than their own. Taken as a whole, the sequencing conveys a sense that *hika* is the authentic register of these speakers and, by extension, of Paotxa radio.

Rude and Crude

Usurbil's programmers were not shy about creating offense. Sometimes they wanted to be downright rude, as befit what one programmer called their *zirikatzaile* [provocateur] identity. Program names like *El Moko Ke Kamina* [The Traveling Booger] and others written with nonstandard spellings on their program flyers signaled this kind of intentionally rude and crude stance in the punklike atmosphere of the radio. Both the *hika* register and colloquial expressions served as resources for crafting rudeness in an authentically *euskaldun* guise. Let us take, for example, the more scandalous program *Alua beti Alu,* which aired dirty dealings in the town. The expression *alua beti alu* is vulgar in tone and, like many slang words, edging toward the misogynistic, as *alua* (alu + the definite article, "-a") is a crude term for female genitals. *Alua,* said the radio programmer, was a colloquial way to call someone a fool. The phrase meant something like "a fool is always a fool." Below is the prerecorded introduction to the program.

EXAMPLE 2
Alua Beti Alu

> **Bold** indicates *hika.*   '*' indicates local vernacular pronunciation.
>
> Musical introduction from The Pogues. Fade down, speaker's voice begins:

(1) Female: **Hi,** ba al **dakik?** Aluba* beti alu
               Hey, did you know? A fool is always a fool

(2) Male: Nola?
               What?

(3) Female: Bai beti **badiagu** salatzeko moduko alukeriaren bat
               Yes, we always have some outrageous act to denounce

(4) Male: Ordun* . . .
               So . . .

(5) Together: Aluba* beti alu
               A fool is always a fool

> Music by The Pogues comes up, closing the introduction.

Alua Beti Alu uses the same dialogue format as that of the news program. The woman initiates and speaks to her partner in *hika*, with the male interlocutor making short responses. As in the previous program introduction, both speakers conclude the sequence by speaking together the name of the program, whose meaning has been "explained" in the preceding phrases. This narrative structure and performance bears a striking resemblance to the performative style of popular improvisational versifying *bertsolaritza* (see Aulestia 1995; Armistead and Zulaika 2005).

In *bertsolaritza*, the content and rhymes of an improvised verse [*bertso*] are always structured around the final phrase. That phrase typically conveys the overarching message. In composing a verse, the improvisational poet has first to think of what will be the last line and then to build a narrative around it, being sure to use rhymes that match the final syllable of the final phrase. This structure is summed up in the popular rhyming expression "*amaia da hasera, atzekoz aurrera*" [the end is the beginning, from back to front] (Aulestia 1995: 32–33). A poem is prized when the last line has an element of surprise, and an attentive audience can sometimes figure out what that line will be before the poet has reached the end. At a *bertso* singing session, audiences and poet will typically repeat the last line, singing it together to signal the close of the verse and a job well done. Thus the introduction to *Alua beti Alu* is reminiscent of versifying in both its narrative structure—that is, revealing the meaning of the program title in the last line—and in its performative style, having the speakers say the last line in unison.

Multiple features conjoin to align the voice of the radio as authentically popular *euskaldun* voice. In *Alua beti Alu*, as well as other Paotxa radio introductions, we find parallels to *bertsolaritza*, a verbal art widely regarded as iconic *euskaldun* vernacular culture. The semiotic link is reinforced by the use of *hika*. Another notable feature contributing to the shaping of this populist voice is the use of markedly local modes of pronunciation that involve the use of contractions [*ordun*, instead of the standard *orduan*] and phonological changes [*aluba*, instead of the standard *alua*].[8] Broadcasters described both of these, particularly the interjection of the bilabial fricative "b," as markers of distinctly local or, as they said, "our" (i.e., Usurbil) Basque. The identity of free radios as unlicensed, intentionally provocative, and local was crafted with vernacular linguistic forms largely absent from mainstream media, where the burden to be translocal, exemplary, and standardized took precedence. As linguistic anthropologists have shown, a certain permissiveness accompanies talk that is keyed "light" or joking, exempting it from the kind of prescriptive rules and norms of politeness applied to other kinds of formal public talk (see Hill 1993, 2008). This was very apparent at free radio. At Paotxa, free-radio programmers exploited *hika*'s connotations of coarseness and potential rudeness to set the frame for a program whose aims were to be outrageous and to make public rumored corruption or wrongdoings in the community. *Hika* was a resource for constructing the voice of the unpretentious, honest people, who cannot be fooled, who can see past appearances and not be tricked.

These program introductions are staged performances, prepared, written out, and practiced in advance. In their staging we can see that, contrary to actual use patterns, *hika* is presented as equally voiced by young men and young women. In *Alua beti Alu,* a women's voice predominates as the rude voice. She is the one who introduces the expression, thereby flaunting norms of female respectability. She occupies the stage as equal partner to her male peers. Outside the radio, the young woman admitted that she was not very comfortable speaking in *hika.* In fact, during the program itself, she said she did not use much *hika* at all.

This can serve as a reminder that the linguistic framing devices we are examining were not so much reflections of popular speech patterns as they were elements in fashioning an identity for the radio. Paotxa radio programs were an early sign of the way in which *hika* was being revitalized and revoiced in the popular culture of politicized urban Basque-speaking youth in the late eighties and nineties. Voloshinov considered linguistic forms of communication to be sensitive indices of social changes in the making. "The word," as he said, "has the capacity to register all the transitory, delicate, momentary phases of social change" (1986: 19). Shifting patterns of *hika* usage are just such an index. I was encountering it not only in free radio, but also among grassroots language activists as well as Basque zines, popular comics, and radical music (Urla 1999; 2001). The recontextualization of this formerly rural vernacular feature signals the emergent voice of radical youth distinguishing itself from the increasingly mainstream nationalist institutions that had gained power after autonomy. At the same time, the gendered connotations of the signs of this voice demand notice. The salience of *hika* as an aesthetic device in Paotxa's introductions is yet another example of the trend for masculine-identified cultural forms to be taken as the "natural" symbols of Basque solidarity, oppositionality, and authenticity (see Echeverria 2003; Del Valle 1994; Bullen 1999; Aretxaga 1988).

Recycling

A second verbal art on display in radio-show titles involves the recycling or creative reanimation of Basque popular-speech forms and colloquialisms.[9] The name of the radio station, Paotxa, is one example. I talked with a couple of the original programmers about why they had chosen this name. To explain its meaning, they pulled out the pamphlet they had produced to announce Paotxa's first broadcast.

It contained two images . One on the front cover announced the station's opening with the phrase *"Azkenean"* [At last!] above the image of an antenna bursting out of a chicken's egg. On the back cover we have another image of the egg now fully open, announcing the name of the station in a rhyming verse: *"Hau duk Paotxa; Ganaduranentzako belar gozoena dena, Usurbildarrontzat sintonia onena"* [This is Paotxa! The sweetest grass for livestock, the best radio for Usurbil](see figures below).

In talking about the naming of Paotxa, programmers seemed pleased at this somewhat atypical and quirky choice, notably different from other stations that took on names like Molotoff and evoking a kind of outlaw status. Sweet grass?

FIGURE 7.1. "Azkenean" [At last]. This image was used in a leaflet distributed by radio programmers to announce the first broadcast of Paotxa Irratia, Usurbil's free-radio station in 1987.

FIGURE 7.2. "Hau duk Paotxa" [This is Paotxa!]. This image from the back cover of Paotxa radio's 1987 leaflet addresses itself to the community using the informal *hika* register. Oppositional Basque-speaking youth culture often marked their identity with informal and colloquial registers of Basque.

As one young man explained to me, "Calling our station *paotxa,* sweet grass, is like saying our radio is great, but not in the usual way." The more "usual" way Basque-speaking youth tended to add emphasis or to signal coolness was though Spanish slang and swear words. Youth drew heavily upon Spanish slang and expletives in everyday talk to say things were cool, great, or horrible: "*la ostia*" and "*de puta madre*" were favorites. In radical Basque posters and zines, these Spanish phrases and words were often written in a "basquified" way. For example, in xeroxed program schedules of free radios I collected, it was common to see the Basque "tx" substituted for Spanish "ch" in words like "*txollo*" [Spanish: *chollo,* meaning a "scam" or "good deal"]; the letter "k" substituted for Spanish "qu" or "c" in "*okupa*" [Spanish: *ocupa,* "squatter"] and in "*ke pasa*" [Spanish: *que pasa,* "what is happening"].

Paotxa programmers did some of this as well, but in naming their radio they drew on Basque vernacular, not Spanish, as their source language. As it was explained to me, *paotxa* is a word farmers used to refer to as a kind of grass that cows apparently enjoy eating. "*Hau duk paotxa!*" [This is sweet grass!], said a young broadcaster, is a phrase for a moment of pleasant surprise, what a farmer might exclaim at encountering something good. The phrase is in *hika,* as we might expect given the association with rural or farming life. The verb morphology *duk* [3rd person singular *ukan,* "to have"] with the final "-k" (allocutive masculine) marks this to be an utterance in *hika* and implicitly addressed to a male. Like other *hika* utterances I have already looked at, this one too connotes unpretentious, spontaneous, and informal talk.

Using this name, then, for the outlaw radio station transferred these values of Basque authenticity and sense of pleasant discovery to the radio station's appearance on the airwaves. In my interview with them in 1994, the programmers laughed heartily. They liked the unexpected juxtaposition of seemingly disparate worlds of the *baserritarra* and pirate broadcaster, electronic media and cow grass. In recycling words and expressions from *euskaldun* rural life into the alternative scene of the free radio, they indirectly showed both the richness and the flexibility of Basque-speech repertoires. They showed Basque to be the house of many possible voices, not just that of the *abertzale,* the patriotic nationalist, the farmer, or the Catholic, but also that of the rude and irreverent youth.

The program title for the radio's popular gossip show, *Txori Guztik Mokodun,* gives us another example of the use of cultural mixing and reanimation of colloquial Basque used in this station. The phrase, written in Gipuzkoan dialect, would be literally translated as "all birds have a beak." The programmer who came up with the title translated it as "no one is innocent." A close equivalent in Spanish, he said, would be the expression "*en todas partes cuecen habas.*" Although it was not widely known, he said it was a phrase he heard his elderly aunt use when he was a child. "I thought it was great; it expressed exactly what we needed to say." He also liked the phrase because of the double meaning of the word "*moko.*" The word for a bird's beak, *moko,* he said, is also a vulgar way of referring to a person's mouth, an apt image for evoking the way gossip and rumors pass by word of mouth. It did not hurt that the Basque word *moko* was also a homonym for *moco,* the Spanish word for booger, a term that programmers seemed to enjoy using with regularity. So the phrase "*txori guztik molodun*" could also mean "all birds have boogers."

These polyvalent meanings, in his view, made the expression a funny and clever title for the gossip show's title.

The segment begins with a *paso doble,* the music that typically accompanies a bullfight. The soundtrack then transitions into an "Olé!" the sound of castanets, and a flamenco song, "Amor Brujo." The music fades and a young man initiates a dialogue with a young woman.

EXAMPLE 3

Txori Guztiak Mokodun

Bold indicates *hika.*   * indicates contractions.

(1) Male: **Aizan,** *nor diñau gaur toreatzeko prest?*

Hey, who do we have ready to bullfight today?

(2) Female: **Jakintzak?** *Ze*,* **ba'kik*,** *txori guztik* mokodun!*

Who knows? Cause you know, no one is innocent!

(3) Male: *Bai, Bai hortan, arrazoi'akan*.*

Yes, yes, about that you are right.

(4) Together: *Txori guztik* mokodun.*

No one is innocent.

The music comes up with an animated Caribbean rhythm.

Several elements of this segment work together to set a very informal and playful tone or mood. Obviously, the dialogue and the music are making an analogy between bullfighting and gossiping. Someone in town is going to be slayed, as it were. As a highly stylized and flamboyant performance, the bullfight is ripe for Basque parodic imitation, having been relentlessly promoted under the Franco regime as a national sport and symbol of Spain. Its use here sets a campy tone to this illicit and perhaps even quasi-effeminate activity of gossiping. *Hika* forms (marked in bold) predominate in this exchange, as in other dialogues, establishing this as very direct unmediated speech, as between close friends. The speakers also use *ze* and other contractions characteristic of informal vernacular talk (*diñau* instead of *dinagu; guztik* instead of *guztiak* and *ba'kik* instead of *badakik; arrazoi'akan* instead of *arrazoi dakan*).

Sandwiched between two musical segments—the *paso doble* and the closing Puerto Rican *plena*—that is, between a signifier of an archetypically "Spanish" event (the bullfight) and the exotic sounds of a Caribbean island rhythm—is the voice of Basque vernacular.[10] Like other colloquial expressions, the message of this segment is communicated metaphorically. That is, its meaning is conveyed not by logical argument or transparent meanings, but via the association of contrasting images or events (Fernandez 1986: 12). This is yet another way that emblematic usages of language echoed the poetics of that most iconic of vernacular *euskaldun* art forms, *bertsolaritza,* improvisational verse. These poetics, recognizable to native speakers of Basque, together with lexical choices and the *hika* register, work together to bring the practices and talk of these free-radio broadcasters into association with vernacular Basque language and culture. In so doing they suggest that vernacular Basque has the elasticity and imaginative resources to be what Kenneth Burke has called "equipment for living" in the contemporary world of urban *euskaldun* youth (Burke, cited in Seitel 1977: 75–76). This is much more than arguing that old "words" are still useful. Rather, Burke was arguing that vernacular culture and its expressions offered wisdom, moral codes, and practical advice for living in the present (see also Basso 1979, 1996).

Uncertain Voices

This sort of creativity in Basque was enabled by Paotxa programmers' language skills, cultural knowledge, and exposure to vernacular culture. But this degree of competency in vernacular forms was not found at all radio stations. At Molotoff in nearby Hernani, only a few programmers had a sophisticated enough command over Basque to engage in puns, and none I spoke with knew *hika* forms. In the last segment, I examine how two second-language Basque learners attempted in their own way to produce a program introduction in which they would frame themselves as a part of the Basque "voice of the street."

Alberto and Rafa were two *euskaldun berri* programmers I interviewed and observed at Molotoff Irratia. Both young men began doing radio in Basque with their classmates at the instigation of their teacher from the *ikastola.* After they finished school, they decided to continue working at the station. I met them in 1994 when they were in their late teens, working together to produce a half-hour weekly show called *Eta Zu Zer?* [What About You?]. In the program Alberto and Rafa read poems, told jokes, played music, and occasionally interacted with each other live on the air entirely in Basque. They began doing radio because it was fun, they said, and because they wanted to continue to develop their skills in Basque. They also wanted to encourage other second-language learners to use Basque. The program title, *What About You?* recalled a well-known slogan of the language movement: "I speak in Basque; why don't you [too]?" Alberto and Rafa liked the phrase, because they saw it as an invitation to listeners to participate in their show and join in their efforts to become *euskaldun.*

This message came across most clearly and provocatively in the prerecorded segment that started off the show. The segment consisted of a song by the late Mikel Laboa, one of the leading figures of the Basque new-song movement. The song they chose is from his *Lekeitio* series of experimental songs. In contrast to the other traditional folk songs and ballads Laboa sang, *lekeitios* were "nonsense" songs, extended stretches of sound and wordplay. In these songs, Laboa was fond of testing the limits of his voice and the boundaries of languages. In some of the songs one often could not decipher what, if any, language he was speaking.

For their program introduction, Alberto and Rafa created a segment in which they played back short bits of one of these songs in which Laboa is heard playing a simple melody on the acoustic guitar and speaking, rather than singing, Basque sentence fragments. From the pauses and disjointed structure of the phrases we hear, it sounds as if we are listening to Laboa having a telephone conversation in Basque, although we can only hear his end of it. The radio programmers splice into this song short recordings of the voices of young people, mostly young men like themselves, talking about their attempts to speak Basque. The overall effect is somewhat chaotic, as the song is interrupted by the voices of recognizably non-native speakers, talking about their experiences speaking in Basque.

EXAMPLE 4

Eta Zu Zer?

[...] indicates pauses.   / / indicates overlapping fragments.
Capitalization indicates emphasis.   **Bold** indicates the voices
of new Basque speakers.   * indicates Gipuzkoan vernacular.

Laboa:

> *Zer?* ...
> What?
> *Nola?* ...
> How?
> *Bai, esan zidaten* ...
> Yes, they told me ...
> *Eh?* ...
> Huh?
> *Nortzuk?* ...
> Who?

(1) Male voice:

> **jode'. . . esan nahi det,*** ...
> Fuck ... I mean,
> **eh jendea . . . me cagüen**
> uh people ... shit [on]
> **/DIOS, ai/**
> God ... ai

(2) Male voice:

> **/Jendea, jendea esnatzeko/**
> The people, to wake up the people

(3) Male voice:

> **/kontzienziatzeko, edo . . .**
> to make them aware, or . . .
> **euskaraz . . . hitz egin behar dala**
> that Basque . . . must be spoken

Laboa:

> *Badakizu zer gertatzen dan hemen*
> You know what goes on here
> *Mm, hasieran bai, konturatu . . . bai*
> Mm, at first, yes, aware . . . yes

(4) Male voice:

> **Bai, nik, kalean,**
> Yes, I, in the street,
> **ez det* euskaraz hitz egiten . . .**
> don't speak in Basque . . .
> **mozkorra nengoenean baizik**
> except when I'm drunk

Laboa:

> *Berak uste zutela . . .*
> He thought that . . .
> *Baina ez zen . . . etzen ere . . .*
> But it wasn't . . . it wasn't even . . .
> *Ez, ez, ez . . .*
> No, no, no . . .
> [laugh, lowers pitch] *ez, ez.*
> no, no.

(5) Female voice:

> **Eh, uste't* gehi'o* e'in behar da**
> Uh, I think more should be done
> **euskararen alde.**
> In favor of Basque.
> **Nik uste't* . . . bueno,**
> I think . . . well,
> **e'iten* det* zerbait . . . e'iten det***
> I do my part, I do a bit

Guitar music begins a new melody and Laboa begins singing.

(6) Male voice:

> **Kalean gutxi, baina gero etxean . . .**
> Not much in the street, but then at home . . .
> **etxean bai . . . etxean ni . . .**
> at home, yes . . . at home, yes . . .
> **aitarekin . . . hitz egin . . .**
> with my dad . . . speak . . .
> **hitz egiten dut ASKO**
> I speak a LOT

Laboa (returns to speaking):

> ez ez ez ez ez
> no, no, no, no, no
> *Berak, eh, bai . . . egia*
> He, uh, yes . . . true
> egia izango zela,
> that would be true,
> *egia izango zela, baina . . .*
> it would be true, but . . .
> *Ez . . . ez . . . ezETZ*
> No . . . no . . . NO WAY

(7) Male voice:

> **Le'no, hasi naiz . . . Naizenean**
> Before, I start . . . When I'm
> **Ba . . . hitz e'iten* det***
> Ba . . . I speak
> **Baino nere problema da HAStea**
> But my problem is STARTing

Laboa:

> *Ezetz*
> No way

The music continues as Laboa shifts into unintelligible sound play.

The fascinating assemblage that makes up this program introduction puts onto the same stage the halting voices of new language learners and a musical icon from the Basque new-song movement. Musicians singing in Basque have been an important voice in the reclaiming of Basque language and cultural identity, and none is more well known and beloved than Laboa. That these young new learners would choose Laboa for their opening is telling. If any musician could represent Basque pride, cosmopolitanism, and populism, it would be Mikel Laboa (Agote 1995). Humble, witty, and renowned for his eccentricities, he was a much admired and celebrated figure among Basque youth and musicians of all generations and genres from radical rock, punk, and heavy metal to ballads. His music offered an unusual blend of political edge, lyricism, and playfulness that managed to be simultaneously tender, ironic, and poetic. His fondness for mixing genres and musical referents, together with his avant-garde experimentalism and imaginative soundscapes, escape categorization and the strictures of what is or is not authentically Basque. He invites exploration into the fuzzy boundaries of what is or is not a "song" and of where one language begins and another ends. His music has offered up spaces of unconstrained experimentation in a political milieu that has been prone to regulation and where the compulsion to transparent exemplary speech was pervasive.

The song Alberto and Rafa chose for their program comes from a performance appropriately titled "Communication/Incommunication," a theme Laboa has played with often in his work. There is no way of deciphering what Laboa is talking about in this song; that is precisely the delight of it. His sentences are fragmented; the other interlocutor is unheard. With the "meaning" of Laboa's conversation unavailable to us, what becomes meaningful is the attempt to communicate itself. Alberto and Rafa productively exploit this theme of disjointed partial communication to set a frame for the struggling utterances of the second-language learners in the pre-recorded segment and for themselves as "new Basques." The snippets of their halting speech find harmony with Laboa's own fragmented conversation.

The talk by the youth in this program introduction has some of the features we saw at Paotxa, except they do not use *hika*. Not knowing *hika* forms, like most second-language learners, they use *zuka*. Their speech, however, is anything but normative "school" Basque. An *herrikoia* (popular) feel is crafted in this case through their use of Gipuzkoan verbal forms and contractions (indicated by asterisks). For example, in statements 1, 4, and 7, speakers use the Gipuzkoan form of the auxiliary verb *"det"* [I have]. The female voice in statement 5 combines this dialectal form of the verb with a contraction to produce *"uste't"* (instead of *uste det*). Other contractions in her speech common to everyday talk are: *"gehi'o"* instead of *"gehiago"* and *"e'in"* instead of *"egin."* A streetlike voice is also signaled through their liberal use of Spanish expletives *"me caguen dios,"* *"jode[r]"* and their gruff intonation. These other features, together with the Laboa song, counterbalance the polite effects of *zuka* and situate these uncertain voices closer to an authentic [*jatorra*] and popular [*herrikoia*] Basque-speaking world.

Conclusion

"We play with language like the *bertsolari*," explained one of Paotxa's programmers when we were discussing their unusual program titles. The comparison was apt, as their radio narratives had elements that parallel the poetics of this improvised form of oral poetry. Paotxa programmers were not alone in aligning urban youth culture with *bertsolaritza*. In the eighties *bertsolaritza* was enjoying a renaissance among radical youth who were, among other things, drawing analogies between this figure of Basque popular culture and the street rapper of hip-hop (Urla 2001). The analogy the Paotxa programmer drew between their productions and vernacular poetry can be a useful one for thinking about the performative effects of the above radio introductions. The *bertsolari* spontaneously composes rhyming verses according to particular melodies. The verses work very much like proverbs, riddles, and other forms of popular expressive culture by constructing a story through the play of tropes and metaphor (Zulaika 1988; Fernandez 1986). Metaphors and expressions that rely on metaphor, explains James Fernandez, generate meanings not by linear argument, but through the images they juxtapose. The skill of the poet, the humor, and indeed the pleasure that verses evoke relies in large part on the unexpected and creative ways the images and sounds they mobilize bring together distinct domains of experience.

Perhaps this is a good way to understand the symbolic work that these experiments in populist media accomplish and their larger contribution to the project of language revitalization. In the domain of deliberately antinormative free radio, there was a greater license to play with language and be antiexemplary. Such a context generated the possibility for expressing a wider range of feelings and stances toward Basque that went beyond patriotism and a commitment to the unity of the nation. It expanded the range of ways to engage with Basque. One cannot help but think that Txepetx would see this as a contribution to language revival, and indeed, *bertsolaritza* is enjoying a growing popularity among young Basque speakers, both male and female.[11] In the specific bits of language play we looked at here, we also see youth knitting together cultural oppositions that have been problematic to the project of language revival. The incorporation of vernacular and the recycling of colloquialisms at Paotxa work to bring together two domains of life that had historically been quite separate in their own town and in Basque society more generally: that of the *baserri*, the world of the farmstead, and *kale*, the world of the street. This distinction at one time indexed a very real and deep disjuncture between rural and urban social milieus that were strongly associated with distinct languages and values. For much of the nineteenth and a good part of the twentieth centuries, the rural world was perceived as historically more conservative, staunchly Catholic, and Basque-speaking, while urban centers, Bilbao in particular, were perceived as the sites of more liberal, cosmopolitan strains in Basque society. The street as a cultural symbol was also a place where immigration and Spanish prevailed. To be a *kaleko umea,* a "child of the street" as people of Usurbil put it, was often to be seen as somewhat less than fully Basque. However, with the rural farmstead becoming more of a tourist attraction than a workplace and the Basque-speaking population now predominantly urban, this contrast no longer made sense to young people. It had lost its social grounding and become fodder for symbolic refiguration and parody in the popular culture of urban youth (Kasmir 1999: 193).[12] The program titles at Paotxa are an example of this. They disrupt the culturally constructed and politically loaded opposition between the rural and the urban that coded the former as the repository of authenticity and the latter as *erdaldun* [non–Basque speaking]. Their musical collages were critical elements in this bridging of cultural boundaries. They were *euskaldun and* they listened to folk, punk, salsa, and jazz. Their location in the transgressive public sphere of free radio allowed them to reanimate vernacular and to capture and broadcast out to their own communities the vitality of informal language that was lacking in the public arena, burdened with modeling a national form. And they took obvious pleasure in it.

If Paotxa played upon the rural and the urban, "Basque" and "non-Basque" music, the introduction to Alberto and Rafa's program, *What About You?* points to and disrupts a different opposition that had emerged in the context of language revival: the one between new speakers and Basque authenticity. The way they set up *What About You?* invites second-language learners into Basque popular culture, a sphere attractive for its vitality but often inaccessible to non–native speaking youth. In the symbolic universe of Basqueness that Alberto and Rafa created in their program, it was possible to be of the street and *euskaldun*; it was possible to be an *euskaldun berri* [new speaker] and also *herrikoia* [popular]. In the zone of free radio as it was practiced in the early nineties, the voice of the street was effected through predominantly masculine-identified linguistic forms. Women performed that voice using forms like *hika* that were more common to men's talk and with which they were not always so comfortable. At least at this point in time, *herrikoia* seemed to be a voice crafted and more authentically represented by men than women. A distinctively feminine *herrikoia* voice had yet to emerge.

As I noted at the start, Basque free radios like Paotxa or Molotoff are not specifically projects in language revitalization. Yet many programs were contributing to language revival's larger goal of expanding the use of Basque into new domains. By the nineties, sociolinguists, language planners, and language activists were becoming increasingly concerned with the question of informal register in Basque (see Garate 2002). They were concerned about how to create venues for expressive creativity and informal expression in Basque for a generation that might only have spoken Basque in school. They were worried that youth, particularly disenfranchised and working-class youth, were alienated from a language that had become for them a sign of political correctness. Researchers on Catalan youth culture report similar dilemmas (Woolard 2003; Pujolar 2001). It seems unlikely, however, that the solutions to these problems can come from language policy and planning. They seem more likely to come from popular culture and activities like free radio, music, or community magazines. Free radios did not try to teach good Basque, but they did provide venues in which youth could experiment in developing their own voice in Basque. One can legislate the language, document it, teach it, preserve it. But a language needs more than that. The cultivation of an expressive culture and popular registers happens in artistic and cultural creations. It happens in everyday life in the ferment of oppositional social currents within a richly varied civil society.

Epilogue

Working in the tradition of what anthropologists have called "the ethnography of resistance," I have drawn on the writings of language advocates and my own observations and interviews from multiple episodes of ethnographic research, exploring what social actors in the movement understand themselves to be doing, their salient practices, and the explicit and implicit assumptions that seem to guide these practices. My questions have been largely questions about cultural meanings—that is, questions about the conceptualizations or logics that inform this type of activism as well as what the movement itself does to reshape understandings of language and identity. Thus my goals have been to explore how language advocates talked about the value of Basque and its relationship to their identity and political beliefs, how they framed their claims; how they understood the forces that worked against the survival of Basque; and what tools they felt they needed to contest the dominance of the state language and preserve a place for Basque. These questions of meaning are central to understanding the dynamics of language politics. After drawing together the threads of my argument, I would like to reflect on the situation language advocacy faces today—quite different from the one in which my research first began.

Although I focused largely on the contemporary language-revitalization movement, particularly after the end of the Franco regime, understanding the logics of today's language advocacy required me to look back in time, to the early moments of the movement, to examine the emergence of what I regard as the two axiomatic premises of the revival movement. The first is the idea that Euskara constitutes the core of a distinctive Basque identity and nationhood; the second, that languages—Euskara included—are to be understood as *social facts,* with speakers whose social characteristics and behaviors can be documented and managed. The story of Basque-language revival is conventionally represented as an outcome of the first premise, but the second is profoundly important. The first premise alone, linguistic nationalism, while very important, could neither explain a good deal of what language advocates argued about, called for, and spent their time doing—measuring, planning, standardizing—nor fully describe what activism produced.

Rather, Basque-language revitalization is shaped by the intersection of the logics of what are arguably the two most significant social discourses of the eighteenth and nineteenth centuries: nationalism and the rise of "the social" as a sphere of knowledge and intervention—in other words, governance.

These premises, fundamental to broader European understandings of languages and nations, shape the ways in which Basque-language advocates articulate their claims and grievances and set about organizing their resistance. After tracing the emergence of these premises in the writings of Basque-language advocates at the start of the twentieth century and again in the sixties, when language advocacy began to regain momentum toward the end of the Franco dictatorship, I considered how these logics continue to operate and evolve in the projects of language standardization, statistical assessments, and the more recent turn to strategic-planning and quality-management techniques. Language revival has implied a kind of "rebirth" of Basque, not only in the sense of increasing numbers of speakers or would-be speakers, but also in the sense of refashioning language into a social object amenable to planning and reform. The necessity for language *planning* was the issue about which all *euskalzaleak* could agree, and it was a key demand of the language movement that took shape in the seventies. In decrying the decline of Basque, modernist language advocates promoted a sociological rather than a philological understanding of language. They argued that the demise of any language was not the result of inherent features of the language (e.g., grammatical or lexical "inadequacies"), but rather the outcome of structural inequalities and knowable social forces having to do with the social status of its speakers and its historically meager presence in social institutions. The crafting and disseminating of the sociological perspective came as much, if not more, from the technologies of documentation that advocates called for and used as it did from explicit political treatises. Technical knowledge and quantitative representations, expert theories and theorists about language are an integral part of the discourses and refashioning of language that formed the foundation for the approaches that emerged to try to save Basque.

Efforts to safeguard the future of Basque have operated as an extended project in remaking how citizens think about language use more generally. They foster recognition of the linkages between language and power. In this sense, language revival operates like the social movements of other disenfranchised groups (e.g., women, blacks, indigenous or disabled people) to expand the field of the political by linking "everyday institutionalized patterns and practices" to exclusion (Hobson 2003: 3). Language revival prompts explicit reflection on how common attitudes and choices about which language to use with the storekeeper or answering the phone, for example, are linked to political ideologies and structures of inequality. In addition, as language advocacy pressed to modernize Basque and contest prejudice, it also advanced new ways of understanding language as a governable object and the speaker as a subject with social impact on the life of the language. Resistance to language domination unfolds not only in legislation and the classroom, but also on the terrain of the self, calling forth a restructuring of subjectivity at more levels than has heretofore been recognized.

This argument aligns with that of social-movement scholars who view collective identity as something that is dynamically shaped within political struggle, rather than something that precedes and exists outside it. As Barbara Hobson has noted, recognition struggles

> name, interpret, and make visible histories of discrimination and disrespect, and thus not only motivate an aggrieved person to become politically active or to resist, but are a crucial part of the process of self-realization or mis- and nonrecognition. The very framing of grievances as injustices and the articulation of group identity shape cognitive processes, by which individuals understand and interpret personal experiences of disrespect and self realization, seeing them as shared with others in a devalued and disadvantaged group. (2003: 5)

I have explored this process by examining the ways language domination was framed and conveyed by language advocates, but also, crucially, how new understandings of Basque language and identity emerged out of advocacy. It is my hope that this will add new dimensions to existing interpretations of the evolution of Basque identity and will correct some misconceptions. For example, while most scholars now agree that Euskara replaced race or descent as the centerpiece of Basque nationality in the twentieth century, my goal has been to show that the transformation went deeper than just a change of "symbols." The notion of language was itself being reworked into a sociological and governable object. In addition, the debates among language advocates reveal the emergence of a pragmatic view of Basque identity. Summed up in the idea that being Basque means speaking Basque, the pragmatic perspective on identity issued a challenge to all Basques, especially nationalists who had abandoned Euskara. It created a nonethnic understanding of Basque identity as something lived and embodied through the acquisition and use of Euskara. The conception of language as a gateway to Basque identity regardless of ethnicity was widely disseminated through the community-based language-teaching schools. Surprisingly, this remains poorly understood if not completely ignored by many outside commentators. A recent book on language policy affirms, for example, that contemporary "Basque-speaking, grass-roots supporters [of Basque nationalism]" have "a desire to exclude outsiders from becoming Basque speakers" (Wright 2004: 212). This claim can hardly be sustained if one actually studies and reads what language advocates say and do. The grassroots movement has consistently sought to expand, not withhold, the teaching of Basque to all citizens. It is a shocking example of how misunderstood the work of minority-language activism can be.[1]

I have examined language advocacy tactics and discourses in order to show their contested and evolving nature, thereby taking seriously anthropologist Sherry Ortner's call for a "thick description" of resistance that explores internal conflicts within resistance movements (1995: 174). Despite the broad support for Basque revival across the political spectrum, advocates have disagreed, sometimes bitterly, over strategy. Standardizing, for example, met with fierce opposition at first. The relationship between standard and vernacular Basque continues to be debated and revised to this day. The goals of modernizing and governing Basque have also repeatedly collided with Basque-nationalist political dynamics. Debate, reassessment, and shifts in tactics have been an ongoing feature of the movement.

In addition to recognizing contestation within the movement, the goal of thick description has also led me to explore the complex and sometimes contradictory entailments of language advocacy. For example, with regard to standardization, this meant examining how the creation of Unified Basque engendered a new kind of prescriptivism, a normative Basque that led some to feel Basque was being corrupted and others to feel as if their spoken dialect was demoted or incorrect. This, in turn, engendered new efforts among language advocates to counteract the stratifying effects of standardization and to reclaim spaces for the use of vernacular Basque. Foucauldian analytics served my goal of thick description in drawing attention to entailments at the level of "subject effects" and the conceptual framing of language (i.e., as a governable object) not usually discussed in assessments of the politics of language revival.

It is not my intention to condemn language planning. While there are certainly elements worthy of critique and caution, and I have articulated some of these, it is not my aim to say that language planning has been either bad or good per se. Rather, it is to peer into the struggle for Basque-language revival to see what it reveals about the logics, modes of power, and conceptualizations that are pervasive in the modern landscape of language and cultural activism. Language revitalization will never be simply a technical problem divorced from politics; it is deeply shaped by the larger political culture, and its very techniques are power-ful. In studying these processes "thickly," it has been my intent to build on the work that advocates of minoritized languages have already done to deepen our collective understanding of the political field of language. My aim has been to denaturalize, not condemn, language planning, measurement, and standardizing—to make apparent the commonsense assumptions that are embedded in these methods of rational governing, so that the priorities and vision of language that derive from them could be considered rather than taken for granted. This, I think, can only be beneficial to the longer-term project of achieving something we might call linguistic democracy.

Ethnographic studies of resistance, writes Ortner, becomes thick to the extent that they can show us the social complexity of resistance struggles, unintended effects, ambivalences, internal differences, and change over time (1995: 173–74). To this I would add that thickness also comes from rendering as best we can the reflexivity and self-criticism that actors have about their own practices. Basque-language advocates—teachers, writers, intellectuals—are keenly aware of the limits of certain strategies and the shifting political and sociolinguistic scenario. They subject their ideas to scrutiny and debate in the pages of the Basque-language press, at conferences, and at public roundtables. A 2003 special issue of *Larrun*, a supplement to the cultural magazine ARGIA (Letona et al. 2003), provides an example. Entitled "Why Be Euskaldun?" this issue of the magazine brought together three important voices in Basque cultural life—sociolinguist Joxe Maria Odriozola, university professor and former *bertsolari* Jon Sarasua, and novelist Bernardo Atxaga—to have a conversation about the future of Basque. Among the topics they addressed was the question of "motivation." The latest survey results on the relatively low rates of Basque usage among young people were very much in the news. What, asked the magazine interviewer, will make this next generation want to speak Basque? Their responses, which I paraphrase below, give us a sense of the ongoing reflection and critique that characterizes language advocacy.

Odriozola, a Basque-language teacher for many years, responded that second-language learners do not speak Basque because they do not actually know it. Schools teach grammar, he explained, but not how to communicate. Second-language learners need to develop fluency in the nuances of register and pragmatics, and this comes ultimately from being a part of a social community of speakers. The key to motivation, he said, lies in expanding the social use of Basque (Letona et al. 2003: 8). Sarasua agreed and took the opportunity to make other criticisms. We have focused our attention on the quantitative dimensions [of revival]: numbers of children in immersion schools, numbers of pages written in Basque, numbers of broadcast hours.

In Sarasua's opinion, it was time to turn more attention to what he called the qualitative dimensions of language. What kind of communicative capacity do people have, he asked? What degree of creative capacity do we have in Basque? To what degree are we just building a translated culture? (ibid). This has been a question with which advocates have repeatedly struggled. In Sarasua's view, language revival urgently needed to reassess the mind-set and goal of achieving parity with

Spanish if it wanted to begin to address this question of usage and creativity. Interest in speaking Basque, he said, will come from the richness of what is produced in it and the unique cultural worlds one can access through it. We should be asking ourselves not whether Basque is as good as other languages, but rather, what does [knowing] Euskara give to me? Our movement, he concluded, has not done enough to convey our capacity for enjoyment, creativity, and experimentation in Euskara (ibid: 15).

This excerpt from a longer conversation gives a sense of the ongoing conversation and reassessment advocates are having about where their strategies have succeeded and where they need to change course (see Azurmendi and Martinez de Luna 2006; Baztarrika 2009). Efforts to legitimate Basque have by and large emphasized regularity, qualities of transparency, parity, and the unity of the language. The poetics of Basque that these commentators allude to—the playful, musical, or even sensual dimensions of language use—have gone largely unarticulated in the rhetoric of an advocacy that had been based on patriotism and rights. Translinguistic blending of languages have tended to be disqualified as incompetency, interference, or corruptions. As linguistic anthropologists have shown (e.g., Pujolar 2001; Rampton 1995; Woolard 1998), studying these translingual or bivalent usages could teach us a great deal about the investments speakers have in language as well as new hybridized forms of social identity that may be emerging. However, to date, funding for research on Basque has been tied closely to planning applications that approach language as a bounded countable "thing." A sign of shifting research approaches is afoot, however, in the work of Basque anthropologist Jone Miren Hernández. Her ethnographic study (2005) of young people's language attitudes asks not how much Basque do young people use, but what does it mean to them to speak Basque? How do they mobilize language in fashioning their identities and relationships with one another? She and Echeverria are among the new scholars who are also asking questions about language use as it relates to gender identity. Central to their work is a departure from a view of languages as stable, grammatically distinct systems toward one in which languages are approached as symbolic repertoires that speakers draw upon to construct and express their identities. It is a very promising new direction that takes us beyond the limited set of questions explored in demolinguistic surveys and linguistic-vitality assessments.

These shifting priorities and new frameworks for understanding the social life of language are apparent in the discourse of governmental language policy as well. A recent example can be seen in the work of the Advisory Council on Basque, a committee formed by the Department of Language Policy that includes writers, scholars, and representatives from the wide spectrum of social organizations working in Basque cultural life and advocacy. A 2009 report by the Advisory

Council entitled "Bases for Language Policy at the start of the 21st Century: Toward a Renewed Social Accord" (Consejo Asesor del Euskara 2009) shows us that the strategies and priorities of the past are not written in stone. The report is a summary of extended debates initiated in April 2008 with a wide range of groups in civil society about the status of language policy today. More than twenty-five years after the Law of Normalization (1982), which had set the basis for language policy for the Autonomous Community, it was time, felt the Advisory Council, to take stock of the results of their efforts, make adjustments, and reaffirm a broad-based social commitment to the normalization of Basque. According to Patxi Baztarrika, Director of the Department of Language Policy and chair of the committee that authored the report, this consultation was a laborious process, yet absolutely necessary. The most decisive factor for the future of Basque revival, in his view, is the establishment of a consensus on its value and purpose. He laid the groundwork for this by deliberately creating an Advisory Council that had members from diverse sectors of the language-advocacy world in order to engage as broad a spectrum of people as possible. Then, in an unprecedented move, citizens were invited to participate in the discussions about governmental language policy via the Internet and numerous public roundtables and presentations.[2]

In this stock-taking document, we find changes in the discourse of official language advocacy worth noting. First, the familiar tropes of linguistic nationalism have been set aside. The goal of language policy for the twenty-first century is not envisioned as a kind of return to a "Basque-speaking nation," certainly not Basque monolingualism. As can be seen in the new statistical categories that have been adopted, there is a definitive move away from a vision of a territory defined by two opposed languages struggling for territory. The project of language revitalization is described as the promotion of societal-wide bilingualism that will allow citizens to live in the language in which they are most comfortable.

Second, the Advisory Council Report recommends dropping the heavy focus adult language teaching used to place on delivering academic certificates and diplomas, an approach they call philologist. The report reveals the impact of new understandings about language that came out of their study groups around *A Future for Our Past*. They advocate adopting a model of continuing education that gives priority to producing practical competency in specific communicative tasks. Language teaching, they say, needs to be tailored to the needs of a language "that is not yet normalized and whose vitality depends on its active usage" (Consejo Asesor 2009: 26).

Third, sensitive to the symbolic significance of classification, the report encourages a more fluid and continuumlike understanding of the Basque speaker, the *euskaldun*. Language policies of the twenty-first century, they say, should drop the term "quasi-euskaldun" used in previous survey and census counts. It may be useful to measure degrees of linguistic competency, but they believe the practice of applying different labels to new and old speakers needs to be abandoned. The label of euskaldun should be expanded to incorporate the range of competencies Basques have, from understanding and speaking a little Basque to full fluency. The authors give two reasons for this. First, doing so would recognize the extraordinary symbolic and practical contribution that passive bilingualism and, indeed, all efforts to learn Basque make to encouraging social harmony between linguistic communities and thereby facilitating the growth of the Basque-speaking community.[3] Second, the idiosyncratic categories Basque advocates and planners once used are no longer needed now that standardized measures and categories are available in the European Framework of Reference for Language Acquisition, Education, and Evaluation.

As this last reference suggests, twenty-first-century language policy is becoming more standardized in its terminology and more friendly to the frameworks and principles of quality management. Efficacy and conviviality (*elkarbizitza* in Basque, *convivencia* in Castilian) have displaced patriotism as the key values in twenty-first-century language policy (Baztarrika 2009). Conviviality [*elkarbizitza*, in Basque, *convivencia* in Castilian] is the key term of twenty-first-century language policy. The 2009 report conveys a more accepting stance toward the linguistic plurality of the Autonomous Community. The first sociolinguistic studies and maps produced by advocates had treated the uneven distribution of Basque speakers as a negative sign of its decline and threatened status. This document, in contrast, presents Basque/Spanish bilingualism as a positive feature of modern life to be managed through realistic policies that aim to reduce monolingualism and facilitate spaces of Basque-language use. Language planning is good government, it argues. But language-promotion policies have to be tailored to the sociolinguistic realities of the specific areas. The report calls upon Basque advocates to accept that normalization will proceed at different paces across the territory. It recognizes Spanish as one language of the Basque Country and presents what it calls "sustainable diglossia" as the goal of normalization (ibid: 28). By this it means that Basque will inevitably prevail in some domains, Spanish in others. The report describes unevenness in usage as an inherent feature of multilingual life. Similar to Jon Sarasua, the report calls for shifting priorities from trying to achieve parity with Spanish in all domains to working instead to strengthen those arenas where Basque usage is vital and habitual (ibid).

The 2009 Advisory Council Report, unanimously endorsed by all its members, indicates significant shifts in some of the most basic premises of linguistic nationalism that once shaped language revitalization. The once inseparable association between ethnicity, patriotism, and speaking/knowing Basque has been set aside. The binary view of the linguistic universe and the aspiration of exact equivalency between Basque and Spanish are being displaced in favor of more flexibility and a pluralistic understanding of the linguistic landscape. Gone, too, is the kind of the anticolonial rhetoric found in texts from the seventies. Instead, there is a very pointed effort to step away from models of languages in conflict in order to situate language planning as enlightened management and language revival as a progressive democratic endeavor. Language revival, says the report, generates discomforts and sometimes inconveniences. It requires economic resources and work. What is undeniable, says the report, is that a social transformation toward balanced bilingualism and harmonious *elkarbizitza* [conviviality] will be successful only if it is based on a democratically achieved consensus and broad participation underlies it.

The elegantly simple statement by poet Joxanton Arze—a language is not lost because those who do not know it do not speak it, but because those who do know it do not speak it—has long been the mantra of the revival movement, reminding Basque speakers that the responsibility and power to keep their language alive has always, in some ways, rested in their hands. This was, no doubt, important to keep in mind during the darkest days of the Franco regime's repression. The Advisory Council reaffirms this fundamental principle, but it also goes beyond it. If the goal of language policy is not just to "save" Basque like a museum object, but to produce a harmonious bilingual society, they make clear that all residents, according to their abilities, have a responsibility and a role to play as citizens to help shape that future and take part in it.

> The key is, therefore, the support of the citizenry. The rest (legal frameworks, public policy, planning) are supporting instruments. In no way can this stance be described as an imposition; it is rather the result of a democratic accord that our society has undertaken on the path to [language] equality. To accuse this project or any other social goal that has the backing of the majority of citizens of imposition is a subversion of democracy itself. (Consejo Asesor 2009: 58)

Language Revival in an Age of Counterterrorism

As Hobson writes, recognition struggles are dynamic processes in which social actors articulate their claims, seize political opportunities, and refashion public discourses. However, as she goes on to say, "claims and claims-makers" exist in political cultures that condition their ability to speak and make their actions more or less dangerous or possible (Hobson 2003: 8). There are, she says, "hospitable and inhospitable fields for recognition struggles" (ibid). The shifting coordinates in the discourse of language revival that I have described and those to be found in the Advisory Council Report show this dynamic refashioning at work. The report's specific emphasis on the democratic nature of Basque-language policy and its direct allusion to accusations of language "imposition" also signal a sociopolitical context that has become more hostile to language normalization. In the last ten years, nongovernmental Basque cultural activists and projects so distinctive to the Basque case have been subjected to police investigations and accusations of reverse discrimination and even terrorism. By way of conclusion, I want to describe some of this larger sociopolitical context and specific challenges to Basque cultural activism that it poses. I will begin by setting the context with a personal story from the pages of my fieldwork.

Dateline: Euskal Herria 2001

The European Union had declared 2001 "The Year of Minority Languages." I traveled to the United Kingdom to attend a conference on the topic in June and, when it ended, made a short visit to Usurbil. It had been a tumultuous three years since my last spell of fieldwork studying the local language associations and community magazines. In September of 1998, ETA had declared a cease-fire. In Northern Ireland the IRA had agreed to the Good Friday peace accords just a few months earlier, and for a while it seemed that the Basques might be able to start a peace process as well. For fifteen months there was a spirit of optimism that negotiations with ETA might finally bring an end to the violence and the dispersion of Basque political prisoners.[4] But as we now know, that was not to be. The failed negotiations and the subsequent end of the cease-fire in December 1999 brought a new round of bombings and assassinations on the part of ETA, more police arrests, more street violence, and massive demonstrations against ETA in the Basque Autonomous Community and throughout Spain. It also brought an intensification of police and judicial investigations and harassment of nongovernmental activism that was literally starting to terrorize the organizations of language revival that I had studied and the people who worked in them.

Olatz Altuna, a young language advocate with whom I had worked, was one of the many targets of this harassment. I use her real name here after consulting with her, because what I recount below is now part of the public record and both she and I think it is important to make cases like hers more widely known. Olatz is a native of Usurbil and the daughter of Basque-speaking parents. Her father, a factory worker, was the mayor of the town for many years and a major figure in helping to create the town's *ikastola* for the town's largely Basque-speaking population. A bright student, she studied political science and sociology at the University of the Basque Country, with a focus on social movements politically identified with the nationalist left. Although it had not been her intention to make a career out of it, upon completing her degree she started to work in an array of language-revival projects, some paid, some as volunteer. One of her first jobs was to help organize and carry out the statistical analysis of the Street Survey, the Kale Neurketa. She was also hired to design Usurbil's campaign to promote Basque in local businesses, and she helped to found and served as director for a while of Usurbil's Basque-community magazine, *Noaua!* Today she works as a researcher for Soziolinguisika Klusterra, a Basque sociolinguistic institute where she coordinates the surveys on Basque-language use. Her diverse experience made her an invaluable collaborator in my research. I spoke often with her, and it was in no small measure due to her assistance—countless conversations, explanations, contacts, and sharing of draft memos and proposals—that I was able to reach a deeper understanding of language-revival strategies. Bright, enthusiastic, and seemingly tireless, Olatz was considering studying for a doctorate in language planning.

On my visit to Usurbil in 2001, however, those plans were permanently on hold. In October 2000, Olatz had been arrested and charged with belonging to ETA. We were meeting up now some eight months after her arrest. She suggested picking me up and offered to take me to visit the offices of the research institute to see the work they were doing and meet the people there. As we made our way down the highway, she told me about the arrest. I listened in shock. Below I paraphrase her story, reconstructed from my notes later than evening.

> It was very late, one thirty or so in the morning. Iñigo [not his real name] and I were asleep. The police came banging on the door of our apartment. He went to open it and they threw him down on the floor and pointed the machine gun at his head. The police wore face masks. They came to get me in the bedroom. They were screaming at us. They told me to get dressed, and then spent the next two hours searching through everything in the apartment. They took my computer. The whole time they kept Iñigo in one room and me in another, so we couldn't talk to each other. When they were finally ready to take me, I asked to speak to Iñigo and they said I could, but only in Spanish. So I did and asked him to tell my family not to worry. I haven't done anything. It was so surreal, talking to Iñigo in Spanish, the masked policemen, the machine guns. I couldn't believe it was really happening. I felt like I was in a movie.

Olatz told me she was taken by car to Madrid in the early hours of that morning, handcuffed and at times blindfolded.

> I was lucky. At least they didn't come in with a television crew, as they did when they came after Carlos.[5] After what seemed like hours in the police station, taking photos and fingerprints, they said they were taking me to Madrid. As we got into the car one

of the policemen told me, "Olatz, by the time we get to Madrid I would like you to have condemned armed struggle." I explained to him that ETA was a symptom, not a cause of the problems. I also told them that what they were doing to me was barbaric: arresting me; taking me to jail. I told them that they knew very well what kind of work I did and that it had nothing to do with ETA. You know what you are doing is wrong, I said to him. You know we are not ETA. But it didn't matter. He wanted me to condemn ETA. We began to argue. He refused to recognize our right to vote for self-determination and instead said the *ikastolak* were to blame for fomenting anti-Spanish feelings. By the time we got to Madrid, we were screaming at each other at the top of our lungs. As I left, still handcuffed, one of them said to me, "it has been very interesting. I have never spoken with a person from the *izquierda abertzale*." And I replied, "well, I have never spoken with a member of the [state's] repressive forces."

Under antiterrorist law the police were permitted to hold Olatz for seventy-two hours incommunicado without access to a lawyer or her family. She was then formally questioned by the presiding judge and released on bail set at 6,000 euros. It was during her questioning that she learned the cause for her arrest was a job she had taken in 1998 at the Zumalabe Foundation, a newly created nongovernmental organization. Olatz's job there was to coordinate and facilitate intercommunication among what in the Basque political culture are called *herriko taldeak,* or populist social movements (e.g., antimilitarists, ecologists, feminists, proindependence youth, free radios). This job was a natural extension of the interest she had developed in Basque social movements during college, and she was excited at the prospect of working with a broad range of progressive groups. This work entailed editing a newsletter with a calendar of the events of various groups, creating a directory of nongovernmental organizations, and developing materials for discussion workshops on nonviolent civil disobedience.

As we drove, she described her arrest to me. She was completely certain that the police had to know that the foundation where she worked was not a part of ETA. Not only did the Zumalabe Foundation not teach or advocate violence, it was widely known that the donor who had created the foundation had denounced ETA's political violence.[6] Nevertheless, Olatz found herself, several other members from the foundation, and dozens other people from various legal political organizations standing before Spain's Audiencia Nacional [National Tribunal] accused of terrorism. Thus began what would turn out to be a long and drawn-out nightmare for Olatz, culminating in one of the biggest prosecutions of Basque social-movement organizations, known as the Sumario 18/98. It took five years for her case to come to trial. In the meantime, she kept working and doing research. She and her partner had a child, moved into a new home. But during the entire five years, she remained under a kind of domestic arrest, unable to leave the country and having to register with the police every week. With such a long wait, many of the accused thought the case would be dropped, but it was not. The trial began in November 2005, and it lasted sixteen months. The conditions were harsh. Olatz and the fifty-one other people indicted were required to be physically present at the court in Madrid for every day of the entire proceedings against all fifty-two people. They had to personally absorb all the cost of transportation back and forth to Madrid every week, housing, child care, and loss of work. They entered a court that re-garded them as enemies of the state and had them sit behind bullet-proof glass. Every day they entered the court, they had to pass before the numerous anti-ETA protestors who shouted death threats and epithets at them as they entered. When it was finally over, in November 2007, Olatz was sentenced to nine years prison. In keeping with its practice of dispersing Basque political prisoners, the state sent her to a jail in Valencia several hundred kilometers away from the Basque provinces.[7] After eight months in jail, she was released when lawyers successfully had the deci-sion against Zumalabe members reversed.

At the time of her sentencing, *Noaua!*—Usurbil's community magazine where Olatz had worked—ran her picture on the front cover with a somber title that read "injustice." Dozens of neighbors and friends stood in solidarity outside her house on a late November evening in 2007 when the police came to take her preemp-tively to jail to await her sentence. She was leaving behind a three-year-old daugh-ter. In protest, residents posted a video of the arrival of the police on YouTube. Thousands of miles away, I watched in disbelief. Olatz was not the only one, but she was someone I knew, not an anonymous "terrorist." She had a face, a history, a family. How could it be that she and so many other people working in political or civic organizations—citizens who had never committed a violent crime—were now finding themselves under suspicion of terrorism and going to jail with sen-tences of ten, twenty, or more years? How did things come to this, and what does this mean for language revitalization?

Sumario 18/98: Everything is ETA

The explanation for the arrests lies in a new strategy the Spanish state had been developing in its war against ETA. Operation "Itzali," the code name for the police operation in which Olatz was arrested, was just one of many authorized police-judicial investigations spearheaded by the Spanish judge Baltasar Garzón, best known as the judge who led the battle to extradite the Chilean dictator Augusto Pinochet from England to be tried for crimes of torture and murder. His investi-gations of Henry Kissinger's role in U.S.–backed military coups in Latin America and, more recently, his criticisms of the U.S. invasion of Iraq and its policies in

Guantánamo, have earned him an international reputation as a defender of human rights. In the Basque Autonomous Community, Garzón's reputation is more mixed. As head of the Central Criminal Court No. 5, a subsection of the Audiencia Nacional, a special court created to prosecute terrorism, organized crime, and corruption, Garzón is the primary architect of a new strategy to defeat ETA by rooting out its alleged support network.[8]

The thesis behind Garzón's judicial strategy was first made public as a prologue to a book on ETA published in 1997 (Garzón Real 1997). In this text he argues that ETA controls and economically sustains itself through a wide network of social, cultural, and financial entities including political parties, unions, businesses, youth organizations, even educational organizations that are aligned with what he calls the *entorno* [orbit] or *entramado* [framework, structure, network] of the radical leftist wing of Basque nationalism, popular referred to as the *izquierda abertzale*. More specifically, his text reconstructs a history of ETA's political evolution in which he claims that the organization deliberately gained political control over two legal political associations of the Basque nationalist left, KAS [Koordinadora Abertzale Sozialista] and EKIN, and the variety of organizations affiliated with them. His claim is essentially that ETA gives directives to KAS and EKIN such that they are defacto all one and the same organization. Any Basque-nationalist political or cultural organization who had high-ranking personnel, especially directors, presumed to be affiliated with either KAS or EKIN were to be regarded as in effect subsidiaries of ETA, and thus their members were to be considered terrorists.

Garzón's thesis set into motion a number of secret investigations and subsequent indictments of various political, education, and media organizations ideologically aligned with leftist Basque nationalism. The first to be shut down were the newspaper *EGIN* and its radio station, Egin Irratia, in 1998, followed by an indictment against Jarrai, a leftist nationalist youth organization. Then came what has been called the "macro indictment," Sumario 18/98, in 2000—a dossier of many thousand pages accusing members of varying nongovernmental groups, popular associations, media, and business enterprises of belonging to or following orders from ETA. These included Xaki, a group working internationally to promote the rights of stateless nations, and Gestoras pro-Amnistia, a group working in defense of the rights of Basque political prisoners and members of the Zumalabe Foundation, where Olatz worked. It is fair to say that these groups were correctly perceived by police to be ideologically supportive of the nationalist-left political program and the right to Basque self-determination. As a shorthand, the various indictments stemming from this general thesis have become known as "18/98 plus."

Language revival was not the target of these prosecutions, but it was inevitably affected by the pursuit of ETA's alleged infrastructure. The grassroots adult language-teaching network, AEK, was the subject of repeated judicial investigations during this period, including accusations of teaching kidnapping techniques in its language classes and of funneling monies for ETA. In February 2003, the Audiencia Nacional went on to indict one of the most significant creations of the Basque linguistic and cultural movement: the independent Basque-language newspaper, *Euskaldunon Egunkaria,* also known simply as *Egunkaria.* Many years in the making, the paper was the first to publish entirely in Basque and was conceived as a critical instrument in both the normalizing of Basque and the creation of a Basque reading and writing public sphere that addressed itself to the entire Basque territory on both sides of the border. In operation for thirteen years, the highly successful newspaper was permanently shut down, its materials confiscated, its bank accounts blocked, its digital edition and archives taken off the Internet, and its board of directors—among them highly respected scholars and journalists—arrested and subjected to interrogation. Several of the arrested, including the newspaper's director, Martxelo Otamendi, subsequently leveled credible charges of torture during their time of interrogation. Demonstrations in the days following the newspaper shutdown brought the capital city of Donostia to a standstill. Protests were issued from respected media organizations in Catalonia and elsewhere in Europe. Although in 2006 the state's official prosecutor recommended dropping the case for lack of evidence, the trial of various members of its top administrative staff was allowed to go forward in December 2009 with an association of victims of terrorism acting as the plaintiff. Once again, they were all required to be present in Madrid for the duration of the trial. In June 2010 the court found in favor of the newspaper for lack of evidence.[9]

Looking at these events, we can say that the first decade of the twenty-first century has been a devastating one for nongovernmental political and cultural organizations particularly, but as the newspaper case makes evident, not exclusively for those ideologically aligned with leftist Basque nationalism. Two of the first groups to begin collecting and disseminating information about the indictments were the Basque human-rights organization Behatokia (The Basque Observatory of Human Rights) and Eskubideak (The Association of Basque Lawyers). In 2002 they published one of the first compendiums of information on the indictments, the groups involved, charges being leveled, and international human-rights treaties.[10] A delegation composed of members of the National Lawyers Guild and Democratic Lawyers of Europe went to Spain to investigate the indictments. They formed the organization called Euskal Herria Watch, with the intention of monitoring the judicial proceedings. In the Autonomous Basque Community, civil society responded with public demonstrations and the formation of a pluralistic

FIGURE E.1. Street demonstration in Bilbao by the Movimiento 18/98 plus against the arrest and prosecution of Basque-nationalist associations, November 2005. Courtesy of Argazki Press.

coalition known as the Plataforma 18/98 plus, comprised of intellectuals, lawyers, journalists, and union leaders as well as representatives from the nonpartisan peace organization Elkarri (see figure E.1).

Concerned about the dangerously eroding boundary between political dissent and terrorism, the coalition organized conferences of legal experts and scholars and mobilized internally and internationally to study the juridical bases and social impact of the indictments (see Ferrer et al. 2005). Of concern is the new and much more expansive definition of ETA underlying these indictments. In these prosecutions it is no longer necessary to prove the use of any violence, any crime, or even an intention to support the terrorist organization. Activist lawyer Carlos Trénor, one of the arrested, had seen this coming. In a conversation I had with him in 1998, shortly after the publication of Garzón's thesis, he explained that the logic of Garzón's reasoning led to the inescapable conclusion that support for Basque self-determination and a distinct Basque identity, regardless of the means, would become tantamount to a crime. Basque nationalists, he said, have become enemies of the state. Trénor is among those now in jail for this crime.

The Spanish state's preemptive closure and prosecution of leftist Basque-nationalist media and cultural and political associations via the above-mentioned judicial proceedings, together with the expanded police surveillance over citizens, make what is happening in the Spanish Basque Country into a compelling example of how Western democracies are usurping basic legal entitlements in the name of security (see Agamben 2005; Crumbaugh 2010: 663). Facilitating this has been the rise to power of the conservative Partido Popular (PP), a party founded by former members and supporters of the Franco regime. In 1996, advocating a platform based on the defense of Spanish national unity and identity and a hard-line approach to ETA, the PP edged the Socialist Party (PSOE) out of the presidency of the Spanish government and then gained absolute majority in the legislature from 2000 to 2004. Coincident with their rise to political power came a worsening of relations between the Spanish central government and Basque nationalist political parties and an increasingly hostile portrayal of both Basque- and Catalan-nationalist political and cultural projects and aspirations.

ETA helped to cultivate a sympathetic audience for this. The organization's campaign of political violence, particularly their decision in the mid-nineties to begin targeting civilians—scholars, journalists, and members of the PSOE and PP political parties, fueled the flames of anti-Basque public sentiment. Their actions created a climate of fear and provoked mass rallies, outrage, and condemnation, in which conflations of legal minority-nationalist parties and terrorism were rampant. A key moment sparking what would become a virtual tornado of anti-Basque criticism was ETA's 1997 assassination of the PP municipal council member Miguel Angel Blanco. Spanish political culture witnessed the emergence of various aggressively anti-Basque nationalist associations: El Foro de Ermua (named after Ermua, the city of Blanco's assassination), Basta Ya! And the Association of Victims of Terrorism (ATV). It was at this time that one began to encounter a new species of extremely inflammatory rhetoric that Zulaika (1999) has called "euskon-azism," in which Basque nationalism and its cultural projects were equated with terrorism, fascism, and Serbian-like ethnic cleansing. In the climate that currently exists, critics like Zulaika who have challenged the outrageousness of these attributions or attempted to explore the perspectives of leftist nationalists have found themselves to be quickly labeled apologists for terrorism.[11]

At a press conference in 2007, Mariano Ferrer, a respected journalist and spokesperson for the "18/98 plus" coalition, traced the origins of the indictments not just to Garzón's thesis, but to this particular political conjuncture. In the aftermath of ETA's ruthless killing of Miguel Angel Blanco, Ferrer argues, the PP-controlled Spanish government saw an opportunity to use antiterrorist law to pursue its long-standing desire to weaken Basque-nationalist political power by going after its weakest link, the *izquierda abertzale,* and by criminalizing and shutting down the array of voices, from youth to newspapers, that make up this diverse sector of Basque civil society.

The expanded definition of ETA operating today, including the political rhetoric associated with it, puts language revival at risk in several ways. It has diminished the freedom of individual language advocates by literally putting many of them in jail and subjecting others to surveillance. It has also instilled fear in anyone involved in nongovernmental activism or oppositional Basque media. This inevitably affects language revitalization. There is and always has been a porous boundary between language revival and other forms of social dissent. Scholarship on language-revitalization movements, whether it be among the indigenous Mayas, the Maoris, or the Irish, shows us that language movements are almost always a part of broader social movements for social justice and political change (Fishman 1991; Hinton 2001; England 1998). It should not surprise us that speakers of minoritized languages are sympathetic to struggles against other kinds of social and political discrimination and are often involved in more than one movement for social change. Language discrimination is typically interwoven with other forms of social inequality.

Prosecuting democratic forms of political dissent exerts a chilling effect on the entire landscape of movements for social change. The material costs of the indictments and trials in terms of loss of income, resources, and years of work are substantial—the Basque newspaper being the most salient example. The elaborate police powers and legal apparatus of antiterrorist prosecution in Spain today make it possible to preemptively close down a political or social group, leaving them very few options but to build again from scratch. The amazing thing is that in many cases, like that of the Basque newspaper, rebuilding is exactly what Basques have done. But even when not attacking language revival per se, these methods put language revival into jeopardy by narrowing the sphere of political debate and weakening civic engagement. As we saw in the Basque-language Advisory Council Report of 2009, effective language policy requires open debate and consensus building. Scholars and experts in language planning similarly underscore that the success of language revival plans depends on popular involvement (Grenoble and Whaley 2006). This involvement has historically been one of the most distinctive features of Basque-language revival in the twentieth century. The Basque population's extraordinary capacity for mobilizing, for fundraising, and for volunteer labor has been nowhere more manifest than in the language movement. It may be some years before we can know how the heightened climate of fear and harsh sentencing has affected the kind of grassroots civic engagement that has for so long supported Basque-language revitalization. The discursive and tactical shifts taking place in language advocacy, have to be understood in relation to these political developments.

Nongovernmental language-revival activism stands to lose ground as collateral damage as Spain's war on terror curtails civil rights. At the same time, the turn to the right in Spanish politics has not been limited to silencing and criminalizing political organizations of the *izquierda abertzale*. It has also spilled over into an explicit attack on both Basque and Catalan schooling and language-normalization policies. As Susan DiGiacomo (1999: 105) has argued, print media are a key locus for language-ideological debates and figure prominently in the backlash against minority-language normalization. A steady flow of op-eds and books penned by public figures such as Fernando Savater, Aurelio Arteta, Antonio Muñoz Molina, Juan Ramón Lodares, Jon Juaristi, José María Ruiz Soroa, and others has cultivated a view of Catalan- and Basque-language normalization as a form of ideological fanaticism that discriminates against Spanish speakers. Joan Mari Torrealdai (1998, 2001), a member of the board of directors of the censored Basque newspaper, provides a meticulous documentation of this backlash in a broad array of newspaper articles and essays. As he shows, one of the first elements to be targeted by conservatives was bilingual education and the mandated requirement to teach a minimum of three hours of Basque per week. *Ikastolak* have been a favored target of critique, accused of having a curriculum that indoctrinated children into an exclusionary Basque identity and fomented a violent and xenophobic youth. This is what Olatz was told by her police guards at the time of her arrest. JoAnne Neff-van Aerstaeler (2006: 180–81) documents the efforts of José María Aznar's administration, particularly in its second legislative period (2000–2004), to reduce the power of regional governments in matters of education and to put in place curriculum requirements that emphasized the primacy of Spanish national unity, flags, and other such Spanish national symbols.

Torrealdai (2001) writes that while many of the criticisms being leveled against Basque-language normalization are not new, they became more pervasive and aggressive in the early part of this century. Like Ferrer, he identifies the aftermath of the Miguel Angel Blanco's assassination as a turning point. In 1997, writes Torrealdai, we see anti-Basque nationalists begin to challenge the entire conceptualization of normalization, suggesting it has gone too far both in the Basque Country and Catalonia and needs to be slowed down and even rolled back. In 2000 anthropologist Mikel Azurmendi, a well-known critic of Basque nationalism, published a monumental tome on the writings of early defenders of Euskara, claiming to trace in their work the beginnings of a deep and abiding "ethos" of racial superiority and xenophobia that he claims persists like a congenital disease in Basque culture today and is the true motivation behind the efforts to preserve Basque (Azurmendi 2000). The policies to protect and promote its historically minoritized languages, policies that have won Spain praise from the European Bureau of Lesser Used Languages and the Council of Europe, are portrayed by Azurmendi and other detractors as a source of social strife, engendering reverse discrimination, weakening the Spanish language and national identity, and encouraging a victimized mentality among Basques.

The accusations currently leveled against Basque and Catalan language-normalization efforts exhibit an aggressive and highly inflammatory terminology. In his book on the backlash, Torrealdai (2001) prints the critiques in their original language to allow the reader to see the tone of contempt with which so many critiques are being written. Not only is Basque-language education routinely described as an "imposition," we also find language normalization described as having created a "dictatorship of *Euskara*" (Torrealdai 1998: 201). While the Observatory of Linguistic Rights, Hizkuntz Eskubideen Behatokia, documents daily infractions of the legal rights of Basque-language speakers to receive basic services in Basque, opponents of minority language–promotion policies claim these policies have instituted a de facto form of "ethnic cleansing," making it impossible for monolingual Spanish speakers to find a job, live, or speak their language in the Basque territory. But the reality is and still remains that the vast majority of jobs have no Basque-language requirements. The language requirements that do exist in public-sector jobs are contingent upon the type of job and proportion of Basque speakers in an area. Employees typically receive paid release time to attain the level of Basque required for their job if they do not already know it. Nevertheless, as Torrealdai (1998, 2001) shows, it is regular fare to find in the press a sense that Spanish speakers are discriminated against. These ideas then get circulated uncritically in the international press, creating yet more misunderstanding and an impression of "language vigilantes," as one author has called them, terrorizing people into learning Basque.[12] The unspoken expectation that comes through these irate accusations is that one should be able to live as a Spanish monolingual in these territories without any inconvenience.

Basque revival has entered a new phase in the twenty-first century. Counterterrorism and the rise of a reinvigorated Spanish nationalism have created a hostile environment for minority-language claims that will affect the future of Basque-language revival in ways yet to be known. They also pose very real and immediate risks for nongovernmental language advocates, as Olatz's arrest and the prosecution of the directors of the Basque newspaper make clear. We see a push back against the gains and framework of the past and a demand that policies of "tolerance" for minority languages should replace language promotion and normalization. One of the more recent examples was the presentation in June 2008 of the "Manifesto in Defense of Castilian" by Fernando Savater, the well-known spokesperson for the Foro de Ermua, and the writer Mario Vargas Llosa. The manifesto decries the discriminatory effects of language normalization. It calls for eliminating regional language requirements for civil servants and a constitutional reform, if need be, making it illegal to require any Spanish citizen, regardless of where he or she lives, to learn any language other than Castilian.[13] The manifesto regards the language normanization efforts currently underway in both the Catalan and the Basque Autonomous Communities to be illegal violations of the 1978 Spanish Constitution, according to which Castilian is the only mandatory language of the state. We can understand, then, why we encounter such pointed commentary in the 2009 Advisory Council Report about the democratic underpinning of language policy and the report's rejection of the use of the word "imposition" in describing bilingual-language education.

What Ralph Grillo (1989: 173) once aptly called the "ideology of contempt" for subordinate languages and their speakers finds fertile ground in the contemporary right-wing challenges to the decentralization and cultural pluralism that Spain initiated after Franco. The rapidity with which minority-language promotion policies in Spain have been recast as reverse discrimination and fanaticism is somewhat breathtaking. It flies in the face of the demonstrable hegemony of Spanish and, interestingly, the overwhelming continued support (81 percent) that societal bilingualism enjoys among residents of the Autonomous Community (Hernández, Olaso, and Martinez de la Luna 2006: 113). Accusations of the "excesses" of language-normalization policies and the resulting "tyranny" of Basque (or Catalan) that Spanish nationalists articulate have been able to gain traction because of the continuing vitality of this ideology of contempt. Fundamental to this ideology is the opposition that is drawn time and again between "local" or "regional" cultural vernaculars and languages on the one hand and "cosmopolitan" civic values on the other. This cultural trope lurks, as anthropologist Charles Briggs (2005) has argued, in many cultural struggles today, from the war on terror to debates over multiculturalism, immigration, and citizenship and, of course, language. Woolard (2008a) and Gal and Woolard (2001) have explored this at length. Minority languages are linked (and chained) to values of authenticity and rootedness to a particular place and ethnicity. Majority languages, by contrast, are perceived as transcending specific roots, being neutral, belonging to no one in particular and thus to everyone. With the institutional, historical, and political forces that led to their dominance erased, majority languages are presented as ethnically and ideologically deracinated and thus inherently more suitable to serve as languages of communal public discourse.

The "Manifesto in Defense of Castilian" is an exceptional example of this ideology at work, though it is not alone.[14] Language debates in Spain display a striking reversal with the end of the Franco regime. Today those who advocate a return to a Spanish-only language policy present themselves as defenders of universal values and democracy. As Woolard (2008) has noted, the critiques mounting against minority-language policies increasingly tend to frame Castilian as a *postnational* language, entitled to its dominance not only by virtue of possessing more speakers and the backing of state institutions, but also because of the language's presumed "privileged purchase on modernity and democracy." Opponents to normalization efforts in Catalonia and the Basque Country, she writes, characterize the protection of minoritized languages as a "rootbound particularism" that strangles modern Spanish democracy and advocate instead what they frame as a democratic cosmopolitanism, better expressible in Castilian as a "common language" (ibid.). Thus we have arrived at a curious moment in which it is in the name of democracy and freedom that calls are made to restrict the policies that Spain put in place during its transition to democracy.

I have taken this detour into developments in Spanish political culture and the fight against terrorism because, as a scholar of the language movement, I feel it is necessary to have an understanding of the wider political context in which the movement is operating and an awareness of the very real and personal dangers that Basque-language advocates have been facing in the last decade. The Basque revival experience—both its successes and the current worrisome moment— shows us what scholars of language revival have said before: that the fate of language revival is inextricably linked to the larger political and economic context and to the freedoms that exist for community activism, political debate, and dissent. Language revival will never be simply a question of good planning. If ETA, as seems increasingly likely, finally abandons armed struggle, social and political life on all fronts will be immeasurably better. But it is unlikely that the hostility to minority-language advocacy will cease, because this hostility does not just emanate from the problem of political violence. Additional obstacles derive from the continued and often implicit adherence to the monolingual nation-state as the natural and preferred order of things.

As we find ourselves in a world of increasing interaction, migration, and traffic across national and linguistic boundaries, the question of how to deal with linguistic diversity is inevitably going to become more acute. We need to continue the work of rethinking the place of language in a liberal political-theory conception of citizenship (Kymlicka 1995; Kymlicka and Patten 2003; May 2001) and to confront what I would call, borrowing from George Lipsitz's (2006) important work on racism, our "possessive investment in monolingualism" as a system that benefits some at the expense of others.[15] Additionally, scholars and advocates need to go beyond simply celebrating multilingualism in order to build an understanding of it as a complex lived reality linked to other forms of structural inequality (Duchêne 2011). In that endeavor, we can profit from closer studies of the dynamic field of minority-language movements, examining not just what they have achieved, but also their debates, dilemmas, and experiments. If the Basque case has taught us anything, it is that collective effort can turn the fate of a language around. It has also taught us that this requires imagination, constant critique, effort, and broad-scale participation on the part of everyone, both majority- and minority-language speakers.

Notes

Introduction

1. "Euskara" is the recommended spelling for the Basque language, as established by the Basque Language Academy. With regard to the spelling of this and other Basque words, I follow the official orthography of standard Basque. It is common to find the Gipuzkoan dialect variant *"euskera"* used interchangeably with *"euskara."* Other dialect variants are *eskuara* and *uskara*. In some Spanish-language texts, the Basque language is called *vasco* or *vascuence,* although in the Spanish-language press we find an increasing tendency to use the term *euskera* instead of *vasco*.

As May (2001) and Grenoble and Whaley (2006) point out, due to processes of language shift, people may claim belonging in a minority-language group who have a very imperfect grasp of the language or do not speak it at all but hope to some day. While this fact has sometimes been used in not-so-veiled ways to imply the inauthenticity of some language-revival advocates—that is, as not real speakers of the language—it seems more useful to recognize language-advocacy groups as essentially political-affinity groupings that overlap with speech communities but whose belonging is one of elective affinity.

2. Percentages of speakers come from the *IV Encuesta Sociolingüística 2006* (Eusko Jaurlaritza 2008). This and other periodic survey data are published on the Web site for the Basque Government's Deputy Ministry of Language Policy: http://www.euskara.euskadi .net.

3. Officially titled Hizkuntz Politikarako Sailburuordetzea, the Deputy Ministry of Language Policy, this office is now incorporated into the Department of Culture. Navarre has its own General Directorate of Language Policy. In the Basque provinces located in France, also referred to as Iparralde (northern Basque country), Basque has no official status and no state-sponsored language-planning entity. For a full discussion of the legal status of Basque in Spain, France, and the EU as well as its status in the larger diaspora, see Totoricagüena and Urrutia (2008).

4. Book-length ethnographic studies directly addressing language revival in Europe include Jaffe (1999), MacDonald (1989), Woolard (1989), and O'Reilly (1999).

5. Skutnabb-Kangas and Phillipson (1992) were among the first scholars to broach the subject of linguistic rights and to create the neologism "linguicism" as a form of language-based discrimination.

6. Foucault's *History of Sexuality* (1980a) and his 1982 essay "The Subject and Power" are key texts for the conceptualization of subjectification as a process emerging out of tech-

niques of knowledge. For particularly clear explications of this analytical approach and its political implications, see Hacking (1986), Rose (1990), and Butler (1992).

7. For insightful analyses of resistance and ironies in language revival, see Roseman (1995), Jaffe (1999), Handler (1988), McDonald (1989), Gal (2006), and the early work by Eckert (1983).

8. My thanks to George Lipsitz, to whom I owe this metaphor of stepping forward for a closer look.

9. All names are fictional.

One • Language Loyalism's Early Roots

1. The view that Basque survived due to the geographic isolation of speakers is a common one. For a contrasting view that stresses the role of speakers in actively maintaining their language, see the work of Xabier Erize (1999).

2. For more on the place of language in debates over foral rights, see Madariaga Orbea (2006).

3. Ostensibly a war over succession to the Spanish crown, the two Carlist wars (1833–40 and 1873–76) pitted a highly religious and conservative coalition of rural notables, clergy, peasants, and artisans against liberalizing capitalist urban centers. The defense of Basque foral regional rights became associated with Carlism, though most historians see the conflict as a broader struggle over the competing forces of liberalism and rural conservatism (Payne 1975).

4. In Gipuzkoa contrasts were less stark; immigration was both quantitatively smaller and more dispersed. Language decline was less severe there as well (Tejerina 1992: 86–104).

5. Evidence suggests that Basque was widely used in the Middle Ages during the height of the Kingdom of Navarre; its use is documented in the regions of Logroño, Zaragoza, and into Huesca. Annexation of Gipuzkoa, Alava, and Bizkaia into Castile initiates a process of decline in part by introducing *romance* as a language of prestige in certain social circles and contexts (Tejerina 1992: 80). See Euskaltzaindia (1977) and Trask (1997) for further description of the history of Basque-language loss.

6. For a somewhat analogous case, see Eckert's classic study (1980) of language shift among Gascon-speaking peasants in France.

7. On the perceived antagonism between the Basque-speaking farmer, *baserritarra*, and the typically hispanicized urbanite, *kaletarra*, see Heiberg (1980: 49–51). Heiberg notes that a vision of "the moral hard working peasant in confrontation with the immoral, effete urbanite" was manifest as early as Larramendi's 1754 text, *Corografía de Guipuzcoa*.

8. The linkage of nationhood to rural culture received its most elaborate expression in the writings of the German philosopher Johann Gottfried Herder, for whom the roots of the nation lay in its *Volk*, or rural peasantry and, in particular, its poetic traditions (Ergang 1966; Wilson 1973). For other examples of the use of ruralist tropes in expressions of nationhood, see DiGiacomo (1987), McDonald (1989), Hobsbawm and Ranger (1983), Fernandez (1962), Gellner (1983), and Fishman (1972).

9. Arana writes this in the magazine *La Patria* in 1902, cited in Corcuera 1979: 396n280. For a rich analysis of Arana's political thought and his ideas on language see Corcuera (1979) and Euskaltzaindia and Fundación Sabino Arana Kultur Elkargoa (2004).

10. In the early part of his work, Arana is most appropriately described as a Bizkaian

nationalist, though later on he was to develop the concept of an independent federated Basque country, for which he invented the name Euzkadi, comprising all seven of the Basque provinces (Larronde 1977; Corcuera 1979).

11. Heiberg and many Basque social and economic historians explain Basque nationalism largely in terms of class dynamics resulting from industrialization (e.g., Beltza 1976; Corcuera 1977; Letamendia 1977; Heiberg 1980). Another important line of argument sees Basque nationalism as a consequence of failed Spanish nation building (Linz 1973; Douglass 1985).

12. Larronde provides the exact wording in Spanish from the 1897 article as: *"nada es el saber el euskera, no siendo patriota. Todo es el patriotismo, aun no sabiendo el euskera. A la Patria no la salvará el euskera; sí y solamente la salvará el patriotismo . . . Propaga el patriotismo, y con él se propagará también el euskera. Si propagas el euskera como lengua sin patria, con él también se extenderán también los enemigos de la Patria"* (1977: 134–35).

13. In somewhat different terms, Zalbide (1988) also traces the call for modern corpus and status planning to the speech Luis de Eleizalde made to the first Basque Studies Congress of 1918. Fishman notes that inaugural language congresses merit greater study as a kind of "embryonic stage" of language planning when people are being rallied so that a course of action can be decided upon, responsibilities allocated, priorities set, and authorities empowered (1993: 2).

14. Reluctant to name names and enter the rancorous and highly personalized political debates over language, Urquijo, who was not a Basque nationalist, directed most of his criticisms to the whole field of Basque-language studies, which he called *euskaralogía*. He was an adamant proponent of separating language studies from politics as a whole (Urquijo 1918: 405). See Crowley (1996) on the cordoning off of political ideology as foundational to the formation of linguistics.

15. For a useful annotated version of this and other key essays by Unamuno, see Unamuno (1997). Villasante (1979: 342) suggests some of Unamuno's ire may have stemmed from having been passed over for the first professorship of Basque established by the provincial government of Bizkaia in 1888. The position was awarded to Resurrección María de Azkue, who went on to become the first president of the Basque Language Academy.

16. The four literary dialects recognized at this time were Gipuzkoan, Lapurdian, Zuberoan, and Bizkaian (Trask 1997: 48). The proposal for amalgamation of the dialects into a single standard was made in Campion and Broussain (1992), who also review the various other options for standardization.

Two • Euskara and Basque Nationhood

1. Resurrección Azkue and Julio Urquijo, neither of whom were Basque nationalists, stayed in Spain and continued to be active in linguistic research.

2. More detailed descriptions of the repression of Euskara under Franco can be found in Pérez-Agote (1987) and Gurruchaga (1985). Euskaltzaindia (1977) and SIADECO (1979) also contain firsthand accounts of how linguistic repression was experienced.

3. Two of the first and most comprehensive histories of ETA's formation upon which I draw are Gurutz Jáuregui (1981) and José María Garmendia (1996). In English, Robert Clark's (1984, 1990) work on ETA is very valuable, using archival sources, firsthand accounts, and interviews. A highly useful source is the multivolume collection published

by the editorial collective Hordago entitled *Documentos,* which contains reprints and brief annotations of many otherwise unavailable pamphlets and articles covering ETA's beginning in 1952 to 1977. For analyses of ETA's evolution into the eighties, see Letamendia (1994), Ibarra Guell (1989), and Sullivan (1988).

4. ETA's first casualty and its first assassination did not occur until 1968.

5. For a detailed analysis of the radicalization of the clergy, see the important work of Iztueta (1981), also Heiberg (1989).

6. Many historians and sociologists have commented on the fact that despite ETA's commitment to secularism, ETA activists retained strong affinities to Catholic faith and discourse (see Gurruchaga 1985: 328–30). Beltza (1977) has argued that the prewar leftist nationalist party Acción Nacionalista Vasca was ideologically a clear predecessor of ETA's leftist form of national liberation.

7. A critique of the racialized concept of the nation had been articulated before the Civil War (see Jáuregui 1981). Krutwig's language-centered argument bore similarity to a well-known prewar text, *Genio y Lengua* [Genius and Language], written by P. Justo Mokoroa under the alias Ibar (1935), which was apparently widely read by ETA recruits at the time (Unzueta 1980).

8. Txillardegi's expertise in Basque linguistics earned him a seat at the Basque Language Academy in 1957. He was forced into exile in 1961 and remained so until 1977, when he returned to Donostia with the transition to democracy. A prolific scholar who earned his first degree in engineering, he later earned a PhD in linguistics and taught in the Philology Department for many years at the Estudios Universitarios y Técnicos de Gipuzkoa (EUTG).

9. Of special interest was an issue of *Zutik* (October 1963) devoted almost exclusively to the issue of Euskara. In this issue, the organization identified four fundamental goals for the language movement: literacy; adaptation of Basque to communicative needs of modern industrial society; creation of a standard unified Basque; and renovation of Basque cultural institutions, in particular the Basque Language Academy. All of these would be key areas of struggle in the language movement (Jáuregui 1981: 271–72).

10. Robert Clark argues that the regime's development projects had as part of their explicit aim the weakening of urban-worker organizations and diffusing the ethnic identity of the Basque and Catalan regions through demographic shift (Clark 1979: 229).

11. From 1940 to about 1973, Rentería in Gipuzkoa grew from 10,106 inhabitants to 37,310; Elgoibar went from 5,683 to over 13,000; and Durango from 8,251 to 22,354 (Heiberg 1989: 94). Gurruchaga estimated in the mid-eighties that roughly one-quarter of the inhabitants of the Autonomous Community were migrant workers or the children of Spanish labor migrants (1985: 216). For further discussion of industrialization and demographic change with attention to differences between Gipuzkoa and Bizkaia, see Gurruchaga (ibid.: 211–35).

12. Too little ethnography has been done of the contexts in which Spanish-speaking immigrants and the Basque-speaking working class did come together in daily life—in the factory, church, market, or town place. Hernández's (2004) historical ethnography of language and identity in Lasarte-Oria is a remarkable exception that reveals a more complex scenario and points of encounter than heretofore suggested by the notion of "two communities."

13. The commitment to these socialist principles is, however, questioned by some authors who argue that ETA's focus, particularly after 1974, began to center more on its military struggle with the state, resulting in an increasingly impoverished vision of its socio-economic program (see Jáuregui 2000: 264).

14. See Clark (1984: 146–52) on the class and ethnic background of early ETA members.

15. Reports and letters Txillardegi sent to the leaders of ETA between 1965 and 1966 detailing his criticisms of its ideological shift are translated and reprinted in Alvarez Enparantza (1997: 213–40). The issues of the journal *Branka: Euskaldun sozialista aldis-karia*, published between 1966 and 1971, were collected and reproduced in facsimile under the title *Branka* by Ediciones Vascas in 1979.

16. Two principal factions had been forming within ETA: the "Trotskyists," who favored a working-class revolution, clustered around the figure of Francisco (Paco) Iturrioz, and the "third-worldists," who drew inspiration from the anticolonial struggles of Algeria, Vietnam, or Cuba. On these factions and tensions, see Jáuregui (1981) and Giacopuzzi (1997).

Three • Making a Modern Language

1. As classically defined by Haugen (1966b), language planning involves code selection, codification, elaboration, implementation, and acceptance.

2. Amorrortu (2000) offers a useful discussion in English of Zuazo's dialectal classification. See Trask (1997) for an overview of Basque dialectal variation using the classification established by linguist Mitxelena.

3. The Basque Language Academy kept a low profile after the war. They continued to name new members (Federico Krutwig among them, in 1941), but it was not until the fifties that the academy became publicly active again and renewed the publication of its journal, *Euzkera*. The Basque Language Academy was not officially recognized by the Spanish state until 1976, the year after Franco died (Gurruchaga 1985: 290).

4. An example of the low status Basque had at the time of the transition was a statement in 1976 by then Prime Minister Adolfo Suarez, who, when asked by a *Paris Match* reporter if there would be a high-school diploma in Basque or Catalan, replied: "Excuse me, but your question is idiotic. Show me first of all where you can find teachers who can teach nuclear physics in Basque" (Torrealdai 1998: 183).

5. In addition to being a political activist and linguist, Txillardegi was also one of the first novelists of this generation. For a brief synopsis of the development of contemporary Basque fiction and some excerpted translations into English, see Lasagabaster (1990) and Olaziregi (2004). Fuller treatments of contemporary Basque literature can be found in Torrealdai (1977), Villasante (1979), Mitxelena (2001), and White (1999). White's research has brought a much overdue appreciation of Basque women writers.

6. The original conceptualization of normalization is attributed to the Catalan socio-linguist Lluis Aracil. For a useful discussion of Aracil's work and ambiguities in the meaning of normalization, see Woolard (1986). See also Zalbide (1998) for a discussion of how the term has been interpreted in the Basque-revival movement.

7. This group claimed to have created an alternative language academy called Eusker-azaintza. They distributed a two-page leaflet at an international conference on the Basque language, as part of the Second World Congress of Basque Studies, which I attended in 1987. Written in English, the leaflet was addressed to the "foreign linguists that have come

to Donostia in order to learn about the present situation of our national language." Beginning with the title "Death sentence for the *Euskera!*" [*sic*], it described Batua as a "dull, soul-less, poetry-less language" that was creating "a rift within many of the Basque speaking families between school age children and their elders whose genuine Basque speech is rejected by the young." The leaflet conveys the passion that Batua elicited from its detractors and some of the negative social effects they felt it was having on native speakers.

8. The term "flagging the nation," as Thomas notes, comes from Billig (1995), which he adopts in part from a reading of Anderson (1991).

9. These phrases appear in an exchange of letters between an industrialist of Lasarte (Gipuzkoa), Ramón de Brunet, and his friend Fermín de Lasalle, Duke of Mandas in 1890. At the end of one of the letters, Brunet explains to his friend in Spanish why he has chosen to write to him in Basque: "This is, my esteemed Don Fermín, the first letter in my entire life that I have written in Basque. And, although I know it to be full of errors, I am motivated to send it to you because I know you are one of the few people of high social status who wish to cultivate this philosophical language [*lengua filosófica*]." My thanks to Jone Miren Hernández for bringing this example to my attention.

10. See Thomas (2007) for a fascinating exploration of the symbolics of "k" in Filipino decolonization.

11. The Basque Language Academy used Arana's orthography with some modifications in its publications until 1964, when it introduced new orthographic guidelines. The use of double "r," tildes, and other spelling conventions including the infamous "z" in Euzkera and Euzkadi, were definitively abandoned in these guidelines. For an in-depth discussion of the origins of the various names for Basques and the Basque Country, see Michelena (1984).

Four • Batua and *Euskalki*

1. On the first uses of Batua in the media, see Díaz Noci (1998).

2. Language advocacy and advocates are not always the most conservative or purist about the language. As Hill's (1985) study of Mexicano speakers vividly shows, purist attitudes can come from other social actors, generated by the interaction of socioeconomic changes with social hierarchies internal to a community.

3. See, for example, Dorian (1981), Eckert (1983), Wong (1997), Jaffe (1999), and Roseman (1995).

4. Vowel harmonies are phonological changes that dialect speakers perform at the end of words when they use the definite article "a" [the]. These harmonies vary in form across the dialects. Batua does not recognize vowel harmonies, and so these become markers of dialect. In Usurbil, a common vowel harmony is the addition of an intervocalic fricative "b" to nouns that end in "u." So, for example, the phrase "the head" in Batua is *buru* [head] + *a* [the], but in Usurbil dialect, this same phrase would exhibit a vowel harmony and be pronounced *buruba*.

5. Lexical innovation was primarily carried out by organizations separate from the Basque Language Academy and received some criticism from it (Mitxelena 1981). The most important of these has been UZEI (Unibertsital Zerbitzuetarako Euskal Ikastetxea [Center for Basque University Services]), created in 1977 with the mission of lexical modernization and the development of technical dictionaries (e.g., in political science, biology, econom-

ics, linguistics) for the incorporation of Basque into university teaching. ELHUYAR, a scientific society, has also played a key role in developing technical terminology in the engineering and physical sciences as well as more general dictionaries. Both of these organizations have entered into formal collaborative agreements with the Deputy Ministry of Language Policy of the BAC, resulting in more coordinated efforts in terminological development. See Urkizu (2006) and http:///www.uzei.com. The Basque Language Academy has now produced an official dictionary, *Hiztegi Batua*. See http://www.euskaltzaindia.net.

6. Echeverria reports similar views in her research in this part of the Basque Country (2003: 395). See Eckert (1989) for a highly useful review and reformulation of the relationship of gender, prestige, and language markers.

7. Euskal Herrian Euskaraz, formed in 1979, used Batua in all of their public communications. This group was notorious for spray painting Spanish-language road signs and billboards.

8. In the late eighties, UEMA (Udalerri Euskaldunen Mankomunitatea), at the initiative of chapters of Euskal Herrian Euskaraz, began presenting proposals to municipalities with majority Basque-speaking populations to take up the option the law gave them to function in Basque. Joxe Ramón Zubimendi, a writer and member of the Basque Language Academy, was hired to coordinate this project.

9. The standard orthography would be *nora hoa*. Speakers of Gipuzkoan dialect do not pronounce the "h" and tend to drop the intervocalic "r."

10. King (1983) was an early example of this kind of critique.

11. Amorrortu used matched-guise tests, asking 298 university students—all educated in Basque—to rank speakers in terms of two contrasting core values: group solidarity and prestige, or what she preferred to call "professionalism." In a previous pilot study among teachers, Batua did gain higher scores in professionalism than vernacular. For a highly useful review of the concepts of prestige and solidarity as well as some of the sources of confusion that surround them, see Woolard (1989: 89–94). See Haddican (2007) for an empirical study of dialect/Batua loyalty. Echeverria (2000) offers parallel work on high-school students.

12. See, for example, the work of the scholarly/activist association Mendebalde Euskal Kultur Alkarte [Western Basque Cultural Association] (2001), whose aim is to promote research and greater use of western (e.g., Bizkaian) Basque varieties. Shortly before its closing, the national Basque newspaper, *Euskaldunon Egunkaria*, began to produce a supplement in Bizkaian dialect.

13. *Galduaz doa hiztun euskaldunaren sortzeko ahalmena, galduaz hizkuntzarekin jolasteko eta gozatzeko gaitasuna, eta hor galtzen denean, hizkuntza bera dago galbidean.*

Five • The Will to Count

1. See Hacking (1999) for a useful review of what it means to say something is "socially constructed."

2. On the difference between this methodology and the history of ideas, see Rabinow and Rose (2003).

3. Foucault described technologies of government as giving rise to "subjects," not identities in the psychological sense. But the two concepts have often been conflated, prompting some degree of skepticism and critique of the assumed "magical" theory of identity

formation (see, for example, Brubaker and Cooper 2000). A "subject" is a product of the discourse and practices of experts. It refers to an epistemological entity produced through technologies of knowledge and reform, as in, for example, the "criminal" subject or "the homosexual" (see Foucault 1980a). While Foucault recognized that these constructions may shape how an individual comes to understand him or herself, the process by which that happens, and how the constructions of the subject intersect with other potential ways of understanding the self, requires inquiry. For further discussion, see Rabinow and Rose (2003: xx).

4. See the two-volume collection, *The Probabilistic Revolution* (vol. 1, Kruger, Daston, and Heidelberger 1987; vol. 2, Kruger, Gigerenzer, and Morgan 1987); see also Hacking (1990), Donzelot (1988), and Rabinow (1989).

5. This census data is collected every five years. The French state does not collect data on language in its census; consequently, information on language in the northern Basque provinces comes via sample survey.

6. *The Continuity of Basque* surveys sort linguistic competency into four categories: "Monolingual Basque speakers," of whom the 1996 survey reports 0.5 percent in all of Euskal Herria; "Bilinguals," defined as people who report being able to function well or fairly well in both languages; "Passive Bilinguals," people who report that they can understand Basque well or fairly well but that they speak it with difficulty; and "Monolingual Erdaldunes," people who know only Spanish or French. The category "bilinguals" is yet further refined into those who report being dominant in Spanish, "balanced," that is, having equal competency; and those dominant in Basque.

7. Basque-language planning has drawn upon the expertise of various international figures in sociolinguistics as advisors. These have included Joshua Fishman, Juan Cobarrubias, A. Taboret-Keller, and most recently Richard Bourhis of the University of Quebec in Montreal, who served as key consultant for *The Continuity of Basque* surveys.

8. The event was a local Basque-language campaign carried out during Usurbil's annual patron-saint day celebrations. The collection and display of language statistics are described at greater length in Urla (1993b).

9. EKB organized the Street Surveys of 1989, 1993, and 1997. After the dissolution of EKB, the survey of 2001 was carried out by SEI (Soziolinguistika Euskal Institutoa) and subsequently taken over by SEI's successor, the Soziolinguistika Klusterra, an independent sociolinguistic research institute. Results are regularly released in the media and are reported and debated in the Basque sociolinguistic journal *BAT: Soziolinguistika Aldizkaria*.

10. A formal relationship between language statistics and language-use rights was established by Decree 250/25 (November 1986), *Uso y normalización del euskera en las administraciones públicas de la Comunidad Autónoma de Euskadi*. This decree establishes the criteria determining whether Basque will be a considered a requirement or simply extra "merit" for certain civil-servant positions in the Autonomous Community. Language requirements are established according to the relative proportion of Basque speakers in each area, along with various other criteria having to do with the nature of the job and the degree to which it requires interaction with the public. See Gardner (1990: 29n3).

11. This approach follows what sociologists of language call the "personality" rather than the "territorial" approach to language rights (McRae 1975). On these approaches and

their differences, see also Williams (1981) and Laponce (1987). On debates over these models in the European Union, see Mar Molinero and Stevenson (1991).

Six • Beyond the Classroom

1. Positions for municipal language technicians began to be created after the passage of the Law of Normalization in 1982. Hired by town halls, they are typically charged with heading up a Basque Service (Euskara Zerbitzua). They provide translation services as needed, develop projects to normalize Basque-language use, and sometimes collect statistical data on language. The creation of Basque Service departments is voluntary, and the majority are in Gipuzkoa and Bizkaia.

2. On the role of experts as producers—not simply observers—of language ideology, see Collins (1998).

3. Web access to the activities of the Deputy Ministry of Language Policy as well as data on language are available at www.euskara.euskadi.net.

4. UEU originated in the late seventies as an annual summer university and "happening" for language loyalists. Typically held in July on the campus of the public university in Navarra, it was a place where for two weeks writers, scholars, teachers, and anyone else with some expertise on a topic offered to teach classes in a range of topics from biology to literature in Basque. Though framed largely as a means of developing technical vocabulary in Basque, UEU continues to be a rich site for discussions about language revitalization.

5. For a discussion of the impact of Txepetx ten years after the publication of *A Future for our Past,* see the special issue of *BAT* 18, June 1996.

6. Linguistic anthropologists tend to favor a more neutral conception of language mixing as a creative verbal strategy that is responsive to unequal power relations. See, for example, Hill and Hill (1986) and Urcioli (1996).

7. My thanks to Jone Miren Hernández for sharing these observations based on her personal experience.

8. The AED representative I spoke with tied the success of this pioneering organization to this associational tradition. "Here in Arrasate and many other towns, we have cooperatives, *sociedades* (gastronomic clubs), . . . people get together, each person puts in their own money and they buy a space and make their own club. They go there to eat with friends. . . . There has always been this inclination for associations. You see it in the *ikastola* phenomenon, the cooperatives, the gastronomic clubs, AED, and many other cultural groups. People come together easily." Like other associations, *euskara taldeak* have dues-paying members. Annual dues in 1998 ran anywhere from four or five dollars in some associations to fifty dollars in others.

9. For a description of these and other strategic-management techniques, see Thompson and Strickland (1984).

10. This is described in the unpublished internal document of Topagunea: *Euskara-elkarteen eta herri-aldizkarien topagunea: 1998ko lan-ildo nagusiak Batzar Nagusirako proposamenak; Durango 1998ko Urtarrila* [Meeting of the Basque associations and municipal magazines. Proposals of the Central Committee on principal work arenas for 1998].

11. In addition to seeking revenues through advertising, some community associations also experimented with other forms of revenue generation. The most successful to date

has been Zenbat Gara, the language association of Bilbo that created a café/theatre, a travel agency, a local radio station, and an *euskaltegi*.

12. The evolution of governmental policies and initiatives to promote language normalization in the workplace is described in Consejo Asesor del Euskara (2005). This text notes the importance that consultations with Quebec-based language planners had for the Basque government planning efforts (ibid: 27).

13. For a much fuller discussion of the various sources besides TQM proper on which he has drawn in his work over the past decade, see Marko Juanikorena (2004, 2010).

14. Miren Azkarate, Basque Minister of Culture, on the occasion of the Bikain certificate, Dec. 17, 2007, pp. 2–3. Accessed at *www.euskara.euskadi.net*.

15. These arguments are presented at greater length in the articles assembled for a special issue of *BAT: Soziolinguistika Aldizkaria* 57 (Dec. 2005), *Euskararen erabilera enpresetan* [Basque-language Use in Business].

16. Hyatt (2001) shows the value of in-depth ethnography to reveal how neoliberal empowerment schemes can fail as they come into conflict with preexisting norms of social life. While it may be true that managerialist discourse and practices are becoming hegemonic, we should not attribute to neoliberalism the same kind of monolithic status that has plagued scholarly discussions of capitalism. See Gibson-Graham (2006).

17. Studies of the public expenditure on Basque-language promotion in the Basque Autonomous Community show that it has decreased slightly from 1.35 percent of the total budget in 2001 to 1.24 percent in 2008 (SIADECO 2010).

Seven • The Voice of the Street

1. Browne (1990) reports that this was always the case for Basque-language radio in the northern Basque provinces located in France.

2. Jakue Pascual, interview by the author, Bilbo, 1994.

3. Some aspects of this program are analyzed in Urla (2001).

4. A third, even more formal term of address in some Basque dialects is *berori*, a term of great respect or deference. In some eastern dialects we also find the pronoun *xu*, a mode of address intermediate between *hi* and *zu*.

5. For descriptions of *hi/zu* usage, see Alberdi (1993, 1995), Echeverria (2000, 2003); Zulaika (1988: 319–20). For some interesting indicators of how *hika* usage may be changing, see Garate (2002).

6. It remains to be seen if this is true for areas beyond this part of Gipuzkoa. Amorrortu's study (2002) of language attitudes among a broader range of youth in the Autonomous Community pursues in greater depth the associations youth have with Unified and vernacular Basque. Like Echeverria, she learns that youth find vernacular socially attractive, but her study unfortunately does not explore *hika/zuka* contrasts.

7. If the speakers had been using *zuka* forms, they would have greeted each other using the same word: "*aizu*" [hey, 2nd person singular "zu"].

8. These phonological changes, referred to as vowel harmonies, are performed at the end of words when using the definite article –a. The changes vary among the dialects. Batua does not recognize vowel harmonies, and so these become markers of vernacular. See Trask (1997) for one of the best overviews in English of Basque linguistic features.

9. I borrow the concept of recycling from Spitulnik's important work on Zambian radio (1996).

10. Curiously, I could find no one who recognized "*txori guztik mokodun*" as a common expression and several who suggested it might have been unique to this family.

11. Though women have always also sung *bertsos,* the public performance of *bertsolaritza* has been almost exclusively male. However, young women are increasingly participating in this practice (Larrañaga 1996). In 2009 Maialen Lujanbio made history in becoming the first woman to win the national *bertsolaritza* competition.

12. On the way radical youth culture closely associated with the free-radio movement created the conditions for new forms of Basque collective identity open to immigrants, see Kasmir (1999).

Epilogue

1. Wright and other authors like Neff-van Aertselaer (2006) who affirm the exclusionary nature of Basque identity appear to base this claim on Conversi's (1997) comparison of the historical development of Basque and Catalan nationalism in the late nineteenth century, rather than on a study of contemporary language-activist practice or discourse.

2. Patxi Baztarrika, interview by the author, March 16, 2011.

3. The full statement in the report is "Anyone who has attempted to learn *Euskara,* even if they have not gotten beyond a passive understanding should be considered an *euskaldun.* Limited though that [competency] may be, the passive bilingual is a form of 'value added' that contributes to social harmony . . . [which in turn] carries extraordinary symbolic and practical value since it enables the growth of the Basque speaking community" (2009: 27). As the report adds, passive bilinguals make possible the expanded use of Basque because they understand it, even if they cannot speak it themselves.

4. On the failure of the cease-fire and the initiative for peace, see Mees (2003) and the insightful essays by Aranzadi (2005).

5. Carlos Trénor, a well-known activist lawyer, was arrested in the same police operation. A private television channel filmed his arrest, and it was apparently shown on television.

6. For more information on the Zumalabe Foundation, see their Web page: http://www .joxemi.org.

7. Of the 52 people accused in the Sumario 18/98, 47 were sentenced to a total of 525 years of prison as members, leaders, or collaborators of ETA. Bails for the accused ranged from 6,000 to 300,000 euros. The practice of dispersion as well as torture of prisoners while they were held incommunicado has been criticized by Amnesty International as a violation of human rights and remains an ongoing source of protest in the Basque conflict.

8. The Audiencia Nacional was created by decree of the Council of Ministers in December 1976 to replace the Tribunal of Public Order, the court notorious for prosecuting political dissidents under the Franco regime. Many people in Basque social movements see direct continuity between the old and the new court.

9. For more information, see the Web site www.egunkaria.info.

10. Available from www.behatokia.info or from www.ehwatch.org. The latter Web site contains the most comprehensive documentation on the trial, complete with the text of

the indictments, declarations by detainees, and statements by a variety of international observers.

11. See also Aranzadi (2005) and Crumbaugh (2010) for highly useful analyses of the inflamed political rhetoric of anti-Basque nationalism and victim discourse respectively. Crumbaugh describes an incident in which "a group of rabid AVT members mobbed Basque director Julio Medem at Spain's Goya awards, calling him a "terrorist" and a "murderer" for having attempted to represent a broad spectrum of perspectives in *La pelota vasca*, Medem's documentary about political violence in the Basque Country" (2010: 662).

12. The term *vigilante* comes from the work of U.S. political scientist David Laitin (1999), who argues that political violence is practiced to intimidate people into adopting the regional language. See a critique of his model in Mansvelt Beck and Markusse (2008).

13. "Savater presenta hoy un manifiesto en defensa del castellano," *EL PAÍS*, June 23, 2008.

14. For an example of this in English, see an article published in 2007 in *the Wall Street Journal* that portrays Basque-language normalization policies as a fanatical enterprise driving out Spanish speakers: "Basque Inquisition: How Do You Say Shepherd in Euskera? Through Fiat, Separatists Bring Old Tongue to Life" (Johnson 2007). The article provoked an immediate response by the then head of the Deputy Ministry of Language Policy, Patxi Baztarrika (press release accessed Nov. 11, 2007, http://www.euskara.euskadi.net.

15. Lipsitz (2006) argues that racism is not just Black people's problem to solve. White people, as its beneficiaries, need to recognize what they gain from racism, or what he calls their "possessive investment in Whiteness," from which they gain materially and symbolically.`

Glossary

abertzale: Patriot, supporter of Basque nationalism.

Adorez eta Atseginez: Group formed to study the sociolinguistic theories of José María Sánchez Carrión (Txepetx)

AED, Arrasate Euskaldun Dezagun: The community language-advocacy group of Arrasate/Mondragon, formed in 1983.

AEK, Alfabetatzen Euskalduntzen Koordinakundea: The adult Basque-language and -literacy organization created by the Basque Language Academy in 1968.

Asociación Euskara de Navarra: The first of a variety of late nineteenth-century Basque cultural associations and magazines that promoted artistic production in Euskara. Members were known as Los Euskaros.

auzolan: Basque rural practice of neighborhood mutual aid or collective work

baserritarra: Farmer

bertsolaritza: Improvised oral poetry

cuadrillas: Spanish term for friendship circles

EITB, Euskal Irrati Telebista: Basque Radio and Television network, created in 1982 by the Basque Autonomous Community.

EKB, Euskal Kulturaren Batzarrea: The Confederation of Basque Culture; a non-governmental Basque-language research and planning organization created in 1983.

erdaldun: (plural, *erdaldun**ak***): Non-Basque speaker

erdera: Language other than Basque

erderismos: Spanish-derived words or constructions

ETA, Euskadi ta Askatasuna: Basque Land and Freedom. Formed in 1959, this armed revolutionary nationalist organization seeks independence for the Basque Country.

*euskaldun (*plural, *euskaldunak)*: Basque-speaking person (noun); Basque-language or Basque-speaking entity (adjective).

euskaldun berria: New Basque speaker; a term used to refer to second-language learners of Basque. Also sometimes spelled as one word.

euskaldun zaharra: Colloquial term for native Basque speaker

euskalgintza: Term language advocates use to refer to the nongovernmental language movement

Euskal Herrian Euskaraz: Basque in the Basqueland; a language-advocacy group formed in 1979.

euskalki: Local or regional dialects of Basque

Euskal Pizkundea: Basque cultural renaissance of the late nineteenth century

Euskaltzaindia: The Basque Language Academy

euskaltzaleak: Basque-language advocates

euskaltzaletasuna: Term used to refer to a person's Basque-language loyalism

Euskara Batua: Standardized or Unified Basque; also called Batua.

euskara elkarteak: Community-based Basque-language and cultural associations

Eusko Ikaskuntza: The Society for Basque Studies, founded in 1918.

fueros: Contractual agreements between the Spanish crown and Basque provinces granting special economic and political rights

gazteen asanblada: Term for youth groups that emerged in the eighties, usually associated with oppositional political ideology.

Hegoalde: "The South"; a term used to refer to the Basque territory located within the Spanish state.

Herri Batasuna: Basque political party formed in 1979, espousing leftist nationalism.

hika: Informal mode of address in Basque. Also referred to as *hitanoa*.

*hitzarmen (*plural *hitzarmenak)*: Basque term for an agreement, pact, or contract.

HPIN, Hizkuntz Politikarako Idazkaritza Nagusia: The primary department responsible for language policy in the Basque Autonomous Community. Renamed the Hizkuntz Politikarako Sailburuordetza [the Deputy Ministry of Language Policy].

ikastola: School that uses Basque as the medium of instruction

Iparralde: "The North"; a term used to refer to the Basque territory located in the French state.

izquierda abertzale: Spanish term for political groups espousing leftist Basque nationalism

jatorra: Basque term meaning authentic or genuine

Kale Neurketa: Street Survey; Basque term for a sample survey of public Basque-language use, which has been conducted periodically since 1989.

kaletarra: Basque term for an urbanite

Kontseilua: The Council of Basque Language Associations, formed in 1997.

korrika: Marathon run organized by the language-activist organization AEK to raise funds and awareness about language revival.

LanHitz: Governmental program that promotes language normalization in the private sector

maketos: Disrespectful term invented by Sabino Arana to refer to Spanish-language immigrant workers

MLNV, Movimiento de Liberación Nacional Vasco: The Spanish acronym for the Basque Nationalist Liberation Movement, also referred to as the *izquierda abertzale*. Both terms refer to political groups subscribing to Basque-nationalist socialism.

PNV, Partido Nacionalista Vasco: The Basque Nationalist Party, founded by Sabino Arana.

PP, Partido Popular: The conservative Spanish nationalist party

PSOE, Partido Socialista Obrero Español: The Spanish Socialist Worker's Party, founded in 1879 by Pablo Iglesias, embraces a social democratic ideology. It has been the governing party of the Spanish state throughout much of the post-Franco era.

SIADECO: Acronym for Sociedad de Investigación Aplicada del Desarollo Comunitario, a progressive Basque sociological-research institute.

Topagunea: Federation of community of Basque-language and cultural associations that produce local media

UEMA, Udalerri Mankomunitatea: Association of municipalities with majority Basque language–speaking population. The association works to facilitate the normalization of Basque-language use in town halls.

UEU, Udal Euskal Unibersitatea: In existence since the seventies, annual Basque summer university has been held every July, offering classes and workshops entirely in Basque.

Urtekariak: Basque term for annual yearbook, commonly published by *ARGIA* magazine and *Egin* newspaper.

vascos: Spanish-language term for people of Basque descent

vascuence: Spanish term for the Basque language

Zazpiak Bat: Slogan meaning "the Seven [provinces] Are One"

References

Abad, Begoña, Javier Cerrato, Gabriel Gatti, Iñaki Martinez de Albéniz, Alfonso Pérez-Agote, and Benjamín Tejerina. 1999. *Institucionalización política y reencantamiento de la sociedad: Las transformaciones en el mundo nacionalista*. Euskal koadernoak/Cuadernos sociológicos vascos. Vitoria-Gasteiz: Eusko Jaurlaritzaren Argitalpen Zerbitzu Nagusia.

Abramson, David. 2002. "Identity Counts: The Soviet Legacy and the Census in Uzbekistán." In *Census and Identity: The Politics of Race, Ethnicity, and Language in National Censuses*, ed. David Kertzer and Dominique Arel, 176–201. Cambridge: Cambridge University Press.

Abu Lughod, Lila. 1990. "The Romance of Resistance: Tracing Transformations of Power Through Bedouin Women." *American Ethnologist* 17, no. 1: 41–55.

Agamben, Giorgio. 2005. *State of Exception*. Trans. Kevin Attell. Chicago and London: University of Chicago Press.

Agote, José Luis, ed. 1995. *Mikel Laboa*. Donostia–San Sebastián: Elkar.

Aizpurua, Xabier. 1995. *Euskararen jarraipena/La continuidad del euskera/La continuité de la langue basque*. Vitoria-Gasteiz: Eusko Jaurlaritza, Kultura Saila.

Alberdi, Jabier. 1993. "Hika tratamendua balore sozio-afektiboak." *Fontes Linguae Vasconum: Studia et documenta* 64: 425–42.

——. 1995. "The Development of the Basque System of Terms of Address and the Allocutive Conjugation." In *Towards a History of the Basque Language*, ed. José Ignacio Hualde, Joseba Lakarra, and Robert L. Trask, 275–93. Vol. 131 of Amsterdam Studies in the Theory and History of Linguistic Science. Amsterdam/Philadelphia: John Benjamin.

Alonso, William, and Paul Starr, eds. 1987. *The Politics of Numbers*. New York: Russell Sage.

Altuna, Olatz, I. Martinez de Luna, X. Aipzurua, and R. Ramos. 2002. "Mahaingurua: Euskararen erabilera." *Larrun* 56: 1–15. Special supplement to *ARGIA* 1860, 2002.

Alvarez Enparantza, José Luis [Txillardegi]. 1979 [1966]. "Hizkuntza eta pensakera." *Saioak* 3: 259–78.

——. 1997. *Euskal Herria en el horizonte*. Tafalla: Txalaparta.

——. 2001. *Hacia una socio-lingüística matemática*. Donostia–San Sebastián: SEI.

Amonarriz, Kike, and Iñaki Arruti. 1993. "Euskararen aldeko mugimendu sozialak gaur egun." Paper presented at the Cursos de Verano of the Universidad del Pais Vasco. Photocopy.

Amorrortu, Estibaliz. 1998. "Dialect Attitudes in the Basque Country: A Pilot Study." Unpublished manuscript.

————. 2000. "Linguistic Attitudes in the Basque Country: The Social Acceptance of a New Variety." PhD diss., University of Southern California.

Anderson, Benedict. 1991 [1983]. *Imagined Communities: Reflections on the Origins and Spread of Nationalism.* Rev. ed. London: Verso.

Anzaldúa, Gloria. 1987. *Borderlands/La Frontera.* San Francisco: Spinsters/Aunt Lute Press.

Appadurai, Arjun. 1996a. "Life After Primordialism." In *Modernity at Large,* 139–57. Minneapolis: University of Minnesota Press.

————. 1996b. "Number in the Colonial Imagination." In *Modernity at Large,* 114–35. Minneapolis: University of Minnesota Press.

Arana y Goiri, Sabino de. 1965. *Obras completas.* Buenos Aires: Editorial Sabindiar-Batza.

————. 1995. *La patria de los vascos: Antología de escritos políticos.* Ed. Antonio Elorza. Donostia–San Sebastián: Haranburu Editor.

Aranzadi, Juan. 2005. *Good-Bye* ETA. Donostia–San Sebastián: Hiria.

Arel, Dominique. 2002. "Language Categories in Censuses: Backward- or Forward-Looking?" In *Census and Identity: The Politics of Race, Ethnicity, and Language in National Censuses,* ed. David Kertzer and Domique Arel, 92–120. Cambridge: Cambridge University Press.

Aretxaga, Begoña. 1988. *Los funerales en el nacionalismo radical vasco.* Donostia–San Sebastián: La Primitiva Casa Baroja.

————. 2005a. "Before the Law: The Narrative of the Unconscious in Basque Political Violence." In *States of Terror: Begoña Aretxaga's Essays,* ed. Joseba Zulaika, 177–200. Reno: Center for Basque Studies, University of Nevada, Reno.

————. 2005b. "Playing Terrorist." In *States of Terror: Begoña Aretxaga's Essays,* ed. Joseba Zulaika, 215–29. Reno: Center for Basque Studies, University of Nevada, Reno.

Arexola-Leiba, Juan Luis. 1993. "Sentsibilizazio arloa." *Jazten* 8: 43–60.

Armistead, Samuel G., and Joseba Zulaika. 2005. *Voicing the Moment: Improvised Oral Poetry and Basque Tradition.* Reno: Center for Basque Studies, University of Nevada, Reno.

Arteaga, Alfredo. 1994. "An Other Tongue." In *An Other Tongue: Nation and Ethnicity in the Linguistic Borderlands,* ed. A. Arteaga, 9–34. Durham and London: Duke University Press.

Atxaga, Bernardo. 1992 [1989]. *Obabakoak.* Trans. Margaret Jull Costa. New York: Pantheon.

Aulestia, Gorka. 1995. *Improvisational Poetry from the Basque Country.* Reno: University of Nevada Press.

Aztiker (Soziologia Ikergunea). 2002. *Euskal Herria datuen talaiatik.* Astigarraga: Udalbiltza.

Azurmendi, Mikel. 2000. *Y se limpie aquella tierra: Limpieza étnica y de sangre en el País Vasco (siglos XVI–XVIII).* Madrid: Taurus.

Bakhtin, Mikhail. 1981. *The Dialogic Imagination.* Trans. C. Emerson and M. Holquist. Austin: University of Texas Press.

————. 1984a. *Problems of Dostoevsky's Poetics.* Ed. and trans. C. Emerson. Minneapolis: University of Minnesota Press.

————. 1984b. *Rabelais and His World.* Trans. Hélène Iswolsky. Bloomington: Indiana University Press.

————. 1986. *Speech Genres and Other Late Essays.* Ed. M. Holquist, trans. M. Holquist and C. Emerson. Austin: University of Texas Press.

Balibar, Renée, and Dominique Laporte. 1974. *Le Français national: Politique et pratiques de la langue nationale sous la Révolution Française*. Paris: Hachette.

Barruso Barés, Pedro. 2005. *Violencia política y represión en Guipúzcoa durante la guerra civil y el primer franquismo (1936–1945)*. Donostia–San Sebastián: Hiria.

Barth, Frederik, ed. 1969. *Ethnic Groups and Boundaries*. Boston: Little, Brown.

Basso, Keith H. 1979. *Portraits of the Whiteman*. Cambridge: Cambridge University Press.

———. 1996. *Wisdom Sits in Places*. Albuquerque: University of New Mexico Press.

Bauman, Richard, and Charles Briggs. 1990. "Poetics and Performance as Critical Perspectives on Language and Social Life." *Annual Review in Anthropology* 19: 59–88.

Baztarrika, Patxi. 2009. *Babel o barbarie Una política lingüística legítima y eficaz para la convivencia*. Irun: Alberdania.

Beltza [Emilio López Adan]. 1976. *Nacionalismo vasco y clases sociales*. San Sebastián: Txertoa.

———. 1977. *El nacionalismo vasco en el exilio, 1937–1960*. San Sebastián: Txertoa.

Bhabha, Homi. 1992. "Double Visions." *Artforum* (January): 85–89.

Bidart, Pierre. 1986. "'Ilustracion' et question linguistique en Pays Basque." *Mélanges de la Casa de Velazquez* 22: 325–44.

Billig, Michael. 1995. *Banal Nationalism*. London: Sage.

Bourdieu, Pierre. 1977. *Outline of a Theory of Practice*. Cambridge, London, New York, Melbourne: Cambridge University Press.

———. 1982. *Ce que parler veux dire*. Paris: Fayard.

———. 1990. "Opinion Polls: A 'Science' Without a Scientist." In *Other Words: Essays towards a Reflexive Sociology*, trans. M. Adamson, 168–74. Stanford: Stanford University Press.

———. 1991. *Language and Symbolic Power*. Ed. and int. John B. Thompson. Cambridge, Mass.: Harvard University Press.

Briggs, Charles. 2005. "Geneaologies of Race and Culture and the Failure of Vernacular Cosmopolitanisms: Rereading Franz Boas and W. E. B. du Bois." *Public Culture* 17, no. 1: 75–100.

Briggs, Charles, and Richard Bauman. 2000. *Voices of Modernity: Language Ideologies and the Politics of Inequality*. Cambridge: Cambridge University Press.

Brown, Roger, and A. Gilman. 1960. "The Pronouns of Power and Solidarity." In *Style in Language*, ed. Thomas A. Sebeok, 253–76. Cambridge: Technology Press.

Brown, Wendy. 2006. *Regulating Aversion: Tolerance in the Age of Identity and Empire*. Princeton: Princeton University Press.

Browne, D. R. 1990. "Finding a Basque Radio Voice: The French Experience." *Intermedia* 18: 39–42.

Brubaker, Rogers. 2004. "'Civic' and 'Ethnic' Nationalism." In *Ethnicity Without Groups*, 132–46. Cambridge, Mass., and London: Harvard University Press.

Brubaker, Rogers, and Frederick Cooper. 2000. "Beyond 'Identity.'" *Theory and Society* 29: 1–47.

Bullen, Margaret. 1999. "Gender and Identity in the Alardes of two Basque Towns." In *Basque Cultural Studies*. Basque Studies Program Occasional Paper Series 5, ed. William A. Douglass et al., 149–77. Reno: University of Nevada.

Burke, Kenneth. 1957. *The Philosophy of Literary Form: Studies in Symbolic Action*. New York: Vintage Books.

Butler, Judith. 1992. "Contingent Foundations: Feminism and the Question of 'Postmodernism.'" In *Feminists Theorize the Political,* ed. Judith Butler and Joan Scott, 3–21. New York and London: Routledge.

Calvet, Louis-Jean. 1974. *Linguistique et colonialisme: Petit traité de glottophagie.* Paris: Payot.

Cameron, Deborah. 1995. *Verbal Hygiene.* London, New York: Routledge.

Campión, Arturo. 1907. "Defensa del nombre antiguo, castizo y legítimo de la lengua de los Baskos contra el soñado EUZKERA." *Revista Internacional de Estudios Vascos* 1, no. 1: 217–41.

Campión, Arturo, and Pierre Broussain. 1922. "Informe sobre la unificación del euskera." *Euskera* 3, no. 1: 4–17.

Caro Baroja, Julio. 1971. *Los vascos.* Madrid: ISTMO.

Carter, Donald. 1997. *States of Grace: Senegalese in Italy and the New European Imagination.* Minneapolis: University of Minnesota Press.

Cenoz, Jasone, and Durk Gorter. 2006. "Linguistic Landscape and Minority Languages." *International Journal of Multilingualism* 3, no. 1: 67–80.

Certeau, Michel de. 1984. *The Practice of Everyday Life.* Berkeley and Los Angeles: University of California Press.

———. 1986. "History, Science, Fiction." In *Heterologies: Discourse on the Other,* trans. Brian Massumi, 199–221. Minneapolis: University of Minnesota Press.

Certeau, Michel de, Dominique Julia, and Jacques Revel. 1975. *Une politique de la langue: La Révolution Française et les patois; L'enquête Grégoire.* Paris: Gallimard.

Clark, Robert. 1979. *The Basques: The Franco Years and Beyond.* Reno: University of Nevada Press.

———. 1984. *The Basque Insurgents: ETA, 1952–1980.* Madison: University of Wisconsin Press.

———. 1990. *Negotiating with ETA: Obstacles to Peace in the Basque Country, 1975–1988.* Reno and Las Vegas: University of Nevada Press.

Cohn, Bernard S. 1987. "The Census, Social Structure and Objectification in South Asia." In *An Anthropologist among the Historians and Other Essays,* 224–54. Delhi: Oxford University Press.

Cohn, Bernard S., and Nicholas Dirks. 1988. "Beyond the Fringe: The Nation State, Colonialism, and the Technologies of Power." *Journal of Historical Sociology* 1, no. 2: 224–29.

Collins, James. 1998. "Our Ideologies and Theirs." In *Language Ideologies: Practice and Theory,* ed. Bambi Schieffelin, Kathryn Woolard, and Paul Kroskrity, 256–70. Oxford: Oxford University Press.

Comaroff, Jean, and John Comaroff. 1991. *Of Revelation and Revolution: Christianity, Colonialism and Consciousness in South Africa.* Vol. 1. Chicago: University of Chicago Press.

———. 2009. *Ethnicity, Inc.* Chicago: University of Chicago Press.

Consejo Asesor del Euskera/Euskararen Aholku Batzordea. 2005. *Criterios y estrategias para la promoción del uso del euskera en el ámbito socioeconómico y para un acercamiento más sistemático y eficaz a la normalización lingüística.* A publication of the Department of Culture, Basque Government. Vitoria-Gasteiz, Spain: Servicio Central de Publicaciones del Gobierno Vasco.

———. 2009. *Bases para la política lingüística de principios del siglo XXI: Hacia un pacto renovado.* Trans. Jorge Giménez Bech. A publication of the Department of Culture, Basque Government. Vitoria-Gasteiz, Spain: Servicio Central de Publicaciones del Gobierno Vasco. http:// www.euskadi.net/euskara21.

Conversi, Daniele. 1997. *The Basques, the Catalans, and Spain: Alternative Routes to Nationalist Mobilization.* Reno: University of Nevada Press.

———, ed. 2002. *Ethnonationalism in the Contemporary World: Walker Conner and the Study of Nationalism.* London and New York: Routledge.

Corcuera, Javier. 1979. *Orígenes, organización, e ideología del nacionalismo vasco, 1876–1904.* Madrid: Siglo XXI.

Cotter, Colleen. 2001. "Continuity and Vitality: Expanding Domains through Irish-Language Radio." In *The Green Book of Language Revitalization,* ed. L. Hinton and K. Hale, 301–12. San Diego: Academic Press.

Crossley, Nick. 2002. *Making Sense of Social Movements.* Buckingham, UK: Open University Press.

Crowley, Tony. 1989. *Standard English and the Politics of Language.* Urbana: University of Illinois Press.

———. 1996. *Language in History: Theories and Texts.* London and Boston: Routledge.

Crumbaugh, Justin. 2007a. "Are We All (Still) Miguel Ángel Blanco? Victimhood, the Media Afterlife, and the Challenge for Historical Memory." *Hispanic Review* 75, no. 4: 365–84.

———. 2007b. "El turismo como arte de gobernar: Los 'Felices Sesenta' del Franquismo." In *Cine, imaginario y turismo: Estrategias de seducción,* ed. Antonia del Rey Reguillo, 145–75. Valencia: Tirant lo Blanch.

———. 2009. *Destination Dictatorship: The Spectacle of Spain's Tourist Boom and the Reinvention of Difference.* Albany: SUNY Press.

———. 2010. "Victim Discourse, Victim Studies and the Biopolitics of Counter-Terrorism: The Case of Iñaki de Juana Chaos." *Revista de Estudios Hispánicos* 44, no. 3: 657–76.

Dávila, Pauli, and Ana Eizagirre. 1995. "Las fiestas Euskaras en el País Vasco (1879–1936): Nuevos espacios de alfabetización." In *Lengua, escuela, y cultura: El proceso de alfabetización en Euskal Herria, siglos XIX y XX,* ed. Paulí Dávila Balsera, 257–311. Bilbao: Servicio Editorial Universidad del País Vasco.

Dean, Mitchell. 1999. *Governmentality: Power and Rule in Modern Society.* London and Thousand Oaks, Calif.: Sage.

DeCicco, Gabriel, and Joel M. Maring. 1983. "Diglossia, Regionalism and National Language Policy: A Comparison of Spain and the Philippines." In *Bilingualism, Social Issues and Policy Implications,* ed. Andrew W. Miracle, 38–53. Southern Anthropological Society Proceedings 16. Athens: Universty of Georgia Press.

Deleuze, Gilles. 1979. "The Rise of the Social." In *The Policing of Families,* ed. Jacques Donzelot, trans. Robert Hurley, ix–xvii. New York: Pantheon.

Díaz Noci, Javier. 1998. "Los medios de comunicación y la normalización del euskera: Balance de dieciseis años." *Revista Internacional de Estudios Vascos* 43, no. 2: 441–59.

DiGiacomo, Susan. 1987. " 'La Caseta i L'Hortet': Rural Imagery in Catalan Urban Politics." *Anthropological Quarterly* 60, no. 4: 160–66.

———. 1999. "Language Ideological Debates in an Olympic City: Barcelona 1992–1996." In *Language Ideological Debates,* ed. Jan Blommaert, 105–42. Berlin and New York: Mouton de Gruyter.

Donzelot, Jacques. 1979. *The Policing of Families*. Trans. Robert Hurley. New York: Pantheon.

———. 1988. "The Promotion of the Social." *Economy and Society* 17, no. 3: 395–427.

Dorian, Nancy. 1981. *Language Death: The Life Cycle of a Scottish Gaelic Dialect*. Philadelphia: University of Pennsylvania Press.

———. 1994. "Purism vs. Compromise in Language Revitalization and Language Revival." *Language in Society* 23, no. 4: 479–94.

———. 1998. "Western Language Ideologies and Small-Language Prospects." In *Endangered Languages*, ed. L. Grenoble and L. Whaley, 3–21. Cambridge: Cambridge University Press.

Douglas, Mary. 1966. *Purity and Danger: An Analysis of Concepts of Pollution and Taboo*. New York: Praeger.

Douglass, William A. 1985. "Introduction." In *Basque Politics: A Case Study in Ethnic Nationalism*, ed. William A. Douglass, 1–17. Reno: Associated Faculty Press and Basque Studies Program, University of Nevada, Reno.

———. 2002. "Sabino's Sin: Racism and the Founding of Basque Nationalism." In *Ethnonationalism in the Contemporary World*, ed. Daniele Conversi, 95–112. New York: Routledge.

Dreyfus, Hubert, and Paul Rabinow. 1982. *Michel Foucault: Beyond Structuralism and Hermeneutics*. Chicago: University of Chicago Press.

Duchêne, Alexandre. 2011. "Néoliberalisme, inégalités sociales, et plurilinguisme: L'exploitacion de ressources langagieres et des locuteurs." *Langage et Société* 136: 81–106.

Duden, Barbara. 1992. "Population." In *The Development Dictionary: A Guide to Knowledge as Power*, ed. Wolfgang Sachs, 146–57. London: Zed Books.

Dyson, Frances. 1994. "The Geneaology of the Radio Voice." In *Radio Rethink: Art, Sound and Transmission*, ed. Daina Augaitis and Dan Lander, 167–188. Banff, Canada: Walter Phillips Gallery.

Earl, Jennifer. 2004. "The Cultural Consequences of Social Movements." In *The Blackwell Companion to Social Movements*, ed. David A. Snow, Sarah A. Soule, and Hanspeter Kriesi, 508–30. Malden, Mass.; Oxford, UK; and Carlton, Australia: Blackwell.

Echeverria, Begoña. 2000. "Basque Schooling: What Is It Good For?" PhD diss., University of California, San Diego.

———. 2003. "Language Ideologies and Practices in (En)Gendering the Basque Nation." *Language in Society* 32, no. 3: 383–413.

Eckert, Penelope. 1980. "Diglossia: Separate and Unequal." *Linguistics* 18, nos. 11–12: 1053–64.

———. 1983. "The Paradox of National Language Movements." *Journal of Multilingual and Multicultural Development* 4, no. 4: 289–300.

———. 1989. "The Whole Woman: Sex and Gender Differences in Variation." *Language Variation and Social Change* 1, no. 1:245–67.

Eckert, Penelope, and Sally McConnell-Ginet. 1992. "Think Practically and Look Locally: Language and Gender as Community-Based Practice." *Annual Review of Anthropology* 21: 461–90.

Eco, Umberto. 1981. "Una nueva era en la libertad de expresión." In *De las ondas rojas a las radios libres: Textos para la historia de la radio*, ed. Lluís Bassets, 213–30. Barcelona: Editorial Gustavo Gili, S.A.

Eisenlohr, Patrick. 2004. "Language Revitalization and New Technologies: Cultures of Electronic Mediation and the Refiguring of Communities." *Annual Review of Anthropology* 33: 21–45.

Eleizalde, Luis de. 1918a. "Metodología para la restauración del euzkera." In *Primer congreso de estudios vascos,* 428–39. Oñate: Eusko Ikaskuntza.

———. 1918b. "El problema de la enseñanza en el País Vasco." *Primer congreso de estudios vascos,* 865–74. Oñate: Eusko Ikaskuntza.

Elliot, J. H. 1963. *Imperial Spain, 1469–1716.* New York: St. Martin's Press.

Elorza, Antonio. 1978. *Ideologías del nacionalismo vasco, 1876–1937: De los "Euskaros" a "Jagi-Jagi."* Donostia–San Sebastián: Haranburu.

———, ed. 1995. *Sabino Arana Goiri: La patria de los vascos.* Donostia–San Sebastián: Haranburu.

England, Nora. 1998. "Mayan Efforts Toward Language Preservation." In *Endangered Languages: Language Loss and Community Response,* ed. Lenore Grenoble and Lindsay Whaley, 99–116. Cambridge: Cambridge University Press.

Ergang, Robert R. 1966. *Herder and the Foundations of German Nationalism.* New York: Octagon Books.

Erize Etxegarai, Xabier. 1999. *Vascohablantes y castellanohablantes en la historia del euskera de Navarra.* Pamplona/Iruña: Gobierno de Navarra.

Estornes Zubizarreta, Idoia. 1983. *La sociedad de estudios vascos: Aportación del Eusko-Ikaskuntza a la cultura vasca, 1918–1936.* San Sebastián: Eusko Ikaskuntza.

Euskaltzaindia. 1977. *El Libro Blanco del euskara.* Bilbao: Euskaltzaindia.

Euskaltzaindia and Fundación Sabino Arana Kultur Elkargoa. 2004. *Sabino Arana Goiri: Euskara eta kultura.* Bilbao/Bilbo: Elkar.

Eusko Jaurlaritza. 1980. *Programa de gobierno 1980–1984.* Colección Informe 1. Vitoria-Gasteiz: Servicio Central de Publicaciones, Gobierno Vasco.

Eusko Jaurlaritza/Gobierno Vasco. 1983. *La lucha del euskara en la Comunidad Autónoma Vasca.* Vitoria-Gasteiz: Servicio Central de Publicaciones, Gobierno Vasco.

———. 1989. *Soziolinguistikazko mapa: Análisis demolinguístico de la Comunidad Autónoma Vasca derivado del padrón de 1986.* Vitoria-Gasteiz: Servicio Central de Publicaciones, Gobierno Vasco.

———. 2008. *IV Encuesta sociolingüística 2006.* Vitoria-Gasteiz: Servicio Central de Publicaciones, Gobierno Vasco.

Ewald, François. 1986. *L'Etat Providence.* Paris: Grasset.

Fanon, Frantz. 1967 [1952]. *Black Skin, White Masks.* Trans. Charles Lam Markmann. New York: Grove.

Fernandez, James W. 1962. "Folklore as an Agent of Nationalism." *African Studies Bulletin* 2: 3–8.

———. 1986. *Persuasions and Performances: The Play of Tropes in Culture.* Bloomington: Indiana University Press.

———. 2001. "Creative Arguments of Images in Culture and the Charnel House of Conventionality." In *Locating Cultural Creativity,* ed. John Liep, 17–30. London: Pluto Press.

Fernandez Fernandez, Idoia. 1995. "La escuela vasca y la larga historia de la Posguerra." In *Lengua, escuela, y cultura: El proceso de alfabetización en Euskal Herria, siglos XIX y XX,* ed. Paulí Dávila Balsera, 159–91. Bilbao: Servicio Editorial Universidad del País Vasco.

Ferrer, Mariano, Manuel Cancia, Jon-Mirena Landa, Félix Cañada, José María Elosua, Xabier Ezeizabarrena, Íñigo Lazcano, and Iñaki Lasagabaster. 2005. *Derechos, libertades, y razón de estado (1996–2005)*. Pamplona: Lete Argitaletxea.

Fishman, Joshua A. 1972. *Language and Nationalism: Two Integrative Essays*. Rowley, Mass.: Newbury House.

———. 1973. "Language Modernization and Planning in Comparison with Other Types of National Modernization and Planning." *Language in Society* 2, no. 1: 23–44.

———. 1989. *Language and Ethnicity in Minority Sociolinguistic Perspective*. Clevedon, Penna.: Multilingual Matters.

———. 1991. *Reversing Language Shift: Theoretical and Empirical Foundations of Assistance to Threatened Languages*. Clevedon, Penna.: Multilingual Matters.

———, ed. 1993. *The Earliest Stage of Language Planning: The "First Congress" Phenomenon*. Berlin and New York: Mouton de Gruyter.

———. 1996. *In Praise of the Beloved Language: A Comparative View of Positive Ethnolinguistic Consciousness*. Hawthorne, N.Y.: Mouton de Gruyter.

———, ed. 2001. *Can Threatened Languages be Saved?* Clevedon, Penna.: Multilingual Matters.

Flores, Juan, John Attinasi, and Pedro Pedraza Jr. 1981. "La Carreta Made a U-turn: Puerto Rican Language and Culture in the United States." *Daedalus* 110, no. 3: 193–217.

Flores, Juan, and George Yúdice. 1990. "Living Borders/Buscando America: Languages of Latino Self-Formation." *Social Text* 24: 57–84.

Foucault, Michel. 1980a. *The History of Sexuality*. Vol. 1, *An Introduction*. Trans. Robert Hurley. New York: Vintage Books.

———. 1980b. "Truth and Power." In *Power/Knowledge: Selected Interviews and Other Writings 1972–1977 by Michel Foucault*, ed. Colin Gordon, 109–33. New York: Pantheon.

———. 1982. "Afterword: The Subject and Power." In *Michel Foucault: Beyond Structuralism and Hermeneutics*, by Paul Rabinow and Hubert Dreyfus, 208–26. Chicago: University of Chicago Press.

———. 1991. "Governmentality." In *The Foucault Effect: Studies in Governmentality*, ed. Graham Burchell, Colin Gordon, and Peter Miller, 87–104. Chicago: University of Chicago Press.

Fraser, Nancy. 1997. *Justice Interruptus: Critical Reflections on the "Postsocialist" Condition*. London and New York: Routledge.

Freeland, Jane, and Donna Patrick, eds. 2004. *Language Rights and Language Survival*. Manchester, UK: St. Jerome.

Fusco, Coco. 1995. *English is Broken Here: Notes on Cultural Fusion in the Americas*. New York: New Press.

Gal, Susan. 1979. *Language Shift*. New York: Academic Press.

———. 1987. "Codeswitching and Consciousness in the European Periphery." *American Ethnologist* 14, no. 4: 637–53.

———. 1989. "Language and Political Economy." *Annual Review of Anthropology* 18: 345–67.

———. 2006. "Contradictions of Standard Language in Europe: Implications for the Study of Practices and Publics." *Social Anthropology* 14, no. 2: 163–81.

Gal, Susan, and Judith T. Irvine. 1995. "The Boundaries of Languages and Disciplines: How Ideologies Construct Difference." *Social Research* 62, no. 4: 967–1001.

Gal, Susan, and Kathryn Woolard. 2001. "Constructing Languages and Publics: Authority and Representation." In *Languages and Publics: The Making of Authority,* ed. Susan Gal and Kathryn Woolard, 1–12. Manchester, UK, and Northampton, Mass.: St. Jerome.

Garate, Katixa. 2002. "Kaleko Hizkeran Hankamotz." *ARGIA,* no. 1850, April 21, 2002, 15–23.

Gardner, Nick. 1990. "Goodwill Language Policies and Language Planning." Paper presented to the Joint Working Party on Bilingualism in Dyfed, Carmarthen, Wales. Department of Education, Universities and Research, Basque Government, Gasteiz-Vitoria.

Garmendia, José María. 1996. *Historia de ETA.* Donostia–San Sebastián: Haranburu.

Garmendia, Mari Carmen. 1994. "El proceso de normalización lingüística en el País Vasco: Datos de una década." *International Journal of the Sociology of Language* 109: 97–107.

Garzón Real, Baltasar. 1997. "Prólogo: 'Con esperanzas en el futuro . . .'". In *ETA entre España y Francia,* by Sagrario Morán Blanco, XV–LIV. Madrid: Editorial Complutense.

Gatti, Gabriel, Ignacio Irazuzta, and Iñaki Martinez de Albéniz. 2005. *Basque Society: Structures, Institutions, and Contemporary Life.* Reno: Center for Basque Studies, University of Nevada, Reno.

Geertz, Clifford. 1973. "Religion as a Cultural System." In *The Interpretation of Cultures,* 87–125. New York: Basic Books.

Gellner, Ernest. 1983. *Nations and Nationalism.* Ithaca, N.Y.: Cornell University Press.

Gerth, Hans H., and C. Wright Mills, eds. 1958. *From Max Weber: Essays in Sociology.* New York: Oxford University Press.

Giacopuzzi, Giovanni. 1997. *ETA p.m., el otro camino.* Tafalla (Nafaroa): Txalaparta.

Gibson-Graham, J. K. 2006. *A Post-Capitalist Politics.* Minneapolis and London: University of Minnesota Press.

Gilroy, Paul. 1993. *The Black Atlantic: Modernity and Double Consciousness.* Cambridge, Mass.: Harvard University Press.

Ginsburg, Faye. 1992. "Indigenous Media: Faustian Contract or Global Village?" *Cultural Anthropology* 6, no. 1: 92–112.

Goffman, Erving. 1979. "Footing." *Semiotica* 25: 1–29.

Gómez Peña, Guillermo. 1993. *Warrior for Gringostroika: Essays, Performance Texts, and Poetry.* Saint Paul, Minn.: Graywolf Press.

Gordon, Colin. 1991. "Governmental Rationality: An Introduction." In *The Foucault Effect: Studies in Governmentality,* ed. Graham Burchell, Colin Gordon, and Peter Miller, 1–52. Chicago: University of Chicago Press.

Gortari, Miguel. 1920. "La estadística en el País Vasco." In *Segundo congreso de estudios vascos,* 235–48. San Sebastián: Eusko Ikaskuntza.

Gould, Steven Jay. 1981. *The Mismeasure of Man.* New York: W. W. Norton.

Granja Pascual, José Javier. 1984. "Divergencias lingüísticas y literarias entre Arturo Campión y Sabino Arana." *Fontes Lingua Vasconum: Studia et Documenta* 43: 155–79.

———. 1985. "La gramática de Arturo Campión y Luis Luciano Bonaparte." *Euskera* 30: 31–49.

Greenwood, Davyyd J. 1977. "Continuity and Change: Spanish Basque Ethnicity as a Historical Process." In *Ethnic Conflict in the Western World,* ed. Milton Esman, 81–102. Ithaca: Cornell University Press.

Grenoble, Lenore A., and Lindsay J. Whaley, eds. 1998. *Endangered Languages: Current Issues and Future Prospects.* Cambridge: Cambridge University Press.

————. 2006. *Saving Languages: An Introduction to Language Revitalization*. Cambridge: Cambridge University Press.

Grillo, Ralph D. 1989. *Dominant Languages: Language and Hierarchy in Britain and France*. Cambridge and New York: Cambridge University Press.

Grin, François. 2003. "Diversity as Paradigm, Analytical Device and Policy Goal." In *Language Rights and Political Theory*, ed. Will Kymlicka and Alan Patten, 169–88. Oxford and New York: Oxford University Press.

Grin, François, Regina Jensdóttir, and Dónall O Riagáin. 2003. *Language Policy Evaluation and the European Charter for Regional or Minority Languages*. Hampshire, UK, and New York: Palgrave.

Guattari, Felix. 1981. "Las radios libres populares." In *De las ondas rojas a las radios libres*, ed. Lluís Bassets, 231–36. Barcelona: Editorial Gustavo Gili.

Gumperz, John J., and Jenny Cook-Gumperz. 2005. "Language Standardization and the Complexities of Communicative Practice." In *Complexities: Beyond Nature & Nurture*, ed. Susan McKinnon and Sydel Sylverman, 268–88. Chicago: University of Chicago Press.

Gurruchaga, Ander. 1985. *El código nacionalista vasco durante el Franquismo*. Barcelona: Anthropos.

Hacking, Ian. 1981. "How Should We Do the History of Statistics?" *Ideology and Consciousness* 8: 15–26.

————. 1982. "Biopower and the Avalanche of Printed Numbers." *Humanities in Society* 5, nos. 3–4: 279–95.

————. 1986. "Making Up People." In *Reconstructing Individualism: Autonomy, Individuality and the Self in Western Thought*, ed. T. Heller, M. Sosna, and D. Wellbery, 222–36. Stanford: Stanford University Press.

————. 1999. *The Social Construction of What?* Cambridge, Mass.: Harvard University Press.

Haddican, Bill. 2007. "Suburbanization and Language Change in Basque." *Language in Society* 36, no. 5: 677–706.

Hale, Kenneth L., Colette Craig, Nora England, La Verne Jeanne, Michael Krauss, Lucille Watahomigie, and Akira Yamamoto. 1992. "Endangered Languages." *Language* 68, no. 1: 1–42.

Hall, Stuart. 1996a. "Introduction: Who Needs Identity?" In *Questions of Cultural Identity*, ed. Stuart Hall and Paul de Gay, 1–17. London, Thousand Oaks, New Dehli: Sage.

————. 1996b [1988]. "New Ethnicities." In *Stuart Hall: Critical Dialogues in Cultural Studies*, ed. David Morley and Kuan-Hsing, 441–49. London and New York: Routledge.

Handler, Richard. 1988. *Nationalism and the Politics of Culture in Quebec*. Madison: University of Wisconsin Press.

Haraway, Donna J. 1991. "Situated Knowledges: The Science Question in Feminism and the Privilege of Partial Perspective." In *Simians, Cyborgs, and Women: The Reinvention of Nature*, 183–201. New York: Routledge.

Harries, Patrick. 1988. "The Roots of Ethnicity: Discourse and the Politics of Language Construction in South-East Africa." *African Affairs* 87: 25–52.

Haugen, Einar. 1966a. "Dialect, Language, Nation." *American Anthropologist* 68, no. 6: 922–35.

———. 1966b. *Language Conflict and Language Planning: The Case of Modern Norwegian.* Cambridge, Mass.: Harvard University Press.

———. 1972. *The Ecology of Language.* Essays selected and introduced by Anwar S. Dil. Stanford, Calif.: Stanford University Press.

———. 1983. "The Implementation of Corpus Planning: Theory and Practice." In *Progress in Language Planning: International Perspectives,* ed. Juan Cobarrubias and Joshua A. Fishman, 269–89. Berlin: Mouton.

Hechter, Michael, and Margaret Levi. 1979. "The Comparative Analysis of Ethnoregional Movements." *Ethnic and Racial Studies* 2–3: 262–74.

Heiberg, Marianne. 1980. "Basques, Anti-Basques and the Moral Community." In *"Nation" and "State" in Europe: Anthropological Perspectives,* ed. R. D. Grillo, 45–60. London: Academic Press.

———. 1982. "Urban Politics and Rural Culture: Basque Nationalism." In *The Politics of Territorial Identity,* ed. Stein Rokkan and Derek Urwin, 355–87. London: Sage.

———. 1989. *The Making of the Basque Nation.* Cambridge: Cambridge University Press.

Hernández, Jone M., Olatz Olaso, and Iñaki Martínez de Luna. 2006. "Theoretical, Social and Political Discourses on the Basque Language." In *The Case of Basque: Past, Present and Future,* ed. Mari-Jose Azurmendi and Iñaki Martínez de Luna, 103–16. Soziolinguistika Klusterra.

Hernández García, Jone Miren. 2004. "Euskara, comunidad, e identidad: Elementos de transmisión, elementos de transgresión." Phd diss., Departamento de Filosofia de Valores y Antropología Social, Universidad del País Vasco.

———. 2005. *Jolasgaraia: Gaztetxeoak, hizkuntzak eta identitateen adierazpenak.* Soziologiazko Euskal Koadernoak/Cuadernos Sociológicos Vascos. Vitoria-Gasteiz: Servicio Central de Publicaciones del Gobierno Vasco.

Herr, Richard. 1971. *A Historical Essay on Modern Spain.* Berkeley: University of California Press.

Higonnet, Patrice L-R. 1980. "The Politics of Linguistic Terrorism and Grammatical Hegemony During the French Revolution." *Social History* 5, no. 1: 41–69.

Hill, Jane H. 1985. "The Grammar of Consciousness and the Consciousness of Grammar." *American Ethnologist* 12, no. 4: 725–37.

———. 1986. "The Refiguration of the Anthropology of Language." *Cultural Anthropology* 1, no. 1: 89–102.

———. 1993. " 'Hasta la Vista, Baby': Anglo Spanish in the American Southwest." *Critique of Anthropology* 13: 145–76.

———. 1995. "The Voices of Don Gabriel: Responsibility and Self in a Modern Mexicano Narrative." In *The Dialogic Emergence of Culture,* ed. Barbara Tedlock and Bruce Mannheim, 97–146. Urbana: University of Illinois Press.

———. 2002. " 'Expert Rhetorics' in Advocacy for Endangered Languages: Who is Listening and What do They Hear?" *Journal of Linguistic Anthropology* 12, no. 2: 119–33.

———. 2008. *The Everyday Language of White Racism.* Malden, Mass., and Oxford: Wiley-Blackwell.

Hill, Jane H., and David Coombs. 1982. "The Vernacular Remodeling of National and International Languages." *Applied Linguistics* 3: 224–34.

Hill, Jane H., and Kenneth C. Hill. 1986. *Speaking Mexicano Dynamics of Syncretic Language in Central Mexico.* Tucson: University of Arizona Press.

Hinton, Leanne, and Ken Hale, eds. 2001. *The Green Book of Language Revitalization in Practice.* San Diego: Academic Press.

Hobsbawm, Eric. 1990. *Nations and Nationalism Since 1780.* Cambridge: Cambridge University Press.

Hobsbawm, Eric, and Terence Ranger, eds. 1983. *The Invention of Tradition.* Cambridge: Cambridge University Press.

Hobson, Barbara, ed. 2003. *Recognition Struggles and Social Movements: Contested Identities, Agency and Power.* Cambridge: Cambridge University Press.

hooks, bell. 1990. "Marginality as a Site of Resistance." In *Out There: Marginalization and Contemporary Cultures,* ed. Russell Ferguson, Martha Gever, Trinh T. Minh-ha, and Cornel West, 341–43. New York and Cambridge: New Museum of Contemporary Art and MIT Press.

Hordago. 1979. *Documentos.* 18 vols. Donostia–San Sebastián: Lur.

Horn, David G. 1994. *Social Bodies: Science, Reproduction and Italian Modernity.* Princeton: Princeton University Press.

Hornberger, Nancy H., and Kendall King. 1996. "Language Revitalisation in the Andes: Can the Schools Reverse Language Shift?" *Journal of Multilingual and Multicultural Development* 17, no. 6: 427–41.

Hyatt, Susan. 2001. "From Citizen to Volunteer: Neoliberal Governance and the Erasure of Poverty." In *The New Poverty Studies: The Ethnography of Power, Politics, and Impoverished People in the United States,* ed. Judith Goode and Jeff Maskovsky, 201–235. New York: New York University Press.

Hymes, Dell H. 1974. *The Foundations of Sociolinguistics.* Philadelphia: University of Pennsylvania Press.

Ibarra Güell, Pedro. 1989. *La evolución estratégica de ETA: De la "guerra revolucionaria" (1963) hasta después de la tregua (1989).* Donostia–San Sebastián: Kriselu.

Inda, Jonathan Xavier, ed. 2005. *Anthropologies of Modernity: Foucault, Governmentality and Life Politics.* Malden, Mass.: Blackwell.

Inoue, Miyako. n.d. "What do Women Want? Gender Equity and the Ethics and Aesthetics of the Self in Neoliberal Japan." Unpublished manuscript.

Iriarte López, Iñaki. 2000. "El legado de los Éuskaros: El discurso sobre el euskara en el "Suplemento" en vascuence de Príncipe de Viana." In *El euskera en tiempo de Los Euskaros,* ed. Roldán Jimeno Aranguren, 317–38. Pamplona: Gobierno de Navarra, Dirección General de Universidades y Política Lingüística.

Irvine, Judith. 1989. "When Talk Isn't Cheap: Language and Political Economy." *American Ethnologist* 16, no. 2: 248–67.

Irvine, Judith, and Susan Gal. 2000. "Language Ideology and Linguistic Differentiation." In *Regimes of Language: Ideologies, Polities and Identities,* ed. Paul Kroskrity, 35–83. Santa Fe, N.M.: School of American Research Press.

Iztueta Armendariz, Paulo. 1981. *Sociología del fenomeno contestatario del clero vasco: 1940–1975.* Donostia–San Sebastián and Baiona: Elkar.

Jacob, James E. 1994. *Hills of Conflict: Basque Nationalism in France.* Reno: University of Nevada Press.

Jaffe, Alexandra. 1999. *Ideologies in Action: Language Politics on Corsica*. Berlin and New York: Mouton de Gruyter.

Jáuregui Bereciartu, Gurutz. 1981. *Ideología y estrategía política de ETA: Análisis de su evolución entre 1959 y 1968*. Madrid: Siglo XXI.

———. 2000. "ETA: Orígenes y evolución ideológica y política." In *La historia de ETA*, ed. Antonio Elorza, 172–276. Madrid: Temas de Hoy.

Jimeno Aranguren, Roldán, ed. 2000. *El Euskera en tempo de los Euskaros*. Pamplona: Gobierno de Navarra,Dirección General de Universidades y Política Linguística.

Johnson, Keith. 2007. "Basque Inquisition: How do You Say Shepherd in Euskera? Through Fiat, Separatists Bring Old Tongue to Life." *Wall Street Journal*, November 6, 2008, p. A1.

Joseph, John Earl. 1987. *Eloquence and Power: The Rise of Language Standards and Standard Languages*. London: Frances Pinter.

Kasmir, Sharryn. 1996. *The Myth of Mondragon: Cooperatives, Politics, and Working-Class Life in a Basque Town*. Albany, N.Y.: SUNY Press.

———. 1999. "From the Margins: Punk Rock and the Repositioning of Ethnicity and Gender in Basque Identity." In *Basque Cultural Studies*, ed. William A. Douglass, Carmelo Urza, Linda White, and Joseba Zulaika, 178–204. Reno: University of Nevada Press.

———. 2002. "'More Basque than You!' Class, Youth, and Identity in an Industrial Basque town." *Identities: Global Studies in Culture and Power* 9: 39–68.

———. 2005. "Activism and Class Identity: The Saturn Auto Factory." In *Social Movements: an Anthropological Reader*, ed. June Nash, 78–95. Malden, Mass.: Blackwell.

Kearney, Richard. 2004. "Postnationalist Identities: A New Configuration." In *Empire and Terror: Nationalism/Postnationalism in the New Millenium*, ed. B. Aretxaga, D. Dworkin, J. Gabilondo, and J. Zulaika, 29–40. Conference Paper Series 1. Reno: Center for Basque Studies, University of Nevada, Reno.

Kertzer, David, and Dominique Arel, eds. 2002. *Census and Identity: The Politics of Race, Ethnicity, and Language in National Censuses*. Cambridge: Cambridge University Press.

Khubchandani, Lachman M. 1983. *Plural Languages, Plural Cultures: Communication, Identity, and Sociopolitical Change in Contemporary India*. Honolulu: University of Hawaii Press.

King, Alan. 1983. "Batua Bai, Euskalkiak ere Bai!" *ARGIA* 11–13. www.argia.com/mendea/hemero/83king.htm.

Kitsuse, John I., and Aaron Cicourel. 1963. "A Note on the Uses of Official Statistics." *Social Problems* 11: 131–39.

Kohn, Hans. 1944. *The Idea of Nationalism: a Study in its Origins and Background*. New York: Macmillan.

Kostelnick, Charles. 2004. "Melting Pot Ideology, Modernist Aesthetics, and the Emergence of Graphical Conventions: The Statistical Atlases of the United States, 1874–1925." In *Defining Visual Rhetorics*, ed. Charles Hill and Marguerite Helmers, 215–42. Mahwah, N.J.: Lawrence Erlbaum.

Kroskrity, Paul V., ed. 1999. *Regimes of Language: Ideologies, Polities and Identities*. Santa Fe, N.M.: School of American Research Press.

Kruger, Lorenz, Lorraine Daston, and Michael Heidelberger, eds. 1987. *The Probabilistic Revolution*. Vol. 1, *Ideas in History*. Cambridge, Mass.: MIT Press.

Kruger, Lorenz, Gerd Gigerenzer, and Mary Morgan, eds. 1987. *The Probabilistic Revolution.* Vol. 2, *Ideas in the Sciences.* Cambridge, Mass.: MIT Press.

Krutwig, Federico. 1979 [1963]. *La nueva Vasconia: Estudio dialéctico de una nacionalidad.* Bilbao: Ediciones Vascas.

Kula, Witold. 1986. *Measures and Men.* Trans. R. Szreter. Princeton: Princeton University Press.

Kulick, Don. 1992. *Language Shift and Cultural Reproduction: Socialization, Self and Syncretism in a Papua New Guinean Village.* Cambridge: Cambridge University Press.

Kymlicka, Will. 1995. *Multicultural Citizenship: A Liberal Theory of Minority Rights.* New York: Oxford University Press.

Kymlicka, Will, and Alan Patten, eds. 2003. *Language Rights and Political Theory.* Oxford: Oxford University Press.

Laitin, David. 1999. "National Revivals and Violence." In *Critical Comparisons in Politics and Culture,* ed. John Bowen and Roger Petersen, 21–60. Cambridge: Cambridge University Press.

Landry, R., and R. Y. Bourhis. 1997. "Linguistic Landscape and Ethnolinguistic Vitality: An Empirical Study." *Journal of Language and Social Psychology* 16, no. 1: 23–49.

Laponce, Jean. A. 1987. *Languages and Their Territories.* Trans. A. Martin-Sperry. Toronto: University of Toronto Press.

Larrañaga, Carmen. 1996. "Ubiquitous but Invisible: The Presence of Women Singers within a Basque Male Tradition." In *Gender and Memory: International Yearbook of Oral History and Life Stories,* ed. Selma Leydesdorff, Luisa Passerini, and Paul Thompson, 4:59–71. Oxford: Oxford University Press,

Larronde, Jean Claude. 1977. *El nacionalismo vasco: Su orígen y su ideología en la obra de Sabino Arana-Goiri.* San Sebastián: Txertoa.

Lasagabaster, Jesús María. 1990. *Contemporary Basque Fiction: An Anthology.* Trans. Michael E. Morris. Reno: University of Nevada Press.

Latiegui, Vicente, and Dionisio de Oñatibia. 1983. *Euskaltzaindia, el batua y la muerte del euskera.* San Sebastián: Lorea.

Le Bras, Hervé. 1986. "La statistique générale de la France." In *Les Lieux de Mémoire.* Vol. 2, *La Nation,* ed. Pierre Nora, 317–53. Paris: Gallimard.

Letamendia, Francisco. 1977. *Historia de Euskadi: El nacionalismo vasco y* ETA. Barcelona: Ruedo Iberico.

Letamendia Belzunce, Francisco. 1994. *Historia del nacionalismo vasco y de E.T.A.: ETA y el gobierno del PSOE (1982–1992).* Donostia–San Sebastián: R & B Ediciones.

Letona, Xabier, Kike Amonarriz, and Nagore Irazustabarrena. 2003. "Hiru ikuspegi euskararen etorkizunaz." *Larrun* 1885: 1–16. (Interview with Bernardo Atxaga, Joxe Mari Odriozola, and Jon Sarasua.)

Lieberson, Stanley. 1981 [1966]. "Language Questions in Censuses." In *Language Diversity and Language Contact: Essays by S. Lieberson,* ed. Anwar S. Dil, 281–303. Stanford: Stanford University Press.

Linke, Uli. 1990. "Folklore, Anthropology, and the Government of Social Life." *Comparative Studies in Society and History* 32, no. 1: 117–48.

Linz, Juan. 1973. "Early State–Building and Late Peripheral Nationalism Against the State:

The Case of Spain." In *Building States and Nations: Analyses by Region*, ed. S. N. Eisenstadt and Stein Rokkan, 33–116. London: Sage.

Lippard, Lucy R. 1990. *Mixed Blessings: New Art in a Multicultural America*. New York: Pantheon Books.

Lipsitz, George. 1994. *Dangerous Crossroads: Popular Music, Postmodernism and the Poetics of Place*. London and New York: Verso.

———. 2006. *The Possessive Investment in Whiteness: How White People Profit from Identity Politics*. Philadelphia: Temple University Press.

Lodares, Juan Ramón. 2000. *El paraíso políglota: Historias de lenguas en la España moderna contadas*. Madrid: Taurus.

———. 2002. *Lengua y patria: Sobre el nacionalismo lingüístico en España*. Madrid: Taurus.

MacClancy, Jeremy. 1988. "The Culture of Radical Basque Nationalism." *Anthropology Today* 4, no. 5: 17–19.

Madariaga Orbea, Juan. 2006. *Anthology of Apologists and Detractors of the Basque Language*. Center for Basque Studies Basque Classic Series 2. Reno: Center for Basque Studies, Unversity of Nevada, Reno.

Maffi, Luisa. 2000. "Language Preservation vs. Language Maintenance and Revitalization: Assessing Concepts, Approaches and Implications for the Language Sciences." *International Journal of the Sociology of Language* 142: 175–90.

Mansvelt Beck, Jan, and Jan D. Markusse. 2008. "Basque Violence: A Reappraisal of Culturalist Explanations." *Archives Européenes de Sociologie* 49, no. 1: 91–118.

Marko Juanikorena, J. Inazio. 2004. "Euskara bultzatzeko erantzukizuna eta enpresak." http://www.erabili.com/aer berri/muinetik/1084208726.

———. 2010. "ENEKUS Eredua, lan-munduko organizazioetan euskararen normalizaziorako eraldaketa kudeatzeko erreferentziazko eredua." *Bat* 76: 125–44.

Mar Molinero, Clare, and Patrick Stevenson. 1991. "The 'Territorial Imperative' Debate in the European Context." *Language Problems and Language Planning* 15: 162–76.

Martínez de Luna, Iñaki. (2002). "Etorkizuna aurreikusten 99: Euskal Herriko gaztetxoak eta euskara; Previendo el futuro 99: Los adolescentes de Euskal Herria y el Euskera." In *IX Jardunaldi Pedagogikoak: Euskararen Erabilera*, ed. Juan Jose Gomez Senande, 361–414. Nafarroa: Ikastolen Elkartea.

Maskovsky, Jeff. 2001. "The Other War at Home: The Geopolitics of Urban Poverty." *Urban Anthropology* 30, nos. 2–3: 215–38.

Mateo, Miren, and Xabier Aizpurua. 2003. "Evolución sociolingüística del euskera." *Euskonews & Media* 201. http://www.euskonews.com.

May, Stephen. 2001. *Language and Minority Rights: Ethnicity, Nationalism and the Politics of Language*. Harlow, Essex, UK; New York: Longman/Pearson Education.

———. 2003. "Misconceiving Minority Language Rights: Implications for Liberal Political Theory." In *Language Rights and Political Theory*, ed. Will Kymlicka and Alan Patten, 123–52. Oxford: Oxford University Press.

McDonald, Maryon. 1986. "Celtic Ethnic Kinship and the Problem of Being English." *Current Anthropology* 27, no. 4: 333–47.

———. 1989. *We Are Not French! Language, Culture and Identity in Brittany*. London and New York: Routledge.

McEwan-Fujita, Emily. 2005. "Neoliberalism and Minority-Language Planning in the Highlands and Islands of Scotland." *International Journal of the Sociology of Language* 171: 155–71.

McRae, Kenneth D. 1975. "The Principle of Territoriality and the Principle of Personality in Multi-lingual States." *Linguistics* 158: 33–54.

Mees, Ludger. 2003. *Nationalism, Violence and Democracy: The Basque Clash of Identities.* Houndsmill, Basingstoke, Hampshire; New York: Palgrave Macmillan.

Melucci, Alberto. 1980. "The New Social Movements: A Theoretical Approach." *Social Science Information* 19: 199–226.

Mendebalde Kultur Alkartea, ed. 2001. *Euskalkia eta hezkuntza.* Bilbao/Bilbo: Mendebalde Kultur Alkartea.

Mendiguren, Xabier, and Joxe J. Iñigo. 2006. "The Social Movement in Favor of the Normalization of the Basque Language." In *The Case of Basque: Past, Present and Future,* ed. Maria-Jose Azurmendi and Iñaki Martinez de Luna, 53–65. Andoain: Soziolinguistika Klusterra.

Menéndez Pidal, Ramón. 1962 [1921]. "Introducción al estudio de la lingüística vasca." In *En torno a la lengua vasca,* 11–57. Buenos Aires: Colección Austral.

Michelena, Luis [Koldo Mitxelena]. 1977. "El largo y difícil camino del euskara." In *El Libro Blanco del Euskara,* ed. SIADECO, 15–29. Bilbao: Euskaltzaindia.

———. 1984. "Los Vascos y su nombre." *Revista Internacional de Estudios Vascos* 29, no. 1: 11–29.

Miguel, Amando de. 1976. *Cuarenta millones de Españoles cuarenta años después.* Barcelona: Ediciones Grijalbo.

Mill, John Stuart. 1861. *Considerations on Representative Government.* London: Parker, Son, and Bourn.

Mitxelena, Koldo [Luis Michelena]. 1981. "Nuestra irresistible ascensión de la poesía a la ciencia." *Muga* 19.

———. 2001. *Historia de la literatura vasca.* Donosita: Erein.

Mocoroa, Justo María [Ibar]. 1935. *Genio y lengua.* Tolosa: Librería de Mocoroa Hermanos.

Muñoz, Pedro. 2000. *España en horas bajas: "La guerra de los nacionalismos."* Madrid: Brand Editorial.

Neff-van Aerstaeler, JoAnne. 2006. "Language Policies in Spain: Accomodation or Alteration." In *Along the Routes to Power: Explorations of Empowerment through Language,* ed. Martin Putz, Joshua A. Fishman, and JoAnne Neff-van Aertselaer, 179–98. Berlin and New York: Mouton de Gruyter.

Nettle, Daniel, and Suzanne Romaine. 2000. *Vanishing Voices: The Extinction of the World's Languages.* Oxford: Oxford University Press.

Ninyoles, Rafael. 1972. *Idioma y poder social.* Madrid: Technos.

Ochs, Elinor. 1992. "Indexing Gender." In *Rethinking Context,* ed. Alessandro Duranti and Charles Goodwin, 335–58. Cambridge: Cambridge University Press.

Offe, Claus. 1985. "The New Social Movements: Challenging the Boundaries of Institutional Politics." *Social Research* 52: 817–68.

Olabuenaga, José Ignacio Ruiz. 1984. *Atlas lingüístico vasco.* Vitoria-Gasteiz: Servicio Central de Publicaciones, Gobierno Vasco.

Olarriaga, Luis de. 1920. "Estadística: Conferencia general." In *Segundo congreso de estudios vascos*, 233–34. San Sebastián: Sociedad de Estudios Vascos/Eusko Ikaskuntza.

Olaziregi, Mari Jose, ed. 2004. *An Anthology of Basque Short Stories*. Reno: Center for Basque Studies, University of Nevada, Reno.

O'Reilly, Camille C. 1999. *The Irish Language in Northern Ireland: The Politics of Culture and Identity*. Basingstoke, Hampshire: Macmillan; New York: St. Martin's.

Ortner, Sherry. 1973. "On Key Symbols." *American Anthropologist* 75: 1338–46.

———. 1995. "Resistance and the Problem of Ethnographic Refusal." *Comparative Studies in Society and History* 37, no. 1: 173–93.

———. 1996a. "Gender Hegemonies." In *Making Gender. The Politics and Erotics of Culture*, ed. Sherry Ortner, 139–72. Boston: Beacon Press.

———. 1996b. "Is Female to Male as Nature is to Culture?" In *Making Gender: The Politics and Erotics of Culture*, 21–42. Boston: Beacon Press.

Orueta, José de. 1920. "Conferencia-Resúmen." In *Segundo congreso de estudios vascos*, 274–79. San Sebastián: Sociedad de Estudios Vascos/Eusko Ikaskuntza.

"Oskillaso" [José Basterrechea]. 1984. *El libro negro del euskara*. Bilbao: La Gran Enciclopedia Vasca.

Ott, Sandra. 2008. *War, Judgment and Memory in the Basque Borderlands*. Reno: University of Nevada Press.

Parakrama, Arjuna. 1995. *De-Hegemonizing Language Standards: Learning from (Post) Colonial Englishes about "English."* Basingstoke, Hampshire: Macmillan; New York: St. Martin's.

Payne, Stanley. 1973. "Spanish Fascism in Comparative Perspective." *Iberian Studies* 2: 3–12.

———. 1975. *Basque Nationalism*. Reno: University of Nevada Press.

———. 1980. *Fascism, Comparison and Definition*. Madison: University of Wisconsin Press.

Pérez-Agote, Alfonso. 1984. *La reproducción del nacionalismo: El caso vasco*. 2nd ed. Centro de Investigaciones Sociológicas, Colección Monografías 73. Madrid: Siglo Veintiuno.

———. 1987. *El nacionalismo Vasco a la salida del Franquismo*. Madrid: Centro de Investigaciones Sociológicas.

———. 2006. *The Social Roots of Basque Nationalism*. Trans. Cameron Watson and William A. Douglass. Reno: University of Nevada Press.

Phillipson, Robert. 2003. *English-Only Europe? Challenging Language Policy*. London and New York: Routledge.

Porter, Theodore M. 1986. *The Rise of Statistical Thinking, 1820–1900*. Princeton: Princeton University Press.

———. 1995. *Trust in Numbers: The Pursuit of Objectivity in Science and Public Life*. Princeton: Princeton University Press.

Pred, Allan. 1990. *Lost Words and Lost Worlds: Modernity and the Language of Everyday Life in Late Nineteenth Century Stockholm*. Cambridge: Cambridge University Press.

Pujolar, Joan. 2001. *Gender, Heteroglossia and Power: A Sociolinguistic Study of Youth Culture*. Berlin and New York: Mouton de Gruyter.

Rabinow, Paul. 1989. *French Modern: Norms and Forms of the Social Environment*. Cambridge, Mass.: MIT Press.

Rabinow, Paul, and Nikolas Rose. 2003. "Introduction." In *The Essential Foucault*, ed. Paul Rabinow and Nikolas Rose, vii–xxxv. New York and London: New Press.

Rampton, Ben. 1995. *Crossing: Language and Ethnicity among Adolescents*. London and New York: Longman.

Reyhner, Jon., ed. 1997. *Teaching Indigenous Languages*. Flagstaff: Northern Arizona University. http://jan.ucc.nau.edu/~jar/TIL Contents.html.

Rijk, Rudolf P. G. de. 1991. "Familiarity or Solidarity: The Pronoun *Hi* in Basque." *Revista Internacional de Estudios Vascos* 36: 373–78.

Rosaldo, Renato. 1989. *Culture and Truth: The Remaking of Social Analysis*. Boston: Beacon Press.

Rose, Nikolas. 1990. *Governing the Soul: The Shaping of the Private Self*. London: Routledge.

———. 1999. *Powers of Freedom: Reframing Political Thought*. Cambridge: Cambridge University Press.

Rose, Nikolas, and Peter Miller. 1992. "Political Power Beyond the State: Problematics of Government." *British Journal of Sociology* 43, no. 2: 173–205.

Roseman, Sharon. 1995. "Falamos como Falamos: Linguistic Revitalization and the Maintenance of Local Vernaculars in Galicia." *Journal of Linguistic Anthropology* 5, no. 1: 3–32.

Safran, William. 1999. "Politics and Language in Contemporary France: Facing Supranational and Infranational Challenges." *International Journal of the Sociology of Language* 137: 39–66.

Samuels, David. 2004. "Language, Meaning, Modernity and Doowop." *Semiotica* 148: 1–27.

Sánchez Carrión, José M. ["Txepetx"]. 1987. *Un futuro para nuestro pasado: Claves de la recuperación del euskara y teoría social de las lenguas*. San Sebastián.

Schieffelin, Bambi, and Rachelle Charlier Doucet. 1992. "The 'Real' Haitian Creole: Linguistics and Orthographic Choice." *Pragmatics* 2, no. 3: 427–43.

Schieffelin, Bambi, Kathryn Woolard, and Paul Kroskrity, eds. 1998. *Language Ideologies: Practice and Theory*. New York: Oxford University Press.

Scott, James C. 1998. *Seeing Like a State*. New Haven: Yale University Press.

Scott, Joan Wallach. 1988. "A Statistical Representation of Work: La statistique de l'industrie à Paris, 1847–1848." In *Gender and the Politics of History*, 113–38. New York: Columbia University Press.

Segal, Daniel A. 1988. "Nationalism, Comparatively Speaking." *Journal of Historical Sociology* 1, no. 3: 301–21.

Seitel, Peter. 1977. "Saying Haya Sayings: Two Categories of Proverb Use." In *The Social Use of Metaphor: Essays on the Anthropology of Rhetoric*, 75–99. Philadelphia: University of Pennsylvania Press.

Sekula, Allan. 1986. "The Body and the Archive." *October*, 3–64.

Shafir, Gershon. 1995. *Immigrants and Nationalists: Ethnic Conflict and Accomodation in Catalonia, the Basque Country, Latvia and Estonia*. Albany, N.Y.: SUNY Press.

Shohat, Ella, and Robert Stam. 1994. *Unthinking Eurocentrism: Multiculturalism and the Media*. London and New York: Routledge.

Shore, Cris, and Susan Wright. 1997. "Policy: A New Field of Anthropology." In *The Anthropology of Policy: Critical Perspectives on Governance and Power*, ed. C. Shore and S. Wright, 3–39. London: Routledge.

———. 2000. "Coercive Accountability: The Rise of Audit Culture in Higher Education." In *Audit Cultures: Anthropological Studies in Accountability, Ethics, and the Academy*, ed. M. Strathern, 57–89. New York and London: Routledge.

SIADECO. 1979. *Conflícto lingüístico en Euskadi: Informe* SIADECO. Bilbao: Euskaltzaindia.

———. 2010. *2008an Euskararen sustapenerako erabilitako aurrekontu publiko, dirulaguntza eta giza baliabideen ikerlana.* Vitoria/Gasteiz: Eusko Jaurlaritza.

Silverstein, Michael. 1996. "Monoglot 'Standard' in America: Standardization and Metaphors of Linguistic Hegemony." In *The Matrix of Language,* ed. Donald Brenneis and Ronald Macaulay, 284–306. Boulder, Colo.: Westview Press.

Singh, Rajendra, ed. 1998. *The Native Speaker: Multilingual Perspectives.* New Delhi; Thousand Oaks, Calif.; London: Sage.

Skutnabb-Kangas, Tove, and Robert Phillipson, eds. 1992. *Linguistic Human Rights: Overcoming Linguistic Discrimination.* Berlin: Mouton de Gruyter.

Snow, David A., Sarah A. Soule, and Hanspeter Kriesi, eds. 2007. *The Blackwell Companion to Social Movements.* Malden, Mass.: Blackwell.

Spitulnik, Debra. 1993. "Anthropology and Mass Media." *Annual Review of Anthropology* 22: 293–315.

———. 1996. "The Social Circulation of Media Discourse and the Mediation of Communities." *Journal of Linguistic Anthropology* 6, no. 2: 161–87.

———. 1998. "Mediating Unity and Diversity: The Production of Language Ideologies in Zambian Broadcasting." In *Language Ideologies: Practice and Theory,* ed. Bambi B. Schieffelin, Kathryn A. Woolard, and Paul V. Kroskrity, 163–88. Oxford and New York: Oxford University Press.

Strand, Thea R. Forthcoming. "Winning the Dialect Popularity Contest: Mass-mediated Language Ideologies, Age-graded Responses, and Local Dialect Revalorization in Rural Valdres, Norway."

Strathern, Marilyn, ed. 2000. *Audit Cultures: Anthropological Studies in Accountability, Ethics and the Academy.* London and New York: Routledge.

Sullivan, John. 1988. ETA *and Basque Nationalism: The Fight for Euskadi 1890–1986.* London and New York: Routledge.

Swift, Jill. A., Joel E. Ross, and Vincent K. Omachonu. 1998. *Principles of Total Quality.* Boca Raton, Fla.: St. Lucie Press.

Tagg, Jonathan. 1988. *The Burden of Representation: Essays on Photography and Histories.* Amherst: University of Massachusetts Press.

Taylor, Charles. 1994. "The Politics of Recognition." In *Multiculturalism: A Critical Reader,* ed. David Theo Goldberg, 75–106. Cambridge and Oxford: Blackwell.

Tejerina Montaña, Benjamín. 1992. *Nacionalismo y lengua: Los procesos de cambio lingüístico en el País Vasco.* Centro de Investigaciones Sociológicas, Colección "Monografías," no. 122. Madrid: Siglo XXI.

———. 1996. "Language and Basque Nationalism: Collective Identity, Social Conflict and Institutionalization." In *Nationalism and the Nation in the Iberian Peninsula,* ed. Clare Mar-Molinero and Angel Smith, 221–36. Oxford: Berg.

Thiong'o, Ngũgĩ Wa. 1986. *Decolonising the Mind: The Politics of Language in African Literature.* London: James Currey.

Thomas, Megan. 2007. "K is for De-Kolonization: Anti-Colonial Nationalism and Orthographic Reform." *Comparative Studies in Society and History* 49, no. 4: 938–67.

Thompson Jr., Arthur A., and A. J. Strickland III. 1984. *Strategic Management: Concepts and Cases.* 3rd ed. Boston: Irwin McGraw Hill.

Thornton, Robert J. 1988. "The Rhetoric of Ethnographic Holism." *Cultural Anthropology* 3: 285–303.

Torrealdai [Torrealday], Joan Mari. 1977. *Euskal idazleak, gaur: Historia social de la lengua y literature vascas.* Arantzazu: Jakin.

———. 1982. "Euskararen zapalkuntza (1936–39)." *Jakin* 24: 5–73.

———. 1998. *El libro negro del euskera.* Donostia–San Sebastián: Ttarttalo.

———. 2001. "Euskalgintza auzitan." Special issue, *Jakin* 123–24.

Totoricagüeña, Gloria, and Iñigo Urrutia, eds. 2008. *The Legal Status of the Basque Language Today: One Language, Three Administrations, Seven Different Geographies and a Diaspora.* Donostia–San Sebastián: Eusko Ikaskuntza.

Tovar, Antonio. 1980. *Mitología e ideología sobre la lengua vasca.* Madrid: Alianza Editorial.

Trask, Robert L. 1997. *The History of Basque.* New York: Routledge.

Tsing, Anna Lowenhaupt. 2005. *Friction: An Ethnography of Global Connection.* Princeton: Princeton University Press.

Ugalde, Martín. 1979. *Unamuno y el vascuence.* San Sebastián: Ediciones Vascas.

Ugalde Solano, Mercedes. 1991. *Las mujeres nacionalistas vascas en la vida pública: Gestación y desarrollo de Emakume Abertzale Batza, 1906–1936.* Madrid: Universidad Complutense de Madrid, Facultad de Geografía e Historia, Departamento de Historia Contemporanea.

Unamuno, Miguel de. 1997. *Crítica del problema sobre el orígen y prehistoria de la raza vasca.* Edited, with introduction and notes by José Antonio Ereño Altuna. Bilbao: Beitia.

Unanue, Amagoia, and Nahia Intxausti. 2002. *Cooperativas y el euskera: Historia y fundamentos de una nueva etapa.* Limited edition publication of EMUN Cooperative and Lanki Research Institute, Mondragon University.

Unzueta, José Luis. 1980. "La quinta asamblea de ETA." *SAIOAK* 4: 3–52.

Uranga, Mikel Gómez. 2003. *Basque Economy: From Industrialization to Globalization.* Reno: Center for Basque Studies, University Nevada, Reno.

Urcioli, Bonnie. 1996. *Exposing Prejudice: Puerto Rican Experience of Language, Race and Class.* Boulder, Colo.: Westview Press.

Urkizu, Koro. 2006. "Basque Language Corpus Planning." In *The Case of Basque: Past, Present and Future,* ed. María-Jose Azurmendi and Iñaki Martínez de Luna, 43–52. Andoain: Soziolinguistika Klusterra.

Urla, Jacqueline. 1988. "Ethnic Protest and Social Planning: A Look at Basque Language Revival." *Cultural Anthropology* 3, no. 4: 379–94.

———. 1989. "Reinventing Basque Society: Cultural Difference and the Quest for Modernity, 1918–1936." In *Essays in Basque Social Anthropology and History,* ed. William A. Douglass, 149–76. Basque Studies Program Occasional Papers Series, no. 4. Reno: University of Nevada Press.

———. 1993a. "Contesting Modernities: Language Standardization and the Making of an Ancient/Modern Basque Culture." *Critique of Anthropology* 13, no. 2: 101–18.

———. 1993b. "Cultural Politics in an Age of Statistics: Numbers, Nations, and the Making of Basque Identity." *American Ethnologist* 20, no. 4: 818–43.

———. 1995. "Outlaw Language: Creating Alternative Public Spheres in Basque Free Radio." *Pragmatics* 5, no. 2. Special issue, Constructing Languages and Publics, ed. Susan Gal and Kathryn Woolard, 245–61.

———. 1999. "Basque Language Revival and Popular Culture." In *Basque Cultural Studies,* ed. William A. Douglass, Carmelo Urza, Linda White, and Joseba Zulaika, 44–62. Reno: University of Nevada Press.

———. 2001. "'We Are All Malcolm X!' Negu Gorriak, Hip-Hop and the Basque Political Imaginary." In *Global Noise: Rap and Hip Hop Outside the USA,* ed. Tony Mitchell, 171–93. Middletown, Conn.: Wesleyan University Press.

———. 2003. "Euskara: The 'Terror' of a Minority European Language." *Anthropology Today* 19, no. 4: 1–4.

Urquijo, Julio. 1918. "Estado actual de los estudios relativos de la lengua vasca." In *Primer congreso de estudios vascos,* 403–27. Oñate: Eusko Ikaskuntza.

———. 1919. "Lengua internacional y lenguas nacionales: El euskera lengua de civilización." *Revista Internacional de Estudios Vascos* 10: 164–80.

Valle, Teresa del, 1994. *Korrika: Basque Ritual for Ethnic Identity.* Reno, Las Vegas and London: University of Nevada Press.

Valle, Teresa del, et al. 1985. *Mujer Vasca: Imagen y realidad.* Barcelona: Anthropos.

Villasante, Luis. 1979. *Historia de la literatura vasca.* 2nd ed. Burgos: Editorial Aranzazu.

———. 1980a. *Hacia la lengua literaria común.* 3rd ed. Oñate: Editorial Franciscana Aranzazu.

———. 1980b. *La H en la ortografía vasca.* Oñate: Editorial Franciscana Aranzazu.

Voloshinov, Valentin. N. 1986 [1930]. *Marxism and the Philosophy of Language.* Trans. Ladislav Matejka and I. R. Titunik. Cambridge, Mass.: Harvard University Press.

White, Linda. 1999. "Mission for the Millenium: Gendering and Engendering Basque Literature for the Next Thousand Years." In *Basque Cultural Studies,* ed. William Douglass, Carmelo Urza, Linda White, and Joseba Zulaika, 134–48. Basque Studies Program Occasional Papers Series, no. 5. Reno: Center for Basque Studies, University of Nevada, Reno.

Williams, Colin H. 1981. "The Territorial Dimension in Language Planning: An Evaluation of Its Potential in Contemporary Wales." *Language Problems and Language Planning* 5, no. 1: 57–71.

Williams, G., and D. Morris. 2000. *Language Planning and Language Use: Welsh in a Global Age.* Cardiff: University of Wales Press.

Williams, Raymond. 1977. *Marxism and Literature.* Oxford: Oxford University Press.

Willis, Paul. 1977. *Learning to Labor: How Working Class Kids Get Working Class Jobs.* New York: Columbia University Press.

Wilson, William A. 1973. "Herder, Folklore, and Romantic Nationalism." *Journal of Popular Culture* 6: 819–35.

Wolf, Eric R. 1982. "Introduction." In *Europe and the People Without History,* 3–23. Berkeley: University of California Press.

Wong, Liliana. 1997. "Authenticity and the Revitalization of Hawaiian." *Anthropology and Education Quarterly* 30, no. 1: 94–115.

Woodworth, Paddy. 2001. *Dirty War, Clean Hands: ETA, the GAL and Spanish Democracy.* Crosses Green Cork, Ireland: Cork University Press.

Woolard, Kathryn. 1985. "Language Variation and Cultural Hegemony: Towards and Integration of Sociolinguistic and Social Theory." *American Ethnologist* 12, no. 4: 738–48.

———. 1986. "The Politics of Language Status Planning: 'Normalization' in Catalonia." In

Languages in the International Perspective, ed. Nancy Schweda-Nicholson, 91–102. Delaware Symposium 5. Norwood, N.J.: Ablex.

———. 1989. *Double Talk: Bilingualism and the Politics of Ethnicity in Catalonia.* Stanford: Stanford University Press.

———. 1998a. "Introduction: Language Ideology as a Field of Inquiry." In *Language Ideologies: Practice and Theory,* ed. Bambi Schieffelin, Kathryn Woolard, and Paul Kroskrity, 3–47. New York: Oxford University Press.

———. 1998b. "Simultaneity and Bivalency as Strategies in Bilingualism." *Journal of Linguistic Anthropology* 8, no. 1: 3–29.

———. 2003. " 'We Don't Speak Catalan Because We are Marginalized': Ethnic and Class Meanings of Language in Barcelona." In *Language and Social Identity,* ed. Richard Blot, 85–103. Westport, Conn.: Praeger.

———. 2004. "Is the Past a Foreign Country? Time, Language Origins and the Nation in Early Modern Spain." *Journal of Linguistic Anthropology* 14, no. 1: 57–80.

———. 2008a. "Language and Identity Choice in Catalonia: The Interplay of Contrasting Ideologies of Linguistic Authority." In *Lengua, nación e identidad: La regulación del plurilinguismo en España y América Latina,* ed. Kirsten Suselbeck, Ulrike Muhlschlegel, and Peter Masson, 303–23. Frankfurt am Main: Vervuert; Madrid: Iberoamericana.

———. 2008b. "Rootbound Community, Rootless Cosmpolitanism, or New Roots/Routes for Post-Post-Transition Catalonia?" Paper presented at the annual meeting of the American Anthropological Association, San Francisco, Calif., November 19, 2008.

Wright, Sue. 2004. *Language Policy and Language Planning: From Nationalism to Globalisation.* Houndsmills, Basingstoke, Hampshire, UK; New York: Palgrave Macmillan.

Zalbide, Mikel. 1988. "Mende-hasierako euskalgintza: Urratsak eta hutsuneak." In *Euskara Biltzarra/Congreso de la Lengua Vasca,* vol. 2, 390–412. Vitoria–Gasteiz: Eusko Jarlaritzaren Argitalpen Zerbitzu Nagusia, Servicio Central de Publicaciones del Gobierno Vasco.

———. 1998. "Normalización lingüística y escolaridad: Un infome desde la sala de maquinas." *Revista Internacional de Estudios Vascos* 43, no. 2: 355–424.

Zalbide, Mikel, Nicholas Gardner, Xabier Erize, and Maria-Jose Azurmendi. 2006. "The Future of Basque in RLS Perspective." In *The Case of Basque: Past, Present and Future,* ed. Mari-Jose Azurmendi and Iñaki Martínez de Luna, 117–39. Andoain: Soziolinguistika Klusterra.

Zallo, Ramon. 1997. *La segunda transición.* San Sebastián: Erein.

Zuazo, Koldo. 1988. *Euskeraren Batasuna.* Bilbao: Euskaltzaindia.

———. 2000. *Euskararen Sendabelarrak.* Irun: Alberdania.

Zuberogoita, Aitor, and Pedro Zuberogoitia. 2008. *Bertan Bilbo: Bizkaiko Hiriburua eta Euskara: XX; Mendeko Historia.* Bilbo: Udala Euskara Saila.

Zulaika, Joseba. 1988. *Basque Violence: Metaphor and Sacrament.* Reno: University of Nevada Press.

———. 1999. *Enemigos, no hay enemigos.* Donosti: Erein.

Index

Italic page numbers refer to illustrations